12 $\frac{50}{}$

D0079117

SOVIET AVIATION
AND AIR POWER

This book is sponsored by the Air Force Historical Foundation. The purpose of this nonprofit foundation is to preserve the traditions and publish the history of aerospace power, with special emphasis on the history of the United States Air Force. In striving to meet these goals, the foundation relies heavily on the publication of the magazine Aerospace Historian *and sponsorship of appropriate educational and cultural activities.* Aerospace Historian *contains articles, book reviews, museum news, photographs, and other features stressing the importance and relevance of the lessons of the past for the present and the future. It appears in March, June, September, and December. For more information about this periodical, write to:* Aerospace Historian, *Department of History, Eisenhower Hall, Kansas State University, Manhattan, Kansas 66506.*

SOVIET AVIATION AND AIR POWER
A HISTORICAL VIEW

edited by
Robin Higham and Jacob W. Kipp

BRASSEY'S
LONDON, ENGLAND

WESTVIEW PRESS
BOULDER, COLORADO

Copyright©1977 by the Air Force Historical Foundation

Copyright©1978 in the United Kingdom by Brassey's Publishers Ltd.

Published in 1977 in the United States of America by
    Westview Press, Inc.
    5500 Central Avenue
    Boulder, Colorado 80301
    Frederick A. Praeger, Publisher and Editorial Director

Published in 1978 in the United Kingdom by
    Brassey's Publishers Limited
    21, Montagu Street
    Portman Square
    London W. 1. England

ISBN (U.S.): 0-89158-116-2
ISBN (U.K.): 0-904609-13-8

Library of Congress Cataloging in Publication Data
Main entry under title:
Soviet aviation and air power.

    1. Aeronautics, Military—Russia—History—Addresses, essays, lectures.
2. Aeronautics—Russia—History—Addresses, essays, lectures. 3. Air power—
Addresses, essays, lectures. I. Higham, Robin D. S. II. Kipp, Jacob W.
UG635.R9S596   358.4'00947   76-30815

Contents

Illustrations

Editor's note: Photographs of Soviet aircraft are extremely difficult to obtain in the West—even, as in our case, with the cooperation of Sovfoto. We have included some photographs of dubious quality because of the importance of the subject matter. Most of the recent photographs were supplied by the U.S. Navy and the U.S. Air Force.

About the Contributors

Kendall E. Bailes received his Ph.D. in history from Columbia University, where he also studied at the Russian Institute. He currently teaches at the University of California, Irvine. The author of articles in *American Historical Review, Technology and Culture, Soviet Studies,* and *Cahiers du Monde Russe et Sovietique,* he is also the author of a forthcoming monograph to be published by Princeton University Press, *Technology and Society under Lenin and Stalin: The Origins of the Soviet Technical Intelligentsia, 1917–1941.*

Otto Preston Chaney, Jr., a colonel in the U.S. Army, holds a Ph.D. in Russian area studies. He is the author of the full-length biography *Zhukov,* published in the United States, Great Britain, and Spain. Recently he was a consultant to the BBC-TV production "The Commanders: Zhukov." He twice served as liaison officer to the Commander-in-Chief, Group of Soviet Forces in East Germany. He now resides in Prague, Czechoslovakia, where he is the U.S. Army attaché.

John T. Greenwood received his Ph.D. from Kansas State University in military history after studying Russian and Soviet history at the Universities of Colorado and Wisconsin. After serving as a historian for the Strategic Air Command at Offutt Air Force Base and for the Space and Missile Systems Organization in Los Angeles, he joined the Office of Air Force History in Washington, where he is currently employed in the study of USAF strategic offensive forces. His work has been published in *Aerospace Historian, Military Affairs,* and *Military Review,* and he is the compiler of the bibliography *American Defense Policy since 1945.*

Neil M. Heyman received his B.A. summa cum laude from Yale in 1959 and his graduate training at Stanford (M.A., 1965; Ph.D., 1972). He attended the Army Language School and served as a Russian linguist from 1960 through 1963. He has contributed articles to *Journal of Modern History, Military Affairs,* and *Army Quarterly and Defense Journal.* Now associate professor of history at San Diego State University, he is writing a book on the military career of Leon Trotsky.

Robin Higham, professor of history at Kansas State University and editor of the publications *Military Affairs* and *Aerospace Historian,* is the author of *Air Power: A Concise History,* a selection of both the History Book Club and the *Flying* Book Club.

David R. Jones lives in Cambridge Station, Nova Scotia. He is currently preparing the *Modern Encyclopedia of Russian Military and Naval Affairs* and the newly established *Soviet Armed Forces Review*. He has been published widely on Russian military affairs in such journals as *Slavic Studies, Soviet Studies, Naval War College Review, Aerospace Historian,* and *Military Affairs.*

Jacob W. Kipp, associate professor of history at Kansas State University, received his Ph.D. from Pennsylvania State University in 1970. Professor Kipp has been a Fulbright-Hays fellow in Poland, an IREX fellow in the USSR, and a Kosciuszko fellow in Poland. He has published articles on Russian and Soviet naval and administrative history in *Jahrbücher für Geschichte Osteuropas, Journal of Modern History, Military Affairs,* and *U.S. Naval Institute Proceedings.*

Joseph P. Mastro holds a Ph.D. from Pennsylvania State University. He is currently an associate professor of political science at North Carolina State University, Raleigh. Specializing in Soviet domestic politics and foreign policy and other Communist systems, he is the author of several papers on the Soviet political elite.

Alfred L. Monks is an associate professor at the University of Wyoming and the author of several articles on Soviet military affairs. He is now writing a book on Soviet military thought and the late Soviet defense minister, Marshal A. A. Grechko.

Phillip A. Petersen is an instructor in university-wide projects at the University of Illinois. He served as foreign armies instructor in the command and staff department of the Army Security Agency Training Center and School, and has published articles about Soviet perceptions of military sufficiency, and about the Sino-Soviet conflict from a military perspective.

Kenneth R. Whiting, chief of the documentary research branch, Academic Publications Division, at the Air University, is a noted expert on Soviet affairs. He received a Ph.D. in Russian history from Harvard in 1951 and has contributed numerous articles and studies on Soviet affairs to a wide variety of publications, including Eugene Emme's *The Impact of Air Power* and Asher Lee's *Soviet Air and Rocket Forces.* He is currently writing a book about the military forces of the Communist powers.

1

Introduction

Robin Higham

The story of Russian aviation blends a number of themes from both outside and inside the Soviet Union. Since Peter the Great, the struggle between Westerners and Slavophiles has affected every aspect of Russian national life, aviation being no exception. The history of aeronautics in Russia reflects both internal and international patterns of technological development.

Traditionally, the Soviet Union has depended upon the West for both aircraft and design. Political and ideological conflicts have not effectively blocked the international flow of scientific and technological information. Technical documents, reports, and papers published in the West have been readily accessible to Russia's many avid flying enthusiasts.

Aviation has thrived in the Soviet Union because the airplane, like the dynamo, is a visible symbol of the modern age and of the Bolshevik revolution. Moreover, no other country, with the exception of the United States, provided such an ideal environment in which to establish aviation. India lacked the space and know-how, if not the will. Australia lacked the necessary capital. In Latin America there were too many conflicting jurisdictions and not enough of a market, and much the same could be said of Africa even after World War II. In China, in spite of the World War II example of the Hump, the civil war and partisan politics combined to stifle aviation development until after Mao gained control in 1949. In Russia, however, vast distances coupled with a limited railway system gave even the airplane of the 1920s a speed advantage over any other form of transportation during daylight hours.

The USSR has some 250 million people (in comparison, the United States has 210 million and Great Britain 52 million). Modern Russia contains some 8.6 million square miles (the U.S. has 3.6 million, Britain 0.9 million). Much of Russia resembles the settled parts of the western provinces of Canada—flat or undulating steppes, sometimes forested, rising in the southeast to the formidable Himalayas. The country's most distinctive feature is the Ural mountain chain, which divides Siberia from European Russia. Until shortly before World War II the population largely lived west of the Urals and was concentrated in the Leningrad, Moscow, and Ukraine areas. In the late Stalinist era, the population spread out, with new concentrations developing just east of the Urals and in a salient running east to Lake Baikal, as the new industrialization and the relocation and dispersion of factories created new productive clusters.

Although Russia did not begin her industrial revolution until late in the nineteenth century, she entered the field of aviation as early as 1910. Aviation found a natural home in Russia even before the Bolshevik revolution placed an emphasis upon technology because of the country's late industrialization and shortage of capital; in contrast to the investment that would have been required to upgrade the country's relatively scant rail network, aviation needed little capital. Although the climate in Russia is harsh—some inhabited areas average fewer than 180 days per year when the temperature rises above freezing —in many areas the building of a landing strip is easy. In fact, an unusual feature of Russian aviation since its inception has been the requirement that all aircraft must be capable of operating from grass airfields. These primitive landing strips may be rock-hard in winter and worse than spongy during thaws. Thus, a typical Russian aircraft has a strong landing gear with weight well distributed on multiple wheels (or on skis, if necessary).

The German Connection

Ever since the days of the medieval Hansa, Germans have acted as a middle-merchant class in agrarian Russia. In the eighteenth century, both Peter the Great and Catherine the Great invited Germans to immigrate in order to staff Russia's growing bureaucracies, which comprised a class above the peasants and beneath the Muscovite aristocracy. Though the French supplied much of the capital for Russia's industrialization, German influence remained great in the years before World War I.

In 1919 Russia and Germany, united by their common defeat, embarked upon a long and mutually profitable collaboration. Deprived of military aviation by the Treaty of Versailles, the Germans found Russia ready and willing to let them operate an airline route across the USSR to Persia and develop training establishments for both Russia's own air force and the illicit German force. Thus, the Russians gained expertise from the more advanced German know-how, and the Germans benefited from being able to keep their military aviation alive and progressive. In some areas— notably heavy bombers, paratroops, and Arctic flight—the Russians even outstripped their mentors, in spite of the fact that two of the former's most capable designers during World War I, Igor Sikorsky and Alexander de Seversky, had fled to the United States.

Though aviation in its early days in Europe was something of an aristocratic enterprise, in Russia it became a middle-level occupation in a "classless" society. (Igor Sikorsky was more typical of the European pattern, in that he was educated in Paris.) Because it was a means of upward mobility, aviation possessed a kind of glamour and an elite status. People with good minds sought to be both leaders and followers in aircraft design teams. For others, merely to be a flier or to be associated with an air service was honor and reward enough. Russia strongly promoted

Figure 1. Tu-144 supersonic airliner and Il-76 cargo plane on exhibit at a Soviet air show.

aviation, which everywhere enjoyed the witch doctor's advantage of being both thrillingly mysterious and highly visible. Even the occasional crashes satisfied a certain perverse human fascination with spectacular disaster.

During the pre-1941 period, Russia aviation efforts were for the most part internal, largely because the Russians had to stay within their boundaries for both physical and political reasons. Before 1917 Russian aircraft were not capable of flying great distances, with the possible exception of the twenty-five Muromets reconnaissance bombers which Sikorsky developed. Tsarist foreign policy after Tsushima (1905) was not expansionist, and the machines of the day were not capable of penetrating more than 150 miles. After the revolution and the civil war, the Soviets tried to mend their wounds and get their economy under control. Trotsky, an internationalist in foreign policy, strongly advocated accepting help from the "decadent" powers in the effort to develop Soviet aviation. Although Stalin was xenophobic, he, too, as a nationalist, accepted aid from the West. Ironically, during this period of self-containment, the United States trusted the Soviet Union sufficiently to permit Russian technicians to visit the Douglas aircraft company and to grant them the rights to manufacture the revolutionary DC-3 under license.

The Five-Year Plans

Aviation, of course, fitted prominently into the Stalinist five-year plans. In a country where the construction of railroads was government-sponsored, air transportation naturally became a state enterprise. The First Five-Year Plan, launched in 1928, was aimed at making Russia an industrial (rather than agrarian) nation and at creating self-sufficiency in defense. Emphasis was placed upon factories, machinery, and transportation, and upon quantity rather than quality. With great psychological shrewdness, Stalin in 1932 announced the plan's achievement, even though the results were marred by many disappointments. The second plan, which was changed after the anti-Bolshevik Hitler came to power, emphasized an increase in the production of war materials, the rational distribution of manufacturing, the establishment of new industries, and improvement of the transportation system, especially of the railways. The result was a great increase in quantity, though quality was still low, and a rate of worker productivity greater than that of tsarist days. The Third Five-Year Plan placed emphasis upon anti-invasion measures, technical perfection and productivity, and relocation of industry to areas east of the Urals. Soviet industrialization during the 1930s resulted in the recognition and creation of a new technical/management middle class into which aviation designers and the air officer corps inevitably began to fit—if, in fact, they had not already mentally identified themselves with that group. By 1941 Russia, apparently the largest industrial country in Europe, enjoyed the exceptional advantage of having within her vast territories all the natural resources she needed to build aircraft except rubber, which she was able to synthesize.

Aircraft design was not a very complex subject, provided that reliable engines were available, until after the technical revolution of the 1930s introduced constant-speed propellers, high-octane fuels, superchargers, all-metal construction, flaps, and retractable undercarriages. In 1936 the Russians, realizing the revolutionary potential of the DC-3, sent engineers to Douglas and contracted to produce the plane under license (as the Li-2). They were not interested in the contemporary Boeing B-17 heavy bomber because they could not foresee any targets for it. Nor were the Russians interested in tactical aircraft, because they were already veterans in the design and operation under wartime conditions of the close-support system. Later, however, in 1945—after they knew the B-29 had dropped atomic bombs on Japan —the Soviets copied the B-29s they had interned, using them as the basis for designing both bombers and transports, just as Boeing developed the 377 Stratocruiser out of the B-29.

The copying of ideas in aviation, if not always so blatant, is a long-established practice. The manufacturing of parts and of whole aircraft under license has always been a standard procedure because some countries have lacked the design and testing facilities necessary to undertake part or all of the work themselves, let alone put up the capital, especially as aircraft have become more complicated. The Russians have been very much a part of the international flow of technology, and in many ways the pattern they set served as a model for the post-1945 new nations. In Russia and Eastern Europe before World War II, in addition to the specialized development of some items, notably of guns in the Balkans and Czechoslovakia and some design and development of aircraft (primarily in Poland), there was a great deal of importation of new aircraft and manufacture of planes under license.

Figure 2. Iliushin DB-3F bombers in World War II. One of the earliest Iliushin designs to see action, this long-range medium bomber was fitted with wooden mainspars in 1942 when there was a shortage of light alloys.

Force and Foresight

Because of the Russians' inherently suspicious attitude toward foreigners, their aviation developed largely within their own country. It is true that Russian aviation was heavily influenced by the Germans between 1919 and 1935, when Hitler ended the liaison, and again after the Russians captured many German technicians and their apparatus after World War II. It is also true that Italian, French, British, and American influence were important at times. Nevertheless, recognition of these influences should not overshadow the fact that the Russians, from the beginning, had a competent design and production organization in which the primary emphasis was placed on serviceability and service, rather than on sophisticated developments or, in the military sphere, strategic bombing.

(Although in the early 1930s the Soviet had the only real bomber force in the world, the leadership of this Douhetian force was later purged.) The Soviets can well argue that their success with using only a tactical air force in World War II—a decision made largely on the basis of bitter lessons learned in Spain and Finland—proves their case. Tactical air forces directly support the people in uniform—a close-to-the-earth, peasant approach to an immediate enemy. If the Soviet air force was ineffective in the long retreat of 1941, this weakness can be blamed upon Stalin's purges of the late 1930s, which removed at least one-fourth of the air-force high command and many of the best aeronautical engineers.

The Soviets had developed aviation primarily because of the desperate need for additional transport in a country where vast, remote regions lacked surface transportation systems, especially in the areas east of the Urals. Through a process of consolidation, the Soviets created Aeroflot as the state airline in 1932, at about the same time that Air France and Lufthansa emerged in Europe and Pan American was founded in the United States. From a technical standpoint, aviation in Russia developed at about the same rate as in Europe, even though, in 1941, the more-numerous Soviet air force suffered substantial initial losses of aircraft to the German Luftwaffe. However, Soviet designers and manufacturers had learned from the Spanish civil war. War against Germany had been anticipated in Stalin's five-year plans since 1928, and much of the aircraft industry had been moved beyond the Urals. Because Russian production had been boosted immensely, the Germans were overwhelmed by the swarms of tactical aircraft that provided effective close support for Red Army tanks, artillery, and infantry after early 1942. Of these new aircraft, some 14,500 mostly obsolete machines came from the United States and Britain, while Soviet factories turned out more than 140,000 (1942-1945) to the Germans' 80,000 and the United States' 257,000.

Because of the foresighted decision to move heavy industry east of the Urals, industrial production in 1945 was only 8.3 percent below that of 1940, though consumer goods, never plentiful, were down by nearly 50 percent. Stalin's first postwar five-year plan continued to emphasize the widespread dispersal of industry, in order both to make it less vulnerable to strategic bombing and to place it closer to raw materials. In aviation, this meant an intensification of Aeroflot activities; the accelerated development of jet fighters, long-range bombers based on the B-29s, and new Russian designs; and the continued transformation of captured German V-2 rockets into intermediate ballistic missiles.

Postwar Progress

World War II had compelled the Soviets to make a supreme effort. The situation called for immediate practical measures; therefore, the Soviet effort was focused on expelling the German armies from Russian soil—thus winning the war on the ground, with emphasis on tactical air forces. The Russians had little to fear, and suffered little, from strategic bombing, although their huge power plants would have made jugular targets. What did affect the Russians' strategy was their growing awareness of the devastating Anglo-American bombing capabilities. Although the USSR could trade space for time, she had an inadequate air-defense system, no fighter force capable of dealing with high-altitude bombers, and no deterrent striking force. (Because of the topography of the territory, most Russian combat sorties had been made below 3,000 feet and many below 1,000.)

If earlier bombing forays had made the Soviets well aware of the power of the Allied bombers from the West, that power was even more dramatically demonstrated by the explosion of the A-bombs at Hiroshima and Nagasaki. Russian fears and distrust of the West were not allayed by the postwar course of American foreign policy. The testing of atomic bombs in the Pacific and the containment policies embodied in the Truman and Marshall doctrines were read, perhaps correctly, as direct and threatening reactions to the Stalinization of Eastern Europe. Relationships were further exacerbated by nationalistic guerrilla movements in other countries, by the successful rise of Mao in China, by the Korean War (with consequent American and British rearmament), and finally, by Russia's detonation of an atomic bomb in 1949.

Figure 3. Fiddler-B interceptor armed with Ash missiles. The Tu-28P, a long-range fighter with three- to five-hour endurance and a "Coke bottle" fuselage, entered service in 1962.

The cold war impelled Russia down a road she was determined to follow out of fear of attack. In the face of rapidly mounting ideological conflict, the Russians felt increasingly vulnerable. They proceeded rapidly to develop both antiaircraft defenses and such long-range bombers as the Tu-20 Bear and M-4 Bison. This protracted, complex program was no less successful than were similar programs in the West. Though the USAF B-47 became operational in 1951, the RAF V-bombers did not enter service until 1955, when the Bears and Bisons joined the Soviet air force. After the reestablishment of the German connection in 1945, the Russians moved ahead rapidly both on the jet and rocket fronts. During the war the Germans had made great progress with jet aircraft,

notably the Me-262; captured German technicians and material later provided the Russians with a fundamental knowledge of jet technology. At the same time, Aeroflot greatly expanded its service, drawing on the large reserve of war-trained fliers and war-tested aircraft. Aeroflot was well equipped to perform its roles, which ranged from bush-hopping with biplanes to flying long-range passenger runs with Li-2 copies of the Douglas DC-3. By the end of the 1950s, passenger versions of jet bombers were in service on Aeroflot's far-flung routes, still operating regularly from grass airfields. The development of a supersonic transport (the Tu-144) closely akin to the Anglo-French Concorde followed naturally. Meanwhile, using German and British jet engines, the Russians had progressed by 1950 to producing jet fighters whose technical performance was at least adequate in the Korean War, a conflict in which Soviet pilots got their first unofficial jet combat experience. Fighter development continued to progress successfully into the Mach 2 range; by 1970 Russia was supplying Egypt, as well as her other allies, with fighter and attack aircraft as modern as the Mig-25 Foxbat.

The sale of British jet engines to Russia only reinforced a technology to which the Soviets already had access. (The Soviets had obtained the V-2 rocket team and its facilities when they overran Peenemunde.) On many occasions the Russians have demonstrated more powerful, if less-sophisticated, technology than the West. Their rocket development shocked the West when they launched Sputnik, the first space satellite, in October 1957, on the fortieth anniversary of the revolution. Thereafter, a race began in missilery similar to the ongoing competition in jets between the United States and the USSR. The former had superiority in numbers and technique, but the latter had the drive of the underdog. Not content with being number two, the Soviet Union had by 1973 surpassed the United States in jet-fighter development and was at least equal in the development and placement of ICBMs and MIRV warheads.

From Stalin to SALT

The years between World War II and Stalin's death in 1953 were of immense benefit to Soviet aviation, since the emphasis was on both development for defense and economic recovery. The momentum of those days continued during the new era after Stalin, which saw a gradual thawing of Soviet attitudes toward outsiders. Their successful testing of a hydrogen bomb in 1953, followed by the launch of Sputnik in 1957, gave the Russians con-

fidence. Their new jet fighters and long-range turboprop and jet bombers enabled them to show the flag abroad and even at sea in neocolonial disputes. In many ways, they emulated the West. The Cuban crisis of 1962 was one consequence of the placement of American missiles in countries bordering Russia, thereby vitiating the IRBM lead of the USSR. But that confrontation also marked a turning point in the interminable international chess game. While the U.S. was becoming involved in Vietnam, which required a return to tactical forces and a concomitant deemphasis of the nuclear umbrella, the USSR began to seriously face the rise of Red China. By 1974, it appeared that the Russians had overshot the American military position at the same time that the U.S. was seeing the need to phase out the cold war and to accept something like the "peaceful coexistence" suggested by Khrushchev in 1956.

The Strategic Arms Limitation Talks (SALT), like the Washington Conference fifty years earlier, were aimed at limiting the stockpiling of massive and costly strategic weapons. As negotiations proceeded, both Soviet and Western military planners came to the realization that weaponry, in the future, would probably emphasize the development and production of tactical weapons for limited wars. Whether the basis for agreement on SALT was the same for both sides—or whether one side signed for political reasons and the other's acquiescence was simply a strategic move in a long-played chess game—remained to be seen; by 1976, doubts had surfaced. Russia's agreement to a joint space adventure, on the other hand, clearly had political as well as scientific motives.

The Great Design Race

Although there has been a tendency in the West to deride Russian material as unsophisticated and therefore slightly inferior, to

Figure 4. Mi-6 Hook helicopter (1961 photo), widely used by the Bulgarians, Egyptians, Indonesians, and North Vietnamese.

do so is a mistake. From the very beginning there has been some originality in Russia; since its establishment in 1918, the Central Institute of Aerodynamics and Hydrodynamics (TsAGI) has focused on design efforts. Although created later than the Royal Aircraft Establishment at Farnborough in England, TsAGI antedates the founding of the National Advisory Committee for Aeronautics (NACA, the forerunner of NASA—1958) in the United States. Furthermore, the Russians developed teams of designers, led by such men as Tupolev the elder, Iliushin, Yakovlev, and Mikoian, who ably took up the legacy of Sikorsky and Zhukovsky and produced aircraft suited to Russia's needs.

Nor were the Russians out of step with world aviation. In the aircraft design race the Germans led slightly at the start, but in both world wars they made the mistake of concentrating upon production (quantity), ultimately to the exclusion and detriment of new design (quality). Consequently, the Germans eventually lost their margin of superiority in the air, just as they did on the ground. For example, in Spain the Me-109 was a generation ahead of the I-16—a situation which, along with other reasons, caused the Russians to withdraw. But by June 1941 the USSR had caught up in design, if not in mass production, and after 1942 they more than held their own in production as well. (By way of contrast, in December 1941 the Americans faced Japanese Zeros and German Me-109s with Boeing P-26s and Curtiss P-40s—both obsolete, by European standards of the day, and neither a match for the Zero.) Though a few Russian designers were purged before 1941, on the whole the Soviet pattern resembles that of aircraft industries in other countries, the caveat being that the Soviet designers are almost a generation younger. Although the entrepreneurs and designers who spearheaded the European and American aircraft industries before World War I were fading from power in the early 1960s, the Russians lasted actively into the 1970s. Tupolev, for instance, died only recently (in 1973) after a long and productive career that extended from biplanes to the Tu-144 supersonic transport.

Soviet aviation has followed the traditional Russian pattern, in that the state has guided technological development. As theoretical scientists and designers, the Russians have been capable, though few have possessed talents that compared favorably with those of their Western European peers. In manufacturing, the Soviets were somewhat less skilled. (In this respect they resembled the British, who, even after World War II—nearly two centuries after the industrial revolution—had trouble organizing production of the superior designs they created.) During the decade and a half after the civil war, the Russians read voraciously in foreign technical periodicals and scientific journals; by 1935, when the I-15 biplane and I-16 monoplane appeared, Russia was ahead of Europe. When Germany invaded Russia in 1941, the latter's Shturmovik ground-attack aircraft, though not yet available in large numbers, proved superior to anything the Germans had.

Nonetheless, the West consistently underrated Russian productive genius, probably because the Western press had widely reported on the chaotic state of Russian industrialization during the 1920s. In fact, Russia had a well-organized production line, designed to concentrate upon a few aircraft types. (The British also underestimated the German aircraft industry in 1935.) Moreover, the Russians were content with less sophisticated but more easily maintained aircraft—a concept they have retained even to the present time. In other words, they design their aircraft to fit the level of their mechanics' ability. Part of the reason for Russia's overwhelming control of the skies after late 1942 was the ability of her squadrons to keep air-

craft in the air for countless sorties every day, while the Germans were not only thinly spread out but also lacking in maintenance and logistics.

War often sets superior technology against sheer numbers, sophistication against maintainability. The Russians chose to rely, in good peasant fashion, on the man, while providing him with a machine that was equal or superior to that of his opponent in ruggedness, maintainability, and speed. Russian pilots did not do better than Americans during the Korean War because (1) the former had had less experience in dogfighting and had lost more professionals than the USAAF during World War II and (2) the Russians lacked sufficient time during the Korean War to apply the knowledge learned from their new combat experience. Despite the heavy losses sustained by the Soviets, however, the Mig-15 was still a formidable early jet.

When Lenin assumed power in 1917, he decreed that science should serve the state. Consequently, aviation fell under this directive. Western observers often overlook the fact that the Soviet policymakers have done a remarkably good job in their management of design and development. Although the designs produced in Russia do not usually compete in the international prototype race, they have been adequate to fill the many diverse needs of the whole domestic aviation system. Furthermore, the traditional view that civil aircraft should be convertible to military uses and vice versa (evident at the Geneva Disarmament Conference of 1932-1934) continues to exist in Russia. Even jet bombers have been used as the basis for transport aircraft —as witness the Tu-16's conversion to the Tu-104, which is unashamed of its ancestry even to the point of retaining a bomb-aimer's position in its nose. By such means, the Russians have frequently been able to place a new civil design into pro-

Figure 5. Tu-20 Bear bomber (foreground) and U.S. Phantom fighter in flight over the North Pacific, 1971.

duction more quickly than the West. Much the same can be said of military designs in which the same fuselage has been used for two different types of planes. Whether Russian airliners are as efficient as those designed in the West is difficult to judge because of the lack of comparable figures. What is known is that, since World War II, Soviet economic planners have ensured that Russia's aircraft industry is fully occupied with domestic production, with minor types of aircraft and allied needs delegated to factories in her satellites—thus avoiding the erratic employment patterns that have been visible in the West.

The Wave Pattern

In my book *Air Power* (1973), I suggested a wave theory to explain the normal business pattern in military aviation, dividing the wave into four parts: peacetime equilibrium, rearmamental instability, wartime equilibrium, and demobilization instability. The model was not intended to be exact, though it probably could be graphed from budgets, aircraft production figures, etc. The wave theory originated as an analysis of the working relationships or contractual aspects of British aircraft production; however, it can be applied to the USSR.

Russian aviation began to develop at about the same rate as Western aviation and encountered similar problems, but it lacked the industrial base found in the West. In anticipation of war in 1914, the Russians imported French and Italian aircraft in order to stimulate the local aircraft industry. During the war aviation remained essentially in the rearmamental instability phase that existed from 1912-1913 onward. In about 1916 wartime equilibrium was reached, with the majority of aircraft unserviceable and new machines on order from abroad. Demobilizational instability began with the revolution and continued through the civil war until about 1923. Peacetime equilibrium was short, consisting largely of building air transport lines and factories with German help. Rearmamental instability came again in 1928 with the five-year plans and lasted until late 1942, when well-organized Russian air forces went over to the offensive. After World War II, while the West experienced a catastrophically rapid demobilizational instability, in Russia only a gradual demobilization took place. During this period Soviet planners emphasized watchfulness, recalling the Allied attacks of 1918 and anticipating the need for air defense against U.S. A-bombs. The cold war again introduced rearmamental instability, which after 1956 tapered off into a peacetime equilibrium in which the pattern was affected in Russia, as elsewhere, by political and diplomatic considerations as well as by economic and social conditions. Any measurement of this phenomenon in budgetary terms must consider both the rising costs of technology in a period of inflation and the fact that, if British experience is a yardstick, the budget for a technical force does not peak until something like twenty years after its prime *raison d'être*. All in all, it can be argued that the Russian wave pattern matches that of its principal opponent of the moment (1977), the United States, but that this pattern may change if a major conflict with the Chinese develops.

The Plateau Effect

Another theory advanced in my book *Air Power* is that technological development continues for approximately three genera-

tions until it hits a plateau caused, not by inability to continue the process, but by political, military, diplomatic, economic, social, and ideological factors. This theory is best demonstrated by the defeat of the American SST and the scuttling of the further development of bombers in the United Kingdom (and possibly in the U.S.). It appears, as well, to have been responsible in part for the SALT talks.

During the last two decades, the main concern of U.S. military planners has been lobbying for legislative appropriations in order to keep up with the Russians. Moreover, especially during the 1960s, the balance of power in such places as the Middle East was thought to be upset by the appearance of a Mig-23 or two. As a result, attention was too often focused upon the newest aircraft or weapon. Whatever prototype was on display in Moscow's Red Square was assumed by many experts to exist in operational form and numbers. On the contrary, an exploration of *Jane's All the World's Aircraft* reveals that in Russia, as in the West, there normally is a long time lag between the appearance of a prototype and the availability of operational squadrons. Thus many of the satellite countries, like the allied countries in the West, have fleets of aircraft which are no longer considered first class.

In order to remain on good terms with the Arabs, the Russians, with their age-old interest in the Mediterranean, have been forced to supply some of their latest aircraft and SAM missiles to the Egyptians and the Syrians. The Soviets have been reluctant to do so for fear that these precious specimens would fall into the hands of their enemies (as indeed happened during the Yom Kippur War in 1973). Yet Egypt has been the only country, since the Korean War, able to give Russian pilots combat experience. It is interesting to note that the combination of Russian suspicions and American scruples has left the field of supplying new nations largely to the French and the British—even though, after the end of the Vietnam conflict, the United States found itself badly in need of markets. Moreover, Russian marketing efforts have been limited because, unlike the French and the Americans, the Soviets have not been able to extol most of their recent designs as combat proven.

Conclusion: What If and What Next?

The history of Soviet aviation and air power, including that of the tsarist period, fits the general pattern of aeronautics and of the wave theory in particular, with due regard for Russian historical experience.

Aviation and its auxiliaries have developed spectacularly in the twentieth century, creating an industry with great potential for peace and war. Yet, because of the mushroom growth of air power during World War II and its general utility and acceptance thereafter, we tend to forget its underdeveloped state everywhere before 1941. Indeed, writers have tended to exaggerate its power, influence, and combat-effectiveness prior to that date by failing to relate numbers to space in wartime and to consider the elite nature of air transport during the peacetime equilibrium between the wars of 1914 and 1941. In only two respects do the Russians fail to fit this pattern: air power was not much used on the eastern front from 1914 to 1918, and the hero worship of the elite fighter pilots of that war did not develop in the USSR. Russian aviation heroes have been more in the Lindbergh tradition.

Few people recognize that the Russians had a three-to-one margin over the Germans in first-line aircraft when Operation Barbarossa was launched by the Germans in June 1941. During the first few hours of the Ger-

mans' surprise attack on Russian airfields along the western frontier, the Soviet military air forces (VVS) lost more than 1,200 of these planes to the Luftwaffe. For the VVS, the battle for air supremacy was lost before it could get its planes off the ground.

In attempting to understand the discrepancy between the Russians' apparent strength and their actual unpreparedness, it is interesting to speculate about the following questions: What if Soviet top military leadership had not been decimated by Stalin's bloody purges? What if Stalin had not ignored the warnings of his intelligence service, and what if he had employed that service more astutely? If any or all of these conditions had not existed the Germans might have been pushed out of Russia by the early winter of 1941. Instead, a full year passed before the VVS was able to recover from the crushing losses it sustained in the early days of Barbarossa: not until after the unsuccessful German summer offensive of 1942 was the VVS able to overwhelm the Luftwaffe to the extent that the Russians achieved tactical superiority over large sectors of the front. Meanwhile, the Allies in the West were helping to waste and attenuate the Luftwaffe by their operations in North Africa and eventually over Italy and the Balkans. By the time the Russians definitely had achieved superiority in mid-1943, the Western air forces were becoming of formidable concern to the Germans, even though the real air battle of Germany did not begin until 1944. Russia benefited, too, from the successful campaign which forced the Japanese to abandon their aggressiveness of the Nomonhan (Khalkhin-Gol) days of 1939 in order to turn their full attention to the Far East.

After the Great Patriotic War of 1941–1945, Russian aviation and air power expanded, as aviation did elsewhere. In spite of the preachings of the emigré de Seversky and the Italian Douhet, the Russians did not adapt and make operational strategic bombing before World War II, although up to 1937 they did continue limited development. (Ironically, although strategic bombing was perhaps one of the Germans' real successes of 1915–1918, they subsequently ignored it in favor of tactical air forces—largely because Goering was a fighter pilot.) After seeing the postwar evidence in Germany and Japan, however, Russia frantically joined the mainstream of air-power thought and began to push strategic defense and attack.

In the 1970s, two historical forces restrained this development: first, the general rule that reform movements usually do not last for more than a generation (twenty years); and second, the tendency for technological development to continue for only about three generations before it reaches a plateau caused by political, economic, social, and ideological forces. Thus Soviet air power entered a new phase at about 1973 in which SALT represented the plateau, even though the Russians had only 140 grand-strategic bombers to the U.S.' 435 in the Strategic Air Command.

In the foreseeable future, although prototype development may continue (as in the cases of the U.S. B-1 and the USSR Backfire), it may well be subject to all the risks of becoming a peripheral weapons system. Deterrence is more likely to be confined to ICBMs and SSBNs, with flying concentrated in such small, versatile, tactical machines as the multirole combat aircraft (MRCA). (However, this pattern may be skewed by Sino-Soviet rivalries and tensions.) Similarly, the development of Aeroflot and of civil aviation in general may be affected to such an extent that the SST (Tu-144) will be limited to freight service and a political role. The bulk of Aeroflot's effort will remain service to all the people. By the 1970s it was carrying 70 million people a year, about as many as the top three (United, Eastern, and Delta) scheduled airlines in the U.S. combined. (In the U.S., thirty-two scheduled airlines, not counting commuter lines, share the job that Aeroflot performs alone in Russia.)

The effect of these two restraints (reform and resistance to technology) on the development of the aircraft industry may be to reduce its importance and flatten the curve of its technological development in favor of aircraft and equipment that can be afforded and maintained not only by Russians but also by less-developed countries. The limitations are not ideological; they are practical. (It might be noted that it was primarily the need for a utilitarian weapon system which led the Russians to pursue the tactically sound line of developing cheap SAMs as an effective way of countering the superior USAF in Southeast Asia and the dominant Israeli AF in the Middle East.) Thus, about sixty years, or three generations, from now will be an appropriate time at which to reexamine the rise of Soviet aviation against the domestic, diplomatic, and developmental background of Russian and international affairs.

2

The Beginnings of Russian
Air Power, 1907-1922

David R. Jones

In mid-August 1910, a group of Russian military officials gathered at Gatchina to observe tests of a new weapon recently acquired by the War Ministry: an Antoinette biplane. Crated and unassembled, it had just arrived from France, accompanied by three French mechanics. The latter were to assemble the plane, but, unfortunately, had brought no tools. Since the Petersburg factories were closed that day and tools were unobtainable elsewhere, the officials dispersed.

By the next morning tools were finally available and the French mechanics set to work. As the assembly neared completion, it was discovered that someone had forgotten to pack the triangular tail rudder. The mechanics hastily reassured the Russians that they could easily build one on the spot. Finally, by 3 p.m., the machine was ready; before the eyes of the impatient spectators, it began its first flight. On the first turn, however, the engine stalled and the steel wing-support cables snapped. The comments of the Russian observers may

well be imagined.

Unfortunately, this was not an isolated incident: dissatisfaction with foreign machines and servicing remained a constant theme in Russia throughout the ensuing decade. For, in spite of the dreams of some military thinkers and the remarkable achievements of some inventors, Russia's primitive technology and limited industrial base made the creation of a powerful air fleet impossible. In 1920, as in 1910, the Russian air services were still largely dependent on foreign machines and anxious to acquire outside technical advice.

The Russians had long been interested in the military potential of aeronautics. In 1831, the military governor of Riazan had attended Russia's first recorded balloon flight—when a subdeacon had been lifted above the birch trees by "the powers of darkness"—and some consideration apparently was given to building a balloon during Napoleon's 1812 invasion. In 1869 this interest became embodied in a lasting and official form when Russia's great war minister, Gen. D. A. Muliutin, set up the Commission on the Use of Aeronautics for Military Purposes. In 1881 the Russian Technical Society established an aeronautics section. By 1895, with fixed balloons being used in maneuvers, these devices were considered important enough to justify the creation of a special aeronautical training park at Volkov Field in St. Petersburg. At that time it was administered by the Main Engineering Directorate; later, in 1910, it served as the basis for the Officers' Aeronautical School.

Fixed observation ballons thus became a permanent, if minor, part of Russia's military establishment, and they played a small but not unimportant role in the Russo-Japanese war of 1904–1905. (At Liaoyang, for instance, a balloonist reportedly spotted a Japanese flanking movement.) As a result, Russia's first aeronautics battalion was formed, and experiments with observation balloons continued during the next few years.

Elsewhere in Europe events moved more rapidly, and patriotic Russians became dissatisfied with their own slow progress. Even the establishment of the Commission for the Planning and Construction of Piloted Aerostats, which began work in 1907, did not silence the critics. As the liberal newspaper *Rech'* acidly remarked in its January 1, 1908, review of military developments during the past year, "In the west they are everywhere flying through the air in piloted aerostats, but we have only just thought of forming a commission on this subject in the Main Engineering Directorate. . . ."

Yet this commission's work did bear fruit, and by 1909 Russia had acquired her first home-built military dirigible in the *Krechet* (Gerfalcon), which carried a crew of six at a speed of twenty-five miles per hour. These efforts received further support from the state Duma's budget commission, which in 1910 insisted on a substantial increase in the expenditures for aeronautics. By that year, the proponents of lighter-than-air dirigibles apparently had won their battle. Mobilization plans now called for thirty-one companies of fixed balloons, with the War Ministry planning for nine long-range and eight short-range airships. Yet, just as victory seemed secure, the public's attention was suddenly diverted by a rival to the airship: the airplane.

After the failure of naval officer A. F. Mozhaisky's heavier-than-air machine in 1894, Russian interest in this type of aeronautics had waned. But by 1906 it had been revived by reports from abroad suggesting that powered airplanes could indeed fly. Although aspiring Russian pilots still had to be trained abroad, by 1908 enthusiasts at home were organizing aeroclubs in Kiev, Moscow, Nizhii-Novgorod, and elsewhere. The most important of these was founded in January of that year, when the Imperial All-Russian Aeroclub was established in St. Petersburg. During the next few years it established branches in Rostov and Kiev, received permission from the tsar to raise funds by public subscription, and, by establishing a flying school in Moscow, did much to popularize aviation and train pilots.

In spite of a not-unnatural skepticism on the part of professional soldiers, the Main Engineering Directorate was also becoming interested in this new invention. In April 1908, for instance, it concluded that, although airplanes "can at present still not make very long flights or rise to any great heights, and while in general they are not suitable for military purposes, in the future they will nevertheless play a tremendous role in military affairs and so will undoubtedly be introduced into the armament of the army" (War Ministry's *Annual Report,* 1908). As a result, seven aeroengines were purchased in France for machines that were to be built by officers of the St. Petersburg Aeronautical Park.

The year 1909 proved to be significant for the airplane, both in Europe and in Russia. Louis Bleriot's cross-channel flight in July demonstrated that heavier-than-air machines had capabilities undreamed of only a few years earlier. Aeroclub memberships grew rapidly, and young officers enthusiastically argued that planes were sounding the death knell of cavalry and that "on the battlefield, a dwarf who can see will conquer a blind giant." So, although many senior military men still saw airplanes as interesting if dangerous toys, the War Ministry nonetheless allotted funds for the acquisition of foreign machines (of which the ill-fated Antoinette was one) and established at Gatchina an aviation branch of the St. Petersburg Aeronautics School (for pilot training).

The man most impressed by Bleriot's feat was the grand admiral, Grand Duke Alexander Mikhailovich. Since the Russo-Japanese war he had headed the Committee for the Strengthening of the Naval Fleet by Voluntary Contributions, which by 1909 had raised the equivalent of some 1.7 million rubles. A few torpedo boats had been acquired, but in 1909 substantial funds still remained. The grand duke, who was spending the summer in France, was immediately convinced that Bleriot's flight meant that "victory in a future war will be impossible without an aerial fleet."

Having decided to use the committee's remaining funds for aviation, the grand duke, an astute politician, obtained approval for his plans by mail from a majority of subscribers and arranged to obtain machines and instructors from the French fliers Bleriot and Voisin. Then he returned to St. Petersburg and publicly defended his policies in an open committee meeting. The resulting vote not only approved his actions but also established a special aviation section of the committee and approved a proposal to petition Tsar Nicholas II for the right to raise further funds. As a result, further machines were acquired, selected army and naval officers were trained abroad, and Russia built a second military flying school at Sevastopol. By September 1910, this school had ten planes and twenty-nine pilots in its training program.

In the grand duke, aviation found a royal patron who, acting in his semiofficial capacity, was able to do much to coordinate the activities of his own committee, the aeroclubs, and the War Ministry. Immediately a series of exhibitions and competitions was scheduled: on May 2, 1910, the first aeronautical exhibition opened in Moscow, the first All-Russian Aviation Week was held in St. Petersburg May 8–15, and the All-Russian Festival of Aeronautics took place in that same city in September and October. By 1911 a St. Petersburg–Moscow air race had been completed, and airplanes were successfully taking part in army maneuvers. So, although interest in lighter-than-air ships did not completely die until 1915, it was already on the decline in 1911. One foreign journal observed in November 1911: "The feature of the last few months has been the development of aeroplanes at the expense of dirigibles" (*Journal of Royal United Services Institution* 55, November 1911, p. 1529).

From 1912 to 1914 the Russian air services made rapid strides forward in equipment, technology, and organization. As of July 30, 1912, the Main Engineering Directorate lost its aerial responsibilities. These were taken over by an aviation section of the General Staff, which had two branches: one for training and service and another for technical questions and equipment. Later the Chief Military-Educational Directorate assumed these responsibilities, but in 1914 Russian aviation was still seeking its proper administrative form.

The rate of increase in actual numbers of aircraft was still more impressive. The 30 to 40 machines available at the end of 1910 had risen to some 250 by April 1913. There were 244 in August 1914, and, while many machines were by this time outdated, new orders had already been placed for 400 more as well as for 10 Sikorsky four-motor heavy bombers. Also, although the number of pilots available was limited, the General Staff estimated that it was more than sufficient for the army's needs; moreover, the training schools were being developed further.

Russian pilots had also obtained some practical experience, apart from maneuvers, in military operations. A handful of volunteers had flown for the Bulgarians in the 1912–1913 Balkan wars, and their experiences contributed to the wide-ranging discussions of aviation's tactical possibilities that took place in the Russian military press. Technical interests were similarly pursued, and experiments with air-to-ground radio communication were carried out. According to one report, even before the outbreak of war, work was already in progress on developing an interrupter mechanism for forward-firing machine guns.

Despite this progress, the basic problem remained unresolved: Russia would only become and remain a great air power when she could, from her own facilities, provide for all her needs in engines, equipment, and personnel. The War Ministry's Main Engineering Directorate was aware of this fact from the first. In 1910 its annual report stressed that "the Aeronautics Section has made every possible effort to see that, wherever possible, all material for the aeronautical units was procured within Russia. During the year covered by this report, a considerable degree of success was achieved in realizing [this aim]." And if this had been the case with regard to dirigibles, it naturally was extended to include heavier-than-air craft as well.

The War Ministry therefore set out to promote the aviation industry, and foreign machines were purchased either as models or to satisfy immediate needs. When it is recalled that Russia's first aircraft company was founded in the summer of 1909, and that her designers and builders were still only gifted amateurs, the tremendous dimensions of this problem are obvious. The creation of an aviation industry in backward Russia was to be a long and difficult task.

Nonetheless, the War Ministry did what it could, sponsoring various aeronautical festivals for the aeroclubs; in 1911, it began to hold its own competitions. These allowed native aircraft to compete with foreign products, and the prizes, along with the promise of government orders, made such competition profitable. But this policy also led to disagreements, with opposition apparently centered in the grand duke and his supporters.

The attitudes of Alexander Mikhailovich, a navy man, toward building an air fleet had been conditioned by his experiences in acquiring naval vessels. Once his attention had turned to the "aerial" fleet, his committee saw the creation of a modern, well-equipped and trained, front-line air service as the first priority. The creation of a native aviation industry was a worthy long-term goal, but in the short term foreign aircraft orders seemed the best use for public money.

The attitude of Nicholas E. Popov, a pioneer pilot and strong supporter of the grand duke, was typical of such views. In

1910, Popov escorted some French officers around the Gatchina flying field, where he was serving as an instructor. There, on display, were a number of Russia's first home-built aircraft. Describing these as being "as solid as barges," Popov recalled:

> I didn't exactly feel like laughing when one Frenchman remarked to me that: "With the money wasted on building these monsters you could have bought 15 excellent machines in France, and still have had your flyers trained, rather than have acquired these ridiculous 'contraptions,' which will fly only when a great pyre is lit beneath them. And then they will rise in the air only as smoke" (quoted in Tikhobrazov, 1964, p. 433).

Such differences of opinion were probably inevitable, but later events were to justify the War Ministry's concern about native production. The flimsy aircraft of that time aged much more rapidly than naval vessels, as new techniques and types of machines followed each other in rapid succession. So, while imperial Russia never developed an industry compatible with her needs, the War Ministry's policy did begin to show results: although the 1911 military competitions were won by foreign machines, by December of that year the government was able to order twenty-four machines from Russian firms.

In the 1912 military competitions, Russian machines took the first three prizes. Second and third places went to Moscow-built French (Farman) designs, but first prize went to the all-Russian Sikorsky biplane. And in June of the same year, the press reported that 140 out of the 150 newly ordered Nieuports were to be built in Russia, not France.

Such orders stimulated the rapid, if limited, growth of the native aviation industry. In 1910 a French firm founded the Duks plant in Moscow, and another company (named for its owner, J. Möller) began work in St. Petersburg. Moscow was also the location of a French Gnome-et-Rhone engine assembly workshop, while in December 1911 another small plant in Riga began to produce the Kalep—Russia's first native aeroengine. Other small factories also sprang up, but the most important development was undoubtedly the association of a young engineer, Igor Sikorsky, with the Russo-Baltic Wagon Factory (RBVZ), a firm engaged in producing railroad equipment.

The Russo-Baltic's first success was the victory of Sikorsky's three-seat S-6 biplane in the 1912 competitions. In 1913 Sikorsky became involved in larger projects, and his four-engine transport, the Grand, which weighed 7,000 pounds, was the result. Work along these lines continued with the support of the War Ministry and Tsar Nicholas II himself. By 1914 Russia had acquired her first two four-engined Sikorsky reconnaissance bombers, which were named after Ilia Muromets, the hero of ancient Kiev. (With the ordering of another ten of these machines, the Russians began to lose interest in large dirigibles.)

By 1914, then, Russia's aviation industry was showing remarkable progress, and the lessons implied by the rapidly changing technology seemed accepted by all. As a result, the mammoth aircraft orders (up to 1,000 planes) planned for the three years 1914-1917 were as much an effort to encourage native production as a measure to renew and standardize outworn equipment. To contemporaries, the air services appeared to be entering a new era.

Such expectations were dashed by the outbreak of war in August 1914. Russia's front-line strength was impressive, comprising 244 aircraft (compared to Germany's 232 and France's 138), along with 12 dirigibles, distributed among six aviation companies and thirty-nine detachments. Yet the machines were largely obsolete or obsolescent, reserves were almost entirely lacking, and Russia's seven aircraft factories were producing only some 30 to 40 machines a month (or about 400 a year, as compared to Germany's production of 1,348 for all of 1914). Engine production was even lower, and its dependence on foreign parts made this branch of the industry particularly sensitive to the effects of the Central Powers' blockade.

The maintenance of available aircraft was obviously of top priority, but here, as elsewhere, Russia was not prepared for a long struggle. As a result, by September 1, after only a month of fighting, only 145 front-line machines remained in service; thus the efforts of the previous four years had been largely negated. In retrospect, the War Ministry has been charged with lacking a clear procurement policy. As proof of this charge, it is pointed out that the 1914 orders had gone to some two dozen factories and included twelve different engine types. But the low productivity of the native aviation industry undoubtedly left little alternative, and the results of efforts to standardize equipment are obvious from an October report: of the 244 original military machines, 133 were Nieuports and 91 were Farmans. Nonetheless, because the maintenance and supply services still found themselves forced to deal with some sixteen different models, the result was confused and inefficient servicing. As the war continued, problems related to railway transport and, according to some sources, graft further complicated the situation.

One of the first signs of strain was the cutback in the "grand" aircraft procurement program in early 1914. Because of the enemy blockade and a shortage of engines, by October only 242 of the original 400 (and 7 of the 10 Sikorsky bombers) had been completed. Yet throughout 1914 and 1915 the government made strenuous efforts to replace losses: the worn-out Nieuports and Farmans by, at first, Voisins and Morance-Gs and, later, Morane Parasols and Spads. Further aircraft and engine orders were placed with both Russia's own overworked plants (expanded and supplemented by new enterprises) and plants in allied and neutral countries (France, Britain, and the United States).

Soviet writers, stressing that the aviation industry remained under the control of foreign firms and Russia's own private capitalists, have continually criticized the imperial government's lack of centralized planning. While this view is not completely unjustified, expansion did occur: by 1917, the number of aero factories had risen from seven (in 1914) to eighteen (seven in the Petrograd region, six in Moscow, and five in the south), employing some 10,000 men. Of these, eleven factories produced aircraft, five produced engines, and two produced propellers, but many remained, in reality, only glorified assembly workshops. Still, production did increase. In 1914, for instance, the RBVZ facilities were producing a mere six machines a month. By 1916 production had risen to twenty-six a month, and by early 1917 to thirty.

The overall production of the twelve leading plants showed a similar growth. In August 1914, they could deliver a paltry 37 machines monthly; this figure rose to 205 in 1915 and in February 1917, to 352. Although some Soviet historians claim that the industry's monthly average reached 230–380 machines, native production probably provided the air services with a total of only 2,200 aircraft.

Russian industry, with its small and poorly trained labor force, was not so effective in the more complicated matter of producing aeroengines. Major General Baranov, a leading figure in the air services, later noted that, while the 1916 aircraft production figure was 1,769, only some 666 engines—of seven different types— were built during that same period. Through early 1917, the situation remained roughly the same: only 110 to 150 new motors a month could be provided.

Domestic production of aircraft and engines was still primarily confined to such foreign (largely French) designs as Farman biplanes, Nieuports, Moranes, and Spads, and the low level of Russian technology meant the Russian-built product was usually inferior to the original. Nonetheless, throughout the war Russian designers remained busy planning their own models or adaptations of captured German machines. The most successful native machine was Sikorsky's RBVZ Ilia Muromets four-engined bomber: by the spring of 1917 some 75 had been accepted, and a fleet of 120 was planned for the future. The same firm also produced Sikorsky's fighters (the RBVZ 17 and 20); the Lebed works provided small numbers of its own reconnaissance and fighter machines (the Lebed 7, 9, 10, and 12); and D. P. Grigorovich's M-9 flying boats were particularly successful.

In spite of these efforts, the aircraft produced within Russia were of low quality, they reached the front in trickles, and they were usually obsolescent by the time they entered service. Further, their number was insufficient to meet the continuing demands for replacement and expansion. So the War Ministry was forced to depend very heavily upon imported equipment; as engine-production figures indicate, imports were necessary even for the majority of native-built aircraft. Recognizing Russia's problems, the French officially promised their ally 14 percent of their own production; up to January 1, 1916, they accepted orders for 586 machines and 1,730 engines. Britain also helped; after a military mission in 1916, the British sent 50 DeHavilland DH-4s and a handful of other types. In all, during the years 1914–1917, imports from the allies provided about 900 of the 3,100 new machines serving in Russian units and a total of 3,600 aeroengines.

As had been the case in 1910, however, the Russians remained far from satisfied with the services of their French allies. After the arrival of the very first French orders, the feeling began to spread that any old machine, however run-down or obsolete, was considered good enough for the Russians. Since that time, both emigré and Soviet writers have been unanimous in condemning the Allied powers in general and the French in particular for both their slowness in delivering and for the second-rate equipment they provided. For example, the commander of the Russian unit defending Warsaw later complained that the obsolescent French machines provided in early 1915 had already seen action on the western front and required extensive servicing before being used. Soviet writers maintain that by January 1, 1915, out of the large orders mentioned previously, only 250 machines and 268 engines had actually been received from France. Admittedly, the problems of communication were tremendous. In the face of these problems, by 1916 the Allies—despite their own needs—were making greater efforts than they had made earlier. Still, it is difficult to entirely discount the Russian complaints, and many Russians never forgot the disadvantages of depending on foreign industry.

These difficulties hindered the maintenance, let alone the expansion, of the Russian air services. In October 1914, the General Staff warned that for the moment only replacements could be guaranteed, and that no new units could begin formation until November or December. After that date, despite the demands of the reequipment program, slow progress began to be apparent. By mid-1915 some 350 machines were in service, and by the end of that year there were 553. Another report maintains that by September 1916 there were 716 aircraft and 502 pilots divided among 75 squadrons. During the next few months, until the outbreak of the revolution, the situation improved rapidly: one archival report notes that by the end of February 1917 an all-time high of 1,039 machines had been achieved, though this estimate probably includes aircraft that had yet to enter actual service.

These figures by themselves are not unimpressive. In view of the high losses occasioned by enemy action and poor servicing, however, the number of available machines was still woefully inadequate. In February 1917 the Russians' western front was reporting a 59 percent shortage in fighters, while on the northern front, which supposedly had a strength of 118 aircraft, only 60 were fit for action. Similarly, the engine situation remained critical: many machines were still being forwarded to front-line squadrons without power plants, and some units had only two engines for every five or six airplanes. Even considering that airframes usually had a shorter service life than engines, such a situation was hardly satisfactory.

Another problem was the shortage and faulty training of air crews. Although by 1914 Russian pilots could fly and navigate well enough, much of their training had been theoretical; they possessed insufficient skills in artillery spotting and in the reporting of enemy positions and maneuvers. The lack of qualified observers remained a pressing problem, despite efforts to entice artillery officers into the air service. In mid-1916, for instance, some 357 observers were available, but only 132 were qualified artillery officers. Meanwhile, the accelerated courses provided for the wartime training of new observers and pilots lowered the standards of instruction; this, in turn, contributed to higher losses and increased inefficiency.

In 1914 the General Staff expressed confidence in the supply of pilots, reporting that the flying units had almost two pilots for each available aircraft. Further, the two main pilot training schools (at Gatchina and Sevastopol) had graduated 130 fliers during that year, making a total of some 300 trained by the War Ministry's own facilities since 1910. Apart from this, pilots were being trained by the aeroclubs at Petrograd, Moscow, and Odessa; all in all, the situation seemed well in hand.

Experience, again, proved these expectations naive. By the late autumn of 1914, the air services were critically short of flyers as well as observers. Although civilian pilot volunteers did step forward, they were few in number—and, surprisingly, they were actively discouraged by the military. (Not only did these volunteers receive extremely low pay, they were also expected to provide their own machines and maintenance.) As a result, the air services were handicapped by shortages of personnel as well as of equipment. In mid-December 1914, for instance, the commander of the squadron attached to the staff of the Ninth Army reported: "There are four machines in the unit, but only two fit fliers, so I must request . . . you give me only two missions a day" (Duz, vol. 2, 1960, p. 125).

Under these pressures, the government

Figure 6. Farman Pushers at the 1914 Imperial Air Review.

made strenuous attempts to provide more personnel both by expanding the training facilities and by shortening the course of studies. In addition to enlarging the Sevastopol and Gatchina facilities, the government founded new schools at Odessa and Moscow. According to one official report, by September 1, 1916, these four schools had trained 269, 125, 47, and 5 pilots, respectively. Other semiofficial facilities at Petrograd, Evpatoria, and elsewhere (apart from those for naval pilots) added a few more, so that by 1917 there were probably about 500 fliers at the front. Given the hasty training, poor equipment, and high losses (25 to 30 percent of the commissioned personnel), it is no wonder that Russia's resources in both training and facilities proved woefully inadequate. For, while all the warring nations had to hastily train replacement pilots, Russia's general backwardness severely limited her manpower reserves for any service requiring technological knowledge or skills and for pilots in particular.

As if all this were not bad enough, throughout the bitter struggle Russia's airmen were bedeviled by another problem: despite all the prewar discussions, senior Russian commanders (like many others elsewhere) were taking a long time to discover the value and potential of military aviation. As A. F. Polovtsov, a

member of the Special Council of State Defense, put it, "no significance was attached to this branch of weaponry" (Duz, vol. 2, 1960, p. 139).

The problems of war did eventually help the Russian air services to achieve administrative autonomy in the form of the Chief Directorate of the Military Aerial Fleet. Yet official neglect of the air services, as demonstrated by slowness of promotion and lowering of morale, continued to plague the Grand Duke Alexander, who assumed command of the new directorate. In 1916, for instance, he complained that his service contained only a single colonel; the rest of his officers were only captains and lieutenants. At the same time, the confusion of authority and the professional jealousies that continued at the top levels of command did little to improve the situation. One senior official later observed:

During the war the aviation units left a great deal to be desired; the business was new and hence the Grand Duke had long theoretical arguments with the representatives of the General Staff at Stavka (i.e., the General Headquarters). So right up to the end of the war a correct diagnosis remained to be made and matters were not corrected. Some aviation units were subordinated to the

Grand Duke, others to Stavka, and so on (Spiridovich, vol. 2, 1961, p. 33).

Although Alexander Mikhailovich was a competent administrator, operation of the air units was subordinated to the army command. Thus each corps had its own reconnaissance unit, while longer-range reconnaissance and, later, fighter units were attached to army and front headquarters. Moreover, although the inadequate antiaircraft defense was usually the responsibility of the ground forces, special squadrons were occasionally formed to protect important cities and targets. Generally, despite the grand duke's early vision of the potential of an air fleet, Russian aviation remained firmly tied to the support requirements of the army. Like the navy, the air force was considered a supplement to the land forces, not an independent arm of war.

With all these drawbacks, it is not surprising that the imperial air services could conduct only limited operations during World War I. Although the length of the front lines allowed neither side a continuous overall supremacy, the statistics for individual Russian aerial combat activity make it painfully clear that the Russians could not gain even a temporary ascendency: from March to May 1915, at the time of the great German offensive, the Second Army's air unit took part in only seventy-five combat flights amounting to 150 hours in the air. By 1917 the situation was undoubtedly much improved—in June, at the time of the abortive Russian offensive, some fifty-two sorties daily were being made on the southwest front. But any real "command of the air," even on a local scale, remained beyond the Russians' reach; their forces on the eastern front never seriously endangered the aerial might of the Central Powers.

In 1914, even though Sikorsky's bomb-

ers were being fitted with machine guns and experiments in aircraft armament were in progress, the Russian high command gave little serious thought to the possibilities of aerial combat: planes were useful for observation, reconnaissance, and liaison. When, a few weeks later, Peter Nesterov rammed an Austrian aircraft and both machines crashed in flames, this was regarded as merely an incidental, if heroic, exploit. By early 1915, however, as enemy raids on Warsaw increased in strength, aerial warfare as a means of air defense became a reality.

The formation in that month of a special aviation detachment for the defense of Warsaw, commanded by N. Voeodsky (later transferred to the Fifth Army), marks the beginning of the Russian fighter forces. Still, only in 1916—as a reaction to the Russian experience on the western front and as a counter to German activity— was serious attention paid to organizing this branch of the aerial fleet. The official basis was laid when, on July 4, 1916, official approval was given to a June 2 report by the director of aviation and aeronautics in the active army. This report argued that German fighter formations must be opposed by similar Russian units that could defend reconnaissance machines, deny the enemy reconnaissance opportunities, and pursue and destroy enemy fighters—a doctrine then being adopted on the western front as well.

Actually, fighter units had already begun formation flying that spring at the army level; at that time, two fighting planes were added to each general army and corps air detachment. In August, the formation by the Eleventh Army of the first large fighter group was officially sanctioned. A month later a second group, under the ace E. N. Krutin, appeared on the southwestern front, with others soon to follow. On the basis of Krutin's observations during a visit to the French front, where large-scale air battles had broken out in 1916, the program was continued in 1917; by May there were four fighter groups with twelve fighter squadrons. But this program, cut short by the revolution, came too late: despite the heroism of Nesterov and other aces (among them A. A. Kazakov, I. V. Smirnov, and V. G. Fedorov), the Russian fighter squadrons never equalled the strength of their opponents.

In other spheres the Russians' limited aerial activity was somewhat more successful. As early as 1913 tests were made on equipment that allowed liaison and reconnaissance machines to "throw" bombs. During the war bombing became a separate activity, if still tied to tactical considerations of ground support. Targets were purely military, with most raids being carried out in daylight (though, after April 1915, night bombing missions were occasionally mounted). By the end of the war, fighter escorts were also being provided.

The best-known Russian bombing unit was the famous "squadron of flying ships," which was equipped with Sikorsky's armed four-engined Ilya Muromets reconnaissance bombers. Because the first experiences with these machines had been disappointing, in December 1914 it seemed that further orders would be cancelled. Then, as a result of the initiative of the Russo-Baltic Works (which had taken over servicing and air-crew training), these machines were concentrated into a separate squadron commanded by Maj. Gen. M. V. Shidlovsky, a former naval officer and RBVZ director who had returned to service for this purpose.

This squadron, whose front-line strength was rarely more than twenty-five machines, made 442 raids and dropped 2,000 bombs between February 1915 and October 1917. Penetrating up to 150 miles into the enemy's rear flank, it carried out raids against railway junctions, troop concentrations, and similar targets. Reconnaissance missions were so successful that during the same period more than 7,000 photographs were taken and analyzed. All of these missions resulted in the loss of only three machines because of enemy action, while the gunners of the squadron of flying ships disposed of some forty enemy aircraft.

In spite of the obvious strengths of these machines and the grand duke's earlier dreams about the possibilities of air power, the squadron's missions remained tactical. Indeed, not even the grand duke's staff was uniformly enthusiastic about the machines; some felt that their main virtue was their "patriotic" Russian origin. Otherwise, they were expensive luxuries, diverting resources from the production of much-needed fighters. Nonetheless, the War Ministry continued its orders and planned a second squadron. Both Soviet and émigré historians, on the other hand, have continued to consider Sikorsky's bomber the high point of early Russian aviation history.

It must be concluded, then, that the imperial air forces were caught unprepared for the long struggle, and that they never really made up the ground lost so rapidly in 1914. By 1917 they were beginning to make slow progress, and the high commanders had themselves come to value the tactical services of the air force. Above all else, however, the war demonstrated the perils inherent in Russia's industrial backwardness and her dependence on foreign imports; though the revolution of 1917 disrupted Russia's air services, the resulting civil war firmly impressed these same lessons upon her new rulers.

The immediate result of the Bolsheviks' seizure of power in November 1917 was the virtual disintegration of the air services along with the rest of Russia's military power. During that year, production in the factories ground to a halt and maintenance services collapsed; even as early as August 1917, most units were only 50 percent equipped. Matters grew worse; by December, with the Soviet regime established in Moscow and Petrograd, the revolutionary chaos had engulfed most units. Both ordinary soldiers and NCOs eyed their officers with suspicion, often drove them from their units, and in some cases actually shot them. (Such, for example, was the eventual fate of Shidlovsky, commander of the squadron of flying ships.)

Although some officers remained, the majority either disappeared into merciful obscurity, joined the organizing Whites, fled to the Allies, or surrendered to the Germans. At the same time, material was often misplaced or (in the early months of 1918) simply destroyed. The motives for such actions varied greatly: thirty Ilia Muromets bombers were destroyed to save them from the Germans at Vinnitsa, while at Sevastopol other aircraft were demolished in an effort to prevent a prolongation of the war. Despite early measures of nationalization, the production of new aircraft ceased as workers turned to politics and service in the Red Guard.

Bolshevik aerial policies were at first hindered by the same contradictions that plagued the army in general. Anticipating the danger of counterrevolution at home, the new regime believed it was necessary to complete the destruction of the now-useless imperial military machine and the last vestiges of its officers' power. Yet, because of this same threat—as well as the threat posed by the Germans—it was necessary to create a new army. Although the form of this "socialist" force was open to debate, even the December 1917 "democratizing" decree that ordered the

election of officers stressed the necessity of preserving the technically trained—and hence the aviation—cadres.

The new government made its first effort to organize an air service when, as ex-Premier Kerensky, along with General Krasnov's Cossacks, advanced on Petrograd, some scratch air detachments were formed to support the defending Red Guards and drop propaganda literature over the enemy's forces. That same day, the Bureau of Commissars for Aviation and Aeronautics, attached to the Military Revolutionary Committee, was set up.

Once the immediate crisis was past and demobilization was under way in its official and unofficial guises, the All-Russian College for the Administration of the Aerial Fleet was established under K. V. Akashev's chairmanship. This group set out to establish some semblance of order so that factories could be reopened, existing equipment preserved, and cadres reassembled. In 1918, when the decision to build a new Red Army was made official by the decree of January 28, the college's work acquired more purpose. The War Commissariat's Order no. 84 of January 25 had already demanded that all measures be taken to collect material and to preserve the aviation schools; in February, the All-Russian Congress on Aeronautics was formed to mobilize support for this work.

The results of this effort are difficult to assess. Although the All-Russian College's writ lacked authority in many areas, it had some success: Soviet sources claim that up to 37 percent of the tsarist regime's equipment and personnel was acquired during this period. In some cases, whole units survived almost intact. The tsarist Twenty-fifth Squadron is a case in point; having purged itself of the "counterrevolutionary" portion of its officer cadres, this unit left the front and eventually passed directly into Soviet service. One of its members main-

tains that twenty-one other units did likewise, and that by April 15, 1918, the
Bolsheviks had an additional ten squadrons
on their newly established fronts. Although
the majority of units were stationed at
such major centers as Moscow, Petrograd,
Tula, and Saratov and equipped with
obsolete and run-down machines, by May
1918 the young Red air service could
manage modest air displays.

Meanwhile, Leon Trotsky had begun
organizing the Red Army along more
traditional lines, and aviation was no
exception. By the authority of the War
Commissariat's Order no. 385 of May 24,
the All-Russian College was replaced by
the Chief Directorate of the Workers' and
Peasants' Red Aerial Fleet, which remained
aviation's main administrative authority
throughout the civil war. On June 20, the
first issue appeared of *Vestnik Vozdushnogo Flota* (Herald of the Aerial Fleet),
which has remained (although renamed
Aviatsiia i kosmonavtika) the official
journal of Soviet aviation.

The renewed outbreak of civil war in
June 1918 and the disasters on the eastern
front caused the Bolsheviks to redouble
their efforts in the military sphere. While
the Red Aerial Fleet had administrative
authority, it now needed operational
guidance. In late summer of that year the
Field Administration of the Aerial Fleet
was created to fulfill this need, and the
experienced military pilot A. V. Sergeev
was appointed its head. The former officers
(controlled by commissars) who served on
this body not unnaturally developed an
operational structure resembling that of
World War I, and once again aviation was
placed firmly under the heel of the land
forces. Later, each *front* (army group) was
given its own chief aviation administration,
beneath which army administrations had
control of individual operational units. At
the divisional level and above, ground-force

commanders had tactical control of aerial
units, although some were directly subordinate to army or *front* administrations.

As of May 1918, the basic air unit was
set at six machines attached to a rifle
division. Although some attempt was
made to create specialized fighter, reconnaissance, and bombing units, the earliest
formations usually contained a mixture
from the stock of available machines. By
1919 the Soviets, like the imperial air
services before them, had begun to return
to the use of more-concentrated formations (as at Tsaritsyn). At the end of that
year, a meeting of army commanders
resulted in a directive "on the employment
of the air force in mobile war." Earlier, up
to 40 percent of the Soviets' air strength
had sometimes been concentrated against
particularly dangerous enemy thrusts (such
as Kolchak's at the end of 1918 and
Denikin's in mid-1919), but by 1920, 70
percent was being thrown into the struggle
against the Poles. Divisions of three or
four squadrons were used, combined with
reserves under a single headquarters, to
break the enemy's resistance (as against
Wrangel in 1920).

At the same time, the Aerial Fleet
showed a gradual numerical increase as
old and captured machines were collected,
reconditioned, and put into service. By
early autumn of 1918, some 260 aircraft
were in action; by November 1919 there
were about 350, divided among sixty-two
squadrons. After that time this strength
was more or less maintained. According to
one Soviet report, at the end of 1920 the
Chief Administration controlled a large
array of units including seven *front* and
sixteen army aviation staffs, eight aviation
parks and warehouses, sixteen aviation
workshops for reconditioning sixty-five
combat units, one division of Ilia Muromets bombers, five aeronautical divisions,
twenty-eight aeronautical units, two naval

aerial fleet staffs, twenty float-plane units, twelve schools and courses, and one engineering institute.

It is doubtful, however, that all these units possessed anything like their full strength; even in comparison with those of the imperial air forces, the supply and maintenance problems faced by the Red Aerial Fleet were gigantic. These problems are revealed by a report on the state of the 1,102 machines in Soviet hands on February 1, 1919. Of these, only 349 were at the front, divided among fifty-nine detachments. Of the remaining 753 aircraft, 34 were allotted to internal military districts and the other 719, in various states of disrepair, were scattered among parks, workshops, schools, factories, and storehouses (167 were without engines, 363 were damaged or incomplete, and 142 were too run-down to be of any use in combat). Further, the figures represent a motley collection of machines—including those inherited from the imperial army as well as those captured from the retreating Germans in 1918 and later from the Whites and intervening Allies—with the result that obtaining parts became a nightmare. For, despite nationalization of the aircraft industry (beginning with individual measures but made general in June 1918), production remained extremely low. After 1918 the Council of Labor and Defense, under Lenin's personal chairmanship, made strenuous efforts to increase production, but in aviation the situation was disastrous: the five factories in the south were in White-occupied areas, and only three out of the seven in Petrograd managed to continue any work. During 1918 new production amounted to only 106 airplanes and 33 engines.

At the end of 1919 the industry was reorganized under the Chief Administration of the Aviation Industry (Glavkoavia), which itself was under the general super-vision of the Supreme Council of the National Economy. Besides attempts to produce synthetic fuel in Kazan, efforts were made generally to increase aircraft production and reopen plants. By December of that year the former Duks plant in Moscow had begun turning out a few Spad-7 fighters, while some float-planes were already in production in Petrograd. Despite all these efforts, however, the output of new aircraft remained minimal: even the most optimistic Soviet figures claim only 669 new aircraft during the years 1918–1920.

The real work of the aviation factories was the refitting of old machines, not the production of new ones. For this work, a large network of maintenance facilities had been developed during the war. By 1920 each unit had its own supply and repair shop, supported by larger workshops situated in trains behind the front or in aviation parks. At the center of this network were the factories that, during the 1918–1920 period, made most of the major repairs. The extent of their work is indicated by the fact that during these years the air industry reconditioned 1,574 aircraft and 1,740 engines. These were only stopgap measures, however; by 1921 the Aerial Fleet badly needed to be re-equipped, and the entire industry needed to be reorganized and expanded.

Similar problems existed with personnel. The Aerial Fleet was always critically short of trained fliers and observers. During the first five months of 1918, recruiting for the air service (as was that for the other branches of the armed forces), was carried out on a volunteer basis. Although some individual fliers (such as the Latvian ace Col. J. Bashko) and even some complete units did pass into Bolshevik service, the response was generally disappointing. Although after June 1918 mobilizations were frequent, in the end the Soviet regime obtained only about one-third of the tsarist air cadres.

The Soviet government was therefore forced to reorganize the old flying schools for its own purposes. On April 20, 1918, the Gatchina school was reopened as the Soviets' first aviation school, and during the following months other practical and theoretical training was offered in Moscow and elsewhere. These training centers were usually staffed by ex-tsarist officer and soldier fliers and mechanics, and during the civil war they produced only a handful of graduates. (One modest Soviet estimate gives the figures of 155 pilots and 75 observers.)

Although these training courses retained the defects of the tsarist regime's accelerated program, exacerbated by the often-insufficient educational level of the students, these drawbacks were to some extent offset by the latters' enthusiasm. Special efforts were made to get Communist volunteers to enter the Aerial Fleet and to ensure that its existing cadres became loyal sons of the party. Thus, by the end of 1919, one-quarter of the personnel were party members; a year later the figure had risen to between 47 and 50 percent. Nonetheless, enthusiasm and dedication could not wholly compensate for defects in training and obsolete equipment, and accidents were frequent. Though statistics for crashes in the schools proper are not available, the general figures are instructive: between April 1, 1918, and April 1, 1920, accidents accounted for 365 of the 422 aircraft lost. A breakdown of causes shows 208 engine failures, 25 fires or explosions in the air, and 132 crashes while landing.

While the total number of Soviet fliers and observers was low, official figures indicate some absolute increase. These data claim that there were 302 pilots and observers in June 1919 and 730 at the end of 1920. Some Westerners consider the

Figure 7. Nikolai Yegorovich Zhukovsky.

latter figure inflated, suggesting one closer to 300, but, in any case, training facilities, like the air industry itself, could be developed extensively only with the coming of peace.

Given such drawbacks, the Red Aerial Fleet could, at best, mount only limited operations. Official figures for the period 1917–1922 maintain that 19,377 sorties were flown, totaling some 27,566 hours in the air, and that 94,508 kilograms of bombs were dropped. From November 1917 onward the Soviets used aircraft as a means of disseminating propaganda; over the same period, 9,000 kgs. of leaflets were distributed from Red airplanes. By the end of 1920, Soviet machines had engaged in 144 aerial battles in which 83 fliers were lost (390 were lost in accidents).

The greater part of this last activity

took place in 1920 against the Poles and Wrangel's Whites. Throughout 1918 and 1919, Soviet units saw action on all the civil war fronts—in the north, against Kolchak in the east and Denikin in the south, in Turkestan, and elsewhere. But, although larger units and greater concentrations of units (the mobility between fronts having been improved by the use of the railways) had been achieved by 1919, only in the following year did Soviet aviation really prove its worth: that year alone accounted for 7,265 official combat sorties (totaling 10,605 hours in the air), 93 aerial battles, and the dropping of 42,304 kilograms of bombs and 5,925 kilograms of agitational literature.

In the course of these campaigns, Soviet military and political leaders acquired a great deal of useful experience that confirmed and supplemented the lessons of 1914–1917. As a result, the Aerial Fleet remained strongly under the control of the land forces' commanders, who fully appreciated the tactical possibilities of the new weapon. During 1919 and 1920 the air force not only had proved useful for bombarding enemy fortifications and supply centers, it also, in the open battlefields of the civil war, had been extremely effective against enemy cavalry. From this time on the Red air force remained strongly interested in developing effective and often heavily armored ground-attack aircraft— a policy which later resulted in the appearance of S. V. Iliushin's famous Il-2 Shturmovik in World War II. Further, while the original strategic promise implicit in Sikorsky's four-engined bombers was never realized, the experiences of 1914–1920 taught the Soviets the advantages of the strategic use of tactical aviation. The rapid concentration, often via railway, of aerial forces on vital fronts or sectors of a front, backed up by reserves that could be thrown into the struggle at the decisive

moment, was a practice that also reappeared in the later Soviet-German conflict. Yet it was air support in the immediate battle zone, not the implications of strategic bombing, that occupied the Reds' attention.

Another painful lesson learned in this early period was the necessity of building standardized, rugged aircraft in order to simplify maintenance and servicing. Given the continual problems experienced with foreign machines, the new regime realized the importance of domestic designs, and in this area the old regime's legacy of aeronautical research was enthusiastically utilized. Although many designers, including Sikorsky himself, had emigrated to continue their work abroad, the research facilities of N. Y. Zhukovsky (see figure 7) and his colleagues remained intact in Moscow.

In December 1918 Zhukovsky's facilities and staff were organized into the Central Institute of Aerodynamics and Hydrodynamics (TsAGI), which received a level of state support unprecedented in Russia's aerial history. Zhukovsky himself headed TsAGI until his death in 1921; in 1919 he was also involved in founding the Moscow Air Technical College, which in 1920 became the Institute for Engineers of the Red Air Fleet and, later, the Zhukovsky Air Academy. The results of all this work and support were soon apparent: by the end of 1920 a native engine was entering production, and the new institutions later helped train such famous Soviet designers as Iliushin, A. S. Yakovlev, and A. N. Tupolev. Indeed, Tupolev's 1922 ANT-1 was designed under TsAGI auspices.

The support given TsAGI and the interest shown by Lenin himself are indicative of the high value afforded aviation in the young Soviet republic. Part of this attitude may be ascribed to the Communist's general enthusiasm for industrialization and modernization—for which the airplane was a fitting and spectacular symbol. As early as spring of 1918 plans had been discussed for developing civil air routes. Although these plans had been postponed when the civil war erupted, the war, in turn, helped to bring home to Lenin's government the military importance of aerial self-reliance.

With an end to hostilities, attention was again paid to both these questions. On January 26, 1921, the Council of Labor and Defense set up a commission to examine the aviation industry and to design a maximum program for aviation construction. In June of that year a report was presented envisaging, among other measures, importation of German machines, and in December 1922 the council approved a plan for the completion of airfields and aircraft factories. Although some administrative confusion existed—the Department of Industrial Enterprises of the Red Air Fleet (Provozduch), established in November 1921, to some extent duplicated the work of the Glavkoavia—the commit-

ment of the state to aviation could not be doubted.

By 1922 the Aerial Fleet was being re-equipped and reorganized and the industry behind it expanded. Although native designers were busy, the Soviet Union, as had been the case with imperial Russia a decade and a half earlier, still needed foreign machines and technical advice. Only then did they turn to the Germans, the other pariahs of Europe, and the latter were to play a significant part in the years to come. Most important of all, Russian aviation now had a government which, with its enthusiasm for industrialization and its appreciation of the lessons of the 1914–1920 conflicts, was committed to creating a technologically independent air force bearing the Red Star—the symbol of the new Russia. Thus, while the problems of 1910 remained to be solved, the determination to solve them was not lacking when the means became available in years to come.

Research Notes

The early period of Russian aviation history is briefly recounted, with varying degrees of accuracy, in a number of general Soviet works. These include N. D. Anoshchenko, *Vozdukhoplavateli* (Moscow, 1960); N. K. Denisov, *Boevaia slava sovetskoi aviatsii* (Moscow, 1953); G. P. Mazokhin, *Aviation,* (Moscow, 1971); V. P. Moskovskii, *Voenno-vozdushnye sily SSSR, 1918–1948* (Moscow, 1948); P. Shadskii, *Sovetskaia aviatsiia v boeviakh*

za Rodinu (Moscow, 1958); L. Shesterikova, *Daty istorii otechestvennoi aviatsii i vozdukhoplavaniia* (Moscow, 1953); and N. G. Stubrovskii, *Nasha strana-rodina vozdukhoplavaniia* (Moscow, 1954).

For general histories in English, the reader should consult R. A. Kilmarx, *A History of Soviet Air Power* (London, 1962); H. J. Nowarra and G. R. Duval, *Russian Civil and Military Aircraft, 1884–1969* (London, 1970); and, for World War

I, N. N. Golovin, *The Russian Army in the World War* (New York, 1939).

Early accounts, memoirs, and biographies in English include Lieutenant Colonel "Roustem-Bek," *Aerial Russia: The Romance of the Giant Ships* (London, 1916); Grand Duke Alexander Romanov, *Once a Grand Duke* (New York, 1938); I. I. Sikorsky, *The Story of the Winged S* (New York, 1938); A. R. Coupar, *The Smirnoff Story* (London, 1960); and F. J. Delear, *Igor Sikorsky: His Three Careers in Aviation* (New York, 1969). Also see J. Alexander, "The Russian Section," in B. Robertson, ed., *Air Aces of the 1914-1918 War* (Letchworth, Herts, England, 1959), pp. 148-160.

Articles in English-language journals should also be consulted, especially T. Stariparloff, "The Russian Military Air Service up to the Revolution," *Air Power* 4 (December 1918): 337-324; various articles in *Air Power Historian/Aerospace Historian;* and the following articles in *The Royal Air Force Flying Review (RAF Review):* J. Alexander, "The Squadron of Flying Ships," *RAF Review* 12, no. 9 (May 1957): 20-22; J. Alexander, "Death or Glory," *RAF Review* 13, no. 10 (July 1958): 16-19; and E. Meos, "Schooner Below!," *RAF Review* 12, no. 1 (January 1957): 44-46.

Contemporary developments in the pre-1914 period were rather haphazardly chronicled in the "Military Notes" and "Aviation Notes" regularly published in the British *Journal of the Royal United Services Institution* during the years 1907-1914. Mention should also be made of Colonel Tikhobrazov's "Un As de l'Aviation Russe: Nesterov," *Miroir de l'Histoire,* no. 180 (December, 1964), pp. 42-51.

Many of the general histories and volumes of memoirs dealing with this period contain useful information. Typical of this massive literature are M. Lichnevsky,

trans., *Lettres des Grand Ducs à Nicholas II* (Paris, 1926); M. V. Rodzianko, *The Reign of Rasputin: An Empire's Collapse,* with an introduction by D. R. Jones (Gulf Breeze, Fla., 1973); M. V. Rodzianko, "Gosudarstvennaia Duma i fevral'skaia 1917 goda revoliutsiia," in *Arkhiv russkoi revoliutsii,* vol. 6 (Berlin, 1926), pp. 5-169; A. I. Spiridovich, *Velikaia voina i fevral'skaia revoliutsiia, 1914-1917,* three vols. (New York, 1960-1962); B. Pares, *My Russian Memoirs* (New York, 1969); and D. A. Kovalenko, *Oboronnaia promyshlennost' Sovetskoi Rossii v 1918-1920* (Moscow, 1970).

Emigré Russian sources are very useful. Apart from the articles and memoirs contained in such journals as *Voennyi sbornik* (Belgrade, 1921-1931), *Voennaia byl'* (Paris, 1952-), *Russkii invalid* (Paris, 1930-1940), and *Chasovoi* (Paris, 1929-1941, and Brussels, 1947-); special mention should be made of K. N. Finne, *Russkie vozdushnye bogatyri I. I. Sikorskago: materialy dlia istorii russkoi aviatsii* (Belgrade, 1930); P. F. L'dovskii (Liapidevskii), *Zapiski voennogo letchika* (Shanghai, 1934), and *Goluboi Fokker* (Kharbin, n.d.); and A. Matveev, *Razbitye Kryl'ia* (Berlin, n.d.). Also of importance are N. S. Karinsky's three volumes of typescript entitled "Istoriia letnago dela v Rossii do padeniia Imperii" (New York, 1944-1945), deposited in the New York Public Library.

Among the Soviet studies, the journals *Vestnik vozdushnogo flota,* known since 1958 as *Aviatsiia i kosmonavtika* (Moscow, 1918-), *Grazhdanskaia aviatsiia* (Moscow, 1930-), and *Voenno-istoricheskii zhurnal* (Moscow, 1958-) contain useful articles, as does the army newspaper *Krasnaia zvezda* (Moscow, 1924-). The development of the Russian aircraft industry is briefly surveyed in A. S. Yakovlev, *50 let Sovetskogo samoletostroeniia* (Moscow,

1958), and more thoroughly reviewed in B. V. Shavrov, *Istoriia konstruktsii samoletov v SSSR do 1938* (Moscow, 1969).

The leading Soviet studies of pre-1917 aviation are P. A. Duz et al., *Istoriia vozdukhoplavaniia i aviatsii v SSSR,* vol. 1, *Period do 1914,* (Moscow, 1944), and vol. 2, *Period pervoi mirovoi voiny,* 1914–1918 (Moscow, 1960), although volume 1 is extremely hard to find. For the early years of Soviet aviation, a useful source is L. M. Shishov, *Na zare Sovetskoi aviatsii* (Moscow, 1970). Also see early Soviet newspapers, including such general political journals as *Pravda,* and such special newspapers as *Krasnaia Armiia.*

Also useful are the biographies of early Soviet aviators. These include F. I. Zharov, *Podvigi krasnykh letchikov* (Moscow, 1963); K. Trunov and M. Golyshev, *Petr Nesterov* (Moscow, 1971); G. V. Zalutskii, *Vydaiushchiesia Russkie letchiki: M. Efrimov, P. Nesterov, E. Kruten, K. Artseulov* (Moscow, 1953); and Kh. S. Petrosiants, *V riadakh Sovetskikh aviatorov* (Erevan, 1969). For memoirs of Soviet airmen, see A. Petrenko, *V nebe staroi i novoi Rossii* (Moscow, 1953); I. K. Spatarel, *Protiv chernogo barona* (Moscow, 1957); and I. T. Spirin, *Zapiski voennogo letchika* (Moscow, 1939); as well as such shorter reminiscences, published as part of larger collections, as S. Krasovskii, "Sotsialisticheskie aviatsionnye otriady," in P. A. Akhlov and P. A. Selivanov, eds., *V boiakh i pokhodakh* (Minsk, 1972), pp. 112–121.

Other articles deserving special mention are "Epizody iz boevykh deistvii Russkoi aviatsii, 1914–1917," *Krasnyi arkhiv* 96, no. 5 (Moscow, 1939): 121–147; and I. S.

Korotkov, "Krasnaia aviatsiia v boiakh protiv Vrangelia," *Voennaia mysl',* no. 11 (Moscow, 1938), pp. 77–94.

Pre-1917 Russian aviation literature is scarce, but mention should be made of A. A. Rodnykh, *Istoriia vozdukhoplavaniia i letaniia v Rossii,* two vols. (St. Petersburg, 1911–1912); and N. M. Glagolev, *Vozdushnyi flot: istoriia i organizatsiia voennago vozdukhoplavaniia* (Petrograd, 1915).

For the most part, however, a researcher must rely on the pre-1917 press, including both such general newspapers as the cadet party organ, *"Rech'"* (1906–1917), and more specialized journals. The most valuable sources for this chapter were *Vozdukhoplavatel'* (St. Petersburg, 1905–1916), *Avtomobil i vozdukhoplavanie* (Moscow, 1911–1912), *Ofitserskaia zhizn* (Warsaw, 1906–1914), *Russkii invalid* (St. Petersburg, 1905–1917), *Voennyi mir* (Moscow, 1911–1914), *Armiia i flot* (St. Petersburg, 1914), *Voennyi sbornik* (St. Petersburg, 1900–1917), and *Voennyi letchik* (Sevastopol, 1916–1917). *Morskoi sbornik* (St. Petersburg, 1905–1914) and *Voina i mir* (Moscow, 1906–1907) were also of use.

Official documentation is also scarce. Apart from those works mentioned above, a researcher should examine the relevant portions of the war minister's annual reports *(Vsepoddanneishii otchet o deistviiakh voennago ministerstva)* for the years after 1885 and the various documents contained in Gen. N. N. Golovin's personal archives at the Hoover Institute.

Finally, this writer must thank the various emigré officers and fliers who have helped him with information and advice.

3

NEP and the Industrialization to 1928

Neil M. Heyman

The Russia of early 1922 offered little hope of rapid progress in aviation. Following nearly a decade of international and civil war, the nation possessed, at best, a shattered industrial base. The government was committed to a gradual form of economic recovery that precluded allocating scarce resources to heavy industry. Instead, economic restoration was to depend upon coaxing increased food production from a hostile peasantry. The military was in the middle of one of history's greatest demobilizations, the Russian armed forces falling from nearly five million to less than 600,000 men. Russia's most articulate military leaders were engaged in a barren, bitter debate over the application of Marxism to military affairs. Visions of a future war, not to speak of the role air power would play, were vague and contradictory. The jockeying for political advantage in the developing struggle to succeed Lenin clouded and complicated both military and industrial planning. Finally,

Soviet Russia lacked a clear-sighted spokesman capable of presenting the case for the development of aviation in compelling terms.

By the conclusion of 1927, several of these barriers had been removed. Industry had been restored and, more important, the Soviet government had agreed on an industrial development program which would provide an indigenous base for, among other things, aviation. The pedantic debates over Marxism's role in military affairs had faded in the face of the harsh practical necessity of defending Soviet Russia, given its limited resources and with the political demise of Leon Trotsky. The political struggle was a thing of the past; Stalin was in firm control. Finally, Russia had profited from six years of close technical and military cooperation with Germany.

The NEP to the Death of Lenin

The dominant feature of Russian political

and economic life in the aftermath of the civil war was the establishment of NEP, the so-called New Economic Policy. The government thereby abandoned its effort to control all industrial production via the Supreme Council of the National Economy and that body's *glavki* (centers) for each industry. The previous system, necessary in the war years, had made the entire economy a mere supply mechanism for the Red military forces. Whatever its accomplishments, it had severely alienated the Russian peasantry, from whom it had seized food for the urban industrial areas and military forces without offering anything in return.

The NEP released the peasant from this form of state servitude and returned much of the industrial sector of the economy to private hands, often in the form of a lease arrangement. State-owned industrial enterprises were gathered into "trusts" free of direct government control and enjoined to operate on an efficient—i.e., profit-making —basis. Lenin himself set the standard by calling in 1921 for the restoration of small, consumer-oriented industry, a task he saw as both vital and feasible. The result, evident by 1922, was a highly uneven economic recovery: industries producing consumer goods improved relatively rapidly; heavy industry lagged hopelessly behind. For example, the metallurgical industry, essential for aviation, was only at 7 percent of its 1912 level in 1922.

Beginning in May 1922, Lenin suffered a series of increasingly serious strokes. His deteriorating health prompted, among the ambitious, a rough jockeying for advantage. Politically charged disputes over the nation's economic development inevitably arose. The year 1922 brought the first good harvest since 1917, and with it bitter controversy within the Communist party over the slow recovery of heavy industry. The basic policy of holding all trusts responsible for operating at a profit was

never consistently maintained; although subsidies still went to such areas as metallurgy and transportation, the real sinews of industrial power remained weak. Because of peasant demand for consumer goods and the prevalence of the profit system, light industry alone was thriving.

By early 1923, Lenin's health had grown worse and the politically flavored debate over the development of heavy industry had grown sharper. Trotsky emerged as an early spokesman for heavy industry and intensive economic development. At the Twelfth Party Congress in early 1923, he called for a transition from NEP to a properly planned economy. But Trotsky was a flawed champion for rapid industrialization. The trade unions remembered with hatred his unsuccessful attempt to "militarize" labor at the close of the civil war. Personal differences separated him from the emerging "industrial opposition," economists like E. Preobrazhensky and S. Strumilin who shared his views. Power now fell into the hands of a triumvirate composed of G. Zinoviev, L. Kamenev, and J. Stalin. They were united by a devotion to the economic purposes and principles of NEP and by a desire to forestall Trotsky from taking Lenin's place at the head of the party. In a typical attack, Stalin castigated Trotsky for favoring a "dictatorship of industry" over the peasant-oriented economic revival in progress.

Notwithstanding the limits imposed by the nation's maimed economy, Russian aviation advanced at least haltingly during the early NEP period. The Soviet regime was acutely aware of the potential of air transportation. Large distances separated Russia's major cities. The railroad system, never adequate, had been crippled by the strain and destruction of wartime. In 1921 the Council of Labor and Defense had created a commission to develop a ten-year program for civil and military aviation. Existing government institutions for research into aircraft design received increased support. A system of air links was created with foreign countries, while a system of domestic airlines was projected, and partly established, to span Soviet Russia. But the nation's weaknesses remained unmistakable in the disorganization of the aviation industry and its consequent dependence upon foreign-made aircraft.

It remains difficult to delineate, with any precision, the organization of the aircraft industry. As Robert Kilmarx, a leading student of Russian aviation, put it, "By 1922, the organization of the nascent aircraft industry had become very complex and unwieldy because the military commissariats and organizations, the economic administration, and foreign firms were all competing to use the limited industrial capacity of the state." Poorly coordinated bureaucracies characterized the period. The Chief Administration for the Aircraft Industry (Glavkoavia), a creation of the civil war period, persisted in the NEP era. It stood below the Main Directorate of Military Industry, which was, in turn, below the Supreme Council of the National Economy.

The government obviously took the lead in promoting aircraft development. The Central Aerohydrodynamic Institute (TsAGI) became the government's coordinating agency for aviation research and design. Glavkoavia directed actual production and apparently controlled most aircraft and engine factories directly, although some remained in private hands. By the end of 1924, most aircraft factories had been gathered under a trust typical of the NEP era, but otherwise the record is far from clear.

The making of airplanes was hampered by unskilled labor, poor tools, and inadequate management. Many factories attempted to produce finished planes or engines instead of components. The results were predictable. Only eight engines and fifty airframes were successfully constructed in Russia in 1922. Between 1922 and 1924, the nation's meager air strength was replenished only by importing 300 planes from Germany, Italy, and Holland. By 1923, however, some progress was evident. A talented group of aircraft designers, including A. N. Tupolev, was working under the direction of TsAGI. Russia had begun to produce aluminum, facilitating the construction of all-metal planes. In late 1923, production began on the R-1. That aircraft, a biplane reconnaissance model modified from the British DeHavilland, was to become, by the end of the 1920s, the basis of Russian military aviation.

The pattern of government leadership and slow progress was evident in the growth of airlines. By late 1921, a jointly owned Russo-German airline, Deruluft, had been formed. In May 1922 this line began regular operations between Moscow and Königsberg, and domestic air travel was only slightly behind. During 1922 the book *Air Communications,* by a Petrograd engineering professor, N. A. Rynin, set out a prospective network of air routes for Soviet Russia, emphasizing the need to connect central Russia with the remote regions of the country. TsAGI was instructed to study the cost of such a system. By the close of the year, the Inspectorate of Civil Aviation had been created, with the intent that it would be aided and supervised by military authorities. In 1923 domestic service began between Moscow and Gorky.

The stunted economy placed obvious limits on such developments. The first airline, Dobrolet, took the form of a joint-stock company, backed both by individuals and by such organizations as Komsomol, the Communist party's youth organization.

Dobrolet got off the ground with aircraft borrowed from military authorities. The planes with which the airline began its service were, without exception, manufactured abroad.

Russia's military system during these years was dominated by tension on the country's western borders and by the rapid decline in the size of its armed forces. Simultaneously, debate raged over the application of Marxism to military doctrine and organization. In such an atmosphere, military aviation, like its civilian counterpart, received theoretical attention but only limited material support from the nation's leaders.

If war came, conflict seemed most likely against Poland. The Russo-Polish War of 1920 had ended with a border settlement that the Russians accepted only with bitter reluctance. Poland continued to serve as a sanctuary for anti-Soviet forces well into 1922. Such Soviet leaders as the young civil war hero Mikhail Tukhachevsky called for a political and military strategy based upon the offensive. The revolutionary state, he contended, would face protracted war until the Red Army spread the new political and social doctrines abroad. Once it had done so, the army could expect to recruit members of the foreign proletariat for its ranks. Despite the complete failure of the Polish proletariat to follow this scenario in 1920, Tukhachevsky persisted in calling for "revolution from without."

He found an ally in Mikhail Frunze, another successful commander during the civil war. The latter argued that the revolution had initiated a new era in military affairs in which the military doctrine of the proletarian state had to be dominated by the offensive. Like Tukhachevsky, Frunze foresaw the possibility of revolutionary wars in which the Red Army would be called upon to aid the struggling workers of foreign nations against their ruling classes.

Trotsky, with typical sarcasm, dismissed such thinking as an unrealistic idealization of isolated features of the civil war. The fact that during that conflict the Red Army had frequently—but not always—taken the offensive was no reason to expect it to do so at all times in the future. Moreover, an army containing mostly Russian peasants could not be expected to rush to the aid of a foreign proletariat. Trotsky temporarily won the day in the debates over military policy at the Eleventh Party Congress in March 1922. The Russian military was to be transformed into a relatively small, mixed force of regulars and territorial militia, clearly best suited to fight a defensive war.

In the fall of 1923, the first mobilization of the territorial forces successfully took place. As John Erickson, a leading student of Russian military affairs, noted, 1923 saw the first sign of "the stabilization of the Soviet military machine in the demobilization period." The 1923 territorial call-up in particular "marked the end of serious stagnation and indecision" that had characterized the period following the civil war.

Against this background of a shrinking military establishment and a bitter debate over the fundamentals of strategy, slow progress in military aviation was to be expected. An investigation conducted by Frunze in 1923 showed military aviation to be more ragtag fiction than fact: the air force used thirty-two different types of planes and many types of engines. The naval air arm had no combat machines on hand; land-based forces were somewhat better off, with 28 percent of their paper strength present.

The role that air power would play in a future war remained uncertain. Only in 1923 did Soviet military leaders begin to speak publicly on the issue. Lenin, ill and devoting his brief working day to party and government operations, made no recorded contribution to the discussion. On the other hand, both Frunze and Trotsky presented major statements. In an article commemorating the fifth anniversary of the Red Army, Frunze made several important points, stressing, for example, the need for a major development of military-related industry as soon as possible. He claimed flatly that aerial warfare would decide the outcome of future conflicts. Frunze seemed to be speaking of tactical operations in direct support of ground combat.

Trotsky was less certain. In the spring of 1923, he insisted that progress in aviation was necessary. In contrast to Frunze, he claimed that the government lacked the resources to develop military aviation. He looked to the "Friends of the Air Fleet" (ODVF) to promote military aviation. That organization, founded in 1923 and backed largely by the Komsomol, promoted aviation in the economically pressed nation by means of propaganda campaigns. For example, ODVF encouraged urban workers to contribute their personal funds to finance the purchase of planes. Trotsky called for the joint development of civil and military aircraft, a suggestion the government put into practice, but he insisted that military needs should not dominate progress in aviation.

While Frunze, whose military theories centered on the offensive, was openly concerned about foreign air strength, Trotsky remained indifferent. In Trotsky's mind, Russia's industrial backwardness and vast distances shielded her from the full force of an attack from the air. The Soviet state, he said, needed an air force linked to the Red Army's ground operations.

Thus, Frunze and Trotsky shared a common interest in tactical aviation. Frunze, however, leaned toward claiming a decisive role for such air operations.

Trotsky discounted military aviation as a potentially decisive element in warfare, but agreed that an air force closely coordinated with the army's movements would dominate Soviet Russia's military use of the skies.

From 1922 Russian aviation enjoyed the advantage of a close link with Weimar Germany, the greatest industrial power on the continent. The two countries found much common ground for an alliance. Both were political outcasts and shared a deep hostility toward Poland. Moreover, the Treaty of Versailles barred Germany from manufacturing war planes and severely restricted civil aviation. The German military, led by Gen. Hans von Seeckt, was enthusiastic about bartering German technical help for the right to produce, on Russian soil, such forbidden items as war planes.

Despite their common interests, the two countries had to overcome major obstacles from the start. Leading German diplomats, including the ambassador to Moscow, Count Brockdorff-Rantzau, opposed a close tie with the Russians as being detrimental to relations with Western nations. Brockdorff-Rantzau continually charged that Seeckt's close relations with the Russians were not bringing Germany concomitant advantages. On the other hand, Russian leaders continued to support a militant German Communist party dedicated to the overthrow of Seeckt and the entire Weimar Republic.

The Russians first of all wanted German aid in training their fledgling air force. Second, Soviet leaders expected that the establishment of German factories in Russia would bridge the gap between Russia's industrial capabilities and its need for modern aircraft. Supplying the Russians with German flight instructors proved to be no problem; Seeckt had covertly kept military pilots on the active list of the

German army. But they were a wasted asset without the kind of flying practice forbidden by the Treaty of Versailles. By September 1922 a considerable number of German pilots had been established near Smolensk. Within a year, arrangements had been completed for a permanent German military mission in Moscow, Zentrale Moskau, to coordinate the passage of German personnel to and from Russia and to supervise their work. German aviators gave badly needed training to Russian flying cadets and even participated in Russian maneuvers.

The industrial effort, in contrast, was a conspicuous failure—a failure that lent force to Frunze's call for Russia to push ahead with its own military plants. A triangular arrangement linking the German government, the Soviet government, and German private industry proved unable to function. Early in 1922 the German military received funds to subsidize arms factories in Russia. In October, Junkers began work on a substantial aviation plant at Fili, near Moscow. Such leading Russian designers as Tupolev of TsAGI were attracted to study there. In early 1923 negotiations between Junkers and the Soviet government led to an agreement: Junkers was to produce 300 planes each year, 60 of which were to be purchased by the Russians. The firm had to equip the plant and to provide skilled labor; the Russians were to supply raw materials and the bulk of the work force.

But the Russians preferred to purchase complex aviation equipment directly from Germany rather than from the hybrid operation at Fili. The epochal German inflation of 1923 and the financial straits of the Weimar Republic made it impossible to sustain the Junkers operation. GEFU, the holding company established by Seeckt to finance armaments factories in Russia, found its capital reduced by

the inflation and its entire functioning hampered by the financial ineptitude of General von Borries, its leader. By the beginning of 1924 the operation at Fili was near collapse for lack of Russian orders. Meanwhile, the Soviet government had bought 60 engines from factories within Germany and had ordered 200 more.

The mutual advantages of the link between Germany and Russia enabled it to survive an even more dangerous strain. In late October 1923 the German Communist party failed in its attempt to seize control of the country, even though the Comintern had been deeply involved in the uprising and members of the Red Army had been dispatched to Germany to provide military advice. On November 7, 1923, only two weeks after the unsuccessful Communist rebellion, large numbers of German officials and business leaders attended a glittering reception at the Soviet embassy in Berlin. The occasion was the sixth anniversary of the Russian revolution.

1924 through 1927

Between early 1924 and the end of 1927, solutions began to emerge to many of the military, political, and economic dilemmas of the preceding period. Under the leadership of Frunze, who replaced Trotsky as commissar of war, the Soviet military establishment took on the basic configuration it retained for a decade. Military aviation, bolstered by German training, increasingly tied itself to the support of ground operations. The gradual but unmistakable decline of Trotsky and the rise of Stalin removed a major barrier to rational examination of the nation's economic priorities. Trotsky's opponents were now at liberty to reconsider the policy of rapid government-sponsored industrialization for which they had condemned him. The need to accelerate the development of Russian industry, including domestic aircraft production, began to dominate official policy. The peasant, especially the affluent *kulak,* was increasingly identified as the main obstruction to industrial progress.

Under Frunze the Soviet military system began to stabilize. He stressed the establishment of one-man command, removing the system of dual control of military units established during the civil war which had often set military commanders against political commissars. He fought for good pay and intensified training in order to attract and maintain a professional officer corps and sought to reorganize the entire military administration. The January 1924 constitution of the Soviet Union established the Military and Naval Commissariat to direct military affairs. Frunze, in an order of March 28, 1924, rigidly defined the role to be played by each element in the commissariat. At the center, formulating mobilization and operational plans and otherwise directing the nation's defense policy, was the Red Army staff.

Frunze and his subordinates preferred a large regular army to meet Russia's needs. Fiscal considerations made the militia system inescapable, however, and the Frunze reforms ended by solidifying the territorial system. By 1926 (Frunze died in October 1925) territorial militia units constituted two-thirds of the army's strength. The Russian military establishment was increasingly based upon the militia; i.e., peasants and workers were given brief military training, then placed in ready-reserve status. Moreover, the limited resources of an impoverished country prevented Frunze from creating a modern, mechanized army. He came to rely upon the Soviet infantry, in view of the paucity of other assets. Russia's sole military advantage, he saw, lay in the abundance of available manpower.

Military aviation, as a result, played only a minor role in Frunze's actual military organization. With his increasing reliance upon infantry, Frunze admitted that military aviation was essentially an adjunct to ground operations but refused to apply the territorial principle, relying instead upon the militia-freed resources for augmenting such technical branches of the military as aviation. Frunze insisted that military aviation remain a permanent, professional element in the nation's armed forces. But it was tiny: in 1924, the aviation establishment amounted to approximately 10,000 men, less than 2 percent of the total armed forces.

P. I. Baranov, a longtime associate of Frunze, took charge of the air force and also supervised the embryonic aviation industry. Military air power was divided into strategic and corps units, the latter to cooperate directly with ground forces. Frunze divided the country into military districts and placed military aviation under the control of district commanders. The role of the air force was clearly spelled out in the Provisional Field Regulations of 1925. These regulations called for the close cooperation of combat arms, and most air units were attached directly to ground formations for tactical support. Massive air strikes closely tied to front-line operations became the order of the day. The theories of the Italian air-force leader Guilio Douhet about the decisive importance of long-range air power capable of striking enemy population centers found no support among Soviet policymakers.

There were loud dissenting voices. A. N. Lapchinsky, a noted air-force theoretician, openly promoted an important role for strategic bombing in a future war. Designers like Tupolev were interested in heavy bombers but found the way blocked by army commanders. German influence only confirmed the Russian army's own inclination. Despite promising 1917 strategic heavy-bomber raids on England, the Luftwaffe of the 1920s was not interested in strategic bombing—a lack of concern that was to cost the Germans dearly in 1940.

In Frunze, however, the Soviets found both a powerful spokesman for military aviation and the industrial base necessary to create it. He called unceasingly for the development of militarily useful industry; aircraft and engine factories to end "aeronautical illiteracy," as he called it, drew Frunze's strong support. Under his urging, Russia produced 100 R-1 reconnaissance planes in 1924, and the following year production began on the more advanced R-3. Simultaneously, Russia began to produce its own fighters, beginning with the I-2. The growth of a domestic aluminum industry now permitted Soviet production of all-metal planes and opened vistas of complete independence from foreign plane makers.

The production of aircraft motors remained a more difficult problem. The Scientific Technical Committee of the air force in 1924 called for the production of an armored "storm plane," or low-flying attack aircraft, but the lack of powerful engines proved an insuperable barrier. In May 1925 Frunze noted that, despite progress, Russia lacked the air force it required. The nation needed to advance in metallurgy and engineering in order to reach the point at which Russian poverty would no longer prevent the realization of the fine ideas coming from its inventors and designers. In 1922, he noted, Russia had purchased 90 percent of its planes abroad; by 1925 the nation had no need to go outside of its own boundaries for aircraft. Engines remained the sticking point: in 1924 Russia had produced only 9 percent of the aircraft engines it needed. Frunze called on ODVF and all of heavy industry to rally against the problem. He suggested following the American and western

European example of making standardized parts at various factories, then assembling the planes and motors at central locations. He pledged that more resources would be available for military industry in the future, since budget limits in previous years had admittedly prevented essential progress.

Frunze's undeniable contribution to the development of Soviet aviation was marred by his uncertainty about the use of air power. He asserted that the development of aviation and chemical warfare had blurred the line between the front and the rear; hence the need to prepare the civilian economy for wartime production. This implied a strategic use of airpower in future wars; e.g., to bomb and gas population centers far behind the fighting front. Frunze never stressed this point, however; thus his own air force remained an ancillary of the army.

While he lauded the growing independence of Soviet aviation from foreign sources and insisted that the general industrial level must rise in order to support military production, Frunze persisted in denying that aviation would be decisive in future wars. Walter Jacobs, in his recent study of Frunze's military thought, has suggested that the Russian leader saw aviation merely as taking over the traditional role of cavalry: destroying railroads and other lines of communication and harassing troop movements and concentrations. In 1925 Frunze pointed to the French campaign against rebel forces in Morocco—the most recent example of military aviation in combat—to show that air power was helpful but not decisive. He condemned excessive reliance upon technology as a necessity for bourgeois states: they could not trust their masses enough to arm them. At the same time, he clouded the issue by suggesting that a nation lacking an air force faced "inescapable defeat."

Thus, seeking consistency in Frunze's pronouncements on aviation is an exasperating pastime. As John Erickson put it, the administrative reorganization and reform of the mid-1920s was "not accompanied by any precision of opinion on the significance of the technical factor in modern war." Such wavering and wobbling, whatever its cause, could hardly lead to innovative use of military aircraft.

The inconsistency may rest in Frunze's growing realization that the future would not see Soviet Russia on the military offensive. The air attacks Frunze foresaw were western-based—probably Polish—raids on the vulnerable industrial complex surrounding Leningrad and other cities in European Russia. The infantry and other ground arms, which he expected to be decisive in the outcome of the war, were the forces that would contain and then repel the invading armies. Frunze was adapting Russia's military establishment to the nation's resources.

Civil aviation likewise showed signs of growth between 1924 and the end of 1927. Dobrolet and its affiliates extended domestic routes into the Ukraine and Central Asia. By the end of 1924, Russian-built planes were beginning to participate in this civil air traffic. An aviation trust, Aviatrest, apparently supervised all the nation's aircraft production by late 1924. Taking its basic directions from Glavkoavia, Aviatrest ordered its plants to produce both military and civilian planes. The aviation industry remained a melange. State-owned factories—e.g., GAZ-1, near Moscow, which played a key role in the production of fighters—existed side by side with privately owned factories such as Dobrolet's own plant in Kharkov.

During the period 1924–1927, foreign military aid to Russia remained exclusively German. The relationship between the two countries continued to be complex and troubled. Old difficulties remained: the reluctance of German industry to participate in a venture offering military and political rather than financial rewards; the mutual distrust between the German diplomats supposedly responsible for directing foreign policy and the military, which actually preempted much of that responsibility; Russian desires not to be drawn into onerous expenditures on behalf of German industry in the Soviet Union.

New elements entered the situation. By the close of 1924, neither Germany nor Russia was the international outcast it had been immediately following World War I. Several major powers—Britain, Italy, and France—extended formal diplomatic recognition to Russia in 1924. That same year, Germany accepted the Dawes plan to govern the payment of reparations. In early 1925 the German government openly sought to reduce tensions along the nation's western frontier; this culminated in the Locarno pacts of October and in Germany's entry into the League of Nations in 1926. Russian discomfort with these developments was evident.

Despite these events, the German tie to the Soviet air force grew stronger. The training of German military personnel in Russia was expanded and intensified. Large numbers of Soviet officers received instruction from the visitors, and Soviet military delegations accepted invitations to Germany.

The center of this activity was the huge airfield at Lipetsk. Located near Voronezh, the base had workshops that could manufacture minor items, but its primary mission was to train German air crews and to test German combat planes. This base was fully financed and operated by the German military. The "Fourth Squadron of the Red Air Force" at Lipetsk was, in fact, a German military unit. By 1925 Lipetsk was offering refresher courses to experienced

German combat pilots. In 1926 cadet training began. Despite the gradual lifting of restrictions on aviation inside Germany, actual combat training required the freedom of action and space available only in Russia.

At its peak Lipetsk housed a permanent German staff of 60; during the summer, 50 pilot-trainees and 70–100 other technicians traveled as "tourists" to the Soviet Union in order to receive instruction there. German officers assigned to Lipetsk or to training duties with the Russians were temporarily placed on the inactive list. The training at Lipetsk included work in fighter combat, fighter bombing, aerial reconnaissance, and artillery spotting.

The precise value of German guidance to the Russian air force remains problematical. Such Russian air-force leaders as the future air marshal Krasovsky still found their new pilots poorly trained. Nor was the Russian air force able to profit from imaginative German thinking. The combat training at Lipetsk gave the Germans an opportunity to catch up with rather than to surpass other military establishments. The Germans only haltingly reexamined the antiquated combat methods of World War I. Moreover, their air force, at it evolved in the second half of the 1920s, was still concentrated heavily on cooperation with ground forces rather than on independent strategic operations.

In contrast to the thriving and mutually appealing training program, German aircraft manufacturing in Russia declined. In early 1924 the German army directed Junkers to cooperate in establishing BMW (Bayerische Motorenwerke) facilities at Fili to aid in the troublesome process of producing engines. Seeckt had to intervene personally in order to overcome Junkers' objections. He reminded the latter that politics and strategy, not economic gain, were the mainsprings of military-financed industrial projects in Russia. The increasingly unwieldy operation collapsed entirely by the end of 1925. However, the Russians felt only a mild concern about the problems at Fili. They were now emphatically interested, as Frunze had indicated, in developing an indigenous aviation industry. In the meantime, they intended to purchase aircraft and engines abroad, and they preferred to avoid restricting themselves to German suppliers.

The Russian commitment to an intensive program of government-sponsored industrialization dominated the period from 1924 through 1927. This commitment was, of course, inextricably entwined with the political rivalries of the time: the decline of Trotsky as a power within the Communist party and the concurrent rise of Stalin. Moreover, party economic policy in 1924 was still centered upon generosity to the peasant. In May, the Thirteenth Party Congress was so encouraged by the recovery of agriculture and by the resulting grain surplus for export that it voted to support a program of heavy industry. The agricultural revival seemed to indicate that the economy could bear the strain. But the basic lines of NEP remained unchanged.

By the close of 1924, however, the calls for a shift in direction were growing louder. Trotsky, despite his political decline, now had firm allies on the question of industrial growth. In August, Preobrazhensky published a seminal article in which he stated that Russia had to develop heavy industry rapidly and at the expense of the peasantry. Russia could not rely on outside aid; the Soviet economy had to carry the cost of its own reequipment. According to Preobrazhensky and his followers in the "industrial opposition," the then-recovering Russian industrial economy would bog down shortly. The recovery had consisted largely of restoring labor to idle existing facilities; in the absence of new investment, such vital areas as chemicals and metallurgy lagged behind and would continue to do so.

The turning point came in 1925, a year variously described as "the high point of NEP" and the point at which "the expansion of heavy industry became the predominant aim of [Soviet] economic policy." The year began with Trotsky's resignation as commissar of war. Party leaders were shocked by the peasantry's efforts to hold back harvested grain from the market in order to obtain higher prices. Moreover, the economic recovery was generating public revenues while a heated debate grew about their use: for tax reduction, for consumer goods, or for investment in heavy industry. Although the metals industry remained a bottleneck, Russia was now producing automobiles and tractors for the first time since 1917, albeit in small numbers. State planning agencies had been active since the earliest days of NEP; the most important of these was Gosplan, directly subordinate to the Council of Labor and Defense. Gosplan now began to explore the possibilities for long-term government investment in heavy industry.

The Fourteenth Party Congress of December 1925, the "congress of industrialization," set the course for the future. The appeasement of the peasant had reached its limit. The party now shifted to give priority to the demands of industrialization, in particular the expansion of heavy industry. The congress' key resolution stated that Russia was to aim at creating the capacity to produce all vital machinery itself. A self-sufficient economy dominated by capital-goods industries was the wave of the future. The political wave of the future was also visible at the congress in Stalin's defeat of his former colleagues, Zinoviev and Kamenev.

Following the Fourteenth Congress, all factors in the party agreed on the need for investment in heavy industry. The debate now centered on the rate at which such a program could be pushed forward. K. Voroshilov, who had replaced the deceased Frunze, kept up the call for an industrial system adequate to the needs of modern warfare. During 1926 the Supreme Council of the National Economy was drastically reorganized so as to permit close control over the boom in heavy industry. Privately owned or leased industrial enterprise, one of the cornerstones of NEP, began to decline under the burden of heavy taxes. In April the party central committee proclaimed the importance of the "planning principle" in the present era of capital construction, and called on the party and the state "to liberate our economy from its dependence on capitalist countries." During the fiscal year beginning that fall, the rate of growth in the production of consumer goods began to lag behind the rate for capital goods. During the four years after 1926, the state budget doubled. Most of the increase went to stimulate the nation's industrial growth.

During 1927 the international scene became more threatening: Chiang Kai-shek crushed his former Communist allies in China and diplomatic relations collapsed between Soviet Russia and Great Britain. In June the party central committee called dramatically for progress in the development of military-related industry. Simultaneously, the great industrial projects that were later to characterize Russian industrialization were approved: the Dnieper dam, the Stalingrad tractor factory, the Sverdlovsk engineering works. The obligation of government trusts to operate at a profit now ended; thus another barrier crumbled between a large segment of the economy and effective government direction.

When the Fifteenth Party Congress

convened in December 1927, the anti-Stalin opposition had been crushed. Trotsky and Zinoviev had been expelled—first from the central committee and then from the party itself. Several variants of a five-year plan for industrial development were available for the party's consideration. Despite heated debate, the gathering—and the year—ended with Russian leaders still undecided about the pace at which to travel the road of industrialization.

Conclusion

Aviation played, at best, a minor role in the Soviet military and industrial development that followed the civil war. By the end of 1927, however, air power was strategically placed to profit from the vast industrial expansion upon which Russia was committed to embark. The country was now endowed with a cadre of experienced aircraft designers. Frunze and then Voroshilov had cogently expressed the need for an industrial system tied to the needs of modern warfare. The internecine party warfare that had hindered agreement on industrial growth ended with Stalin's resounding defeat of Trotsky. The German tie, despite its manifest limitations, had provided Russia with trained personnel to operate and to direct a future air force. In short, Soviet Russia had made progress in planning and preparing, if not yet in realizing, its strength as an air power.

Research Notes

Some material on the development of the Soviet aircraft industry and air force during the NEP can be found in Robert Kilmarx, *A History of the Soviet Air Force* (New York, 1962) and Asher Lee, *The Soviet Air Force* (New York, 1962). Neither work, however, provides a thorough treatment of the place of the aircraft industry in the Soviet national economy. E. H. Carr, *Socialism in One Country*, Vol. 1-3 (Baltimore, 1970), and *Foundations of a Planned Economy*, Vol. 1 (Baltimore, 1974) in his monumental *A History of Soviet Russia,* does place the aircraft industry in this context. On the theme of German-Soviet collaboration during the 1920s, see G. Castellan, "Reichswehr et Armée Rouge, 1920-1939," in J. B. Duroselle, ed., *Les relations germano-soviétiques de 1933 à 1939* (Paris, 1954).

On the formulation of Soviet military doctrine and the place of air power in it, see John Erickson, *The Soviet High Command* (New York, 1962). Regarding Mikhail Frunze's role in the development of the Red Army and Air Fleet, see Walter D. Jacobs, *Frunze: The Soviet Clausewitz, 1885-1925* (The Hague, 1969). On the role of Soviet volunteer organizations in technological modernization of the society, especially the Society of the Friends of the Air Fleet, see William E. Odom, *The Soviet Volunteers: Modernization and Bureaucracy in a Public Mass Organization* (Princeton, 1973). Soviet works to be consulted are: V. B. Shavrov, *Istoriia konstrktsii samoletov v SSSR do 1938* (Moscow, 1969); M. V. Frunze, *Sobranie sochinenii* 3 vols. (Moscow, 1929); and L. L. Kerber, *TU—chelovek i samolet* (Moscow, 1973).

4

Soviet Aviation and Air Power under Stalin, 1928-1941

Kenneth R. Whiting

By 1928, on the eve of the First Five-Year Plan, Stalin, his commissar of war, Voroshilov, his outstanding military adviser, Tukhachevsky, and other military leaders were extremely dissatisfied with the cadre-militia Red Army and especially with its lack of modern weapons. The Red Air Force, for example, was small and equipped only with a very mixed bag of foreign-made and obsolescent aircraft. This burning desire to eliminate the militia part of the Red Army in favor of regular troops, as well as the longing for the weapons needed to modernize the armed forces, could lead to little, however, until the Soviet industrial base had been greatly enlarged. During the NEP, the domestic production of food and consumer goods had risen to prewar levels and even heavy industry had made some sporadic gains, but the latter was still not sufficient to serve as an adequate base for producing the armaments capable of transforming the Red Army into a force able to cope with the military forces of the major western European nations and Japan. Furthermore, to a large extent the heavy-industrial sector of the economy was expending its tsarist heritage, as could be seen in its deteriorating transportation system, its worn-out machinery, and its aging technicians. If it were to go forward with any vigor, it needed massive injections of capitalist investment.

Although the founding fathers of communism (Marx, Engels, and Lenin) had little to say about the place of a professional army in the future workers' paradise, they were aware that any military force is dependent upon the economic condition of the nation. Marx, referring to the "manslaughter industry," pointed out that the development of the forces of production and productive relationships postulates the development and conditions of military art. Engels stated that a nation in arms must be predicated upon the high productivity of its national industry. Lenin agreed with Engels that with a change in military materiel the method of warfare will change accordingly, and that there is an intimate connection between the economic and cultural structure of a country and its military organization. Frunze worked assiduously to promote the close integration of industry and military needs, with the latter as the prime consideration.

Stalin, in his political struggle with Trotsky, had come up with the thesis of "socialism in one country"; i.e., that Russia could go it alone without the immediate extension of the revolution to the more industrialized countries of western Europe, and that the Soviet Union should be built up as the bastion of socialism until more favorable conditions for the expansion of communism occurred. The immediate task was to raise the combat capabilities of the Red Army to match those of its potential enemies in western Europe and Japan, thus ensuring the defense of the fortress of world communism. This situation dictated the industrialization of the Soviet Union at a forced tempo.

In October 1928, Stalin announced the beginning of the First Five-Year Plan, the main thrust of which was to speed up the development of a modern military force. Frunze could not have asked for more in the integration of military needs and economic planning. But the overwhelming emphasis on heavy-industrial growth was bound to impose grievous burdens on the Soviet people. The production of consumer goods was cut to the bone, and the peasants were dragooned into collectives in order to ensure the supply of grain both for the burgeoning industrial labor force and for export to obtain necessary foreign technical equipment and knowhow. A measure of the tempo of this rush into industrialization can be gleaned from the

rate of increase in steel output. In 1920 the output was down to the unbelievable figure of slightly over 100,000 tons, and by 1929 it had risen only to the 1913 level of 4 million tons. By the end of the First Five-Year Plan (1932), however, steel output was more than 6 million tons, and by 1937, the end of the Second Five-Year Plan, it had risen to almost 20 million tons a year. Comparable growth rates occurred in other basic products needed for the development of heavy industry.

In 1929, at the beginning of the First Five-Year Plan, the Red Army was in a parlous condition, as is pointed out in the following passage from an official Soviet history:

Up to this time our army was significantly backward in quantity and quality in armaments and military technology compared to the armies of the strong bourgeois nations because of the economic backwardness of the country inherited from tsarist Russia.

Arms and combat techniques were little advanced over the technology of the First World War. There was an absolute insufficiency of weapons. In 1929 the entire Red Army had around 26,000 machine guns, 7,000 guns of various calibers, 200 tanks and armored vehicles, and 1,000 combat aircraft of old construction. Aviation, armored, and technical personnel made up only 10 percent of the armed forces of the USSR (*Istoriia Velikoi*, 1960).

The "1,000 combat aircraft of old construction" referred to in this excerpt was a sore point with the Soviet regime. As befitted a government that prided itself on its scientific outlook, it was air-minded. Lenin had helped Professor Zhukovsky establish the famous TsAGI (*Tsentral'nii aero-gidrodinamicheskii institut*)—the Central Institute for Aerodynamics and Hydrodynamics, devoted to research and development in aeronautics, and Zhukovsky had managed to collect a cadre of bright aeronautical experts, including such men as Tupolev, Mikulin, Kalinin, and Grigorovich. Later the work of TsAGI was supplemented by other institutions, the most outstanding of which were TsIAM (*Tsentral'nii nauchnoissledovatel'skii institut aviamotorostroenniya*), the Central Scientific Research Institute of Aircraft Engines; and VIAM (*Vsesoiuznii nauchno-issledovatel'skii institut aviatsionnykh materialov*), the All-Union Scientific Research Institute of Aviation Materials. Zhukovsky also founded in Moscow the Soviet Air Technical School, which was subsequently named the Zhukovsky Military Air Academy and is now one of the outstanding educational and research institutions in the USSR. But being air-minded alone, however, could not overcome the country's two great lacks: an adequate industrial base and an extensive pool of skilled personnel.

The Soviet regime between 1922 and 1933 was able to get some support from the Germans in the training of personnel, the result of a strange collaboration between the Red Army and the Reichswehr. The idea that some mutually beneficial relationship might be developed between the two armies seems to have arisen almost at the origin of both—a natural reaction to the Versailles settlement that sought to emasculate the German military and to quarantine the Red Army behind the *cordon sanitaire*. In addition, fear of the newly created Poland, established at the expense of both Germany and Russia, was in itself a *raison d'être* for some type of collaboration.

Karl Radek, while imprisoned in Germany, held conferences during 1919 with a number of highly placed Germans about the possibility of closer Soviet-German relations. When Radek left Germany in 1920 the seed had been well planted, and Hans von Seeckt, commander in chief of the new Reichswehr, opted for an *Ostpolitik* and organized a secret group (Sondergruppe R), to look into the matter of collaboration with the Red Army. Trotsky, then commissar of war in the Soviet Union, showed an interest in the scheme, since it would mean German military-industrial assistance in rebuilding his badly run-down Red Army; therefore, a German technical mission was invited to come to Moscow. The negotiations resulted in an agreement by which Junkers was to build a plant at Fili, near Moscow, to manufacture all-metal aircraft, spare parts, and engines. This part of the collaboration came to little, however; by 1925 the Junkers agreement to produce 300 aircraft a year, 60 of them going to the Red Army, had floundered as a result of monetary difficulties at the German end and the desire for indigenous military production at the Soviet end.

The personnel-training side of the collaboration, however, was much more successful. As early as February 1922 Radek, in a conference with Seeckt, suggested that the Reichswehr assist in training senior Soviet officers, and the Treaty of Rapallo (April 16, 1922) promoted more intensive collaboration. A provisional agreement of August 1922 listed the German requests: military bases in the Soviet Union from which to carry out exercises with aircraft, motorized troops, and chemical-warfare forces, as well as the exchange of military information with the Soviets.

The mutually advantageous arrangements worked out well. During the 1926-1933 period of this collaboration, about 120 senior Soviet officers received training in Germany with the Reichswehr, some of them in the secret General Staff course. In return the Reichswehr, severely restricted by the Versailles Treaty, found space and security in the Soviet Union to develop and to experiment with forbidden weapons, especially aircraft. In 1924 an air-force training station was established at Lipetsk (250 miles south of Moscow) with 60 German instructors and 100 technicians. Regular flying training began in 1925. The German and Soviet flying and technical staffs worked in close cooperation, with Soviet ground crews undergoing technical training under German instructors and Soviet fliers learning their trade from their German counterparts. The whole business was camouflaged under the rubric "Fourth Squadron of the Red Air Force." Although the Red Army–Reichswehr collaboration included a tank school at Kazan and a poison-gas school at Volsk (200 miles southwest of Kuibyshev), neither of which worked out very well, it was at Lipetsk that the joint endeavor worked best. One reason was that the creation of the aviation school at Lipetsk coincided with the almost desperate Soviet effort to develop its military aviation.

Difficult as it may be to pinpoint the precise extent to which the Red Army benefited from this collaboration with the Reichswehr, there can be no doubt that it was of great value. At a time when the Red Army command was facing the problem of modernization, it was able to lean on the Reichswehr, which was devoted to the exploitation of the newest in military technology. A good deal of the professional *savoir faire* typical of the German officer corps rubbed off on the Soviet commanders who were trained in Germany, with the result that the reading of German military literature became *de rigueur* for the ambitious Soviet officer.

The goal of the First Five-Year Plan was to end dependence on the importation of aircraft, engines, and spare parts. Although

the goal turned out to be overambitious, by 1932 the Soviet need for foreign aircraft had been so drastically reduced that the mixed bag of obsolete foreign planes in the air force was being phased out. Soviet designers and engineers were coming into their own. Tupolev had designed and produced the I-4, a single-engine biplane; Grigorovich came up with his single-engine fighter, the I-2*bis*; and Polikarpov had designed a whole series of two-seater ground-attack planes, the DI-2, DI-3, and DI-4.* Tupolev had designed and developed a number of transports prior to the First Five-Year Plan: the ANT-1 in 1922, the ANT-2, an all-metal aircraft, in 1924, and the ANT-3 in 1925. During the first plan, he came up with the TB-1 and the TB-2, twin-engine medium bombers, and by the end of the plan in 1932 he had designed and developed the TB-3, a four-engine heavy bomber that weighed more than 40,000 pounds and could carry as much as two tons (the transport version was designated the ANT-6). The TB-3 was the only long-range bomber produced in large numbers during the rest of the 1930s. The Tupolev ANT-2 (called the R-3 in its reconnaissance version) and a Polikarpov plane, the R-5, were the best of the reconnaissance aircraft available to the Soviet air force in the mid-1930s. TsAGI also encouraged the design and development of a number of different seaplanes for the navy but became disillusioned with their potential in the late 1930s. Mikhail Mil, who later became a famous helicopter designer, was

---

*The Russian designations used in this chapter have the following meanings: the "I" stands for *Istrebitel'*, Russian for pursuit or fighter aircraft; "DI" (*Dvukhmestnii istrebitel'*), a two-seat fighter; "ANT" signifies the name Andrei Nikolaevich Tupolev; "TB" (*Tiazhelyi bombardirovshchik*), heavy bomber; "SB" (*Skorostnoi bombardirovshchik*), fast bomber; "DB" (*Dal'-nii bombardirovshchik*), long-range bomber; and "R" (*Razvedchik*), reconnaissance plane.

beginning to play with autogyros during this period.

None of these aircraft was up to the best being produced in Europe and America, and, as Soviet historians admit, the biggest obstacle to the production of better aircraft was the Soviet backwardness in engine design. Although V. Ya. Klimov, A. D. Shvetsov, and A. A. Mikulin were tinkering with indigenous designs, most engines used in Soviet aircraft were either foreign or Soviet copies. One cause of this backwardness was the Soviet weakness in metallurgy, particularly in special steels and alloys.

For all its teething problems, however, the Soviet aviation industry was on the move; the output of aircraft during the period of the First Five-Year Plan increased remarkably. The average yearly output in the years 1930 and 1931 was 860 machines; this increased to an average of 2,595 in the years between 1932 and 1934. Quality, however, was not on a par with the quantitative successes. The lack of skilled personnel, the "storming" technique (pushing production at too fast a rate), and the poor quality of the components going into the assembly of the aircraft—all these problems combined to make it a sporting proposition as to whether a newly built plane would fly.

Soviet aviation may be said to have begun its "takeoff" phase, to use Rostowian jargon, during the last years of the First Five-Year Plan, and was to come into its own during the Second Five-Year Plan (1933-1937). In 1933 the Polikarpov design group produced the I-15 fighter, a biplane with a 480-horsepower engine, armed with four 7.62mm machine guns and capable of climbing to 16,000 feet in six minutes, according to Soviet accounts. Further development of the aircraft resulted in the I-15*bis* in 1934, whose more-powerful engine (775 hp) enabled it to

attain a maximum speed of 230 miles per hour. Still further modifications on the I-15 produced the I-153 (Chaika, or Sea Gull), whose 1,000-hp engine increased its speed to 275 mph. The I-15, in its various forms, was widely used in the Soviet air force for the next six or seven years. The Polikarpov group also designed and developed the I-16 figher, a low-wing monoplane with a 1,000-hp engine. This plane had a top speed of 280 mph and sported two 20mm cannon along with two 7.62 machine guns. The I-15 and I-16 were the main fighters in the Soviet inventory until 1940.

The bomber category—which was made up mainly of the TB-1, the TB-2, and the TB-3 until the mid-1930s—received a valuable addition when the SB-2 went into production in 1935-1936. This was a twin-engine, all-metal, low-wing monoplane with 750-hp M-25 (Wright Cyclone) engines. This "fast bomber" (which is what the "SB" stands for) had a maximum speed of 260 mph and a range of 500 miles, and carried a 1,000-pound bomb load.

The I-15 series, the I-16, the SB-2, and the TB-3, plus the R-5 reconnaissance plane, were the best machines available to the Soviet air force in its subsequent adventures in Spain, China, and Mongolia during the late 1930s. By 1937, the end of the Second Five-Year Plan, the Soviet military air forces (VVS) had a front-line strength of around 2,500 aircraft, organized in forty to fifty brigades. In November 1936, V. V. Khripin, deputy chief of the VVS, claimed that his air force was the strongest in the world and that its combat strength had quadrupled since 1932. He also stated that 60 percent of the combat aircraft in the VVS were bombers—which brings up the subject of the role and mission of the bomber in the VVS, as visualized by the Soviet strategists of that era.

For some time a group of Soviet military theorists had favored the development of independent bomber operations. This faction probably was influenced by Gen. Giulio Douhet's theories, which were popular in the late 1920s and the 1930s among a number of military theorists throughout the world. Douhet saw the strategic bomber as the preeminent weapon of future wars. A. N. Lapchinsky, an early Soviet theorist on air power, pointed out the importance of strategic bombing in the mid-1920s, although he did not go all the way with Douhet's thesis that it was the be-all and end-all in determining the outcome of war. Lapchinsky also saw aviation as an integral part of the combined arms of the country and favored a very heavy commitment to providing close support for the ground forces. Khripin, in the mid-1930s, held similar views—especially since the two most likely potential enemies of the Soviet Union, Germany and Japan, presented such tempting industrial targets. In an era of relatively poor antiaircraft weapons and before the advent of radar, even the rather primitive bombers of the VVS appeared to have potentialities as means of penetrating to the enemy's industrial heartland. For example, the Soviet strategic bomber force in the Far East, although small, did have the capability of reaching some Japanese cities, and, in the West, German targets were within range. The adventure in Spain (1936–1938), however, was to disillusion these early enthusiasts of strategic bombing, with its city-busting potential.

During the first two five-year plans, military leaders found another use for their proliferating aircraft: namely, to carry paratroopers and their support equipment behind the enemy lines in order to disrupt an opponent at some depth. The parachute troops, an idea which Tukhachevsky pushed vigorously, were first organized in 1931 in two small units. The first available aircraft, such as the TB-1 and R-5, were

not adequate for anything beyond small operations, but the introduction of the TB-3, the four-engine bomber, and its transport version had sufficiently changed the picture by 1934 so that buildup of the airborne forces could proceed apace. By 1935 the military leaders had enough confidence in their airborne troops to inject them into the main maneuvers at Kiev —and before foreign military observers, at that. The TB-3s dropped some 600 paratroopers to secure a defense perimeter; then successive waves of planes brought in infantry and support equipment so as to consolidate the area seized. In 1936 the paratroopers again proved their effectiveness in maneuvers held in Byelorussia and in the Caucasus.

Although the parachute troops had their troubles during the purges between 1937 and 1939—especially with the execution of their mentor, Tukhachevsky—their strength steadily increased. By 1938 the airborne troops were organized into four brigades of about 1,000 men each, with three brigades being stationed in the military districts facing the Baltic countries and Poland and the fourth being sent to the Far East.

One of the most serious problems that inhibited the creation of a bigger and more potent VVS in the 1930s was that of training the pilots and technicians needed to keep the aircraft operational. Although a Soviet calculation in 1933 that it would take more than 100 trained men to keep one airplane serviced and operational was certainly an exaggeration, the demand for trained manpower was bound to increase exponentially as aircraft poured off the assembly lines and were sent into operational units. However, two developments contributed to the solution of this problem. For one, the ongoing mechanization of agriculture as a result of collectivization was providing a reserve of potential mechanical literates, as peasants learned from

Figure 8. Mass parachute drop from a TB-3 four-engine bomber, a gimmick used in the 1930s to publicize Soviet air power.

tinkering with and operating tractors and trucks. In addition, the Society for the Promotion of Defense, Aviation, and Chemical Warfare (Osoaviakhim), a voluntary organization dedicated to training young people in skills needed by the armed forces, taught tens of thousands of youth how to operate, maintain, and repair engines, radios, and motor vehicles. Osoaviakhim also saw to it that the young enthusiasts learned how to shoot straight, and even had its own aircraft in which future pilots could learn the rudiments of flying. In spite of all this outside help, however, the VVS was forced to become one great technical training institution, with academies and flying schools mushrooming all over the country.

In the mid-1930s, the Soviets went in for seeking world publicity for their aeronautical exploits, a sign of their growing confidence in fliers and machines. The first publicity break came in February 1934, when the icebreaker *Chelyuskin*, with a party of scientists aboard, was caught in the ice and sank. The government pulled out all the stops in launching an air-rescue mission, and, using an ANT-4 and some R-5s, the Soviet airmen managed to get everyone off the ice floe upon which they were stranded. On April 20 the government created a new medal, Hero of the Soviet Union, to bestow on seven of the pilots involved in the mission, and nineteen other fliers and support personnel received the Order of Lenin.

In September 1934, M. M. Gromov,

pilot, and I. T. Spirin, navigator, flew an ANT-25 on a closed-circuit route of 12,411 kilometers in seventy-five hours. The ANT-25—a Tupolev creation, as the designation "ANT" indicates—was a low-wing monoplane with a retractable landing gear, equipped with a 950-hp M-34 Vee liquid-cooled twelve-cylinder engine. It had a maximum speed of 150 mph and a flight duration of sixty-five hours. This aircraft gave the Soviets a chance to indulge in some spectacular long-distance flying during the next couple of years.

In 1936 and 1937 the Soviets sought all kinds of records. V. K. Kokkinaki, A. B. Yumashev, and M. A. Niukhtikov garnered a total of ten altitude records in 1936. In July 1936, V. P. Chkalov and G. F. Baidukov, both test pilots, along with their navigator, A. V. Beliakov, flew an ANT-25 from Moscow along the Arctic coast and over Kamchatka to Udd Island (now Chkalov Island) in the mouth of the Amur River, a distance of 9,374 kilometers, in fifty-six hours and twenty minutes. In June 1937, the same trio flew their ANT-25 from Moscow to Portland, Oregon, via the polar route, a 9,130-kilometer flight that took sixty-three hours, sixteen minutes. A month later, the pilots Gromov and Yumashev, with navigator S. A. Danilin, also in an ANT-25, made the transpolar flight from Moscow to San Jacinto, California, covering 11,500 kilometers in sixty-two hours, seventeen minutes.

There were other feats in 1937, and in 1938 three women—V. S. Grizodubova, P. D. Osipenko, and M. M. Raskova—flew their ANT-37, named *Rodina* (the Motherland), 5,908 kilometers in twenty-six hours, 29 minutes to establish a world record for women. The achievements in long-distance flying and in breaking world records in altitude and speed did much to bolster Soviet confidences in both flying personnel and Soviet aircraft, with the en-thusiastic assistance of the Soviet media—the whole business resembled the later arduous Soviet approach to the Olympic games.

While Stalin was busy pushing industrialization and building up a formidable military force in the late 1920s and early 1930s, he was trying to follow a relatively nonbelligerent foreign policy. The disaster that befell the Soviet intervention in Chinese affairs in 1924–1927, the diminution to the zero point of any chance of revolution in western Europe in the early 1930s, and the concentration upon the "building of socialism in one country"—all these contributed to a semiisolationist period in Soviet foreign policy. There was, however, some apprehension about Japanese objectives in the Far East—apprehension that led to the formation of the semiautonomous Special Far Eastern Army, which included an air force, in August 1929.

The only Soviet military action in the Far East in this period was a conflict with the Chinese over the Soviet rights to comanagement of the Chinese Eastern Railway, which crossed Manchuria between Manchouli and Vladivostok. The situation in Manchuria was unbelievably complicated in the late 1920s. The Japanese had tried to use the warlord of Manchuria, Chang Tso-lin, to further their aspirations in that area, but when Chiang Kai-shek defeated him in 1928 and Chang was forced to flee to his base of operations in Manchuria, the Japanese assassinated him by blowing up his train near Mukden. They had hoped his son, Chang Hsueh-liang, "the Young Marshal," would be more malleable, but they soon discovered their mistake when he threw his lot with the new Kuomintang government in Peking.

Chang Hsueh-liang, like his father, was intensely anti-Communist. He began a campaign to drive the Russians out of the

Figure 9. Crew of the ANT-25 which in June 1936 was flown nonstop from Moscow to Udd (now Chkalov), Siberia: G. Baidukov, V. Chkalov, and A. Beliakov. In 1937 the same crew flew nonstop from Moscow to Portland, Oregon.

Chinese Eastern Railway administration, a campaign that increased in virulence in 1929. Bliukher, the commander of the new Special Far Eastern Army, had built his force to about 100,000 men, supported by tanks and aircraft. Moscow instructed him to prepare for action against the Young Marshal, a campaign that needed to be swift and effective in order to keep the Japanese from getting too worried about the Russians' plunging into a bailiwick the Japanese hoped to acquire for themselves. The Japanese Kwantung Army (named after its location on the Kwantung Penin-

sula in Manchuria), which had been "leased" from the Chinese, was keeping a wary eye on the Russians. In October Bliukher's forces hit the Chinese along the Sungari River and also encircled a large force near Manchouli, and in about six weeks Chang Hsueh-liang's troops were beaten. The Soviets used thirty-two aircraft in the operation, the first real blooding of the VVS. Although there were some snafus and mistakes, the Soviet forces looked so effective in the operation that the Kwantung Army leaders began to speed up their plans for a complete takeover of

Manchuria before the Russians got any stronger in the Far East. The Japanese took over Manchuria in September 1931, a move that put their soldiers right on the Soviet borders in the Far East as well as on the Mongolian border.

The Soviets, extremely worried about the Japanese belligerency in northern China and along the Soviet borders, feverishly increased their military strength in that area. Tanks, fighter aircraft, and bombers were added to Bliukher's Special Far Eastern Army, and the Trans-Siberian Railway's efficiency was augmented by intensive efforts in doubletracking. By late 1934 Bliukher's army consisted of fourteen rifle and three cavalry divisions, 950 aircraft, and 900 tanks. The Japanese General Staff estimated that, in addition, the Soviets had about 150 bombers in the Maritime Territory capable of hitting the Japanese homeland. These facts tended to quiet the hotheads in the Kwantung Army for the time being.

By 1934 it was obvious that Stalin was going to have to shelve his semiisolationist policy and seek foreign allies, for, in addition to the Japanese expansionism in the Far East, Hitler was becoming a threat in the West. In January 1934 the latter signed a ten-year nonaggression pact with Poland and began to mutter about German designs on the Ukraine—a subject more than adequately covered in *Mein Kampf*. Something had to give, since the Soviets faced potential enemies in both the East and the West— the perennial nightmare of Russia's policymakers, tsarist or Communist. In September 1934 the Soviet Union joined the League of Nations, began to angle for alliances with France and Czechoslovakia (both signed in 1935), and at the Seventh, and last, Comintern Congress in July–August 1935 adopted a "united front" policy which called on all Communist parties to cooperate with any antifascist

party, whatever its leanings otherwise. Stalin had opted for a collective security system, anchored on Great Britain and France, to offset the German and Japanese threats.

Hardly had Stalin moved toward collective security when his partners began to look less than reassuring. When Mussolini invaded Ethiopia in October 1935, the League of Nations responded with little more than a mild scolding. When, on March 7, 1936, Hitler remilitarized the Rhineland, France and Great Britain— which had specific authority to act—did nothing. Then came the civil war in Spain. Franco revolted against the Republican government on July 19, 1936, a move that threatened to put France in the middle of three fascist states if he won. But France and Britain went for cover under a "nonintervention" facade, and Germany and Italy cynically gave lip service to this policy while covertly helping Franco. Stalin was in a dilemma: failure to support the Republicans would alienate the popular fronts in many countries, especially in France, but too open an intervention would frighten the French and British governments. If he intervened in Spain, it would have to be a cautious intervention.

Stalin found a way out of the dilemma by avoiding making a large commitment of Soviet troops in Spain. Communist agents recruited the International Brigade from all over Europe and the Western Hemisphere; some volunteers were Communists while others merely sympathized with the Republican cause. Although the International Brigade probably totaled some 60,000 men during the course of the war, there were never more than 30,000 in Spain at any one time. The only direct Soviet involvement came in supplying aircraft, tanks, and artillery with support equipment. Moreover, Red Army specialists flew the aircraft, operated the tanks, and acted as in-

Figure 10. Tupolev TB-3 heavy bombers of the 1930s. This early all-metal aircraft had a corrugated wingskin.

structors to the Republican troops in those weapons. The first Soviet aid began in October 1936, when a Norwegian freighter delivered some Soviet aircraft, tanks, and artillery to Spain.

Just how many men Stalin sent to Spain is an unanswerable question. According to one official Soviet account, he sent "557 Soviet volunteers, including 23 military advisers, 49 instructors, 29 artillery experts, including antiaircraft specialists, 141 aircraft pilots, 107 tank drivers, and 29 sailors; communications specialists, engineers, and doctors totaled 106, and there were 73 interpreters and other spe-

cialists." Other sources, equally unreliable, give much higher figures.

In aircraft, the Soviet assistance was approximately 1,500 machines, although in any one month not more than a third of that number were operational. Of the thousand or so fighter aircraft, around 500–600 were I-15s or I-15*bis*es and the rest were I-16s.* There were more than

---

*The I-16 had many nicknames applied to it during the Spanish civil war. It was called *rata* (rat) by the Franco forces and *mosca* (fly) by the Loyalists, while the Soviet fliers referred to it as *ishak* (donkey). With its short, barrel-like configuration, it was an easy plane to identify, and everyone in Spain got to know it.

200 SB-2 bombers; the rest were R-5 reconnaissance planes. Soviet aircraft made
up more than 90 percent of the Republican
air force by early 1937, with the result that
the Republicans had air superiority until
late that year. At that point the Nazis
equipped the Condor Legion in Spain with
Me-109 fighters and Ju-87 dive bombers,
which were superior to the Soviet I-15s and
I-16s. The obvious inability of the Soviet
fighters to oppose the Germans successfully led Stalin to begin phasing out the
Soviet air force in Spain in mid-1938, so
that by the end of the year all Soviet aircraft were out of the country.

Although Soviet fliers gained valuable
combat experience in Spain, the lessons
they learned were mostly negative. For example, the VVS came to the conclusion
that strategic bombing was an ineffective
use of fliers and machines—a conclusion
the Germans also drew from their Spanish
experience. In retrospect, considering the
modesty of the bombing effort in each case
and the rather primitive equipment involved in that effort, it is not surprising
that neither the Luftwaffe nor the VVS
was favorably impressed by the results
achieved in the Spanish adventure. The
Soviet pilots were also made painfully
aware of the inferiority of their machines
in combat against the German Me-109s. All
in all, the Soviet involvement in the
Spanish civil war, especially in the air war,
was far from successful.

The Soviets, while trying to consolidate
a united front against Germany and Italy in
Europe and aiding the Spanish Loyalists
in their own peculiar way, were not neglecting the Far East region threatened by
the Japanese expansion into Manchuria,
Northern China, and Inner Mongolia. Every
effort was put forth to make the Special
Far Eastern Army as self-sufficient as possible, so as to be able to face Germany and
Japan simultaneously if worse came to

worst. The Japanese estimated that
Bliukher's army east of Lake Baikal had
quadrupled its strength between 1931 and
1936, and that in the latter year it consisted of nearly twenty rifle and four cavalry divisions plus 1,200 aircraft and an
equal number of tanks. When the Japanese
began their all-out attempt to conquer the
rest of China in July 1937, the Soviets
added still more men and equipment to
their Far Eastern forces, and the number
of aircraft rose to nearly 2,000 in 1938.

Relieved that the Japanese thrust was
against China and not against the USSR,
Stalin saw much to be gained from helping
the Chinese in their struggle, thereby keeping the Japanese busy enough in China to
discourage any serious incursions into
Soviet territory. The main Soviet contribution in the Sino-Japanese War was aircraft
and pilots.

The Chinese Air Force (CAF) had fewer
than a hundred first-line planes in July
1937; four months later, the Japanese had
just about eliminated those. Thus, when
Soviet aircraft begain arriving in October
1937, the CAF was at its nadir and had
nowhere to go but upward. At first the
Soviets tried flying the aircraft from the
Turk-Sib Railroad in Kazakhstan across
Sinkiang to Lanchow in Kansu province,
where the aircraft were prepared for
combat and then dispersed to other air
bases. But the air route was so hazardous
and so lacking in navigational aids and airfields that the Soviets discontinued the
ferrying practice and began to ship the
dismantled planes by truck over a road
built by tens of thousands of Chinese in
late 1937 and early 1938. By mid-1938 the
trucks were able to travel from the Soviet
frontier as far as Chengtu and Chungking in
Szechwan province, a distance of more
than 3,000 miles. Travelers in China in
1938 reported seeing thousands of Soviet
trucks hauling aircraft, weapons, and

Figure 11. Soviet fighter pilots in front of I-16 during a lull in the fighting around Lake Khasan in 1938.

ammunition.

The Soviets not only delivered aircraft to the beleaguered Chinese, they also set up and maintained depots and assembly plants, trained Chinese pilots, and sent in "volunteer" Russian pilots to engage the Japanese in combat. For example, on April 29, 1939, in an air battle against a Japanese bombing attack on Wuhan, more than half the 65 Soviet-built fighters in that engagement were flown by Russians. The Japanese lost most of their bombers and a high percentage of the accompanying fighters in that battle, causing the Japanese ambassador in Moscow, Shigemitsu, to protest the Soviet involvement, claiming that the Soviet Union had sent to China (up to May 1938) some 500 planes and 200 pilots.

The Soviet aircraft sent to China were I-15 and I-16 fighters, SB bombers, and a few TB-3 heavy bombers (the last were used mostly as transports). The I-15s and I-16s, which had shown up badly against the Me-109s in Spain, did much better against the less-effective Japanese fighters of that period, and the Soviet pilots in China were able to evaluate the ability of the Japanese pilots, study their air tactics, and observe their equipment. In 1938 China was the ideal area for testing Soviet

aircraft and for trying out air tactics under actual combat conditions. It was in China that the Soviet pilots realized that the 7.62mm machine gun was a very inadequate weapon for making bomber kills, and as a result began the installation of the 12.7mm gun, the equivalent of the American 50-caliber gun. Control of the air, easily acquired by the Japanese following the near-annihilation of the CAF in 1937, was getting more difficult to maintain in 1938 as Soviet aircraft and pilots entered the fray.

Soviet activity in China slowed down somewhat in early 1939, although the air war was intense in the Lanchow-Sian area in February and March, when the Japanese made a serious attempt at interdicting deliveries coming over the highway from Sinkiang. During the May–September period, the Soviets were busily engaged in an open confrontation with the Japanese along the Mongolian border and thus had less equipment to spare for the CAF. After September, however, the deliveries were increased. At this time the Soviets moved units into Chengtu and Chungking and took over the air defense of those cities. In September 1939 the American ambassador in Moscow claimed that the

Russians had sent at least 1,000 aircraft and 2,000 pilots to China. Since Moscow limited its pilots to a maximum of six months in China, the latter figure does not seem out of line with the facts.

The Winter War with Finland in late 1939 and early 1940 slowed down Soviet deliveries to China, but they picked up again in mid-1940. Although the Chinese were anxious to get newer and better fighters from the Soviets, especially since the new Japanese planes were making things more and more difficult for the old I-15s and I-16s, the Russians ignored their plea. By late 1940 the Russian pilots had been withdrawn from China, partly because the CAF by then had enough trained pilots to man the available aircraft and partly because Stalin was now anxious to pacify the Japanese in order to concentrate on the western front, a policy that culminated in the Soviet-Japanese neutrality pact of April 1941.

There can be no doubt that between late 1937 and the end of 1940, for well over three years, the CAF was mainly dependent upon Soviet assistance. A U.S. State Department report in 1941 estimated that the Soviets had supplied China with more than 700 aircraft and about 40,000 tons of weapons and ammunition. On the other hand, Stalin's policy had helped keep the Japanese military bogged down in mainland China, had enabled a large number of Soviet pilots to gain combat experience, and had provided a laboratory in which to test Soviet aircraft and equipment under combat conditions.

While the Soviets were engaging the Japanese indirectly in China in the late 1930s, they found themselves in direct confrontation on two occasions: at Changkufeng, or Lake Khasan, in 1938, and at Khalkhin-Gol in 1939. On both occasions it would seem that the Japanese were

feeling out Soviet resolve and capability, and in both confrontations the Soviets demonstrated an ability to defend their borders. In order to have succeeded, the Japanese would have had to draw upon forces committed in China—a price they were unwilling to pay for dubious gains against the Soviet Union.

The Lake Khasan engagement, to use the Soviet terminology, began in early July 1938 when the Japanese protested the Soviet fortifying of Changfukeng Hill, a point between Lake Khasan and the Tumen River on the Korean-USSR border, an area under dispute. The line defined in the Hunchun Protocol of 1886 was no longer easy to determine, since the old wooden boundary posts had long since rotted away, and both the Japanese and Russians claimed the area—although why either wanted it is hard to understand. When the Japanese attacked on July 29, the frontier skirmish rapidly escalated into a "limited war" of some proportions. For almost two weeks both sides increased their commitments until the Soviets had a force of twenty-seven infantry batallions plus several regiments of artillery and tanks. The Japanese had either to reinforce or to cease operations; they took the latter option. In their opinion, the engagement was getting beyond a "limited" one, as can be surmised from the fact that the Japanese later admitted to incurring 1,439 casualties. Hostilities ceased on August 11 and the Soviets were left in command of Changfukeng Hill and the surrounding terrain east of the Tumen, the line originally claimed by them.

The VVS component of the First Independent Red Banner Far Eastern Army, which confronted the Japanese at Lake Khasan, was commanded by P. Rychagov, who was executed in 1941 as one of the scapegoats for the massive Nazi destruction of Soviet aircraft. His airmen, facing light

Figure 12. Soviet heroes of Khalkhin-Gol, 1939. S. I. Gritsevits and G. P. Kravchenko pose with a marshal of the Mongolian People's Army.

Japanese opposition, were able to penetrate the enemy positions in depth and demonstrated considerable capability. But the Soviet aviators also found that aviation was not very effective against a well-entrenched enemy whose artillery was well protected.

The Lake Khasan incident stimulated further increases in the size of Soviet military forces in the Far East, including the dispatch of the Fifty-Seventh Special Corps to Outer Mongolia to implement the Soviet-Mongolian treaty of mutual assistance signed in March 1936. On May 31, 1938, Molotov, speaking before the Supreme Soviet, stated clearly that "in virtue of our treaty with Mongolia, we shall defend its frontiers as energetically as our own. . . . "

The boundaries between Outer Mongolia and Manchukuo were badly defined, as befitted semidesert grazing areas inhabit-

ed by nomads who followed their flocks with little regard for international boundaries. What with the Japanese undertaking the guarantee of the boundaries of Inner Mongolia and Manchukuo and the Soviet Union supporting Outer Mongolia's territorial integrity, and what with the Soviet Far Eastern Army commanders boasting over their victory at Lake Khasan and the Japanese Kwantung Army leaders thirsting for revenge, it took no prophet to foresee a clash between the two guarantors. This was the atmosphere in which a frontier incident took place on the Manchukuo–Outer Mongolia border in May 1939. The war that ensued is called the Khalkhin-Gol incident by the Russians and the Nomonhan incident by the Japanese. The actual territory under dispute was ridiculous: a small stretch of utterly useless semidesert lying between the Khalkhin-Gol River and a small village called Nomonhan, about ten miles east of the river.

On May 11, 1939, a force of Japanese cavalry, supported by forty aircraft, attacked the Outer Mongolian frontier guards at Nomonhan and forced them to pull back to the Khalkhin-Gol. The Soviets jumped into the fray and sent troops to hold the region east of the river, a situation that led to intense fighting from May 12 to May 22. Kwantung headquarters responded by dispatching a large contingent of infantry from Hailar in Manchukuo, thus escalating a frontier incident into a "limited war." On May 28 the Japanese tried to cut off the Soviet-Mongolian forces east of the river, but Soviet artillery superiority and close air support wrecked their strategy. It was now obvious to Kwantung headquarters that only a major force could dislodge the Soviets, and they accordingly began such a buildup, but it was more than offset by Soviet reinforcements.

The war was characterized during June by an expansion of air activity, with each side using up to 100 aircraft on occasion. On June 27, for example, the Japanese used 80 fighters and 30 bombers to attack a Soviet air base in Outer Mongolia. Tokyo, not nearly so enthusiastic about escalating the Khalkhin-Gol conflict, ordered a cessation of such large-scale air attacks. In spite of Tokyo's desires, however, the Kwantung Army leaders launched a furious two-day attack on July 2 and another on July 23.

The Soviets responded by creating a greatly reinforced First Army group in Mongolia with G. K. Zhukov in command. When Zhukov launched his counteroffensive on August 20, his superiority was 1.5 to 1 in infantry and cavalry, 2 to 1 in artillery, 4 to 1 in tanks, and 1.6 to 1 in aircraft. He insisted on a very close ground-air cooperation; this was developed by having the pilots study the terrain along with the infantry and armored troops and by creating special reconnaissance groups.

By the end of August the Japanese had been pushed over the Mongolian version of the border and an armistice agreement had been reached, to go into effect on September 16.

The Khalkhin-Gol "incident" was really a small war, with the Russians using thirty-five infantry battalions, twenty cavalry squadrons, 500 tanks, and 500 aircraft—the Red Army's first test involving a massive use of artillery, tanks, and aircraft, in which it acquitted itself with distinction. Zhukov, who won his spurs at Khalkhin-Gol, used his aircraft successfully to inhibit enemy reinforcement of the battlefield. The Kwantung Army leaders were impressed by the Soviet performance; indeed, it may have been very influential in the later Japanese decision to go south in 1941 instead of moving north against the Soviet Union.

While the Red Army and its VVS were fighting as far afield as Spain, China, and on the Mongolian border during the 1937-1939 period, Stalin was ruthlessly butchering its top leaders in almost insane fashion. The Great Purge had hit civilians as early as 1934, but the military were immune from arrest until 1937. Then, on January 23, 1937, the trial of the "anti-Soviet Trotskyite Center" began. In the course of the trial, Radek, one of the main defendants, mentioned Marshal Tukhachevsky's name some ten times. Since this was a "show trial" meant for public consumption, Radek's constant references to Tukhachevsky could not have been accidental, and it was obvious that the latter was in deep trouble. In retrospect, it seems obvious that Stalin had lost confidence in the political reliability of the Red Army command, and that he felt it was necessary to strike down the top commanders first and then get at their underlings later. Tukhachevsky was arrested on May 22. On June 11, he, along with six other top commanders, was tried by a special military tribunal made up of such high-ranking officers as: Alksnis, the VVS chief; Budenny, the commander of the Moscow Military District; Blyukher, head of the Far Eastern Army; and Shaposhnikov, chief of the General Staff. The defendants, having been found guilty of treason and other crimes, were shot the following day.

The execution of Tukhachevsky and his companions was only the first step in a senseless blood purge of the Red Army which all but eliminated the top echelons of the officer corps. During the purge, the Red Army lost 3 marshals, 11 deputy commissars for defense, 57 corps commanders, 110 divisional commanders, and 186 brigade commanders. Guesses as to the fatalities among the 75,000 or so officers in the Red Army range from 15,000 to 30,000. No army could stand a blood purge of that dimension without suffering pernicious anemia in its command system.

Soviet aviation was especially hard hit by the purge. Ya. I. Alksnis, who had succeeded Baranov as commander of the VVS in 1931, was arrested in 1937, probably dying in 1940. His deputy, V. V. Khripin, also disappeared in 1937. Alksnis was succeeded by a nonentity named A. D. Loktionov, who in turn gave way in September 1939 to Ya. I. Smushkevich. The latter, a veteran of the Soviet air activities in Spain who had made quite a reputation as an air commander in the Far East, was later destined to be shot as a scapegoat during the debacle of June 1941. In addition to Alksnis and Khripin, such outstanding VVS officers as I. A. Lopatin, commander in chief of the Leningrad Air Command, and R. A. Muklevich, a senior general in frontal aviation, were also victims of the purge. About 75 percent of the senior officers in the VVS had been eliminated by the end of 1939. The purge also extended to the aircraft industry, to

such research organizations as TsAGI, TsIAM, and VIAM, and to some of the design bureaus. Even Tupolev was under arrest for a short period. It would seem fair to say that the poor showing of the VVS in the Winter War with Finland and in the early phase of the Great Patriotic War could be at least partially attributed to Stalin's blood lust in the late 1930s.

While Zhukov was whipping his First Army group into shape to finish off the Japanese, some delicate negotiations were going on in Moscow: Stalin was negotiating with his "collective-security" partners, Britain and France, on one hand while simultaneously conducting secret talks with the Germans on the other hand. The British and French military missions were in Moscow to argue with Voroshilov about how far they would go in supporting the Soviet Union in the event of war with Germany. The debate seemed to hinge on Poland's willingness to allow Soviet forces inside its national boundaries, in order to carry out a forward strategy against the German attack, and on the French and British attitude toward Soviet hegemony over the Baltic countries. Stalin felt that the Poles, French, and British were dragging their feet during the talks, and also suspected that the French and British were inclined to push Hitler to the east. The upshot of these negotiations was the surprise announcement of the Soviet-German Non-Aggression Pact on August 23, 1939.

The most important part of the pact was a secret protocol which divided eastern Europe into German and Soviet spheres of influence. Poland was to be divided along the Narew-Vistula-San river line, and the Soviet sphere also included Finland, Latvia, and Bessarabia. The Germans were to dominate everything west of the line, and each was to be boss within his own sphere with no questions asked. Having insured himself against a two-front war,

Hitler seized his share of the booty on September 1 when he attacked Poland. World War II was under way.

The Russians, flabbergasted by the rapidity of the German advance, realized that they had to speed up their own preparations if they were to seize their share of the Polish spoils. Activating the Byelorussian and Ukrainian fronts, the Red Army hit the Poles from the rear on September 18, covering some sixty miles on the first day. Soviet historians have found it difficult to explain this Russian-Nazi collaboration in the murder of Poland, and they have tried to rationalize it by using euphemistic terminology. The official designation for this invasion is "The Liberation of the Western Ukraine and Western Byelorussia." Although Soviet accounts say it was a twelve-day campaign, actually the Red Army reached the agreed-upon line of demarcation by September 21; the rest of the campaign was a mopping-up operation. As for aviation, although the frontal aviation units assigned to the ground forces flew cover for them, there was no real test of their capabilities because the Germans had already annihilated the Polish armed forces.

A much-greater test of the VVS occurred two months later in the Winter War with Finland. The Soviets had been badgering the Finns since 1938 about allowing the former to fortify certain islands in the Gulf of Finland and about Finnish relinquishment of some territory near Leningrad. During a conference in Moscow which lasted from October 12 to November 3, 1939, the Finns refused to bow to Russian hectoring, and Molotov finally stated that it would be up to the military to clarify the situation. On November 30 the Red Army began its attack on Finland to "clarify the situation."

Over the next 104 days, the Red Army succeeded in bludgeoning its Finnish opponent into submission through massive expenditures of men and metal, but it was a costly and hardly glorious war. The Finns had only 200,000 inadequately equipped troops, a few antitank and antiaircraft weapons, no tanks, and a tiny air force composed of a Heinz-57 mixture of obsolescent foreign-made planes. To overcome Finnish resistance, the Soviets used forty-five rifle divisions, 1,500 tanks, 3,000 aircraft, and a plethora of artillery. The casualties admitted to by the Soviets— some 200,000—were the equivalent of the entire Finnish armed forces.

The VVS faced a Finnish air force that, although doughty, was not equipped quantitatively nor qualitatively to do more than offer a stubborn holding action, a resistance doomed to be swamped by sheer numbers. When the war began, the Finns had a total strength of 145 aircraft, of which only 100 or so were airworthy. Their fighter aircraft consisted of 65 Fokker C-10s, C-5s, and D-2s, 10 Bristol Bulldogs, and 15 Blackburn Ripons. Only the Fokkers could be called even adequate to face the Russians. They also had 15 Blenheim-I bombers. During the Winter War the Finns received 200 aircraft from foreign countries, but some of them, like the Gloster Gladiator-IIs, were not able to cope with the Soviet I-153s and I-16s. By the end of the war, the Finns had just over 100 serviceable aircraft to face some 2,000 to 2,500 Soviet planes.

The VVS, apparently underestimating the enemy, initially assigned only 900 aircraft to the Finnish front, but heavy losses in I-15 and I-15*bis* fighters as well as SB-2 bombers forced the VVS to double the commitment. The I-153 and I-16 fighters, arriving in overwhelming numbers, were able to decimate the obsolescent Finnish fighters, thus enabling the Soviet bombers (mostly SB-2s and the faster DB-3s) to drop 150,000 explosive and incendiary bombs for a total of 7,500 tons. However,

Mannerheim, the Finnish commander in chief, claimed that Russian air power, either in bombing or in a close-support role, was not a factor of decisive importance.

Be that as it may, the Soviets paid heavily in aircraft. The Finns claim to have destroyed, in air combat, by antiaircraft fire, or on the ground, more than 700 Soviet aircraft. If "unconfirmed" kills are added, the figure rises to more than 900. On the other hand, the Finnish pilots noted that their Soviet counterparts improved steadily during the war, apparently learning their trade as they went along. When, two years later, the Soviet fliers had to operate in similar winter conditions in the defense of Moscow and Leningrad, they had their experience in the Winter War to fall back on—something their Luftwaffe opponents lacked.

The overall miserable performance of the Red Army, including the VVS, in the Winter War was just one more reason for the frenetic activity that characterized the Soviet defense industry between 1939 and June 1941. Zhukov's candid appraisal of Soviet shortcomings at Khalkhin-Gol, close observation of German efficiency in Poland, and the horrors of the Winter War alerted Stalin to the need for both better organization in the armed forces and better weapons. Of course, many of the troubles were derived from the purge; for example, the wholesale slaughter of high-ranking officers trained to handle large masses of men led to their replacement by junior officers who had yet to learn their trade. Furthermore, the managers of industrial plants devoted to military output were so afraid of being accused of "sabotage," "wrecking," and other blanket charges used in the purge that they avoided decision-making if at all possible.

Voroshilov, who had not measured up in the war with Finland, was replaced as commissar of defense by Marshal S. K. Timoshenko, and Zhukov, fresh from his exploits in Mongolia, became chief of the General Staff. The new bosses immediately recommended a reorganization of the VVS, and in late 1940 work was begun on expanding the school system and reequipping combat formations with new types of aircraft—all in an effort to come up with an expanded and modernized VVS capable of holding its own against the awesome Luftwaffe. But, as Zhukov observed in his memoirs, when the Germans attacked, the VVS was in the midst of its reorganization; its pilots were not yet fully trained to use the new aircraft that had come into the inventory, and only 15 percent of them were trained for night flights.

In January 1940, A. I. Shakurin replaced M. M. Kaganovich as head of the Aviation Industry Commissariat, and the former went to work with a will. According to Shakurin, his job was to accelerate the output of better aircraft at literally breakneck speed—an instruction he received from Stalin himself. His job was helped by the completion of the new TsAGI, replete with new laboratories and wind tunnels, an expansion and modernization that had been under way since 1935.

In 1940 three new fighters were put into series production: the Mig-3, designed by A. I. Mikoian and M. I. Gurevich, with a 1,350-hp AM-35A engine, armed with two 12.7mm and two 7.6mm guns and capable of a maximum speed of around 400 mph; the Yak-1, designed by A. S. Yakovlev, with a 1,050-hp VK-105P engine, armed with a 20mm cannon and two 7.62mm guns, which had a top speed of 365 mph and was constructed mostly of wood and fabric on a steel-tube frame; and the Lagg-3, designed by the team of S. A. Lavochkin, V. P. Gorbunov, and M. I. Gudkov, built almost entirely of wood, with a 1,050-hp M-105P liquid-cooled engine, armed with a 23mm cannon and two 12.7mm guns, which could reach a top speed of about 350 mph. Also going into series production at that time were two dive bombers, the Pe-2 and the Il-2. The Pe-2, designed by V. M. Petliakov, was a twin-engine, 1,100-hp, Vee, liquid-cooled machine that carried a crew of three, was armed with three 12.7mm and two 7.62mm guns, could carry 1,200 pounds of bombs, and had a top speed of 340 mph at 16,000 feet. The Il-2 Shturmovik (the Iliushka, to Soviet pilots) was destined to become one of the most celebrated Soviet aircraft in World War II and the tank-destroyer par excellence. Designed by S. V. Iliushin, the Il-2 was a heavily armored ground-attack plane with a 1,600-hp AM-38 engine; it had two 23mm cannons plus one 12.7mm and two 7.62mm guns, could carry 800 pounds of bombs, and had a top speed of 260 mph.

According to Shakurin, during the second half of 1940 all the old fighters were taken out of series production. Since by that time there were twenty-eight aircraft, fourteen engine, and thirty-two aircraft component factories in operation, Shakurin had every right to anticipate a VVS adequately equipped with modern machines within the next few years. Marshal Zhukov, in his memoirs, reported that the Red Army received 17,745 combat planes, including 3,719 of the latest types, between January 1939 and June 22, 1941, an average of more than 7,000 aircraft a year. Unfortunately for the VVS, the overwhelming bulk of the aircraft it received was obsolescent, since the newer types did not begin to flow into combat units until early 1941—just before the Nazis destroyed most of them on the ground.

The VVS, on the very eve of the Nazi invasion, must have had a total stength of around 10,000 aircraft. The Soviets admitted losing more than 5,000 planes in the early days of the war, and they still had a VVS of sorts fighting at the end of the year. But in June 1941, the VVS was an air force undergoing intensive reorganization, a force with an inventory of mostly obsolescent planes.

Research Notes

Overall coverage of the Soviet air force during the 1928–1941 period can be found in the following standard works: John Erickson, *The Soviet High Command* (New York, 1962); Asher Lee, *The Soviet Air Force* (New York, 1962); a collective work edited by Lee, *The Soviet Air and Rocket Forces* (New York, 1959); and Robert A. Kilmarx, *A History of Soviet Air Power* (New York, 1962). An excellent account of the development of Soviet aircraft, replete with pictures, is to be found in Heinz J. Nowara and G. R. Duval, *Russian Civil and Military Aircraft, 1884-1969* (London, 1970). The Soviet confrontation with the Japanese in the late 1930s is covered in *The Memoirs of Marshal Zhukov* (London, 1971). From the Japanese point of view, the so-called incidents as Changku-feng and Nomonhan are well covered in *Japanese Studies in Manchuria,* vol. 9, part 3, books A and B, "Small Wars and Border Problems: The Nomonhan Incident" and "The Changkufeng Incident" (Tokyo, 1956). This work also includes an English translation of a Soviet account: S. N. Shishkin's *Khalkhin-Gol* (Moscow, 1954). Gordon Pickler's unpublished doctoral dissertation, "U.S. and the Chinese Nationalist Air Force, 1931–49" (Tallahassee, Fla., n.d.) is an excellent work on the Soviet involvement in the Sino-Japanese War. The Finnish view of the Winter War is dealt with in *The Memoirs of Marshal Mannerheim* (London, 1953) and in a more vivid form by the Finnish ace Eino Luukkanen in his *Fighter over Finland* (London, 1963).

For those who read Russian, the available literature is more plentiful. *Istoriia velikoi otechestvennoi voiny Sovetskogo Soiuza, 1941-1945* [The History of the Great Fatherland War of the Soviet Union, 1941–1945] (Moscow, 1960), the nearest thing to an official account of the Soviet experience in World War II, is a six-volume cooperative work published between 1960 and 1965. Volume 1 gives the background from 1917 up to 1941. A rather small book by B. L. Simakov and I. F. Shipilov, *Vozdushnii Flot Strany Sovetov* [The Air Fleet of the Land of the Soviets] (Moscow, 1958), covers the Soviet air force up to the middle of the 1950s; for a specific account of the state of the Soviet aviation industry on the eve of the Great Patriotic War, see an article by A. I. Shakurin, "Aviatsi-onnaia promyshlennost' nakanune velikoi otechestvennoi voiny" [The Aviation Industry on the Eve of the Great Fatherland War] in *Voprosy istorii,* no. 2 (1974), pp. 81-99.

5

The Great Patriotic War, 1941-1945

John T. Greenwood

Early on Sunday, June 22, 1941, 30 specially selected Luftwaffe Heinkel bombers struck ten forward airfields housing fighter units of the Red Air Force (Voenno-vozhdushnie Sili, or VVS). Timed to coincide with the start of the massive blitzkrieg, these predawn attacks succeeded brilliantly in confusing the numerically superior VVS, which was too stunned and disorganized to cope with the full fury of the German aerial assault on the main airfield complexes in the western frontier military districts. By noon, the VVS had lost more than 1,200 first-line aircraft; the majority were destroyed on the ground. Within days, the Luftwaffe had firmly grasped aerial supremacy in the east.

In April and May 1945, less than four years after that disastrous June, the Red Air Force victoriously concluded a long and bitter air war over Berlin. As a measure of its nearly total dominance in the air, the VVS mustered more than 7,500 combat aircraft in the final struggle for Berlin,

while the once-vaunted Luftwaffe was little to be seen. With well over 15,000 aircraft in front-line service by May 1945, the VVS emerged as the world's third-strongest air force, with the world's largest and most proficient tactical air arm.

Plans, Purges, and Preparations: 1928-1941

The roots of the VVS' ultimate triumph over the Luftwaffe, as well as those of the crushing defeats of 1941, lay in the crucial years from the launching of the First Five-Year Plan in the fall of 1928 to the opening of the German invasion. When the Germans struck in June 1941, the Soviet Union was caught in the midst of an extensive and fundamental reorganization, rearmament, expansion, retraining, and redeployment of its armed forces. Begun in 1939, spurred on by the shoddy performance against Finland in the Winter War (1939–1940), and given renewed urgency by the stunning German victory in the west in May–June 1940, the entire program was still well short of its goals when the war started. In no branch of the Red Army was this more apparent, nor with such nearly fatal consequences, than it was in the VVS.

Never developed as an independent air arm, as were the Royal Air Force and the Luftwaffe, the VVS was from its inception considered an auxiliary of the Red Army and an essential part of the ground-air team. In this role, the air units were always subordinate to ground-force commanders, though a separate air-force chain of command stretched down from the chief of the VVS for administration, personnel, training, and logistics.

During the 1930s, the VVS had grown steadily in size and strength until it had well over 4,000 aircraft and 100,000 men by 1938. Possessing some of the finest aircraft then in service—the I-15 biplane and I-16 monoplane fighters and the SB-2 and SB-2*bis* twin-engine bombers—the Red Air Force in both quantity and quality was one of the world's premier air forces. This very fact, however, contributed to a sense of complacency that hampered the design and development of more modern aircraft.

In the early and mid-1930s, during a brief but serious flirtation with the strategic bombing ideas of Giulio Douhet, the VVS had built the largest fleet of multiengine bombers in the world. This infatuation soon faded, as a result of both the purging in 1937–1939 of the leading exponents of strategic air operations and the Soviet air experiences in the Spanish civil war (1936–1939). To Soviet leaders, the generally ineffective use of bombers and the conversely heavy stress on ground-support operations in Spain seemed to disprove Douhet's concepts and to reaffirm the more traditional Soviet emphasis on tactical air operations.

As Soviet involvement in Spain drew to a close, it was clear that front-line Soviet aircraft were increasingly hard pressed to match the newer German aircraft, the Bf-109s, He-111s, Do-17s, and Ju-87s then making their combat debuts with the Condor Legion. With the combat aircraft of 1935–1937 swiftly approaching obsolescence, the Soviet government in 1939 largely discontinued the production of multiengine bombers in favor of increased output of fighter, attack, and light-bomber aircraft, and directed its designers to create new generations of military planes. The decision to concentrate on tactical air operations and new aircraft reflected a realistic appraisal of productive capacity, resources, geographic and strategic position, and military requirements.

Even as Soviet designers labored on their new aircraft, Soviet forces were thrown against Finland in November 1939. Neither the ground nor air forces performed well. Leadership at almost all levels of command was poor and hesitant, still suffering badly from the recent purges.

Despite a huge numerical superiority, the VVS units that engaged the miniscule Finnish air force were poorly organized and trained as well as extremely inefficient and ineffective. Second-line units and the now-expendable bomber force were employed extensively, but the better air units remained in the west to guard against possible German reactions. Ground-support operations were confused and poorly coordinated until the last days of the fighting. Bomber performance and results were so miserable that they only confirmed the correctness of the earlier Kremlin decision to give up strategic bombing. Unready for war in the harsh winter climate, both air and ground units suffered heavy losses. In the process, however, the VVS and the army learned much that proved invaluable in 1941.

While the Red Army eventually won

Figure 13. Prewar Soviet naval fighter, an I-153, over Sevastopol.

early in 1940, the overall performance of the armed forces profoundly dismayed Soviet leaders. They realized that the Red Army badly needed an extensive program of reorganization, rearmament, and retraining in order to place it on a satisfactory combat footing. Gen. S. K. Timoshenko, who had taken command of the northwestern (Karelian) district in January 1940 and brought the war there to a swift and successful conclusion, was promoted to marshal on May 7, 1940 and subsequently replaced Marshal K. E. Voroshilov as commissar of defense. Aided by the astute Marshal B. M. Shaposhnikov, chief of the Army General Staff, Timoshenko energetically set about rebuilding and revitalizing the Soviet armed forces, spurred on by German victories in the west.

Timoshenko's efforts extended to the VVS, which was even then revising its basic organizational structure. Until the late 1930s, the basic tactical units of the VVS were squadrons of from twenty to thirty planes, grouped into air brigades assigned to the territorial military districts of their ground armies. In July 1940, regiments of from sixty to sixty-four aircraft became the basic tactical units. The former flights were redesignated as squadrons, three or four of which were usually assigned to each regiment. In turn, from three to five regiments made up the new air divisions that replaced the former air brigades. These divisions could operate independently, assigned directly to a military district (*front*) or army, or they could be grouped into air corps that were similarly assigned.

The new air regiments were either integral (homogeneous) or mixed (composite). The former consisted of one type of combat aircraft, although different models could be found in various squadrons. The latter, and most common, kind of regiment had various types of aircraft and provided a full range of air support. Air divisions were normally composite, with mixed regiments or various combinations of integral units, because of their wide-ranging tactical responsibilities. There were some homogeneous fighter and bomber divisions, but the air corps were composed of long-range bombers and air-defense fighters (IA/PVO), such as the Sixth Fighter Air Corps (FAC) guarding Moscow. The regiment/division structure of 1940 was refined somewhat as a result of wartime experience, but remained substantially unaltered during the war.

The 1940 reorganization also included a functional restructuring and redistribution of the entire VVS. Excluding the Naval Air Force (VVS/VMF), the Air Landing Force (Vozhdushno-desantnye voiska, or VDV), and Civil Air Fleet (Grazhdanskii vozhdushny flot, or GVF), the air force was realigned into five major components—the Long-Range Bomber Aviation (Dal'nebombardirovochnaia aviatsiia, or DBA) unit of the High Command, a new air-reserve component of the High Command replacing the former Aviation of Special Assignment (Aviatsiia osobogo naznacheniia, or AON), Front Aviation (VVS fronta), Army Aviation (VVS armii), and Corps Aviation (Korpusnye aviaeskadril'i). The long-range and medium bombers, especially the DB-3s and Il-4s, combined in 1940 with the remaining TB-6 and TB-7 (Pe-8) heavy bombers, formed the five air corps and three independent air divisions of the DBA. Of this force, three air corps with 29 air regiments and 1,000 aircraft were stationed in the western frontier military districts in 1941.

Front, Army, and Corps aviation units—all tactical—were assigned to army units for direct and indirect support of ground operations. A Front Aviation unit normally consisted of three or four bomber, attack, and/or fighter air divisions, each with 200–250 aircraft, and was assigned for opera-

Figure 14. SB-3 medium bomber, 1941. Designed by Tupolev, it carried a crew of three at 280 mph.

tional use and control to a major military district that would become a *front,* or army group, when mobilized for war. The primary mission of Front Aviation was to conduct air operations for the entire *front,* and more than half of the unit was usually reassigned to provide additional air support for the combined-arms ground armies. Army Aviation consisted of one or two mixed air divisions attached directly to each ground army to support combined-arms and mechanized units on the battlefield. Corps Aviation squadrons, usually liaison aircraft, were assigned directly to each rifle, mechanized, and cavalry corps and came under the immediate operational control of the corps commander. This reorganization was still incomplete when the war began. Most of the *front* air divisions were established and assigned to designated military districts, but only a few of the ground armies as yet had their air divisions attached.

The desire to increase the cooperation between the air and ground forces prompted these changes. By aligning air-force unit organization with that of the ground forces and assigning air units directly to the ground units they supported, the Soviet command believed that improved coordination and cooperation would be fostered. Unfortunately, this change also so dispersed the tactical air units among subordinate formations that it seriously hampered centralized control and concentration of all tactical aviation for major *front* air operations. This particular weakness, however, became apparent only in the war's early months.

The restructuring of the VVS before the war was intended to facilitate its combat employment. Soviet air doctrine carefully delineated the basic tasks of the VVS in air warfare and the respective responsibilities of the various combat elements. The VVS had three main objectives: (1) achieving air supremacy, both tactical and strategic, (2) supporting of army ground forces and the navy in conducting their operations, and (3) performing air reconnaissance. The struggle for air superiority was the most important VVS task, with ground-support and aerial reconnaissance of lesser significance and dependent upon the attainment of air control.

The primary mission of the fighters was to gain air supremacy so that the other branches could operate against the enemy on the battlefield and in the immediate rear areas. *Front* fighters were also to escort the ground-attack and bomber aircraft that carried the full burden of close air-support operations. Long-range bombers were to be used against strategic targets in the enemy's deep rear areas, but they could also be employed to augment the striking power of tactical aviation in major ground operations and for interdiction of the battlefield. Although the VVS had to be able to conduct independent air operations against enemy supply depots, railways, and airfields, air operations in cooperation with the army ground forces always took precedence.

The Finnish war revealed some serious shortcomings in the Rear Services (Tyl VVS)—logistics, airfields, and maintenance. After a detailed examination, the VVS Rear Services were reorganized on an area principle in April 1941. Air-base regions (*raion aviatsionnogo bazirovaniia,* or RAB) were created; each supported three or four air divisions with one air base allotted per division. Depending upon the number of regiments in the division, the airfield would have three or four airfield maintenance (technical) battalions (*batal'on aerodromnogo obsluzhivaniia,* or BAO). One BAO could support a two-motor aircraft regiment or two single-engine regiments.

Airfields and BAOs sustained air opera-

tions and the operational and base personnel, while providing necessary munitions, petroleum-oil-lubricants (POL), logistics, and maintenance facilities and services. Slated for completion in August 1941, only half of the BAOs were functioning in the Western Special Military District when the war began, and the Kiev Special Military District had not even started to revise its base structure.

Russia's seizure of additional territory in 1939–1940 enlarged the problems caused by the reorganization programs. The acquisition of a huge chunk of eastern Poland in September 1939 and of certain border areas from Finalnd, the incorporation of the Baltic states, and the annexation of Bessarabia and northern Bukovina—these moves had, by June 1940, pushed the Soviet border westward, adding important buffer areas. But they had also seriously dislocated military dispositions; such prepared positions as the Stalin line, as well as the established base network, were left behind. A large number of new airfields had to be built. Although more than 200 airfields and landing strips were rushed into construction and renovation in 1940–1941, the air units deployed to these newly acquired areas were crowded onto a limited number of primary airfields in the Western and Kiev special military districts. Under such conditions, aircraft could not be dispersed effectively or camouflaged; thus vulnerability to surprise attack was greatly enhanced.

Late in 1940, the Commissariat of Defense, the Army General Staff, the chief of the VVS, and the Main Directorate (headquarters) of the VVS submitted their plans for the expansion and complete reequipment of the VVS. Approved on February 25, 1941, the decree "On the Reorganization of the Red Air Forces" authorized the formation of 106 new air regiments to fill out the VVS' new structure.

Figure 15. Mig-3 long-range interceptor designed by Mikoian and Gurevich for World War II.

Most of these units were to be equipped with the new types of aircraft and were to be combat-ready in early 1942. To support this expansion, the VVS training system was to be enlarged and greater emphasis placed on the primary pilot resources of Osoaviakhim. By June 1941, only 19 of the 106 regiments had been formed.

In the reequipment program, the fighter units of the Air Defense (IA/PVO) were given priority because of their vital mission. As they rolled off the production lines, the new Mig-1 and then Mig-3 interceptors, as well as the air-superiority Yak-1s and Lagg-3s, were delivered to IA/PVO regiments. The first improved Mig-3s were received in the regiments in March 1941, and more became available as weekly Mig-3 output climbed to 75 in April. However, early technical problems encountered by the three new aircraft prevented many air regiments from completing conversion training, so many retained their I-153 and I-16 fighters. As of June 22, the VVS units of the western frontier districts—the Baltic, Western, and Kiev—had 1,762 I-16 and 1,549 I-153 fighters but as yet only 886 Mig-3s and 107 Yak-1s.

Only 20 percent of the VVS units had been equipped with new aircraft by June 22, and few of these were combat ready. The case of the Western Special Military District provides an excellent example of the slowness with which the new aircraft were reaching the operational units. When the war started, that district's air units had 1,560 aircraft, of which only 402 were new models—233 of them Mig-3s. The bulk of the fighter force consisted of 424 I-16s, 262 I-153s, and 73 I-15*bis* models, while the 377 SB bombers formed the backbone of the bombing force. Conversion training moved slowly, not only in this district but in the VVS in general. On May 1, 72 percent of the pilots in Pe-2 units and 80 percent of those in Mig-3 regiments were trained, while only 32 percent of the pilots in the Lagg-3 units had received training.

Despite these serious deficiencies, the growth of the VVS between 1938 and June 1941 was nothing short of spectacular. From 4,000 aircraft and 100,000 men, the VVS grew to an estimated 12,000–15,000 aircraft and more than 400,000 men. Nevertheless, the VVS in June 1941 presented an extremely vulnerable and inviting target. Its first echelon of defense was composed mostly of obsolescent aircraft packed onto a few congested forward airfields, with virtually no reliable early-warning system. The production and deployment of modern aircraft were only beginning to reach sizable proportions. Expanding in manpower and aircraft, the VVS was involved in a complicated organizational restructuring and redefinition of its tactical role. Its leadership was shaky; the morale of its officers and men questionable. All preconditions for disaster were present, and on June 22, 1941, the Luftwaffe sought to make it complete.

Disaster to Recovery:
June 22, 1941 – November 18, 1942

Just before midnight on June 21, Stalin gave the alert for an imminent German attack. For the vast majority of Soviet units, this warning came too late. As the first Heinkels roared in low over their assigned targets, they found the Soviet aircraft neatly parked wingtip to wingtip, row upon row. Surprise was complete; the results were devastating.

Thus, the VVS in the west was largely incapable of any organized opposition to the main wave of attacking aircraft that followed at first light. Throughout the day the Luftwaffe concentrated its major effort against the main Soviet airfields, military headquarters, and communications centers from the Baltic to the western Ukraine. By noon the bulk of the VVS in the frontier areas—well over 1,200 aircraft—lay shattered and burning. In this bold stroke, the Luftwaffe achieved one of the swiftest and tactically most decisive aerial victories in history.

Operation Barbarossa: Summer 1941

In Directive 21 of December 18, 1940, authorizing Operation Barbarossa, Hitler and the German High Command stressed the overriding importance of destroying the Soviet armed forces before the onset

of winter. The directive emphasized the necessity of the immediate destruction of the numerically larger VVS and the rapid seizure of air superiority, so that the Luftwaffe's full strength could be shifted to support of ground operations. Any concerted strategic air offensive against either the Soviet defense industry or lines of communication would be postponed pending the satisfactory outcome of the mobile phase of ground operations.

From the first, the Luftwaffe's role in Barbarossa was limited to tactical air support. To accomplish its mission, the Luftwaffe decided to launch surprise attacks in an effort to eliminate a sizable part of the VVS on the ground and paralyze the rest, thus neutralizing the Soviet numerical edge at the outset. Approximately 2,800 of its front-line strength of 4,300 aircraft were assigned to the four air fleets (*Luftflotten*), facing an estimated 7,500 VVS aircraft. The Germans realized, however, that the Soviet numerical superiority was more illusory than real. Most of the Soviet fighters were inferior I models; the modern Mig, Lagg, and Yak aircraft were just beginning to reach the operational units. Moreover, the Luftwaffe's veteran crews possessed skills and experience far exceeding those of the VVS flyers.

On June 22, the Northwestern and Western *fronty* bore the brunt of the initial German air assault. The VVS of the Western Front, under Lieut. Gen. I. I. Kopets, suffered disastrous losses—528 aircraft destroyed on the ground and 210 in the air, a total of 738 (47.3 percent) of its 1,560 combat aircraft. Many aircraft damaged in the early raids were soon lost as rapidly advancing German troops overran airfield after airfield. These losses were even more staggering in view of the fact that some of the VVS' best-trained fighter air regiments, equipped with 233

Mig-3s and 20 Yak-1s of the 886 Migs and 107 Yaks then in the west, were assigned to the Western Front. So grievous were his losses that Kopets committed suicide on June 23.

The Northwestern Front was also quickly rendered impotent. Indeed, the German advance into the Baltic states toward Leningrad was so swift that some forward airfields had to be abandoned on the very first day. The VVS commander there, Lieut. Gen. P. V. Rychagov, was soon executed as a scapegoat for the huge losses. In the Ukraine, the VVS of the Southwestern Front suffered the smallest losses of the three border districts, losing only 277 aircraft by June 22.

While the Germans were systematically smashing Soviet air power on the North-western, Western, and Southwestern *fronty,* the more distant Northern and Southern *fronty* at first escaped relatively unscathed as the Luftwaffe focused on the immediate border areas. The Odessa Military District (Southern Front) was fortuitously involved in an operational readiness exercise when the war began, with its aircraft on alert, dispersed, and camouflaged; it lost only six aircraft on June 22.

In the midst of the carnage and confusion, some VVS units tried to carry out their assigned offensive air operations according to the VVS' prewar plans to wage the battle for air supremacy with the enemy. Unescorted SB-2 and DB-3 bombers, operating in regiment-sized groups, pressed suicidal attacks against the Luftwaffe airfields only to be slaughtered by fighters and flak. When able, Soviet fighters rose to challenge German formations only to suffer further losses in unequal aerial duels with prowling Messerschmitts. Though skilled pilots flying the inferior yet highly maneuverable Soviet fighters would have had at least some slight chance against the experienced Luftwaffe pilots, few pilots in the VVS had such skills. The VVS fliers, however, did not lack reckless courage and foolhardy determination; they were even known to ram enemy aircraft on occasion.

The Luftwaffe soon established control and swept the VVS from the sky. The Germans later claimed 1,811 Soviet aircraft destroyed on the first day—1,489 on the ground and 322 in the air—for the loss of 35 planes. Three days after launching Barbarossa, air superiority rested so securely in German hands that the Luftwaffe shifted almost exclusively to supporting ground operations. Although the exact dimensions of the early VVS losses will probably never be known, the German Armed Forces High Command (Oberkommando der Wehrmacht, or OKW) claimed 4,017 Soviet aircraft destroyed at the cost of 150 German planes through June 30. This figure was probably close to being correct, inasmuch as the VVS of the Western Front lost 1,163 of its 1,560 aircraft—74 percent of its initial combat strength—between June 22 and 30. Despite these horrendous losses, comparatively light crew casualties were sustained because so few aircraft got off the ground. For the moment, however, the immensity of the destruction and the ensuing chaos obscured this important fact.

The opening German attacks shattered the VVS' command structure in the west, thoroughly uprooted its base and logistics system, and scattered its support and crew personnel. Tactical control, and thus the ability to conduct effective air operations, disappeared. The VVS had lost the battle for command of the air before it began, and with it air cover and support for the hard-pressed Red Army. Air reinforcements were rushed to the front from DBA units; the interior military districts could not redress the balance and were soon lost.

The struggle for survival now became the VVS' paramount task, for it had been thrown into a savage defensive battle that it was ill prepared to fight.

On June 29, the Stavka reorganized the VVS command structure, appointing Gen. Pavel F. Zhigarev to fill the newly created post of commander of the VVS (komandui-ushchii VVS krasnoi armii) and deputy commissar of defense. His express duty was directing the overall recovery of the air force.

The formation of the State Defense Committee (Gosudartsvennyi komitet oborony, or GKO) under Stalin on June 30 and the subsequent reorganization of the fighting *fronty* into three large groups, or "directions," in early July were intended to facilitate recovery and reestablishment of control in the conduct of defensive operations. New air force commanders were appointed to the "directions" in an effort to enhance the coordination of tactical air operations, but in reality little could then be done to stop the German armored and mechanized forces as they rolled eastward. The Soviets went over to the strategic defensive in July and began trading space for the time necessary to recover and regroup. The VVS shifted its now limited forces from fighting for air control to ground support.

Aside from leadership and aircrew ability, the most important gap between the Luftwaffe and VVS in the summer of 1941 was in fighter aircraft. Because of its losses and the evacuation of many aircraft plants eastward, the VVS relied upon the I-153 and I-16 against the superior German Bf-109E and Bf-109F. Even the few Yak-1, Mig-3, and Lagg-3 fighters that were available were outperformed. The lack of modern tactical fighters compelled the VVS to use the more numerous Mig-3 high-altitude interceptors at medium and low altitudes, where they were placed at a grave disadvantage and suffered heavy losses.

In contrast to the situation in the other sectors, the VVS maintained a fairly effective level of air operations on the southern part of the frontier throughout the summer, hampering the German and Rumanian advance into the Ukraine and toward the Dnieper River. Bombers were especially effective against German ground troops until a lull on the *front* engaging the German Army Group Center allowed Mölders' JG-51 forces to be shifted south. During the September fighting around Kiev, in which the Germans destroyed Gen. M. P. Korponos' Southwestern Front and reportedly captured 665,000 Soviet soldiers, Soviet air units flew more than 10,000 sorties. When the Luftwaffe subsequently withdrew a number of its units to reinforce the Second Air Fleet for the drive on Moscow, the VVS in the south once again reasserted itself.

During the summer of 1941, the Stavka had the patience and foresight not to rush everything to the front to stem the German advance. Instead, it began to painstakingly create both ground and air reserves for use in later defensive and offensive operations. Beginning in August, units of the DBA and those of the remaining military districts were drawn upon to form air reserves of the Stavka (rezerv Stavki verkhovnogo glavnokomandovaniia, or Rezerv VGK) which could be moved rapidly and concentrated in critical sectors of the front. From three to eight air regiments of various types of aircraft made up each reserve air group (RAG). By carefully husbanding its scanty resources and even withholding new aircraft and personnel from the front, the Stavka by October had assembled six reserve air groups and assigned them to various *fronty*. In addition, a special mobile strike air group (udarnaia aviatsionnaia gruppa, or UAG) was formed as part of the Rezerv VGK.

Figure 16. Yakovlev Yak-1 fighter taxiing for takeoff on a typical grass Soviet airfield during World War II.

In July and August, the Soviet High Command undertook a number of expedient organizational changes in an attempt to reestablish and strengthen centralized control of the armed forces and improve combat efficiency. The reverses suffered by the air forces showed that the structure of *front* aviation had numerous weaknesses. The dispersion of air units down to the army level prevented centralized control, exploitation of opportunities for the mass use of air power, and concentration of strength on the main sectors of the front. Equipment losses and operational requirements forced changes and reductions in air-unit organization. Each air division was cut from three or four regiments to two, with regimental strength slashed from a nominal sixty aircraft to twenty-two planes in two ten-plane squadrons.

Largely smashed and scattered in June and July, the VVS Rear Services organization in the west had to be reconstructed and streamlined before effective air operations could be undertaken. The tremendous losses had vividly demonstrated that the reforms of April 1941 had been inadequate. The VVS' immobility, in both its air and ground organizations, was partly at fault for the early losses and was principally due to the inflexible structure of the Rear Services.

Accordingly, thoroughgoing changes were made in August 1941. As a first step, a VVS Rear Services Command with overall authority was established directly under General Zhigarev. In a subsequent directive of August 24, VVS Rear Services was altered so that the air-base regions (RABs) were more flexible and not attached to definite territories or air units. The intermediate air-base administrations were abolished, and each RAB now included administration, staff, communications, miscellaneous technical services, and from six to eight airfield maintenance battalions (BAO) to support three or four two-regiment air divisions. A complete aviation depot (golovnoi aviatsionnyi sklad, or GAS), airfield construction battalion, mobile railroad workshop, and road-mobile maintenance battalion were also attached to each RAB, providing a mobile logistical formation modeled after the revised BAO. In its new form, a BAO could be transferred easily from one airfield to another and could easily service any type of aircraft. The expansion of the BAO organization was seen as the first step toward recovery. By September 1, 351 BAOs had been established to support front and district VVS units, while a number of poorly manned battalions had been disbanded.

These alterations were essential to re-establishing the centralized control and strengthening the logistical service and base structure upon which the VVS' future expansion and fighting capabilities would depend. The ground organization emerging from the August reforms remained basically the same throughout the war. While considered primitive by the Germans, it was simple, flexible, mobile, generally satisfactory, and capable of further refinement in a war with few permanent airfields.

After the opening days' attacks, the bulk of the Luftwaffe's strength was thrown into tactical support of the ground forces, with medium bombers providing most of the required close support. Confined increasingly to this limited role, the German bomber forces suffered heavily. Given the ever-dwindling resources available, the Luftwaffe found it impossible to maintain air superiority while simultaneously providing a sufficient level of tactical support for the army. The latter need prevailed, and the still-vulnerable Soviet strategic targets were neglected. Thus the Soviet Union was able to re-locate much of its key defense industry to the Urals, Siberia, and Central Asia, where full-scale production could proceed unhampered.

The Luftwaffe fixation on tactical support provided the respite necessary for VVS recovery. Despite continued German superiority, the Soviet air units put in more than token appearances and inflicted some serious damage on German ground forces in the fighting around both Leningrad and Kiev during August and September. The VVS' astonishingly quick recovery was as much the product of German actions as of Soviet efforts. The Luftwaffe had gained a false confidence from its crushing early victories, but the VVS had retained a pool of trained crews for the modern aircraft that would soon be produced in large numbers by the expanded and relocated aircraft industry. The delivery of Lend-Lease aircraft and aid from the western Allies did not begin until the fall of 1941, when the VVS' recovery was already under way.

The speed of this recovery seems even more remarkable in view of the heavy Soviet losses that continued through the fall of 1941. However, German losses through early August were not exactly light—1,023 aircraft lost and another 657 damaged—out of 2,800 initially deployed. With fewer aircraft in service along the front and with operations mostly in the south and near Leningrad during August and September, German losses fell off to 580 planes.

The Battle for Moscow and the Winter Campaign: September 1941–April 1942

When Guderian ordered Army Group Center to advance on Moscow on September 30, the Luftwaffe possessed a marked superiority over the VVS from the Western, Reserve, and Bryansk *fronty*, which had been deployed to protect the capital. Although mustering only 545

Figure 17. Yak-3 fighters ready for combat at a Russian air base.

mostly obsolete operational aircraft against more than 1,000 German planes, the Soviet air units were much more active than they had been previously—a clear indication of VVS recovery. Nevertheless, the Germans quickly broke through the Russian defenses and encircled large Soviet forces at Vyasma and Bryansk in early October. Then, on October 7, the autumn rains began to fall, turning the roads and fields into impassable quagmires and bogging down the Panzer armies by October 20. Stuck in the mud, Army Group Center now had to await the first freezes before resuming its advance.

On October 5, Stalin recalled Zhukov from Leningrad to assume command of the battered Western Front and to direct the defense of Moscow. In an effort to enhance the conduct of defensive operations, during October all IA/PVO units in the Moscow Defense Zone, DBA bomber units, and the VVS of the Western Front were combined under a single VVS commander, Maj. Gen. S. A. Khudiakov, whose headquarters was located alongside Zhukov's at Perkhushkovo. During the October fighting, the VVS grouping flew 26,000 sorties—fully 80 percent of them in support of ground forces—and claimed 228 German aircraft destroyed at the

cost of 120.

To reduce the Luftwaffe's numerical edge at the front, the Stavka ordered counter-air operations against German airfields supporting the offensive. From October 11 to 18 and again from November 5 to 8, air units from the DBA and the Northwestern, Bryansk, Western, and Southwestern *fronty* participated in a series of day-and-night attacks against these fields. The Soviets claimed that 500 German aircraft were destroyed along the entire front in the initial operation and claimed 600 more in the second. These operations were an important factor in the air force's subsequent achievement of operational air superiority at Moscow.

In early November, Stalin and the Stavka were sufficiently confident about Japanese intentions in the Far East to begin transferring troops and equipment from the Far East Military District in order to reinforce the defenders around Moscow for a planned counteroffensive. Four air divisions and more than 1,000 aircraft were thus added to the VVS strength deployed in the west. In mid-November, the VVS gained a numerical superiority over the battlefield, outnumbering the Luftwaffe 1,138 (738 operational) to 670 aircraft.

With the frosts of November, the Germans resumed their push toward Moscow. Many German aircraft were inoperable, while others were made serviceable only with great effort. The Luftwaffe was unprepared for winter. The front-line troops were now without adequate air cover at a critical time, though snow, ice, and subzero temperatures resulted in a marked decline in air operations on both sides. Being more accustomed to such weather, the VVS gained an important edge over the Luftwaffe.

Poor flying weather and fewer sorties further reduced the Luftwaffe's wastage to 489 aircraft lost and 333 damaged from late September through the beginning of the Soviet counteroffensive in early December. Total German losses since June 22 amounted to 2,092 aircraft, with another 1,361 damaged. Simultaneously, the Germans claimed to have destroyed nearly 16,000 Soviet aircraft by late November. (The Soviets admit to losses of 6,400.)

On December 6, the day Zhukov launched his attack at Moscow, Stalin designated six air regiments as "Guards" regiments—the first VVS units so honored—for their performances during the defense of Moscow. This coveted designation was reserved for those units distinguished for their proficiency and excellence in combat as well as their organization and discipline. As was the case with the ground formations, the VVS Guards units typically were vastly superior to the average Soviet units and received the best personnel, newest aircraft, and most-extensive fringe benefits. German pilots considered Guards units equal to the best they had faced in any theater.

Early in December, the German offensive had stalled short of Moscow. The Stavka ordered G. I. S. Konev's Kalinin Front to assume the offensive on December 5,

to be followed the next day by Zhukov's Western Front and the right wing of Marshal S. K. Timoshenko's Southwestern Front. The Soviet winter offensive caught the Germans off guard, overextended, and at the point of exhaustion. Only through Hitler's desperate "no retreat" measures did the Germans avert a greater disaster than actually befell them on the road to Moscow.

These conditions permitted the VVS to seize limited operational superiority over the Luftwaffe. Thanks to the Stavka's measures and the weather, the VVS mustered 762 aircraft (excluding Moscow Defense Zone planes) against 615 for the Luftwaffe. The bulk of the aircraft were obsolete I-model fighters and ground-attack planes and some Mig-3s, reinforced by a sprinkling of Pe-2s, Il-2s, Yak-1s, and Lagg-3s. But weather kept much of the Luftwaffe grounded, leaving the skies mostly to "Stalin's eagles." The weather grew progressively worse in December, finally forcing even the most ardent VVS flyers into inactivity and hampering plans to support the offensive. Only 380 sorties were flown in support of the Western Front's left wing over one eight-day period, and for the entire Western Front, only 2,360 sorties were completed during December 17–24.

Despite the obviously critical situation in the east, Hitler went ahead with his earlier decision to permanently withdraw Kesselring's Second Air Fleet from Russia in order to meet increased air commitments in the Mediterranean area. Gen. Wolfram Freiherr von Richthofen's Eighth Air Corps, also slated for redeployment, was retained in the east only because of the severity of the defensive fighting around Moscow. This marked the end of the Eastern Front's top claim on air resources, and according to Asher Lee, was the turning point in the air war in the east.

Figure 18. La-5 fighters taking off from a snow-covered airfield.

The Soviet counteroffensive that had begun north of Moscow on December 5 had pushed the Army Group Center back to its line of November 15 by Christmas. The success scored here prompted Stalin to launch a general winter offensive along the entire front in mid-January. However, both the army and the VVS then simply lacked the strength for an operation on such a large scale, and the dispersion of effort prevented decisive success anywhere. By the end of February, the crisis for the Germans had passed; the front had held, although it had been forced back many miles at numerous places. Fighting continued on a diminished scale through March and April, when exhaustion and the spring thaws brought an end to the winter's activities and turned the opponents toward preparing for the coming summer.

The lull that now fell over the entire front provided a welcome and needed period of rest, recuperation, and refitting for both sides. The Luftwaffe was particularly in need of this breather in order to replace the equipment and crews lost during the winter months and reorganize its air effort for 1942. So far the Luftwaffe could count 2,951 aircraft lost and 1,997 damaged—a total of 5,048. These losses nullified a large portion of the 8,082 new combat aircraft built in 1941.

The Stavka and VVS learned much from the fighting at Moscow and in the winter campaign. Air power was employed most effectively in defensive operations when central direction existed, but the concentrated use of units in the initial stages of the winter offensive was not sustained through ensuing operations. Thus the powerful reserves needed to ensure superiority for the duration of the offensive had to be saved for a decisive thrust rather than squandered, as the Stavka had done. In addition, air-ground coordination and fighter operations, though improved, still left much to be desired. Despite the August changes, the VVS Rear Services was still deficient, especially in providing continuity and mobility of maintenance during ground-air redeployments. The air operations at Moscow had confirmed the basic tenets of Soviet air doctrine: concentration of air power on major attack zones, use of reserves, coordination of frontal units, and employment of DBA and IA/PVO in support of frontal aviation.

Tactics: 1941–1942

In 1941, Soviet air tactics were outdated, inadequate, stereotyped, and rigid. Soviet fliers, especially fighter pilots, tended to lack initiative and flexibility—though once engaged, they were usually tough, stubborn opponents. The Germans attributed these basic deficiencies to the VVS' tactical and technical inferiority: the individual pilot's lack of confidence, combat experience, and training; and the paucity of qualified commanders at all levels.

Whenever confronted by Germans, VVS fighters either adopted the "defensive circle" *(krug samoletov)* to cover each other or headed for their own lines in the "snake" formation *(zmeika),* flying on the deck and drawing German pursuers into Soviet flak guns. The high percentage of Soviet aircraft shot down over their own territory amply confirmed the generally defensive posture of Soviet pilots and their lack of aggressiveness in the air during the early years of the war. Soviet fighters, reluctant to attack escorted German bombers, showed little ability to escort or cooperate with other VVS arms and rarely engaged in ground-support activities.

Not all Soviet pilots conformed to this general image. Lieut. Aleksandr I. Pokryshkin of the Fifty-fifth FAR, Southern Front, greatly influenced the development of Soviet combat tactics. Pokryshkin was the second-ranking Soviet and Allied ace of World War II, with fifty-nine confirmed victories. His innovations played an important role in breaking the tactical hold of outdated horizontal maneuvering and in introducing vertical tactics that took advantage of the best qualities of Soviet aircraft. In early battles, though they could outmaneuver the faster Germans, the obsolete I-16 and I-153 fighters fell like flies. As the better Yak-7B and La-5 arrived, the transition to vertical maneuvers took place. Pokryshkin developed a formula that was simple and direct—"altitude, speed, maneuver, fire." Sudden, swift attacks were the key to success and survival.

Early in the conflict, Soviet fighters used two or three aircraft in each *zveno* (flight). Eventually, the VVS largely adopted the German tactical organization of the *Rotte, Schwarm,* and *Staffel* in a form modified to fit Soviet conditions. The *para* (pair) of two aircraft, one attacker and one defender, became the basic element upon which the tactical structure was built. Two *para,* one offensive and one defensive, made up a *zveno;* three or four *para* formed a *gruppa* (group) of six to eight aircraft, the most common combat formation after 1942. Tactically, the group normally flew with each successive flight of four aircraft echeloned slightly higher than its predecessor. Adoption of the German "four-finger" organization, with each squadron in two flights of two pairs, fitted the reduced size of regiments and squadrons. The reduction to ten aircraft per squadron allowed the formation of two four-plane *zveno* and one *para* made up of the squadron commander and his wingman. The change to this *zveno-para* structure gave greater tactical flexibility. First used extensively at Moscow, the four-plane flight became standard in September 1942, and the transition began in October. For the rest of the war, the *para, zveno,* and *gruppa* were the basic VVS fighter combat elements. Squadrons and regiments operated in several effective combat groups, using strike, cover, and reserve elements.

Soviet air doctrine stressed the role of the fighter arm in gaining air superiority so that all other VVS missions could be effective. To regain the superiority lost in the summer of 1941, Soviet leadership devoted full attention to turning the VVS tactical fighter force into an elite arm. Emphasis was given to fighter production; output of ever-better aircraft was pushed; and the best pilots were grouped into fighter units, especially the Guards. The best aircraft and units were always committed on the most important sectors to confront the Luftwaffe's best.

With Mig-3 production largely discontinued in favor of Il-2s, fighter aircraft output dropped from more than 5,100 in July–December 1941 to 3,871 in January–June 1942 before jumping to 5,973 in the last six months of that year. Thus, during 1942, despite relatively high losses, the VVS fighter force was gradually rebuilt. Such modern aircraft as the Yak-1, Yak-7B, and later, La-5 and Yak-9 gave fighter pilots a new self-assurance that resulted in a more aggressive attitude in aerial combat. Fighters came increasingly to use "free hunt" (*svobodnaia okhota*) tactics on wide-ranging patrols, with "hunters" (*okhotniki*) usually operating in pairs. Such sorties accounted for an ever-larger share of fighter missions and represented the primary fighter tactic after Stalingrad.

Soviet bombers conducted both day and night operations, but the latter came to predominate early in the war as a result of German day fighter strength. After the first two weeks, bombers normally operated under 3,000 feet in tight formations of from six to eight (rarely more than ten) aircraft. At such altitudes, they could most easily find and attack targets and were less readily spotted by German fighters. Their doggedness in attacking, strict formation flying, and slowness and lack of maneuverability caused these units to suffer heavy losses to German ground and fighter defenses.

Normally formed into squadrons of nine aircraft with three *zveno* of three aircraft each, both frontal and long-range (DBA) bombers employed the "wedge" and "line" tactics that provided better defense, flexibility, and bombing accuracy. The "wedge," or V-formation, of three to twelve aircraft, with one following another and echeloned in altitude, was preferred. Eventually, an average of twelve to thirty aircraft or more came to fill the wedge, but the pilots' lack of basic flying skills hindered formation discipline. Tight formations were stressed in order to ease the burdens on inadequately trained crews, improve defense, cut losses, and provide concentrated attacks against assigned targets. The Germans found that as a rule only the bomber formation leaders were thoroughly briefed on targets and routes or had maps. Consequently, shooting down the leaders forced the group to turn back or break up, though formations were usually maintained despite losses.

As a group, Soviet bombers—frontal and DBA, night and day—proved ineffective in most cases until late 1942 because of early heavy losses, poor tactics and flying skills, and the emphasis on fighters and ground assault. As was the case with the Luftwaffe, bomber attrition ran high for frontal bomber units because of their constant employment in ground-support missions. Horizontal bombing was the most common Soviet bombing tactic, simply because most crews lacked the basic navigation and flying skills and instruments for dive bombing. Only the more proficient Pe-2 units attacked high-priority point targets.

Like its fighter operations, VVS bomber operations more and more came to resemble those of the Germans. Concentrating on close-support missions, they reinforced artillery and attack aviation and only rarely attacked deep, rear-area targets, with the result that the distinction between tactical battlefield support and interdiction disappeared.

As did the bomber crews of 1941, the Soviet ground-attack aircraft pilots, in contrast to the fighter pilots, presented notable exceptions to the general Soviet lack of aggressiveness. They usually pressed home their attacks with relentless and fearless determination—if not always with tactical skill and success, for maturity was gained only at great cost. Although badly battered and little in evidence during the early stages of the war, ground-attack aviation made an astonishingly quick recovery and gained steadily in importance and effectiveness. This fact was especially true after the introduction of the Il-2 in July–August 1941. Until the Iliushins were available in large numbers, the obsolete I-16, R-10, and Su-2 aircraft labored on, despite their obvious inferiority and unsuitability for close-support operations.

In 1941, ground-attack aircraft operated in groups of from three to five, usually in three-plane Vs. Then, during 1942, the basic operating element became the *para,* working in a flight of four aircraft or in a *gruppa* of from six to eight. Experience confirmed the pair as the basic combat element and the six plane group as the optimum size for defense and maneuver-

ability. As the basic element changed, ground-attack tactics shifted from the wedge to the line formation that had become standard by the fall of 1942. Although large V-formations were still preferred for approaches, units deployed into attack formations before reaching their targets, which were attacked by either individual aircraft or flights at ground level or from below 1,000 feet. In making their attacks, VVS assault pilots came to show considerable flexibility in tactics, approach angles, altitudes, directions, timing of strikes, and formations. At Stalingrad, attack aircraft operated in groups of four to six aircraft escorted by two to four fighters.

Fighter-escort activities in 1941–1942 were sparse or poorly executed, with fighters frequently departing quickly for Soviet lines when they encountered German fighters. The paucity of fighter escorts until late 1942 forced attack units to operate mostly without cover, suffering severe losses in the process. These circumstances prompted the addition of the rear-seat machine gunner to the Il-2 in 1942.

Persistent to the end, unescorted ground-attack pilots either continued on their way or formed the familiar "defensive circles." Indeed, even when carrying out ground attacks, the aircraft formed such circles until the attacks were finished. The appearance of more Il-2s in 1942 allowed concentrated attacks by groups of several squadrons instead of the small groups formerly employed. With the greater confidence gained in 1942 and the introduction of the Il-2m3 two-seater, the Iliushins also began to use free-hunt tactics, especially in the bad weather that grounded the Germans.

Reorganization and Recovery: Spring–Summer 1942

Combat operations in 1941 and during the winter campaign of 1941–1942 indi-

Figure 19. Soviet DB-3F heavy bomber of the long-range forces.

cated that the organizational structure of the VVS and frontal aviation had serious flaws (see figure 23). VVS experiences during the Moscow operations revealed that air units were too scattered among the ground armies and *fronty* to permit the concentrated employment of air power. The operational requirements for such massed use in the coming offensives, in combination with the increased output of the Narkomaviaprom plants, produced a major reorganization of the VVS structure during the spring of 1942.

In March, the GKO disbanded the DBA and established the Long-Range Air Force (Aviatsiia dal'nego deistviaa, or ADD) directly under the operational control of the Stavka. Maj. Gen. A. E. Golovanov assumed command of the ADD which included long-range medium and heavy bombers and transports formerly assigned to the DBA and frontal aviation. As a favorite of Stalin, it was hoped that Golovanov could make the ADD into an elite, independent bomber force designed to attack strategic and rear-area targets, while also being extensively employed for interdiction and front-line missions in major offensive operations. However, although it eventually numbered more than 1,500 aircraft in fifty air regiments, the ADD had only limited usefulness during the war because of continued Soviet emphasis on tactical aviation and the struggle for air superiority over the battlefield.

On March 15, 1942, Gen. Pavel Zhigarev, the VVS commander, informed Stalin that the VVS must be reorganized in order to provide unity of organization and command as well as the large air units necessary for future offensive air operations. Stalin agreed, and appointed Gen. A. A. Novikov to replace Zhigarev in April. An outstanding VVS commander in the northwest and at Leningrad, Novikov, under Stavka leadership, directed the reorganization of the VVS, its rebuilding for offensive air operations, the establishment of air armies and integral air divisions, and the fleshing-out of the air corps of the Stavka Reserve.

Novikov's first step combined *front* and army VVS units into air armies (vozdushnie armii, or VA) thus allowing frontal aviation to concentrate its strength more effectively on the main sectors in support of ground-force operations and to conduct coordinated, independent air operations by one or more air armies.

An air army was assigned to each *front,* with the VVS leader under the *front* commander and serving as his air adviser. Acting on Stavka instructions, the Commissariat of Defense on May 5 ordered the Western Front's VVS units consolidated into the First Air Army under Gen. T. F. Kutsevalov. On May 8, its composition was specified as two fighter and two composite air divisions, a night-fighter regiment, a U-2 training regiment, a reconnaissance squadron, and a communications squadron. During the summer an attempt was made to form even larger integral (homogeneous) air armies—the First Bomber and First and Second Fighter air armies. This move did not solve any basic tactical problems, however, and these units were soon disbanded. By November 1942, thirteen air armies had been created and all tactical aviation had been removed from the ground armies.

Basic to the entire spring 1942 reorganization was the restructuring of the frontal VVS under the new air armies into homogeneous air divisions. The shift from the mainly composite units used since 1940 to integral bomber, ground-attack, and fighter air divisions and regiments was a significant step in the development of the VVS. At the same time, air regiments were converted to a single model so that all squadrons had the same composition. More important, as more aircraft became available in 1942, fighter and ground-attack regiments were increased from twenty-two to thirty-two aircraft, allowing a third ten-plane squadron to be added. Each regiment was kept to 170–200 personnel but had no organic equipment to facilitate movement and rapid redeployment.

Many operational and logistic problems were resolved with these changes, and coordination with the ground forces was enhanced by the increased flexibility of air units. The transition to integral air divisions simplified operational, supply, training, maintenance, and command problems. Now only ground-attack air divisions retained the composite structure of 1940–1942 (one fighter regiment and two or three attack regiments). Previously scattered among the combined-arms armies, the attack units were now gathered into divisions—a move that greatly increased their effectiveness. These overall changes transformed the air armies into balanced tactical combat organizations composed of fighter, bomber, attack, and reconnaissance units and fully capable of fulfilling the demands of ground armies. Moreover, their strength and exact composition could be altered swiftly and easily in order to meet shifting frontal requirements. The new organizational structure of 1942 provided the operational mobility and flexibility required for successful air operations. In addition, the new system improved Stavka coordination of the VVS in strategic offensive operations.

The size of air armies varied throughout the war, depending on the growing

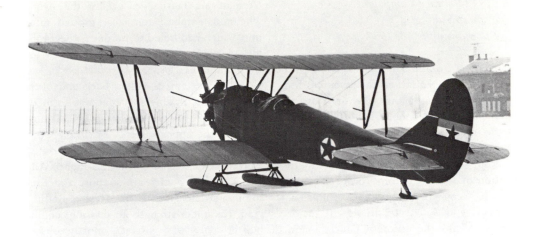

Figure 20. General-purpose Po-2 of World War II period. This model was adapted for winter operations.

availability of aircraft and units as well as on the relative importance of various operations. The average air army numbered 900 to 1,000 aircraft in 1942–1943, 1,500 in 1943–1944, and as many as 2,500 to 3,000 in 1945. In a structure that became more standardized as the war progressed, the fighter, attack, and bomber air corps in an air army could number from one to seven air divisions (each containing three or four air regiments), but normally had two or three.

Another of Novikov's important reforms was the creation of the air corps of the Stavka Reserve. In March 1942, the Stavka had ten reserve air groups of about 100 aircraft, each either operating independently or attached to a front. After Novikov's reforms these air corps, representing between 32 and 43 percent of the frontal air force, provided a significant reinforcement for the air armies on the main sectors of the front. They prepared new air units for combat and rehabilitated worn-down veteran regiments; more important, they made possible the massing of powerful air forces for strategic defensive and offensive operations.

On August 26, 1942, the Commissariat of Defense ordered the formation of additional reserve air units with new aircraft. In November, during the buildup for Stalingrad, ten air corps of the Stavka Reserve were formed, representing more than 30 percent of available tactical aviation. Each reserve air corps normally had three air divisions of three regiments; each fighter and attack regiment had thirty-two aircraft and each bomber unit twenty. As was the case with the ground forces, these reserves provided the mobility and concentration of force required for successful operations—something clearly lacking before.

The large operational formations and reserves created in 1942 allowed the development of a new and more-effective form of operational use—the air offensive. Epitomizing the Soviet concept of air power, the air offensive was the combined, massed action of VVS and ground forces, with continuous air support in operation from preparation of breakthrough to pursuit.

The 1942 Summer Campaign:
Kharkov to Stalingrad,
May 12–November 18, 1942

In contrast to the situation in 1941, the Germans in 1942 lacked the resources for a general offensive along the entire Russian front. Stressing economic factors, especially the importance of Kuban wheat and the Caucasian oilfields at Grozny, Baku, and Maikop, Hitler earmarked the southern portion of the front from Voronezh to the Sea of Azov for the summer campaign. Army Group A was to deliver the major thrust toward the northern Caucasus and the oilfields farther south, while Army Group B would cover it by moving down the River Don and then eastward to cut the Volga River supply routes at Stalingrad.

Stalin beat the Germans to the trigger, attacking north and south of Kharkov on May 12 in what eventually became a vain and costly attempt to preempt the German offensive. Just the reverse resulted, and the Soviet forces were severely mauled and weakened. Gen. Hermann Hoth's Fourth Panzer Army opened the German summer offensive when it struck eastward on June 28 toward the Don and Voronezh. For this campaign, the Luftwaffe had rebuilt its strength in the east to 2,750 aircraft, approximately the level of June 1941. Of these, 1,500 were attached to the Fourth Air Fleet and Eighth Air Corps, supporting Army Groups A and B in the south.

Although the offensive developed quickly, the crushing victories of the previous summer eluded the Germans this time. Rather than fighting unwinnable battles, the Soviet forces withdrew eastward over the Don, trading abundant space for valuable time. In this situation the depth and width of the front, together with diminished German air reserves and vastly improved Soviet strength and expertise, prevented the repetition of the swift defeats of 1941.

German air tactics, especially the overwhelming emphasis on close ground support which had failed to produce a decision in late 1941, were equally unproductive in the summer of 1942.

As Soviet forces pulled back and over the Don, the Stalingrad Front was formed on July 12 under Marshal S. K. Timoshenko to oppose Gen. Friedrich von Paulus' German Sixth Army and Hoth's Panzers. Gen. T. T. Khriukin's Eighth Air Army provided the air support for the summer's defensive fighting west of Stalingrad. His under-strength air divisions could muster only 454 aircraft, mostly obsolete, to confront the 1,200 in Richthofen's Fourth Air Fleet, but the Stavka soon began funneling air reinforcements to the Eighth Air Army. Along with the 150-200 long-range bombers of the ADD and the 50–60 fighters of the 102nd FAR (PVO), ten frontal air regiments—75 percent of which were composed of new Yak-1, Yak-7B, Il-2, and Pe-2 planes—provided an important addition to the Soviet air forces.

VVS air activities in the early days had been narrowly constrained as a result of technical and numerical inferiority. Although they were performing much better now, the VVS units still suffered heavy losses; however, reinforcements were available. From July 20 to 17 August, 447 aircraft arrived, followed by another 984 during the next three months. Nevertheless, attrition was so heavy that in early August Khriukin was compelled to gather all his serviceable aircraft into a single operational group.

Somehow, the Stavka was able to keep dribbling in enough ground and air resources to keep the defensive battle going in the Don bend without adversely affecting the slow buildup of reserves. On August 5, the Stalingrad Front was divided into the Stalingrad and Southeastern *fronty*, with the new Sixteenth Air Army (under

Figure 21. Tu-2 light bomber, first mass-produced in 1942. Its handling characteristics made it a favorite of Soviet air crews.

Gen. P. S. Stepanov) assigned to the former. On August 20, three days after the Germans crossed the Don at Vertiachii and Peskovatka, the Stavka sent more ADD air divisions from their home bases near Moscow to participate in the Stalingrad fighting. The same day, Col. P. S. Danilin's 287th FAD, the first unit to reach the front equipped with the new Lavochkin La-5 fighters, arrived to reinforce the Eighth Air Army.

The new fighters were apparently effective, but they were incapable of preventing the continuing deterioration of the situation around the beleaguered city. In an attempt to bolster the VVS, the GKO ordered an immediate increase in fighter production while transferring many of the most experienced VVS fighter pilots and newest aircraft to the air armies in the area. Despite these efforts, the Luftwaffe controlled the skies over Stalingrad and incessantly pounded the Soviet positions. Severe air fighting continued to make such heavy claims on the VVS that Khriukin had only 188 operational aircraft by early October.

Even as the Germans hacked their way into Stalingrad through September and into October, the Stavka busily prepared a counteroffensive against the now dangerously exposed German salient. On September 28, S. I. Rudenko took command of the Sixteenth Air Army in a general reshuffling intended to clear the way for the planned offensive operations. K. K. Rokossovsky took over the former Stalingrad Front (renamed the Don Front), with A. I. Eremenko retaining the new Stalingrad Front (formerly the Southeastern Front). The Seventeenth Air Army (under S. A. Krasovsky) was created and assigned to N. F. Vatutin's newly organized Southwestern Front. From north to south, the Seventeenth, Sixteenth, and Eighth Air Armies made up the VVS force. The Stavka now summoned up the VVS reserves so carefully accumulated during the summer and fall, while K. N. Smirnov's Second Air Army was temporarily assigned from the Voronezh Front to Vatutin for the impending offensive operations. General Novikov, the VVS commander, was assigned responsibility for the proper concentration on the decisive breakthrough sectors, air-ground coordination, centralized control of air operations, maintenance of adequate reserves for continuation of the offensive, and effective reconnaissance for air and ground operations.

During the savage defensive fighting that ended with the opening of the Soviet counteroffensive on the morning of November 19, the VVS units flew more than 77,000 sorties and claimed 2,100 enemy aircraft destroyed. Of these, tactical aircraft flew 45,325 sorties, more than 77 percent of which had ground-support objectives.

The launching of the Stalingrad counteroffensive concluded the first, or defensive, period of the Great Patriotic War. VVS had recovered sufficiently from the 1941 debacles to play an important role in the fighting. Through November 1942, the VVS flew 858,000 sorties—803,000 by frontal aviation and the rest by the ADD. Of the former, 184,686 protected ground forces and other targets, 69,397 served as escort missions, 22,851 were directed against enemy airfields, and the remainder (526,066, or 66 percent) directly supported ground forces. During the first year alone, the VVS claimed to have destroyed the incredible total of 13,156 enemy aircraft, and by November 1942 it claimed some 15,700.

Nearly 34,000 of the 41,000 aircraft built during 1941-1942 reached the front. To man them, 90,000 men—41,224 of them flight personnel—were trained during the first eighteen months, and 570 air units were manned, trained, equipped, and sent to the front.

Between June 22, 1941, and November 18, 1942, the Red Army, VVS, and the Soviet Union had struggled to survive the period of greatest peril. After November 19, the tide of battle turned and the Red Army took the initiative. The VVS' recovery during these months of trial was as almost as remarkable as the 1941 disasters.

The Seizure of Air Superiority: November 19, 1942–December 1943

Stalingrad: November 19, 1942–February 2, 1943

Reflecting the changing nature of the war in Russia, the revised Soviet field regulations issued on November 9, 1942, detailed new forms of air and artillery support. Designed to assist the main infantry and tank offensives, the "air offensive" was to provide air preparation for a planned breakthrough and to support the actual attack and exploitation phases. The initial use of the air offensive was slated for the Stalingrad counteroffensive, Operation Uranus, which was set to begin on the morning of November 19.

A November 12 Stavka directive outlined the VVS' numerous assignments at Stalingrad. Aviation forces, concentrated in the offensive areas, were to neutralize the Luftwaffe and cover Soviet ground forces, to prepare breakthrough zones for attacking ground units, and to harass enemy forces attempting to regroup. To gain air superiority, the Eighth and Sixteenth air armies and ADD planned to strike thirteen German airfields beginning on the night of November 16. But, adverse weather conditions prevented these operations and continued to interfere with VVS air plans for Uranus.

As the Stavka polished its Stalingrad plans, more and better aircraft, equipment, and crew personnel flowed into the VVS combat units. When the offensive began, VVS strength had grown to 24 air divisions and 99 regiments. The 1,327 operational aircraft out of 1,828 planes assigned to the front, excluding PVO and ADD, accounted for more than 40 percent of the entire Soviet front-line air strength of 3,254 aircraft. Such numbers represented more than a tripling of the aircraft available to Khriukin in late July and gave the VVS an important, if narrow,

Figure 22. Lagg-3 single-seater of 1941–1942. The engine later proved to be underpowered.

tactical edge over the Luftwaffe's Fourth Air Fleet, whose actual operational force of less than 600 aircraft was far below its paper stength of 1,200 planes. The reforms of the previous spring and summer had begun to pay handsome dividends.

Just as important as the numbers was the fact that the expanded output of new aircraft had given the VVS a vastly improved force, qualitatively better suited to fight the Luftwaffe. By November, a full 73 percent of all planes at the front and 97 percent of all fighters were newer models, whereas less than 33 percent had been new during the summer.

The Sixteenth and Seventeenth air armies and three air divisions of the Second Air Army were massed to carry out their carefully planned air offensives when the Don and Southwestern *fronty* attacked southward against the Rumanian Third Army on November 19. That morning, however, low clouds, fog, and light snow made operations impossible. Some ground-attack aircraft supported the Fifth Tank Army's thrust against the Rumanians, but in general the weather negated Soviet air plans, sorely disappointing many VVS leaders anxious to employ their new theories and smooth out unanticipated problems.

The Luftwaffe was relatively helpless at a time when Paulus' Sixth Army desperately needed all the air support and reconnaissance it could get. Despite the virtual absence of the VVS, Soviet infantry and tank forces swept aside light opposition and closed the trap on the Axis forces, linking up west of the city at Sovetskii on November 23. After the Soviet spearheads met, the reduction of the Stalingrad pocket and the prevention of external relief became the main Soviet objectives.

Improved weather conditions allowed the three Soviet air armies engaged in Uranus to fly 5,760 combat sorties from November 24 to November 30. As the Soviet armies moved west, the Luftwaffe lost many of its forward airfields. This, together with heavy equipment losses, limited German air activity to about 115 sorties per day through November 30. Obviously, such a low level of air support could neither help the Sixth Army hold off the Russians nor provide sufficient aid for projected relief attempts.

To sustain the Sixth Army until it could be relieved, Hitler authorized the Luftwaffe to mount an airlift into the pocket beginning on November 25. However, the Ju-52 transports and He-111 bombers were unable to deliver the 500 tons of supplies per day required to keep Sixth Army functioning. During December, Manstein's newly created Army Group Don tried to break into the pocket from the southwest, but met stubborn opposition. Finally held at the Myshkova River by Rodion Malinovskii's Second Guards Army, Manstein abandoned his relief attempt as new Soviet operations to the west threatened to cut off not only Army Group Don but also Kleist's Army Group A, which was still in the Caucasus.

While consolidating the inner ring around the Stalingrad pocket, the Soviet High Command, showing its steadily maturing strategic capabilities, shifted the focus of operations farther to the west for the second phase of the winter counteroffensive (Operation Little Saturn). On December 16, as the Germans fought to patch up their front, regroup, and free the Sixth Army, Vatutin's Southwestern Front struck south and southwest, smashing Army Group B's Italian Eighth Army. Strongly supported by the Second and Seventeenth air armies, Soviet forces plunged into Army Group Don's rear, throwing German units even farther back from the beleaguered pocket, disrupting the airlift, and relieving Manstein's pressure against Eremenko. By early January, the Luftwaffe had been forced off the Morozovsk and Tatsinskaia airfields, thus further cutting back the supplies dribbling into Sixth Army.

The strain of conducting continuous air operations and the drain of resources needed to shore up the crumbling situation in North Africa and the Mediterranean weakened the Luftwaffe in Russia and allowed the VVS to gain the initiative over the southern sector of the front. Compelled to redistribute its dwindling forces in the east to counter Soviet offensive operations in the south, the Luftwaffe handed the VVS the advantage in other areas, notably Leningrad and the Caucasus. By the end of 1942, German single-seat fighter strength in the east had ebbed to 375 planes as a result of wastage and the large number of aircraft abandoned in the retreat.

In mid-January 1943, F. I. Golikov's Voronezh Front, along with parts of the Bryansk and Southwestern *fronty,* unleashed the third blow of the winter, this time on a 300-mile front against the Hungarian and German Second armies. Shattering Army Group B, Golikov's tank and mechanized forces swept westward to Kursk and on to Rylsk under the umbrella provided by Second and Seventeenth air armies. Belgorod and then Kharkov fell as Soviet forces rolled over the Donets River and toward the Dnieper. The fate of the Sixth Army was sealed, and the German position in the Ukraine tottered on the verge of complete catastrophe.

Following Paulus' rejection of Rokossovskii's surrender ultimatum of January 8, 1943, ADD bombers softened up the rear areas and Sixteenth Air Army elements worked over the front lines. Through the ensuing operations that culminated in the German surrender on February 2, the Sixteenth Air Army and ADD assumed an ever-larger role in the fighting, flying more than 10,000 sorties.

During the operations from November 19,1942, to February 2, 1943, the Second, Eighth, Sixteenth, and Seventeenth air armies, plus the ADD units, flew 35,929 sorties against some 18,500 for the Luftwaffe. German losses, especially in transport aircraft, were quite heavy; the Ju-52 losses alone added up to nearly 50 percent of the functioning transport force. Conflicting claims make it impossible to clearly estimate Soviet and German losses, but the Soviet figure of 1,160 may not be far off when fighter, attack, and miscellaneous aircraft losses are counted. Whatever its actual

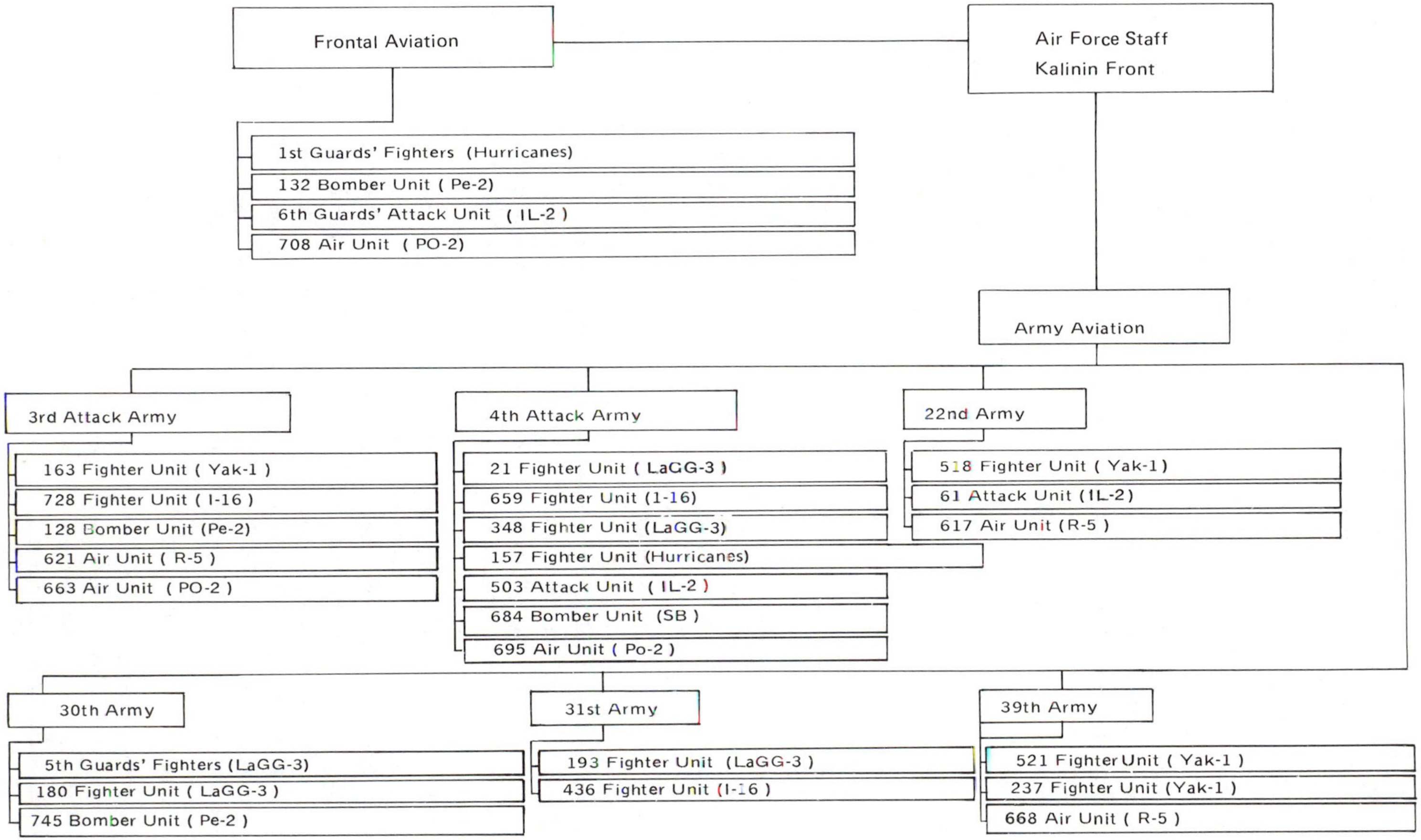

Figure 23. Organization chart of VVS on Kalinin front prior to the reforms of March-May 1942.

losses were, the Luftwaffe was so badly weakened that, for the first time, overall air superiority over an entire major sector passed to the VVS. Stalingrad was the turning point of the war in the east. The strategic initiative passed to the Soviets; only once more would the Germans seriously challenge them. For the first time during the course of the war, the VVS had organized cooperation between its various arms in strategic operations involving a group of *fronty* whose single aim was the encirclement and destruction of a major enemy grouping. At Stalingrad and through the ensuing operations of the winter, the VVS took a giant stride toward air superiority; but it could not as yet seize strategic air superiority over an entire front permanently.

After November 19, 1942, the Red Air Force gained valuable operational experience that greatly aided its subsequent development. The air offensive was introduced—if only as a concept, because of the poor flying weather. Soviet fighter units were especially active in "free hunting," patrolling, protecting ground forces, and interdicting the German airlift. The continuing rehabilitation of the fighter air arm profited immeasurably, in both morale and tactical experience, from the successes scored at Stalingrad. Ground-attack forces also operated much more effectively, although heavy losses, scarcity of replacements, and limited crew experience hampered their impact. However, the appearance of the Il-2m3 Shturmovik helped to offset these shortcomings while demonstrating considerable potential for improving ground support.

Kharkov to Kursk: February–July 1943

In March 1943, the Soviet general offensive that had begun in mid-November 1942 finally came to a halt 500 miles west of its starting point. Under Manstein's direction,

German troops pushed back the now-overextended Soviet forces, recapturing Kharkov and Belgorod in mid-March. But the Kharkov counteroffensive was to be the last example of the successful army-Luftwaffe cooperation that had produced repeated victories from September 1939 through late 1941, in part because of Richthofen's skillful use of his Fourth Air Fleet in support of Manstein. However, a contributing factor was that the Soviet forces had outrun their air cover, because VVS ground units could not move forward quickly enough to establish suitable operational airfields. Combined with the spring thaw, the German recovery in the eastern Ukraine brought all movement in the south to a halt.

The stabilization of this front endured only briefly, as planned German and Soviet offensive operations collided in the Kuban in April. The Luftwaffe shifted some 600 aircraft to support further operations from the Taman bridgehead into the Caucasus, while Soviet air forces were massed to back the North Caucasus Front's projected drive to clear the Taman Peninsula and Novorossiisk of the German Seventeenth Army. The air war now entered a new phase, as Luftwaffe and VVS units struggled for air superiority over the battlefield. The VVS held the upper hand through late May, when the Luftwaffe reasserted itself. From April 17 to June 7, the VVS flew some 35,000 sorties and claimed 1,100 German aircraft—800 in aerial combat.

Operations in the skies over the Kuban influenced the development of VVS tactics and employment. Fighter tactics were improved, largely because of the assignment of better fighters to the frontal units and the adoption of the two-aircraft *para* as the standard combat formation. Fighter employment in the Kuban area changed after commanders discovered that pilots tended to engage Luftwaffe fighters, not

Figure 24. Pe-8 heavy bomber down for maintenance at a U.S. airfield during World War II.

bombers. Interceptors were thereafter directed to attack bombers before they reached the front lines. To accomplish this, fighter escorts for bombers were reduced and greater number of fighters were sent over the battlefield, better protecting the ground forces from enemy air attacks. Despite the heavy air and ground actions, the spring operations in the Kuban were merely an inconclusive prelude to a major offensive on the central sector of the front that summer.

The losses resulting from the operations at Stalingrad, in the eastern Ukraine, and in the north Caucasus had dropped the Luftwaffe's first-line strength in the east to about 1,700 by early 1943. Continuing operational attrition, diversions to other theaters, and the growing proportion of such clearly obsolescent aircraft as the Ju-87 Stuka, He-111, and Bf-110 further weakened the Luftwaffe's position *vis-à-vis* the VVS, which grew stronger each day. Allied operations in North Africa and the Mediterranean drew off ever-larger Luftwaffe forces from the eastern front, compounding the equipment problems. In February 1943, an estimated 70 percent of the German fighter force was in the Mediterranean and the west.

The setbacks of the winter of 1942–1943 notwithstanding, the first six months of the new year brought a period of general recovery for the Luftwaffe. Increased fighter production had pushed overall Luftwaffe strength from under 4,000 aircraft late in 1942 to its wartime high point of 6,000 by June 1943. German air strength in the east began to climb upward and soon topped 2,500 aircraft. However, numerical increases in front-line strength did not necessarily imply improvements in quality, because training problems kept the output of air crews from matching that of the expanded aircraft inventory and heavy combat attrition cut the pool of experienced crews. The VVS, in stark contrast, enjoyed an increasing flow of new aircraft; the Soviets had more than 8,300 aircraft by July 1943. The VVS was clearly winning the struggle for air superiority in the factories and on the training fields; it was only a matter of time before the VVS won it over the battlefield.

The Battle of Kursk: July 1943

When the front finally coalesced in late March 1943, the Soviet Central (Rokossovsky) and Voronezh (Vatutin) *fronty* held a bulging salient centered on the Ukrainian town of Kursk. German forces occupied salients on each flank—Kluge's Army Group Center in the Orel area and Manstein's Army Group South in the Kharkov-Belgorod area. The Kursk bulge soon became the magnet for German plan-

ning in regard to offensive operations. Unlike those of the previous two years,
German objectives for 1943 were strategically defensive because chances of out-
right victory had died in Stalingrad's
rubble. If armored attacks launched from
Orel and Kharkov-Belgorod could snip off
the Kursk bulge, a sufficiently large
number of Soviet forces might be encircled
and destroyed to rebalance the scales
temporarily. But grave doubts about
Operation Zitadelle (Citadel) were present
from the very start.

German plans for Citadel called for large
concentrations of armor, supported by the
Luftwaffe, to carry out the most important
tasks. Originally scheduled for mid-April,
Citadel was postponed in order to await
the arrival of new Tiger and Panther tanks
and heavy Ferdinand self-propelled guns.
The delay proved fatal, for Soviet intelligence agents meanwhile acquired the
basic plans from their contacts in the
"Lucy ring" (Rudolph Rössler) in the
German High Command. This information
led the Stavka to cancel its own offensive
plans and prepare extensive defensive positions.

Heavy emphasis was placed on Luftwaffe support in planning Citadel; Germany, France, Norway, and other sectors
of the eastern front were drained of air
resources after March 15. With Goering
promising a maximum Luftwaffe effort,
more than 1,800 aircraft were gathered
for Citadel. The German air forces
massed there represented 70 percent of all
German forces on the eastern front and 40
percent of the Luftwaffe's total air
strength. Jeschonnek, the Luftwaffe chief
of staff, had devoted the major part of the
Luftwaffe's strength in Russia to the Kursk
operations because he believed that Citadel
would succeed only with a maximum aerial
effort.

The Stavka set out not only to defeat

Citadel but to follow up closely with its
own general summer offensive. A central
role in these operations was allocated to
the VVS, and the Stavka made every effort
to gather a powerful air grouping on the
Kursk front.

The Luftwaffe's operations in preparation for the summer offensive escalated in
May and June with attacks against the
Soviet lines of communications, railway
junctions, bridges, supply depots, and
other critical targets. The VVS countered
with its own efforts to interfere with the
German buildup for Citadel and to disrupt
German air operations. Well before the
actual offensive began, the Luftwaffe and
VVS were locked in a bitter struggle for
air superiority. Soviet frontal and PVO
fighters battled the German attackers while
frontal and ADD aircraft went after
German lines of communications, airfields,
depots, and other facilities both day and
night.

Increasingly, independent air operations
into the enemy's rear areas came to play an
important part in VVS operations. Attacks
were particularly concentrated on Luftwaffe airfields during the months preceding
Citadel, as part of counter-air operations
intended to whittle down the German air
strength deployed in the offensive zones.
From May 6 to May 8, the VVS struck
about twenty airfields in four concentrated
strikes, forcing the Germans temporarily to
pull back their air units. Then, from
June 8 to June 10, three air armies plus
ADD elements hit another twenty-eight
airfields in an effort to check German long-
range bomber attacks against Gorki,
Saratov, Yaroslavl, and other industrial
centers. These pre-Kursk air operations
significantly weakened, but certainly did
not destroy, the Luftwaffe strength
gathering for Citadel. In that respect, they
were an important measure of the VVS'
continuing maturity and strength, for now

Figure 25. Pe-2 dive bomber, designed in 1939 and mass-produced during the war.

the battle for air superiority was being carried to the Germans prior to major operations.

Soviet air strength was not, at first, well organized. The Fifth Air Army (under S. K. Goriunov) of I. S. Konev's Steppe Front (then in reserve behind the salient), the First Air Army (under M. M. Gromov) of V. D. Sokolovsky's Western Front, and the Fifteenth Air Army (under N. F. Naumenko) of M. M. Popov's Bryansk Front were all earmarked for the offensive operations that were planned to commence once Citadel was stopped. The real possibility that these forces might be drawn into the defensive fighting convinced the Stavka of the need for closer planning of the overall air effort. Moreover, the Seventeenth Air Army (under V. A. Sudets) of the Southwestern Front was assigned to operate with the Second Air Army on the Voronezh Front's defensive zone, thus injecting yet another complicating factor. As had been done at Stalingrad, the Stavka dispatched A. A. Novikov to oversee VVS planning and to coordinate the air activities of the Second, Sixteenth, and Seventeenth air armies during the defensive phase of the Kursk fighting. With the commanders of the two primary air armies (S. I. Rudenko of the Central Front's Sixteenth Air Army and S. A. Krasovsky of the Voronezh Front's Second Air Army), the Stavka team worked out defensive plans to cover the various attack options open to the German forces. Strict attention was paid to coordination and support of the ground forces' defensive operations. So that maximum air-ground cooperation was assured, VVS officers were assigned to the ground and tank armies that would be involved in the fighting.

Through the Stavka's efforts, the VVS forces facing the Germans on the Kursk sector had a marked superiority over the Luftwaffe. Two PVO fighter divisions shared air-defense duties and cooperated closely with the frontal fighters. More than 500 ADD bombers operated in the area to assist the Central and Voronezh *fronty* and to strike targets in German rear areas. The Stavka also brought up sixteen reserve air corps to reinforce the frontal air forces during both the defensive and planned offensive phases. The Second and Sixteenth air armies each received several corps before the fighting began. By early July, the three air armies designated to support the defensive operations numbered 2,650 aircraft—881 assigned to the Second, 735 to the Seventeenth, and 1,034 to the Sixteenth. In addition, the First and Fifteenth air armies readying for the offensive against the Orel salient had another 2,200 aircraft, while the Fifth Air Army of the Steppe Front had 550 more in reserve. Thus, the six air armies massed in and around the Kursk sector had more than 5,400 aircraft available for use, without counting PVO and ADD elements. Against this force, the Germans had approximately 2,000 aircraft.

Late in the afternoon of July 4, probing attacks against the Sixth Guards Army marked the opening of the southern phase of Citadel. German Eighth Air Corps forces were massed on sixteen airfields in the Kharkov area to support the main attacks on the morning of July 5. Alerted to the German plans, the VVS staged a surprise bomber raid against these airfields early that morning, in the hope of catching the Germans on the ground preparing for the first strikes and thus crippling the Luftwaffe at the start. But German "Freya" radar had detected the massing Soviet formations long before they crossed the front lines, and 270 fighters (JG-3 Udets and JG-52 Mölders) repulsed the attackers in a fierce aerial engagement. The German fighters downed 120 of the more than 400 Soviet bombers for comparatively light losses.

The first full day of Citadel witnessed some of the heaviest, most confused, and most hectic air action of the war in Russia. The Luftwaffe won the first round with the VVS in the south, destroying more than 400 Soviet aircraft during the day and thus establishing an early edge that lasted for some days to come.

In the north, air activity was just as fierce, although the first large-scale appearance of the VVS did not come until the afternoon of July 5. The VVS' tardiness in engaging the attacking German units left the defending ground forces without air cover or support for three or four critical hours. On both attack sectors, the

Luftwaffe gained the upper hand as a result of its initial victories and the VVS' deficiencies, especially in fighter operations. As in the early Kuban fighting, Soviet air operations left much to be desired on July 5: too often, fighters went after German fighters instead of attacking enemy bombers and ground-support aircraft. Moreover, the VVS frequently dissipated its efforts and thus lost its ability to deliver massed attacks, as the Sixteenth Air Army did on July 5 by attacking too many ground targets.

Although it grasped control over the battlefields, the Luftwaffe definitely could not establish the air superiority it had enjoyed during the previous two summers. The pressing demands of close support often prevented the Luftwaffe from challenging the VVS in the air. Lacking the forces to provide adequate air support across the entire expanse of the battlefield, the German air effort shifted daily from sector to sector. The Eighth Air Corps flew 1,700 sorties on July 6, but it could not both support the Forty-eighth and Second SS Panzer corps and oppose the VVS. Furthermore, German bombers and attack aircraft were no longer free to operate with their former impunity, as VVS fighters performed with greater aggressiveness in patrolling and "free hunting." Many of the precious few German fighters had to be diverted to escort duty from air-superiority missions.

On the Soviet side, the VVS began on July 6 to correct its opening day errors. Rudenko's Sixteenth Air Army used a fighter division to clear the way for a massed bomber and ground-assault attack against the German Ninth Army units that were pressing the Thirteenth Army on the Okhlovatka sector of Rokossovsky's Central Front. The results were so good that Rokossovsky requested and received continuing support from small groups of

Figure 26. The Pe-2 bomber or its derivative, a long-range high-altitude fighter, on the ground. About 500 of the latter were built during 1941–1942. Turret guns are wrapped for protection. Note guard's marking on the nose.

Il-2s until another massed strike was readied about three hours later. Both attack and bomber support became much more effective after July 6, as air control teams gained experience in directing aircraft to the hardest-pressed areas.

At first the Luftwaffe put up as many as 3,000 sorties a day. Within a few days, however, a combination of Soviet resistance and heavy operational attrition had cut the number to 1,000 sorties daily. By July 8–9 Citadel was clearly in trouble in both attack zones, as both the fierce Soviet resistance on the ground and the roving Shturmoviks took an awesome toll of German armor. Unable to meet the vastly increased demands for close air support, the Luftwaffe lacked the strength to affect the outcome of the ground fighting. On the

Ninth Army's sector south of Orel, German air operations dropped from 1,162 sorties on July 7 to 350 on July 9. Conversely, Soviet air operations intensified as more and more reserves were thrown into the fighting. Tenacity and greater numbers allowed the VVS to wear down the Luftwaffe and capture a slight operational advantage that was an important prerequisite for the successful outcome of the defensive fighting at Kursk.

From the first day, Soviet ground-attack aircraft played a conspicuous role in Kursk air operations. Initially operating against the German armored and infantry units in the standard groups of six to eight aircraft, they soon switched to groups of 30–40 or more aircraft—thus enhancing their overall effectiveness, simplifying escort protection,

easing suppression of ground fire, and improving attack concentration. Il-2m3s of
all VVS air armies enjoyed good hunting
against German armor, especially the new
Il-2m3 Modified aircraft, which mounted
the twin 37-mm Il-P-37 or Nudelman-
Suranov NS-37 antitank cannon first used
at Kursk. In a concentrated twenty-minute
attack on July 7, these new Shturmoviks
destroyed seventy armored vehicles of the
Ninth Army's Ninth Panzer Division.
Another new weapon, the small PTAB
hollow-charge antitank bombs, was employed effectively even against the heavy
Panther and Tiger tanks. German armored
units lost heavily to swarming Shturmoviks,
which pushed their attacks despite Luftwaffe air control. The appearance of the
Yak-9T tank buster, with a NS-37 cannon
mounted between the cylinder banks and
firing through the propeller hub, added
another dimension to the antitank war.

The fighting at Kursk reached a climax
on July 12 at Prokhorovka, when more
than 1,500 German and Soviet armored
vehicles engaged in a confusing and savage
battle while hundreds of Luftwaffe and
VVS aircraft fought each other and the
enemy armor. Although each side lost
more than 300 vehicles, the Germans held
the field when the day ended.

Meanwhile, the Bryansk and Western
fronty launched the first Soviet summer offensive of the war against the Orel salient,
forcing Model to break off his stalled offensive and pull back. The cumulative effect of the heavy losses in both attack
zones, the Soviet offensive against Orel,
and the Allied landings in Sicily on July 10
prompted Hitler to cancel Citadel on July
17. When all operations had ended in the
Belgorod sector on July 23, the Voronezh
Front had reoccupied its July 5 positions
and was preparing to deliver the second
phase of the Soviet summer offensive.

In the defensive fighting against Model

and Manstein, the Second, Sixteenth, and
Seventeenth air armies flew more than
28,000 sorties and claimed 1,500 enemy
aircraft destroyed. As in other major actions in the east, Soviet losses probably exceeded German losses, but exact figures are
impossible to determine. The important
fact was that the German air losses, especially in personnel, were irreplaceable,
while those of the VVS were not. The
Luftwaffe could not afford such attritional
warfare, faced as it now was with the
mounting pressures of the Anglo-American
strategic bombing offensive and the invasion of Sicily. The demands of multifront
air war were stretching the small Luftwaffe
to the point where it was inferior in all
theaters. In the aerial fighting at Kursk, the
VVS at last grasped a definite superiority
in the air that it never relinquished. The
Battle of Kursk was as decisive in the air as
it was on the ground—Germany's ultimate
defeat was now only a matter of time.

Seizing Control in the Air: July–December 1943

The Stavka hoped to launch the major
thrusts of the summer offensive simultaneously north and south of the Kursk salient
once the Germans were stopped. Continued heavy fighting on the Belgorod-Kharkov sector, however, frustrated Soviet
plans. Without waiting, the Central,
Bryansk, and Western *fronty* went ahead
with their planned attack on the Orel salient on July 12. The Sixteenth, Fifteenth,
and First air armies supporting the fronts
threw more than 3,000 aircraft against the
now-depleted forces of the Sixth Air Fleet.
Orel fell on August 5, and by August 17
Model had withdrawn to the "Hagen line"
at the base of the former Orel salient after
losing 20 percent of his strength in six
weeks.

Far to the south, secondary Soviet offensives begun on July 17 diverted German

Figure 27. Camouflaged Pe-2 dive-bomber group in flight during the Stalingrad counter-offensive in November 1942.

armored and air forces from the main concentrations in the Belgorod-Kharkov area. Instead of one major Luftwaffe concentration in the Kursk front, German air strength was split into three roughly equal groups of 450–500 aircraft: one group covering the Orel salient, another for the Belgorod-Kharkov sector, the third in the south at Stalino. By forcing such a dispersion of the Luftwaffe, the Soviet command assured the VVS' growing superiority. This proved beneficial for the success of subsequent Soviet offenses, because they could be prepared and conducted with the assurance that strategic air superiority was in Soviet hands.

With Army Group South distracted, the southern blow of the summer offensive fell on August 3. Vatutin's Voronezh Front punched a gaping hole in the Fourth Panzer Army's lines west of Belgorod, while Konev's Steppe Front struck toward Khar-kov from the east. Supported by 1,311 aircraft of the Second and Fifth air armies (a 2:1 edge over the Luftwaffe), Vatutin's forces occupied Belgorod on August 5—the day Orel fell—and Konev's troops liberated Kharkov on August 23. This marked the end of the two-pronged Kursk counteroffensive, but only the beginning of the Soviet summer-autumn offensives.

The counteroffensive operations at Orel and Belgorod-Kharkov (July 12–August 23) were significant milestones in the development of Soviet air power. For the first time the VVS began a strategic offensive with a definite superiority in fighters—better than 3:1. Also, for the first time this advantage cleared the way for the air armies to conduct a complete air offensive in both preparatory and support phases. Backed by ADD and PVO units, frontal aviation concentrated on narrow sectors of the offensive zones in order to achieve maximum effect. On the Belgorod-Kharkov breakthrough sectors, for example, all attack and bomber aircraft and more than half of the fighters of the Second Air Army massed in support of the First Tank and Fifth Guards Tank armies on August 3, flying 2,370 sorties. When P. S. Rybalko's Third Guards Tank Army entered the fighting at Orel on July 20, Naumenko's Fifteenth Air Army provided 200 fighters, 112 bombers, and 120 attack aircraft for support—well over 63 percent of its effective strength. Although primarily used for direct support against German tanks, artillery, and strong resistance hindering the advance, air units also ranged out against enemy reserves, regrouping efforts, and movement of reinforcements.

Central to the success of both these operations were air cover and support for the tank armies that carried the burden of the major Soviet offensives after 1943. The VVS provided the most mobile, flexible, powerful, and effective means of supporting tank armies during offensive operations. Once fighters had assured control and cover, air support fell principally to the attack units and tactical bombers. Covered by one or two fighter divisions, one or two attack divisions usually worked in depth with specific tank armies during breakthrough and exploitation. In some instances an entire attack air corps—ordinarily a fighter division and two attack divisions—was assigned such duty.

The techniques of the Soviet air offensive in the summer campaign showed vast improvements over previous efforts. Prior to offensive operations, air units moved as close as possible to the front so that a maximum number of sorties could be flown and so that effective time in action was lengthened before forward redeployment was necessary. Fighters were normally sited on fields from twelve to twenty-five miles from the front and bombers/attack units some thirty to seventy-five miles. To prevent alerting the Germans to the imminence of attack, the fields were never occupied until just before an offensive. For each major operation, air armies created reserve airfield maintenance battalions (BAO). As the offensive unfolded, they shifted forward with first-echelon armies to restore captured air bases or build new fields, thus allowing the rapid redeployment of combat air units and preserving continuous air cover and support for ground forces. Battlefield employment was also enhanced through the use of more efficient radio networks for controlling attack aviation units directly on the battlefield.

After August 1943, the Germans fought to regain some control over the situation in the east, but to little effect since sufficient forces were no longer available. Allied pressure in the west prevented the reinforcement of the eastern front while constantly draining it of the best units, leaving the Luftwaffe in an ever-worsening position. Growing Luftwaffe commitments, especially for Reich defense against Allied bombers, led the new chief of staff, Günther Korten, to accelerate these tendencies. More and more, Korten drew off units from the east—primarily fighters, which were seldom if ever returned or replaced—thus virtually abdicating air control to the increasingly aggressive and already numerically superior VVS fighter force. In these circumstances, Soviet dominance in the air became more marked with every passing day.

Skillfully exploiting the strategic initiative it now held, the Stavka varied its thrusts along the front throughout the remainder of 1943, exempting only the Leningrad-Karelian sector. Operating without adequate reserves, German ground and air units were shifted quickly from sector to sector in desperate attempts to meet the

Figure 28. Il-2 Shturmoviks taking off during winter operations on the eastern front. This aircraft became one of the finest ground-attack planes of World War II.

cleverly applied Soviet pressure. In August–September, the Kalinin and Western *fronty* pushed forward against the weakened Army Group Center. The Western Front took Roslavl and Smolensk on September 25, while the Kalinin captured Nevel and stopped just short of Vitebsk.

On the east bank of the Dnieper, Army Group South pulled back to the Melitopol-Dnieper line on September 30 in the hope of holding along it. Following up swiftly, forces of the Central, Voronezh, Steppe,

and Southwestern *fronty* cleared the left bank and crossed the Dnieper at many points before the Germans could establish their defenses.* From these initial footholds, solid bridgeheads were built up on the west bank. Kiev fell to the First Ukrainian Front on November 6. Farther south along the river, the Second and Third Ukrainian *fronty* expanded their bridgeheads until they formed an enclave running Cherkassy- Kremenchug-Dneprpetrovsk- Zaporozhe. Meanwhile, the Fourth Ukrainian Front pushed westward to the Black Sea coast, isolating German forces in the Crimea. Movement in the southern Ukraine halted temporarily until late December, but then Rokossovsky's Byelorussian Front struck in the center in late November, took Gomel, and moved across the Berezina River before coming to a stop. By the close of 1943, Army Group Center held a bulge of Byelorussia along the line Vitebsk-Orsha-Mogilev-Bobriusk, Army Group South having been forced back across the Dnieper along its entire frontage,

---

*On October 20, the structure of the Soviet *fronty* was slightly revised and renamed. The four *fronty* in the Ukraine—Voronezh, Steppe, Southwestern, and Southern—were redesignated as the First, Second, Third, and Fourth Ukrainian *fronty* and retained their air armies—the Second, Fifth, Seventeenth, and Eighth. On October 10, the Bryansk Front was split between Rokossovskii's Central and Sokolovskii's Western *fronty*. On October 20, Central became the Byelorussian Front while the Kalinin Front became the First Baltic Front and the recently established Baltic Front became the Second Baltic Front, receiving the Fifteenth Air Army from the disbanded Bryansk Front.

with the Russian First Ukrainian Front once again on the move westward from Kiev, while the German Seventeenth was incarcerated in the Crimea. Only Army Group North was spared in 1943.

For the Luftwaffe, the results of this constant pounding were inevitable—its meager forces were stretched to the limit and its crews and equipment worn out by repeated movements and heavy attrition. Despite a significant increase in the Luftwaffe's front-line strength during the year (from 3,955 to 5,585 aircraft), the eastern front benefited little. At the close of 1943, Luftwaffe fighter strength in the east totaled a mere 385 aircraft, of which only 306 were operational.

December 1943 ended the second period of the war, which had begun with the Stalingrad counteroffensive on November 19, 1942. In little more than thirteen months, Soviet forces seized the initiative from the Germans and then solidified their dominant position through extensive offensives that pushed the enemy far to the west. The VVS played a significant role in this change, completing 796,000 sorties. From 3,254 aircraft in November 1942 the VVS had grown to 8,818 combat aircraft and more than 408,000 men in January 1944. Including ADD and naval air forces, 124 air divisions were in operation, with 4 others in the Stavka Reserve. Along with these numerical gains went important qualitative improvements in aircraft, tactics, air-ground cooperation on the battlefield, and attitude and morale. The best Luftwaffe and VVS pilots were equally matched, though the average Soviet flier still lacked the skill of his German counterpart. What the VVS lacked in skill, however, it more than made up for in numbers—a factor that proved to be decisive.

Tactical Development: 1943–1945

The technological and industrial achieve-ments that resulted in more and better Soviet aircraft after 1943 were paralleled by steady improvements in VVS tactical employment and air crews. Combined, these advances produced a powerful and effective instrument of modern air warfare which was neatly tailored to the particular requirements of the ground war in the east.

It is only natural that the VVS fighter arm, upon which the most attention was showered, showed the most significant development. As modern fighters appeared in increasing numbers at the front, the VVS fighter pilots were infused with a greater confidence that was clearly reflected in their growing aggressiveness in patrol and penetration, counter-air, escort, and even ground-support operations.

Training deficiencies, lack of experience, heavy personnel losses, and inadequate aircraft had handicapped the Soviet fighter pilots through 1942. Thereafter, the combination of a realistic combat-training program in frontal air-training regiments and increased combat exposure produced improved individual tactical skills and flying ability. By late 1944, the deficiencies mattered little because of the overwhelming Soviet numerical superiority and the general deterioration of the Luftwaffe in the east.

Soviet fighter tactics closely resembled those of the Luftwaffe, from which the VVS had borrowed freely but never blindly. The combat *para* (pair) consisting of offensive and defensive aircraft, operating in a four-play *zveno* (flight) of two pairs or a *gruppa* (group) of three or four pairs, formed the basis for Soviet tactics. *Zveno* pairs flew in relatively loose formations, using wide frontal spacing and alternating attack and cover positions. Formations were always echeloned upward because altitude carried advantage in aerial combat. Pokryshkin and other Soviet aces always taught that alti-

Figure 29. Shturmoviks attacking a German armored column. Massed attacks at altitudes of less than 300 feet were favored in Soviet tactics.

tude was a primary tactical consideration and the key to survival in the air.

The growth of the air regiment to thirty-two aircraft in 1942 and to forty in 1943 provided greater flexibility, strength, and concentration. Regiments were eventually restructured into three twelve-plane squadrons, each with three *zveno* of four aircraft. Attack groups of thirty–fifty Soviet fighters were common late in the war, but they were made up of individual squadron-sized elements of 8–10 aircraft.

The struggle for air superiority over the Luftwaffe was always the overriding mission of the Soviet fighter arm. In 1943, air armies specifically employed one or two fighter air divisions in the effort to achieve air superiority over the Germans. By 1944–1945, three or more divisions were used to gain control over the battlefield, as a result of increased aircraft production and decreased losses. The narrow edge gained in the summer of 1943 constantly widened, until by mid-1944 the fighter arm had finally and fully achieved its top-priority mission: the seizure of strategic air superiority.

Operations of the VVS fighter force were closely coordinated with those of the ground forces. For major operations, the former shielded the assembly and subsequent breakthrough of tank and ground armies from German air reconnaissance and attack while other VVS units provided air cover against fighter interference. The normal procedure called for the large-scale use of patrols and roving fighters to seal off the entire battle sector, with each regiment committed to a specific zone of operations. As the Luftwaffe became less of a threat, radar detection and radio-controlled fighter operations came increasingly to replace the standing patrols.

Soviet fighter pilots favored the free-hunt tactics of freewheeling offensive air patrols. This preference was so strong that fighters on close-escort duty often left their charges to "hunt" for German aircraft. Once engaged in aerial combat, the pilots tended to open fire at excessive ranges, but their fire discipline and gunnery improved steadily. They also showed a decidedly defensive reaction to attack, preferring to form defensive circles to cover each other until they were safely back within their own lines.

The air war in the east was fought almost exclusively below 10,000 feet, out of preference as well as tactical emphasis. The Yak-3, Yak-9, La-5FN, and La-7 fighters were at least the equals of the advanced Messerschmitts and Focke-Wulfs by 1944, but VVS pilots still preferred to operate between 5,000 and 8,000 feet. At these lower altitudes the Yaks and Lavochkins performed best and gave the VVS the edge in combat.

Whereas the use of Soviet fighters in a ground-support role was nil from 1941 through 1943, such operations became common after January 1944. The decline in German air activity allowed the fitting of bomb and rocket racks. After "free hunting" over enemy-held territory without encountering the Luftwaffe, fighters could attack any targets of opportunity. Older Yaks and Lavochkins were often found in this role or attached as escorts. Such newer aircraft as the Yak-9M and La-5FN were adapted equally for fighter and support operations, while the Yak-9B, 9T, and 9K were specifically designed for attack missions but also capable of fighter operations.

Ground-attack aircraft carried the burden of the Soviet tactical air mission throughout the war. Only slightly less-favored than the fighters, they made steady progress in tactics, equipment, and effectiveness through 1945. With more aircraft available, units increased in number and strength, producing a corresponding impact on the battlefield. The Shturmovik remained the basic attack aircraft, but it was upgraded in performance and armament and was only slowly beginning to give way to the new Il-10 in early 1945. Attack aviation's primary function was always the direct support of army ground operations, to which it was closely tied. But by 1945

the range of targets had expanded beyond the immediate battle area to include such rear-area objectives as rail and road traffic, supply depots, and Luftwaffe airfields. Once Soviet forces had initiated offensive action, ground-attack aviation became the predominant element of the air war, clearing the way for and supporting the tank armies upon which the ultimate outcome rested.

As had the fighters, attack aviation showed definite tactical refinement and maturity after 1943. Its basic operational principles had remained unaltered because it essentially consisted of flying artillery, tied closely to ground operations and requirements. Attack units operated in support (*podderzhka*) or under assignment (*pridacha*) in most instances. Support, the more standard form for tactical air employment, stressed the centralized control of air units. When operating under assignment, attack units were attached to specific ground formations, usually tank and mechanized units. Unlike those operating in support, air commanders on assignment were allowed a relatively free choice of targets.

Ground-attack operations became fairly standardized. Concentrated strikes by large formations of regiment and division strength were used mainly against a single target or during the preparatory phase of an air offensive. Beginning in 1943, formations of from twenty-five to sixty aircraft were employed over the battlefield, with waves of four to twelve aircraft continuously attacking enemy positions and equipment. Coming in low and often from unexpected directions, the attack units struck quickly in strength and returned to their own territory before German fighters could arrive. The emphasis in both forms was on direct tactical support in the immediate frontal area. However, Stalin had become dissatisfied with the effectiveness of deep-interdiction

Figure 30. Il-2m3 Shturmoviks over Stalingrad in 1942. Note addition of rear gunner.

missions prior to the Kursk operations; so, on May 4, 1943, he ordered the creation in each air army of an attack regiment specializing in "hunting" operations. The "hunters" had no specific targets but were sent against German lines of communication and concentrated on railroads, roads, and traffic. Such operations came to play a larger role in attack operations, further blurring the already-vague distinction between direct support and interdiction.

As German fighter opposition weakened and VVS escorts improved, attack aircraft loitered longer over enemy lines and drove their strikes farther into German rear areas. These attacks beyond the tactical zone, primarily against Luftwaffe installations and lines of communication, never rivaled front-line operations in either size or intensity. They did, however, clearly indicate the great distance that the VVS had come since 1941. By the last year of the war, it was not unusual for groups of from forty to sixty attack aircraft to carry out such raids, escorted by as many fighters.

The enhanced use of radio communications vastly improved the attack effectiveness of the VVS. Air officers in communication with ground units coordinated operations and directed attackers to the most critical targets. Voice communications were "in the clear" to prevent confusion, but these direction efforts were frequently frustrated by poor tactical discipline. Nevertheless, improved air-ground and air-air communications made the attack arm more effective and responsive to ground-force demands.

Air support for offensive operations was the basic VVS mission during the closing years of the war. The developed form of the air offensive provided this support in two phases: preparation and support. *Front* and air army commanders carefully worked out plans for air support because it was an integral part of each *front*'s offensive.

Direct air preparation came immediately before the ground attack and lasted for anywhere from fifteen minutes to two hours. Concentrated bomber strikes followed by massed employment of attack aviation in groups coincided with artillery preparation and was directed against artillery, tanks, reserves, and any strong points beyond Soviet artillery range which might hold up the impending advance. Such support was carried over into the actual ground attack and after the introduction of the second echelon into the offensive.

The most important phase of air support came with the commitment to battle of the armored and mechanized forces. These mobile groups were usually committed on relatively narrow fronts, highly concentrated and in dense formations—all of which made them vulnerable to German air action and to flank attacks or obstruction by defenders. During this critical time, fighters covered the armored columns while bomber, attack, and fighter units struck German airfields and defenses. Once in the open, the mobile groups operated as much as seventy miles ahead of the combined-arms armies and thus depended heavily on the air forces for fire support, cover, reconnaissance, and resupply. Strangely, the VVS attack aircraft apparently performed poorly in preventing or interfering with German withdrawal movements after the breakthrough was completed and the pursuit-exploitation phase had begun. In the massive, deep-penetration operations of 1944–1945 that chewed up entire German armies, however, the VVS did provide the strength that the mobile groups lacked to contain encircled German formations after their envelopment.

Soviet bomber and reconnaissance forces, although considerably behind the fighter and attack arms, made significant strides during the period 1943–1945 as a result of strenuous efforts at improvement. Nevertheless, inadequacies in equipment and training hampered the effectiveness of both forces. Like other VVS arms, they were principally tools of tactical warfare dedicated to the support of ground operations.

The frontal bombers were primarily used against targets along the front lines or in immediate rear areas. They flew, almost exclusively, direct and indirect support missions for ground forces, although increasingly the tactical bombers came to be employed against targets in the German rear after 1943. Deficiencies in equipment and training hindered their use in bad weather, at night, and for long-range strikes. On the whole, Soviet bomber

operations were better planned and executed, ranged more deeply, and were more effective in 1944–1945 than in previous years.

Bomber tactics underwent only modest changes, with emphasis placed on perfecting existing tactics rather than evolving new forms. Operations were conducted in large formations protected by fighters. Waves of regiment strength (thirty aircraft), with squadron following squadron at short intervals, normally made horizontal bombing attacks from altitudes of 6,000–13,000 feet. With the achievement of air superiority, the bombers operated at lower attack altitudes, thus increasing their accuracy and impact. Moreover, the favorable air situation of 1944–1945 also meant that bombers operated continuously in daylight, ranging ever deeper into German rear areas to conduct massed attacks. In its bomber operations the VVS adhered to the use of concentrated strikes for maximum effect and protection. Generally, the bombers were employed soundly and to good effect in the support of ground operations, in many respects facilitating and enhancing them. For deep operations they were less successful because of insufficient training and other inadequacies, but they showed marked improvement.

Although Golovanov's Long-Range Air Force (ADD) had been intended for independent, quasi-strategic operations, it was more frequently committed to the direct and indirect support of the ground forces. The ADD normally concentrated on frontal sectors where major operations were impending and made raids against targets deep in the German rear as well as those in front-line defense zones. While not specifically a tactical force, the ADD played a significant role in all major offensive operations after Stalingrad. This fact at least in part explains why the ADD

Figure 31. Pe-8 bomber at a U.S. air base in 1942. Note machine gun mounted in rear of the inboard nacelle.

was redesignated the Eighteenth Air Army in December 1944, lost its former semi-independent status, and was placed directly under the authority of the commander of the VVS for operations against Poland, East Prussia, and Berlin.

For tactical and battlefield reconnaissance, the VVS extensively used fighter and attack aircraft. In effect, the principle was that every aircraft over the battlefield had a reconnaissance responsibility. That this system produced mediocre results was not too important so long as operations were conducted over Soviet territory, with its extensive networks of agents and partisans. Once outside Russia, however, greater attention had to be paid to air reconnaissance. Better qualified pilots were then selected from fighter and attack units for training in reconnaissance operations. After 1943, the level of cooperation between reconnaissance squadrons and ground operations improved, but lingering deficiencies continued to prevent timely action against suitable targets.

The Soviets modified existing equipment for reconnaissance missions rather than developing entirely new aircraft. Standard models, specially equipped (such as the Pe-2, Il-2, La-5, Yak-7B, and Yak-9) were most frequently used for tactical reconnaissance. The Pe-2 and Lend-Lease B-25s and A-20s were used principally for long-range sorties.

The Maturation of the Red Air Force: 1944

Liberation of the Ukraine and the Crimea: December 1943–May 1944

Whatever hopes the Germans may have had for a respite in the winter of 1943–1944 were quickly shattered on December 24, when the First Ukrainian Front struck to the west and southwest from its positions around Kiev. Supported by 750 aircraft of the Second Air Army, Vatutin's forces plunged forward in the first of the major hammer blows of the winter offensive that would liberate the right-bank Ukraine. On January 5, Konev's Second Ukrainian Front and Goriunov's Fifth Air Army (550 aircraft) joined in the battle and by the middle of the month had liberated Kirovograd. In a concerted operation, the two fronts then encircled and eliminated a large German group at Korsun-Shevchenkovskii between January 24 and February 17, 1944. While these operations were in progress, farther south the Third and Fourth Ukrainian *fronty,* backed by the Seventeenth Air Army (552 aircraft) and Eighth Air Army (811 aircraft), cleared the German salient in the Dnieper bend during February.

With Zhukov now commanding the First Ukrainian Front and its regrouping along the Pripet Marshes completed, Soviet armies in the Ukraine were on the move once again in early March.* Zhukov delivered a slashing blow to the rear of Army Group South, cutting across Manstein's lines of communication to take Chernovitsy on March 29. The Second Ukrainian Front struck westward on March 5, took Uman on March 19, and was quickly over the Bug River. Konev's forces linked up with Zhukov's to encircle Hube's First Panzer Army north of Kamenets-Podol'sk on March 26. On April 9, Hube broke out of the encirclement, but only after sustaining heavy losses in men and equipment. The Luftwaffe transport fleet had kept the pocket resupplied sufficiently to allow the breakout, but most of the sorties were flown at night because of Soviet air superiority and lack of German fighter protection. Although the VVS could be faulted for not striking the transport supply fields, it was having its own troubles operating, as a

result of bad weather and the spring thaw. Only by virtue of great efforts by ground-support personnel were airfields kept in operation and supplies brought up to allow the VVS to continue flying. Moreover, the air armies also transported supplies and gasoline to tank groups that were far forward and short of supplies.

Hitler's insistence that the Crimea be held had left the German Seventeenth Army and First Air Corps isolated on the peninsula since the previous fall. The Stavka decided to remove this German-Rumanian outpost during the spring campaign once the western Ukraine was cleared. A formidable array of air power was gathered for the operation. Indeed, Khriukin's Eighth Air Army (of Tolbukhin's Fourth Ukrainian Front) and K. A. Vershinin's Fourth Air Army (attached to Eremenko's Independent Coastal Army) had been at work against the German and Rumanian forces in the Crimea since October 1943. By April 1944, more than 50,000 sorties had been flown for reconnaissance, air defense, interdiction of shipping, and bombing. For the liberation of the Crimea, F. Ya. Falaleev was assigned as Stavka representative to coordinate the air operations of the two air armies, the Black Sea Fleet Naval Air Force, the PVO, and the ADD bombers that would be involved. The air units deployed totaled 2,255 aircraft. Against this force, the German First Air Corps could throw at most a few hundred aircraft.

On April 8, Tolbukhin's *front* struck from the north with the Fifty-first Army. Initially, 108 attack aircraft of the Eighth Air Army hit the forward German defense lines. Then they switched to groups of four to six aircraft which operated constantly over the battlefield. During the heavy fighting of the next few days, the VVS provided air support for the Fifty-

---

*Vatutin was wounded by a Ukrainian nationalist partisan on February 29 while on a motor tour and died soon afterward. Zhukov, then Stavka representative to coordinate operations of the First and Second Ukrainian *fronty,* assumed command of Vatutin's *front* because of his familiarity with the upcoming Proskurov-Chernovitsy operation. The Second Byelorussian Front was formed on February 24 to cover the Pripet Marshes between the First Ukrainian Front and Rokossovsky's now-redesignated First Byelorussian Front.

Figure 32. Il-4 long-range medium bomber at a Russian airfield in 1944.

first Army until it broke through the defenses south of the Sivash on April 11. While this fighting was going on, the Second Guards Army breached the Perekop positions and moved south. To the east, Eremenko opened up his operations on the night of April 10. Both the Eighth and Fourth air armies harassed the withdrawing German and Rumanian units. The Fourth Ukrainian Front reached the Sevastopol area on April 15, and Eremenko's forces arrived two days later.

With well over 1,000 aircraft assembled for the final push on Sevastopol, the Eighth Air Army's tactical aircraft, ADD bombers, and naval aircraft softened up the enemy's defenses and tried to cut off the evacuation route by sea to Rumania. On May 5, the Second Guards Army attacked in the north in an effort to draw the Germans away from the main thrust planned by the Fifty-first and Coastal armies at Sapun Hill on May 7. Effectively supported by attack aircraft, Soviet forces broke through German defenses and had completed the destruction of the Seventeenth Army by May 12. During the entire operation, more than 36,000 sorties were completed, 60 percent for direct support.

The ADD flew 1,865 of these against rear-area targets. Although the Germans were able to evacuate more than 150,000 men from the peninsula during the fighting, most of the equipment was lost, along with probably more than 80,000 men.

The Byelorussian and L'vov-Sandomir Offensives: June 22–August 29, 1944

In the late spring of 1944, the Germans' Army Group Center (under Field Marshal Ernst Busch) still held a dangerously exposed 650-mile-long salient that bellied eastward toward Smolensk and Moscow. While it occupied a vulnerable strategic position, the army group threatened the rear of the Soviet *fronty* in the Ukraine and their further movement westward. Moreover, these German forces occupied the last large parcel of prewar Soviet territory—Byelorussia—and blocked the most direct route to the heart of Germany. Thus the Stavka made the destruction of Army Group Center a major objective for its 1944 summer campaign.

By mid-May the Stavka had worked out a two-phase operation to snip off the bulge, destroy Army Group Center, and

Figure 33. Yak-3 fighter with bubble canopy added late in the war.

liberate Byelorussia. Code-named Operation Bagration by Stalin, this offensive was one of the most carefully planned and prepared of all Soviet operations during the war. It its first phase (June 22–July 15), six major attacks were to be delivered by four *fronty,* with overwhelming forces concentrated on narrow attack sectors along a 488-mile section of the German front. Once Busch's defenses were smashed, armored and mechanized units carried the offensive westward through Byelorussia to the Baltic states, East Prussia, and Poland during the second phase (July 15–August 15). Neighboring forces in the north (the First and Second Baltic *fronty*) and the south (the First Ukrainian Front) joined in during this phase.

The rapidly expanding flow of new equipment into the ground, tank, and air armies greatly aided the buildup for the Byelorussian offensive. During the first five months of 1944, the number of aircraft assigned to frontal air armies, the ADD, the Naval Air Force, and Stavka Reserve air units jumped from 8,818 to 14,787—an increase of 5,969 aircraft, or 68 percent, over the January 1 strength. VVS and ADD personnel grew from 408,000 in January to 447,000 in June, while air divisions (including those of the ADD and Naval Air Forces) went from 128 to 153. When translated into actual air strength, these numbers gave the twelve frontal air armies at total of ninety-three divisions and thirty-two independent regiments, with 8,798 operational combat

Figure 34. La-7 UTI trainer on the ground.

aircraft and 1,046 R-5 and Po-2 light night bombers. This vast expansion of the VVS came at a time when the Luftwaffe was increasingly hard pressed to fend off the Anglo-American air offensive in preparation for the impending Allied invasion of France.

Actually, in late spring of 1944 the Luftwaffe on the eastern front was in better shape than it had been for some time, as a result of the German emphasis on aircraft production. Front-line strength stood at 2,085 aircraft in June, with the bulk assigned to the Sixth Air Fleet (775 aircraft) attached to Army Group Center and to the Fourth Air Fleet (845 aircraft) covering Army Groups North and South Ukraine. But, reflecting the need for fighters in the Reich's defense and in the west, only 395 single-engined fighters were in the east, as compared with 405 bombers and 580 ground-support aircraft. Despite the improved situation, the Luftwaffe was still outnumbered at least 7:1 in total aircraft, more than 6:1 in operational aircraft, and more than 10:1 in fighters.

Because the First and Third Byelorussian *fronty* had the most difficult assignments, their air armies received the most

reinforcements from the eleven Stavka Reserve air corps and eight independent air divisions; more than 3,000 aircraft were brought up during early June. Khriukin's First Air Army of the Third Byelorussian Front (under I. D. Chernyakovsky) had 2,005 aircraft, and Rudenko's Sixteenth Air Army of Rokossovsky's First Byelorussian Front was the largest in the operation with 2,096 planes. To assist the frontal air armies, the Stavka dispatched eight ADD air corps (sixteen divisions) and 1,000 bombers to the Byelorussian front. This brought the total VVS strength for Bagration to 6,683 aircraft, 49.8 percent of Soviet operational air strength in early June. Such a concentration of air power was tailored to the Stavka's overall strategic plan, which stressed achievement of great numerical superiority in the direction of the main efforts.

The German defenses in the Bobruisk sector were so heavily fortified that Rokossovsky wanted a particularly powerful preparatory air attack mounted against them. To provide the needed strength, the ADD would have to be used; but this meant depriving the other *fronty* of adequate preparation, since all four were to attack simultaneously on June 23.

Zhukov requested and received Stalin's permission to delay Rokossovsky's attack until June 24 so that ADD support could be provided to the other *fronty* and then shifted south to the Bobruisk sector. With this problem solved, Rudenko and the other air army commanders finally completed their plans on June 21. The German defenders would receive the full brunt of the "air offensive" in its developed form.

Against these Soviet air forces, Ritter von Greim's Sixth Air Fleet had 775 aircraft, not all of them combat-ready, and only 100 of his planes were single-seat fighters. Thus, the VVS buildup for the Byelorussian operation gave it a nominal numerical air superiority of nearly nine to one and an edge in fighters of probably twenty to one or more. Because much of the Luftwaffe's strength had been drained off to oppose the Allied landings in Normandy early in June, the Sixth Air Fleet was almost nonexistent when the Soviet offensive opened. Indeed, it had only 40 fighters available to face the VVS. The VVS exploited this gift of air superiority to the fullest.

With little to stop them west of Minsk, the Red Army units regrouped and then raced toward East Prussia and Poland without slackening their pace of ten to fifteen miles a day. The success against Army Group Center had cleared the way for the opening of the second phase of Bagration and for Konev's L'vov-Sandomir operation. The left wing of the First Byelorussian Front struck in the Kovel area on July 18. Supported by 1,305 aircraft of Polynin's Sixth Air Army, most of them transferred from Rudenko's air army, the operation developed quickly alongside that of Konev to the south. On July 23, Lublin in southeastern Poland fell. By mid-August, solid bridgeheads had been established over the Vistula at Pulawy, Deblin, and Magnuszew south of Warsaw. To the north, the First,

Second, and Third Byelorussian *fronty* pushed west and northwest and were joined by the First and Second Baltic *fronty*. Soon most of Latvia and Lithuania had been cleared, and the German Army Group North was nearly isolated from the rest of the eastern front. The left and right wings of the First Byelorussian Front joined east of Warsaw, occupying the east bank of the Vistula, the Narev River line, and Warsaw's eastern suburbs.

The rapid advance of the tank armies, however, outstripped the ability of the VVS air armies to redeploy its units to forward air bases. Early in August, only a few fighter regiments of the Sixth and Sixteenth air armies were available to cover the First Byelorussian Front's Vistula bridgeheads against the revived Luftwaffe's attacks. Even when the VVS was able to redeploy units to new fields within range of the front, logistics were difficult to maintain over the long, unrepaired roads. On July 23, the Sixteenth Air Army had only enough aviation gasoline for a single refueling of its aircraft, thus leaving ground forces vulnerable to German counterattacks.

In the battle for Byelorussia proper, the German army suffered one of the worst defeats in its history: at least twenty-eight of Army Group Center's thirty-eight divisions were smashed; more than 350,000 irreplaceable men were killed, wounded, or captured; and vast quantities of equipment and supplies were lost. Among other factors, the magnitude and swiftness of the Soviet victory in Byelorussia must be credited to the decisive and extremely effective role of the VVS.

The air operation of the Byelorussian offensive were a good measure of the improved skills of VVS commanders and units. The nature of the operation, which was characterized by several phases and widely separated drives, meant that air

Table 1. VVS Air Operations in the Byelorussian Offensive (June 22–August 29, 1944)

	1st Air Army	*3rd Air Army*	*4th Air Army*	*6th Air Army*	*16th Air Army*	*Long-Range Air Force*	*Total Forces*
Number of sorties in the first phase of the operations (June 23–July 4)	13,741	13,438	8,195	—	13,992	5,645	55,011
Number of sorties in the second phase of the operations (July 5–August 29)	21,254	22,167	20,736	13,848	13,647	6,882	98,534
Total sorties for the entire operation	34,995	35,605	28,931	13,848	27,639	12,527	153,545

Statistics from Rudenko, "The Byelorussian Air Offensive," translated in *Aerospace Historian*, March 1973, p. 25.

support for the various offensive tasks could be provided only through swift but careful maneuvering of air units, both along the front and in depth. Such maneuvering was greatly complicated by the high rates of advance achieved in 1944–1945, which tended to outrun redeployment of air units and supplies. The maneuvering, or redeployment, of air strength along the front was used to achieve the desired concentration of planes for air operations during major thrusts. After the Third Byelorussian Front cracked the German defenses, forces were shifted to other *fronty*. Using these methods of maneuvering air units, the VVS could assure itself of both numerical superiority in key sectors and the support required by the different ground-force operations along the front and in depth.

The VVS air armies and ADD com-

pleted 153,545 sorties, an average of more than 2,250 sorties daily, during the Byelorussian operation (see table 1). Unmatched in any other wartime operation, this numerical accomplishment was an excellent indication of the VVS' new role in the Soviet war effort. More important, the impact of the tactical air forces on the outcome of the ground fighting was becoming more decisive with each successive offensive operation.

Backed by the 3,052 aircraft of S. A. Krasovsky's Second Air Army, Konev's forces opened their two-phase offensive against Army Group North Ukraine on July 13. By the end of the month the First Ukrainian Front, drained of strength, went over to the defensive in order to hold its gains. During the course of the offensive, the Eighth Air Army moved up on August 2 to temporarily join the Second Air

Army. On August 5, however, the Fourth Ukrainian Front, under I. E. Petrov, was reestablished. Along with units of Konev's *front* and the Eighth Air Army, it was assigned to a frontal sector in the Carpathian foothills between Konev and Malinovsky's Second Ukrainian Front. From July 13 through August 29, the Second Air Army flew 48,725 sorties.

Victory: January–September 1945

The Vistula-Oder Operation: January–February 1945

From June through December 1944, Germany had suffered one disaster after another on the eastern front. In rapid succession, Army Groups Center and North Ukraine were smashed in the Byelorussian and L'vov-Sandomir operations, Finland was knocked out of the war, Rumania and its invaluable oil fields were lost in August and September, Bulgaria pulled out of the war, Greece and most of Yugoslavia were evacuated, Budapest was invested, and Hungary was occupied as far west as Lake Balaton. Pinched from both east and west, Hitler gambled on mounting the Ardennes offensive in December in an effort to drive back the British and Americans and thus free his forces for operations against the Soviet armies in the east. Although this gamble enjoyed fleeting success, it chewed up irreplaceable forces and reserves; its ultimate effect, in combination with the results of Hitler's vain attempt to retake Budapest early in January, was to set the stage for the great Soviet victories of January–May 1945.

The situation in the air by January 1945 ran completely against the Luftwaffe. Although its numerical strength was not much less than it had been in the previous year, it was absolutely outnumbered by the VVS and Allied air forces. Further-

more, what aircraft it had were more often on the ground than in the air because of lack of fuel–the result of the loss of the Rumanian oil fields at Ploesti and Anglo-American bombing of German refineries and transportation systems. On January 1, 1945, the Luftwaffe had 1,900 aircraft (1,200 fighters) in the west, 1,700 fighters for the Reich's defense, and 1,875 (360 fighters) deployed against the Soviet forces. The Sixth Air Fleet, with 1,060 aircraft (but only 190 fighters), possessed by far the most planes, but it had to cover the front from the Baltic and East Prussia to Czechoslovakia. With the Ardennes offensive a failure, the Luftwaffe began transferring aircraft from west to east, where Soviet forces had been preparing another series of offensives for some months. But the 650 single-engine fighters and 100 attack aircraft slated for redeployment could in no way alter the inevitable outcome in the east.

In January 1945, the Soviet armed forces numbered 7,109,000 men in front-line and reserve ground, naval, and air units. On the Soviet-German front the Red Army had 55 combined-arms, 6 tank, and 10 air armies, with 6 combined-arms armies and an air army in Stavka Reserve. The 11 air armies and 155 air divisions (including the naval air divisions) had 15,815 aircraft (excluding 975 Po-2s), of which 1,875 were naval and 275 were in reserve, to pit against 1,875 (1,960, by Soviet estimates) planes of the Luftwaffe. What made the difference, both on the ground and in the air, during 1944–1945 was not so much Russia's edge in manpower as her vast numerical superiority in equipment. From January 1944 to January 1945, although tank and mechanized units actually dropped from 81 to 64, tanks and self-propelled guns increased from 5,628 to 15,100. Air divisions grew from 128 to 155, while aircraft increased from

Table 2. VVS Deployment for Vistula-Oder Operation

	16th Air Army	*2nd Air Army*	*Total*
Air corps/air divisions			
Fighter	3/9	3/10	6/19
Attack	2/6	3/6	5/12
Bomber	1/6	2/5	3/11
Total	6/21	8/21	14/42
Operational aircraft			
Fighter	1,131	1,172	2,303
Attack	735	775	1,510
Bomber	327	417	774
Night bomber	172	120	292
Reconnaissance	94	104	198
Total	2,459	2,588	5,047

8,818 to 15,815. Frontal VVS strength grew to 29 air corps, 121 divisions, and 29 independent regiments, with 11,530 operational combat aircraft and 980 Po-2 light night bombers. This growth was accomplished with the modest addition of 59,000 men, VVS manpower going from 408,000 in January 1944 to 467,000 a year later.

Since September 1944, the First Byelorussian and First Ukrainian (Konev) *fronty* on the central sector of the front in Poland had quietly but busily planned and prepared for another major offensive. On November 12, the Soviet western front from the Baltic to the Carpathians was divided into three main sectors for future operations against the heart of the Third Reich. Rokossovsky was transferred to the Second Byelorussian Front deployed against East Prussia to make way for Zhukov who now assumed command of the First Byelorussian Front. Zhukov's reappearance as a front commander was significant, for the Stavka intended nothing less than the final destruction of Germany in its winter offensive. The two-part plan called first for the clearing of Poland and

East Prussia and then the capture of Berlin and a Soviet advance to the Elbe River.

As the first step, the Stavka and frontal staffs planned two closely coordinated operations for the latter half of January, one to liberate Poland and drive to the Oder River and the other to cut off and destroy German forces in East Prussia. For the Vistula-Oder operation, the First Byelorussian and First Ukrainian *fronty* were built up to 163 divisions, 6,460 tanks and self-propelled guns, and 2,200,000 men. On their designated breakthrough sectors, the two *fronty* held tremendous superiority over the German defenders— nine to one in men, nine or ten to one in artillery, and ten to one in tanks and self-propelled guns (see table 2).

Rudenko's Sixteenth Air Army, which was slated to support Zhukov, was enlarged from 1,265 aircraft in November to 2,459 aircraft by January 10, 1945, giving the VVS a superiority of more than twenty to one over the Luftwaffe on the important Warsaw-Berlin axis, where Zhukov's main blow would fall. Krasovsky's Second Air Army, assigned to Konev's *front,* had 2,588 operational

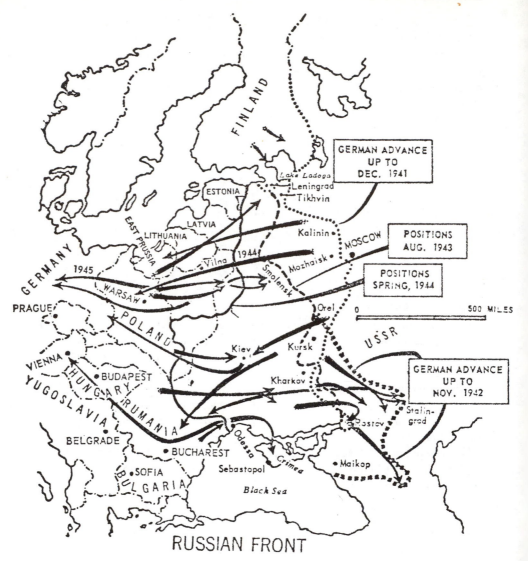

Figure 35. Major military offensives on the Russian front.

aircraft. To the north, Vershinin's Fourth Air Army supporting Rokossovsky had 1,593 operational aircraft, and Khriukin's First Air Army with Chernayakovsky's Third Byelorussian Front had 1,504. With 3,097 tactical aircraft and the Eighteenth Air Army supporting the East Prussian operation and 5,047 for the Vistula-Oder offensive, the VVS mustered 8,144 aircraft (excluding the Eighteenth Air Army) against 1,875 of the Luftwaffe's Sixth Air Fleet.

At the request of the Western Allies, Stalin advanced the date of the Soviet offensives from January 20 to January 12 in order to relieve the pressure in the Ardennes. To gain maximum effect, the operations were carefully staggered. The First Ukrainian Front opened the Vistula offensive on January 12. The next day,

Chernyakovskii attacked toward Königsberg; then on January 14, Rokossovsky's Second Byelorussian Front began its left hook east of the Vistula to the Baltic in an effort to cut off East Prussia while Zhukov forged ahead north and mainly south of Warsaw.

On January 17, Warsaw fell to the Polish First Army, which the Sixteenth Air Army had supported with 6,656 sorties. Two days later, Lodz was taken. Bydgoszcz was reached on January 23, Poznan was invested on January 25 (although it did not surrender until February 23), and Soviet forces crossed the German border on January 29. As had happened in the south, an unexpected thaw late in January and overextended lines of communication, combined with the exposed position of the long right flank stretching back to the Vistula, which was vulnerable to German forces in Pomerania, brought Zhukov to a halt. By February 2, however, the First Byelorussian Front had liberated virtually all of central and western Poland and pushed an armored salient to Küstrin and Frankfurt on the Oder River, just forty miles east of Berlin.

In these operations, according to Soviet figures, thirty-five German divisions were destroyed, another twenty-five suffered 60–75-percent losses, and 147,400 officers and men were captured along with 1,377 tanks and assault guns, 8,280 guns, 5,707 mortars, 19,490 machine guns, and 1,360 aircraft. The two *fronty* had advanced 310 miles along a 500-mile front in twenty-three days at an average rate of 12–14 miles a day, although the tank armies had hit a pace of 25–30 miles a day at their peak. At the conclusion of the Vistula-Oder operation, the Red Army was within easy striking distance of Berlin and thus of the end of the war. (See figure 35 for map showing major offensives on the Russian front and the situation in the spring of 1945.)

The Battle for Berlin: April–May 1945

After the Vistula-Oder operation had been completed and before the final drive on Berlin could be undertaken, the Stavka decided to finish the East Prussian matter and clear the flanks of the First Byelorussian and First Ukrainian *fronty*. Rokossovsky and Vasilevsky (who had replaced Chernyakovsky, killed on February 18) had squeezed the German forces tightly into the area around Königsberg and along the Frisches Haff by early March. The Third Byelorussian Front assumed responsibility for the final reduction of the fortress area of Königsberg, a goal which was accomplished by an April 4–9 assault. Rokossovsky had already shifted his forces to the west in an attempt to clear eastern Pomerania, the Polish Corridor, and Danzig of German troops by early April. The First Byelorussian Front completed the western phase of the Pomeranian operation against Army Group Vistula during the first half of March. Meanwhile, it had pinched out the German bridgehead over the Oder at Küstrin and then forced the abandonment of the German position in Küstrin's *Alte Stadt* west of the river in an effort to straighten its line and strengthen its bridghead over the Oder. While Zhukov and Rokossovsky removed the exposed right flank of the First Byelorussian Front, Konev swept the Germans out of most of Upper and Lower Silesia, invested Breslau, and had pushed up to the Neisse River by March 31.

When Stalin, the Stavka, and the frontal commanders began their final planning conferences in early April 1945 in preparation for the attack on Berlin, the Soviet front line ran along the Oder River from the Baltic to its confluence with the Neisse and then down the Neisse to a point north of the Czech border. The repositioned

Second Byelorussian Front, along with the Fourth Air Army, held the northern section of the line; Zhukov's First Byelorussian Front was in the center, directly east of Berlin, with the Sixteenth and Eighteenth air armies, and the right flank of the First Ukrainian Front, with Krasovsky's Second Air Army, was deployed along the Neisse. Their combined forces held a clear superiority over the defending German forces.

As far as the air forces were concerned, the situation was not much different. The loss of aircraft factories and training facilities to the Soviet advances of January–March had further weakened the Luftwaffe, whose command structure and logistic system were on the verge of complete disintegration. Many of its pilots were barely trained, little fuel was available for combat flying, and what airfields were operational were under constant Soviet and Allied attack. In an attempt to protect Berlin, perhaps more than 2,200 aircraft had been crammed on the fields around the city by late March.

The VVS prepared carefully for the Berlin operation because of its great importance and because of the projected intensity of Luftwaffe resistance. The Stavka reinforced the air armies with thirteen air corps and thirteen independent divisions, bringing Soviet air strength to 7,496 operational combat aircraft by the time the offensive began, while Polish air force units added 216 more aircraft.

To sustain this force of 209 regiments in 19 air corps and 65 divisions of the Second, Fouth, and Sixteenth air armies, 23 air-base regions (RAB) and 163 aviation maintenance battalions (BAO) were established at the 290 bases and fields that had been set up for these air units. All of the fields were sited within sixty-five miles of the front, except for those of the Eighteenth Air Army's units that were located around Poznan in western Poland. The logistics buildup for such a large-scale operation was of major significance; at the Sixteenth Air Army's fields alone, 16,600 tons of air munitions and 15,300 tons of fuel were stocked for the impending offensive.

As always, the VVS units had as their primary mission the preparation and support of ground-force operations. Because Zhukov's First Byelorussian Front had been assigned the lead role in capturing Berlin, and because it had the strongest defenses to penetrate on its planned path to the city, it received the majority of the air force support. Besides the 3,384 tactical aircraft in the Sixteenth Air Army, 800 bombers of Golovanov's Eighteenth Air Army were assigned to this *front,* so that their full impact would be concentrated for Zhukov's operations. The Sixteenth Air Army conducted extensive reconnaissance missions (2,600 sorties) prior to the attack from the Küstrin bridgehead in order to pinpoint enemy defenses and dispositions. Heavy day-and-night bombing attacks were planned for the preparatory and breakthrough phases. Attack aircraft and tactical bombers were to closely follow the massed strike of the Eighteenth Air Army's 800 bombers against strong points and secondary defenses which was planned for just before sunrise. For the actual attack and breakthrough, 90 percent of Rudenko's air strength was assigned to support the ground units. Seven air corps and eight independent air divisions (2,458 aircraft, or 78 percent) of the Sixteenth Air Army VVS units were lined up to support the Fifth Shock and Eighth Guards armies, which were assigned to open the road to Berlin, and the First and Second Guards tank armies, which had been designated to take the city.

When the Fifth Shock and Eighth Guards armies launched Zhukov's attack

Figure 36. P-63 King Cobra in Soviet markings on Lend-Lease duty in November 1944.

on April 16, a thick fog hugged the marshy river bottomlands of the Oder and Alte Oder. Mingling with the smoke and dust thrown up by the barrage, the fog prevented close air support except by small groups of Il-2s. The attacking infantry units were soon hung up in the bottomlands, and the two tank armies piled up behind the infantry units. By early afternoon the fog had burned away, and Pe-2s and Il-2s began operating in large numbers. Without the VVS, this situation could have proved very uncomfortable for the ground forces, because the Luftwaffe was very active. Although the Sixteenth and Eighteenth air armies flew 6,550 sorties, the attacking forces made little progress that day.

By April 17 Zhukov had still made no progress, despite the four ground and two tank armies crammed into the attack zone. Air support was strong but hampered by continuing foggy conditions. Finally, on April 18, ground was gained west of Wriezen and southwest of Seelow. By April 19 the German Ninth Army was cracking, as Soviet forces pushed west as far as Muencheberg while the Second Guards Tank Army had broken out to the west of Wriezen. On the next day the

Fourth Air Army shifted its support from the central sector to the north as the Second Byelorussian Front struck across the Oder from Schwedt to Stettin. Meanwhile, Konev's and Zhukov's forces moved forward on Berlin against waning German resistance. On April 25 the Second and Fourth guards tank armies linked up west of the city, just northwest of Potsdam, to complete the encirclement of the capital.

As the Soviet forces closed the ring around Berlin, the Luftwaffe's activity slackened considerably because of the loss of most of its fields. This factor greatly eased the tasks of the VVS. In preparation for the storming of the city, Rudenko worked out Operation Salute (*Saliut*) for the Sixteenth and Eighteenth air armies. More than 100 heavy bombers of the Eighteenth Air Army began this operation on the night of April 24. On the following day, the Sixteenth Air Army staged two massive raids with a total of 1,486 aircraft, 560 of them Pe-2 dive bombers that attacked defensive positions. That night, 563 bombers of the Eighteenth Air Army concluded Salute by dropping 569 tons of bombs on Berlin. After heavy artillery preparation and with full air support, Soviet forces jumped off on

April 26 to complete the conquest of Berlin. As soon as airfields in the city fell to advancing Soviet troops, fighter regiments were moved in to provide better and more continuous cover against the sporadic attacks of the Luftwaffe.

After Hitler committed suicide on April 30, what little organized resistance was left soon collapsed. Just after noon on May 1, May Day, K. V. Novoselov of the 115th Guards Fighter Regiment and I. A. Malinovsky of the 1st Guards Fighter Regiment, both of the Second Air Army, dropped red banners by parachute over the Reichstag. Looking down, the fliers could see the red banner that Sgts. M. A. Egorov and M. V. Kantariia of the Third Shock Army had placed on the roof of the gutted Reichstag on the previous evening. Gen. Helmuth Weidling, commander of the Berlin defenses, crossed the Soviet lines early the next morning and surrendered the city to V. I. Chuikov, commander of the Eighth Guards Army and defender of Stalingrad, where the long and bloody road to Berlin and victory had begun two and one-half years before.

During the seventeen-day Berlin operation, the VVS units flew 91,384 sorties, fought 1,317 air combats, and claimed 1,232 enemy aircraft destroyed in the air and on the ground, in addition to sizable numbers of other military equipment, for a loss of 527 aircraft. As Soviet forces advanced and the Luftwaffe fields fell, the VVS was unchallenged in the air over Berlin, striking powerfully where and when it wanted or was needed. Air operations at Berlin and to the south in Austria and at Prague concluded the third and final period of the Great Patriotic War against Germany. From December 1943 to May 1945, the VVS flew 1,470,000 combat sorties—a graphic illustration of the extent to which it had matured as a carefully honed instrument of tactical air warfare

which had played a decisive role in the victory over Germany.

Manchuria: August–September 1945

The unconditional surrender of Germany on May 8, 1945, ended the war in Europe. The Red Army and VVS, however, had one more campaign to fight before peace was restored. At Yalta in February 1945, Stalin had agreed to enter the war against Japan within several months after the conclusion of the European fighting. In mid-May he ordered A. M. Vasilevsky, former chief of the General Staff, to the Far East to assume control of the planning and preparation of the Trans-Baikal (under R. Ya. Malinovsky) and Far Eastern (under M. A. Purkaev) *fronty* for conducting military operations against the Japanese Kwantung Army in Manchuria. To carry out his mission, Vasilevskii was appointed commander in chief of Soviet forces in the Far East, operating directly under Stalin and the Stavka.

Because of the length of the front and the complexity of the offensive tasks, K. A. Meretskov's Primorsk Group was redesignated the First Far Eastern Front on August 2 and Purkaev's command became the Second Far Eastern Front. Thus, three *fronty* and three attached air armies were poised for action against the Japanese forces—Malinovsky's Trans-Baikal with the Twelfth Air Army (under S. A. Khudiakov), the Second Far Eastern with the Tenth Air Army (under P. F. Zhigarev), and the First Far Eastern with the Ninth Air Army (under I. M. Sokolov). In addition, the Pacific Fleet and its naval air forces, under P. N. Lemeshko, were available for operations against the Kuriles, southern Sakhalin, and northern Korea.

Veteran combat units and equipment were transferred from Europe to the Far East during May, June, and July to

Figure 37. American Lend-Lease aircraft awaiting delivery to the Soviet Union at Ladd Field in Alaska. Among them are P-39s, Airacobras, A-20 Havocs, and Mitchells.

augment the buildup that had begun in February. Because the Trans-Baikal and First Far Eastern *fronty* carried the burden of the offensive, the Twelfth and Ninth air armies received the bulk of the air reinforcements coming from Europe. To organize the air operations for Vasilevsky, Stalin sent A. A. Novikov, chief of the VVS, to the Far East as Stavka representative for aviation.

Although a sizable and formidable force on paper, the Kwantung Army's best units and equipment had been withdrawn long before to fight in China or in the Pacific or to defend the home islands. The forces remaining in the summer of 1945 (790,000 men, 1,215 armored vehicles, 1,800 aircraft, 6,700 guns and mortars) presented little serious opposition for the battle-hardened, bountifully equipped, and well-led Soviet ground, naval, and air forces. With 1,577,725 men, 26,137 guns and mortars, 5,556 tanks and self-propelled guns, and 5,366 aircraft, Vasilevsky had overwhelming superiority for the planned "blitz" against the Kwantung Army by the Trans-Baikal Front from Mongolia and the First Far Eastern Front from the Maritime Territory. Yet significant problems were encountered in planning the Manchurian operation. Most of these were related to the extreme length of the fronts and distances separating

attacking forces and to the barren desert and mountain terrain that dominated the main attack routes toward Changchun, Kirin, Tsitsihar, Harbin, and Mukden.

The geographic and climatic factors required a particularly heavy emphasis on air reconnaissance and on air transport for resupply of the tank and combined-arms armies once they were in action. Such resupply was especially important for the Trans-Baikal Front's Sixth Guards Tank Army (under A. G. Kravchenko) which would have to cross desert plains and the Great Hsingan Mountains in a nonstop, 500-mile drive toward Changchun and Mukden. Two transport air divisions (189 Li-2 and C-47 aircraft) were assigned to Khudiakov's air army to ensure aerial resupply. Moreover, the rapid rate of advance contemplated would require the Twelfth Air Army to maintain six air divisions, not only to disrupt Japanese communications and troop movements but also to provide air support once the ground units had moved beyond the range of fighter and attack aircraft.

Given the prospect of Japan's imminent collapse and his own knowledge of the atomic bomb (knowledge he had acquired at the Potsdam Conference), Stalin moved up the date of the Manchurian operation from September to early August. Although not fully ready, the Soviet offensive began on the night of August 8, just minutes after Japan was notified of the Soviet declaration of war and two days after the first atomic bomb was dropped on Hiroshima. To ensure complete surprise, the Trans-Baikal Front struck without preliminary artillery or air preparation. During the following day, VVS bombers of the Ninth and Twelfth air armies hit military and industrial targets at Changchun and Harbin as well as railways, stations, airfields, and command centers in Manchuria and northern Korea. Air opposition was virtually nonexistent. By the fourth day, the Sixth Guards Tank Army had advanced 280 miles through the Great Hsingan range and into the central Manchurian plain on the way to Mukden and Changchun. Advanced elements entered those cities on August 20–21.

While Malinovsky pushed eastward against weak Japanese forces, Meretskov's First Far Eastern Front attacked Suifenho on the night of August 8 in heavy rain. By August 11, Meretskov's forces had broken through the city's defenses, but they were still engaged in heavy fighting when the capitulation occurred on August 20. Meanwhile, the Second Far Eastern Front had crossed the Amur River south of Blagovshchensk, and on August 20 Kirin and Harbin fell to Soviet forces.

During active military operations from August 9–20, VVS and naval air units flew 14,030 combat and 7,427 noncombat sorties despite the heavy rains of August 11–20, which restricted air activity. The large number of sorties flown for noncombat purposes (35 percent of the total) —mainly for reconnaissance, communications, and transport—was an unusual feature of these air operations, but these missions were required by the nature of the theater and by the concept of operations adopted for the campaign. Novikov

and the VVS staffs again showed their ability to adapt air support to the needs of ground-force operations.

On August 19, Gen. Hikosaburo Hata, chief of staff of the Kwantung Army, surrendered the Japanese forces in Manchuria and Korea, as specified in the Imperial Rescript of August 16. Stalin declared the Manchurian operation successfully terminated on August 23, although Soviet troops continued to move forward to occupy Dalny and Port Arthur on the Liaotung Peninsula and on into north Korea. The formal document of surrender was signed aboard the *USS Missouri* in Tokyo Bay on September 2. At long last, the war was over on all fronts.

The Role of the Red Air Force in World War II

While sadly oblivious to their own culpability, Soviet historians and military writers have valid reasons for their frequent attacks on Western "bourgeois falsificators" who have neither understood nor given proper credit to the Soviet Union's principal role in the defeat of Germany. The simple fact is that the weight of historical evidence falls on the Soviet side. The Soviet-German front was undoubtedly decisive in the war's final outcome. Drawn into a savage, exhausting war of attrition for which they were militarily and economically unprepared, the German armed forces had suffered huge losses in men and material which had weakened them to the point where defeat was inevitable even before the first Allied soldiers set foot on French soil in June 1944. Smashed at the opening of Barbarossa in 1941, the Red Air Force made a recovery that must stand as one of the most remarkable achievements in modern military history. By 1944, a rehabilitated Red Air Force dominated the skies over the front. Just as the Soviets have always stressed, the

Figure 38. Li-2 at Orly airport, Paris, in 1945. This aircraft was the licensed copy of the Douglas DC-3.

ultimate victory over Germany was a victory of combined arms—ground, sea, and air forces each contributing vitally to the eventual triumph over Hitler and the Wehrmacht. In this context, the VVS' wartime role must be evaluated.

During the years since 1945, however, the exact role of the Red Air Force in World War II has defied precise evaluation. Partly, this has been the result of a myopic, if natural, Western concentration on the American, British, and French involvement in the war against Germany. Little was known about the war in the east, and wartime propaganda—especially that concerning Lend-Lease aid to the Soviet Union—exaggerated the significance of Allied assistance in stopping the German onslaught. Many postwar German works frequently attempted to exonerate the military leaders, blaming Hitler and the Nazis for the

military reverses or attributing Soviet victories to numbers rather than skill. Also contributing to the failure of understanding were the paucity of solid, factual Soviet histories of the war or of the VVS, at least until the post-Stalin era, and the continuing lack of access for Westerners to Soviet military archives. Even today, more than thirty years after the war, Soviet works remain riddled with questionable, incomplete, and misleading information, and they are strangely silent on such subjects as the disasters of June–November 1941, aircraft and crew losses, and serviceability rates of aircraft. Unfortunately, such statistics apparently are still considered indictments of the Communist party, the socialist system, and Soviet military leadership rather than historical facts that reflect the level of Soviet effort and sacrifice.

World War II was essentially a war of

Table 3. Troops and Weapons in Strategic Operations
(Battle for Moscow as base of 100)

Operation	Divisions	Men	Guns & Mortars	Tanks & Self-Propelled Guns	Aircraft
Moscow	100	100	100	100	100
Stalingrad	80	100	190	128	108
Belgorod-Kharkov	61	96	183	385	125
Byelorussia	171	209	500	860	666
Vistula-Oder	155	209	423	950	466
Berlin	179	227	520	894	666

Statistics from V. D. Sokolovsky, ed., *Soviet Military Strategy,* p. 242, table 5.

materiel, and the Soviet Union and its Western Allies won largely because they were better organized and better equipped to fight and win such a conflict. The Soviet victory over German forces in the east was won as much in the factories as on the battlefields, and this was particularly true of the air war. As a result of German blunders and miscalculations, the basic Soviet defense industries continued to function after the trying evacuation of 1941–1942. Under far greater strain than either its U.S. or British counterparts, the Soviet aircraft industry had to improvise in order to build combat aircraft in large numbers. Soviet aircraft designers and plant managers responded with unusual flexibility and innovation in resource allocation and utilization, production, and management so as to achieve maximum output with the limited skilled labor force and supplies of raw materials available. The best measure of their success was the 137,271 aircraft built from January 1941 through June 1945 (the total was 158,218 from 1939 to 1945), because these provided the VVS with the means to attain air superiority.

The plethora of combat aircraft poured forth by Soviet aircraft plants eventually allowed the Red Air Force to match the Luftwaffe in quality and to far outstip it in quantity. With the aid of more and better aircraft, more seasoned and well trained crews, and hard earned combat experience, the VVS recovered to seize command of the air over the eastern front. The abundance of troops and weapons available after 1942 enabled the Stavka to plan carefully and concentrate great masses of men and equipment for the offensive operations that broke the Wehrmacht in the east (see table 3).

The size of Soviet wartime aircraft production dwarfed the U.S. and British Lend-Lease contributions in aircraft, especially during the crucial 1941–1943 period. The U.S. delivered only 1,311 aircraft to the Soviet Union from October 1, 1941, to June 30, 1942, while 3,816 planes arrived from July 1, 1942, to June 30, 1943. Although helpful to the VVS, these aircraft hardly made the difference between victory and defeat. Total deliveries from the United States amounted to 14,018 aircraft (13,209 combat types), but most of the planes were Bell P-39 (Airacobra) and P-63 (King Cobra) and Curtiss P-40 fighters that were unwanted in the U.S. Army Air Force because of their inadequate performance.

Despite their shortcomings, Soviet pilots put the aircraft to good use. Many VVS Guards units, including that of A. I. Pokryshkin, flew Airacobras or King Cobras until late in the war with excellent results. More important than the actual aircraft provided through Lend-Lease were the stocks of basic goods and components that the Soviet Union could use for its own aircraft output but was unable to produce. Lend-Lease aid had the most profound impact in basic goods—gasoline, machine tools, trucks, boots, canned food, radars, and so on—rather than in such military hardware as combat aircraft, tanks, and guns. In neither area, however, was its impact discernible before the middle of 1943—that is, after Kursk.

Except for strategic bombing operations, the war provided the VVS with invaluable experience in all types of air operations. In the absence of any actual large-scale combat involvement during the past thirty years, the Soviet air force has drawn heavily on the experience of the Great Patriotic War to provide the doctrinal, tactical, and organizational foundations for the continuing development of Soviet air power. Indeed, the presence of so many wartime air leaders in positions of authority after the war reinforced this tendency. The air war of 1941–1945 also figured prominently in the debate on military strategy and policy within the Soviet military establishment. The "traditionalists" have looked back to the Great Patriotic War for valid historical reasons to enlighten and guide present-day military doctrine, while the "modernists" have seen little applicability of past lessons to the conditions to be faced in nuclear warfare. Whatever the shifting currents of Soviet military thought, the experience of the war has been burned indelibly into the Soviet military memory and remains the foundation for postwar developments, in both theory and practice.

Some Western observers have frequently, and unjustifiably, criticized the overwhelming Soviet emphasis on tactical aviation during the war. Clearly, though this decision was made prior to the war and was reinforced by the early reverses, it eventually proved to be correct. With little immediate prospect of any substantial aid from its allies, the Soviet leadership knew that the battle against the Germans was a life-or-death struggle to be won or lost on the ground in the vast expanses of the Soviet Union. The pressing frontal requirements, along with the inherent Soviet tactical and doctrinal inclinations, resulted in an even greater emphasis on the development of a tactical air force that could be built quickly in large numbers and which could have a direct influence on the battlefield. In these circumstances, the fighter and ground-attack air arms received the greatest attention because of their direct relationship to the ground fighting.

The fighter force had the principal role in the Soviet doctrine of air warfare; thus it had the number-one priority in production and crews. Soviet fighters battled for and held air superiority, thereby preventing German air operations while permitting VVS attack and bomber units to operate more freely and effectively. The fighter arm developed slowly despite its elite status, but by 1943 the crews and aircraft were available in numbers and quality sufficient to take control over the front. Soviet fighter dominance grew steadily from then on, finally reaching a superiority of forty to one or more by 1945. Although escort and attack operations became more common late in the war, the struggle for air superiority always remained the Soviet fighter arm's overriding responsibility, accounting for 35 percent (slightly more than 1 million) of all VVS combat sorties. During the war, more than 1,500,000 fighter sorties were flown for all purposes and 44,000 enemy aircraft claimed—approximately 57 percent of all hostile aircraft destroyed on the Soviet-German front.

At first, support operations for the Soviet ground forces were small, poorly coordinated, and conducted in the face of nearly total German air supremacy. Although the ground forces suffered accordingly, it was not from lack of effort on the part of attack units, which—often without fighter escort—took severe losses. By Stalingrad the VVS had recovered sufficiently to begin effective cooperation with the ground forces. Thanks to the growing number of Il-2 Shturmoviks—the best attack aircraft of the war—the Stavka was able to plan the first "air offensive" for Stalingrad, although poor weather conditions prevented its consummation. The VVS continually refined the air-offensive concept until, during the major operations of 1944–1945, it could provide heavy, continuous air support from preparation through exploitation. These air operations normally involved overwhelming superiority—sometimes as many as 2,000 tactical aircraft were concentrated in narrow attack zones—and often caused devastating results, as in the Byelorussian offensive of June–August 1944. Tactical bombers and fighter-bombers took part in these operations, but the Il-2 "Ilies" dominated the ground-support mission. The best indicator of the VVS' tactical emphasis and of the importance of attack aviation in the overall Soviet air effort was that more than 46 percent of all combat sorties were flown in support of the ground forces.

The VVS was most notably deficient in strategic bombing operations. Of the 3,124,000 combat sorties flown during the war, the Long-Range Air Force (ADD and later Eighteenth Air Army) completed 215,000 (7 percent), of which only 6,607 (0.2 percent) were classed as independent air operations against industrial-economic targets. Lacking a true strategic role, the ADD became, in essence, an adjunct to the frontal bomber force; it completed 168,000 sorties (5.4 percent) against such tactical targets as lines of communication, reserves, and supply depots. The Luftwaffe, too, became enmeshed in the tactical air war to the extent that its medium bombers were drawn into ground support, to the detriment of possible strategic air operations against lines of communication and industrial objectives. Many Western observers have denigrated Soviet air operations against Germany because the Soviets employed no strategic bombing offensive, as did the Royal Air Force and the U.S. Army Air Force. Yet the Soviet decision to opt for a tactical air force had a definite strategic objective—to provide the air support necessary for ground forces to stop the German advance and then defeat the German armed forces on the battlefield.

Certainly the statistics of the air war waged by the VVS are impressive. Frontal and ADD elements flew 3,124,000 combat sorties—858,000 from June 1941 to November 18, 1942; 796,000 from November 19, 1942, through December 1943; and 1,470,000 from December 1943 through May 1945. From an average of 48,000 sorties per month in 1942, the VVS jumped to 68,000 monthly in 1944 and 147,000 in 1945. Conversely, the Luftwaffe dropped from 41,000 monthly in 1942 to 39,000 in 1943 and finally to 15,600 in 1945. While these figures reflect the reversals of fortune taking place in the air war, they do not adequately show the entire picture. All VVS arms completed 3,808,136 combat sorties, in which 696,268 tons of bombs and 1,628,059 tons of fuels and lubricants were expended. In addition, VVS logistics units built 8,545 airfields and thousands of aircraft shelters, command posts, ammunition and fuel depots, and miscellaneous structures.

Wartime experience demonstrated the inherent flexibility and adaptability of Soviet air power, which became increasingly evident as the VVS' organizational structure changed in response to the shifting demands and circumstances of the front, available aircraft and crew resources, and tactics. Forced into a series of improvisations as a result of the early losses, the Stavka and the VVS in 1942 established the air army as the main organizational element of the frontal air war. Formed of integral air divisions and regiments, the air army provided a simple and effective structure that could be expanded easily and quickly so as to conduct the wide variety of air activities required for offensive and defensive operations. With an air army attached to each front, air-ground cooperation and air support were vastly improved, and the Stavka could more readily concentrate its air forces and coordinate the air operations of several fronts. Thus, the VVS' organizational refinement after 1941 resulted in the more effective application of air power because it provided the proper framework for using available aircraft and crews as well as for developing new tactics.

As the Red Army eviscerated the German army during nearly four years of savage ground fighting, the Red Air Force recovered from its opening debacle to gut the Luftwaffe and make a great contribution to the ground war. At various times during the war, the Eastern Front accounted for between 38 and 67 percent of the Luftwaffe's strength. Expecting another blitzkrieg victory according to Hitler's designs, the Luftwaffe was drawn inexorably into a tactical air war for which it had neither the long-range plans nor the crews and equipment. Soon embroiled in a mass war of attrition that favored the USSR, the Luftwaffe eventually found itself subordi-

nated to the army's demands, badly outnumbered, and relegated to an auxiliary role in the fighting. The constant pounding and attrition in the east consumed crews, aircraft, and support equipment, devouring many of the best units and sapping the strength of the Luftwaffe. The heavy losses sustained in the Russian campaign played a significant part in reducing the once-powerful Luftwaffe to a state of atrophy. From June 22, 1941, through December 1943, when the main German air and ground effort was in the east, the Luftwaffe air-crew losses ran to 30,483 killed and missing and 10,827 wounded and injured—41,670 out of a total of 81,403 wartime casualties.

The total losses on both sides in the east are impossible to assess. The Soviet Union claimed 77,000 enemy aircraft destroyed or captured during the fighting. Of these, VVS fighters are credited with 44,000 (57 percent of all German aircraft destroyed), 13,000 were destroyed in attacks on airfields (17 percent), and flak, capture, and miscellaneous causes accounted for the remaining 20,000. From December 1943 to the end of the war, the VVS claimed 21,000 aircraft—15,000 destroyed in the air, 2,500 on airfields, and the rest lost to antiaircraft artillery, capture, and other means. (Comparisons of Soviet claims with German aircraft production figures raise more questions than answers.) Soviet losses are much more difficult to ascertain, because little has ever been officially said about either total losses or losses in specific operations. However, some idea of the magnitude of the Soviet losses can be gained from the fact that Luftwaffe fighter pilots were credited with 45,000 aircraft destroyed on the eastern front. If this figure is accepted as reliable, the VVS' total losses during the war probably ranged between 70,000 and 80,000 aircraft.

Because of the huge number of kills

Table 4. Soviet Aces with more than 50 Victories (1941–1945)

Kozhedub, Ivan N.	62
Pokryshkin, Aleksandr I.	59
Rechkalov, Grigorii A.	58
Gulaev, Nikolai D.	57 (4 before June 1941)
Vorozheikin, Arsenii V.	52 (6 in Mongolia)
Yevstigneev, Kirill A.	52
Glinka, Dmitrii B.	50
Klubov, Alexsandr F.	50

recorded by German aces—103 claimed more than 100 victories, 13 claimed more than 200, and 2 more than 300, many of which were achieved against the VVS—Soviet fighter pilots have received scarce attention or recognition. The German totals, while certainly indicative of skill, were more the result of the particular conditions of the air war in the east. The abundance of VVS aircraft, the small size of the Luftwaffe fighter force, the use of the pair system (an ace protected by a covering wingman), the large number of missions flown (because of the proximity of German airfields to the front), the short duration of most missions (due to the short range of German fighters), and the inadequate preparation and training of VVS fliers and units in the early years—all these factors contributed to the high scores racked up by the Luftwaffe aces. Although attrition and strain took a bloody toll of German crews and aircraft, Soviet fighter pilots must be credited with more than holding their own against the more skilled Luftwaffe fliers. Even the greatest of the German aces were shot down several times, and some with more than 200 victories were lost in aerial combat. In an air war so ferocious and massive as was that on the eastern front, mere survival was a measure of skill. Erich Hartmann, the leading fighter ace of the war with 352 victories (345 in the east), flew 1,405 sorties, engaged in 825 aerial combats, and was shot or forced down 16

times. In contrast, A. I. Pokryshkin, the second-ranking Soviet and Allied ace with 59 victories, flew 560 combat sorties and engaged in 156 air combats, while the leading ace, Ivan N. Kozhedub, racked up 330 sorties, 120 air combats, and 62 victories. The records of the leading Soviet aces—all of whom easily topped the British, U.S., and French aces—verified the German contention that they were equal to any in the war (see table 4).

The Red Air Force certainly was a major contributor to the defeat of the Luftwaffe and the eventual destruction of Nazi Germany because of its important role in the Soviet victory in the east. Contrary to Soviet contentions, however, neither the VVS nor the Eastern Front were the decisive factors in the defeat of the Luftwaffe. When the war began, the Soviet Union was just learning how to employ the great potential of military air power, a potential whose full development was prevented by wartime circumstances. The nature of the fighting in the east and the VVS' rapid recovery forced the Luftwaffe into a tactical air war that it was unprepared to fight, bled it unmercifully, prohibited the concentration of German air effort on any one front or against the Anglo-American strategic air offensive, and helped the Allied air forces gain air superiority in the Mediterranean and western Europe. Adolf Galland, one of the Luftwaffe's earliest and most respected fighter aces, pinpointed the Russian campaign after the failure of Barbarossa in 1941 as "the real point of departure of the decline of the Luftwaffe.... The eastern front held Luftwaffe units in its clutches for three and a half more years and methodically ground them down. Luftwaffe effectiveness became nothing more than air support of ground forces on a numerically inadequate scale." Perhaps Luftwaffe Gen. Klaus Uebe best summed up the role of the Red Air Force in World War II:

As events show, Russian reactions to German Air Force operations, however primitive and makeshift in character, and however crude they might have first appeared to their more enlightened Western opponents, proved throughout the course of the war to be highly efficient, effective, and ultimately an important factor in the defeat of Germany.

During the Great Patriotic War of 1941–1945, the Soviet state, the Communist party, and the Soviet armed forces endured a terrible ordeal and emerged victorious from the most crucial period in Soviet history. For the Red Air Force, this trial by fire marked its transformation into a first-class, battle-hardened combat force and laid the foundations for the postwar development of Soviet air power.

Research Notes

In contrast to the scant research material available on some areas in the history of the Soviet air force, a vast body of literature exists about its performance during the Great Patriotic War. For the sake of convenience, these materials can be divided into two major groupings: Western and Soviet. Within each major group are several important subsections: general histories of the war, studies of major campaigns and battles, military memoirs, and studies of air operations, organization, and equipment.

Western histories of the war on the eastern front include George Blau, *The German Campaign in Russia, Planning and Operations: 1940–1942* (Washington, 1955); Paul Carell, *Hitler Moves East, 1941–1943* (Boston, 1965), and *Scorched Earth: The Russian-German War, 1943–1944* (Boston, 1965); Alan Clark, *Barbarossa: The Russo-German Conflict, 1941–1945* (New York, 1965); Barry Leach, *German Strategy against Russia, 1939–1941* (Oxford, 1973); John Erickson, *The Road to Stalingrad: Stalin's War with Germany* (New York, 1975); Albert Seaton, *The Russo-German War, 1941–1945* (New York, 1971); Alexander Werth, *Russia at War: 1941–1945* (New York, 1964); and Earl Ziemke, *Stalingrad to Berlin: The German Defeat in the East* (Washington, 1968).

Western studies of the major campaigns on the eastern front tend to concentrate on the German summer offensive of 1941, the Battle of Moscow, the Siege of Leningrad, Stalingrad, Kursk, and the final battle for Berlin. The Blau, Leach, and Erickson volumes treat the summer campaign of

1941 in some detail. Geoffrey Jukes has written three volumes on major campaigns: *The Defense of Moscow* (New York, 1970), *Stalingrad: The Turning Point* (New York, 1968), and *Kursk: The Clash of Armour* (New York, 1968). There are numerous accounts of the Leningrad blockade and siege, including Harrison Salisbury's *The 900 Days: The Siege of Leningrad* (New York, 1969) and Alan Wykes' *The Siege of Leningrad* (New York, 1968). Albert Seaton's *The Battle for Moscow, 1941-1942* (New York, 1971) treats the Soviet counteroffensive in detail. Few Western studies have examined the Soviet advance into eastern Europe. The best Western account of the final offensive against Berlin is Earl Ziemke's *Battle for Berlin: End of the Third Reich* (New York, 1968). The essays by Rudolf Hofmann, Hermann Gackenholz, and Walter Görlitz in *Decisive Battles of World War II: The German View,* ed. Hans-Adolf Jacobsen and Jürgen Rohwer (London, 1965), treat Moscow, Stalingrad, and the collapse of Army Group Center with judicious balance.

Western works on the air war over Russia and eastern Europe owe a heavy debt to German sources and accounts. A starting point for the study of air operations can be found in the many accounts of the rise and decline of the Luftwaffe. These include Werner Baumbach, *The Life and Death of the Luftwaffe* (New York, 1967); Cajus Bekker, *The Luftwaffe War Diaries* (New York, 1969); Adolf Galland, *The First and the Last: The Rise and Fall of the German Fighter Forces, 1938-1945* (New York, 1954); and the British Air Ministry's *Rise and Fall of the German Air Force, 1933-1945* (London, 1948). On specific aspects of German air operations against the USSR, see Paul Deichmann, *German Air Force Operations in Support of the Army,* USAF Historical Study no. 163 (Maxwell

AFB, Ala., 1962); Oleg Hoeffding, *German Air Attacks against Industry and Railroads in Russia, 1941-1945* (Santa Monica, Calif., 1970); Fritz Morzik, *German Air Force Airlift Operations,* USAF Historical Study no. 167 (Maxwell AFB, Ala., 1961); Richard Suchenwirth, *Command and Leadership in the German Air Force,* USAF Historical Study no. 174 (Maxwell AFB, Ala., 1969), and *Historical Turning Points in the German Air Force War Effort,* USAF Historical Study no. 189 (Maxwell AFB, Ala., 1969); Harry R. Fletcher, ed., *The German Air Force versus Russia, 1941,* USAF Historical Study no. 153 (Maxwell AFB, Ala., 1965), *The German Air Force versus Russia, 1942,* USAF Historical Study no. 154 (Maxwell AFB, Ala., 1966), and *The German Air Force versus Russia, 1943,* USAF Historical Study no. 155 (Maxwell AFB, Ala., 1967). Roberto Gentili's "The Italian Air Force in Russia," *Air Classics* 8, no. 12 (October 1972):20–27, provides one of the few accounts of the activities of German-allied air power on the eastern front. Hans Ulrich Rudel offers a personal account of ground-support operations in *Stuka Pilot* (New York, 1958).

Western works about the Soviet air force, in comparison to those about the Luftwaffe, have been few and superficial. Soviet air operations are treated in these general histories of Soviet air power: Robert A. Kilmarx, *A History of Soviet Air Power* (New York, 1962); Asher Lee, *The Soviet Air Force,* first ed. (London, 1950), second ed. (London, 1952), and American ed. (New York, 1962); and Robert Jackson, *The Red Falcons: The Soviet Air Force in Action, 1918-1969* (London, 1970). More specialized treatments of important aspects of Soviet air power during the war include Raymond Garthoff's "The Organization of Soviet Air Power" in Asher Lee, ed., *Soviet Air and Rocket Forces* (New York, 1959);

Oleg Hoeffding, *Soviet Interdiction Operations, 1941–1945* (Santa Monica, Calif., 1970); and Klaus Uebe, *Russian Reactions to German Air Power in World War II,* USAF Historical Study no. 176 (Maxwell AFB, Ala., 1964).

A few major studies of Soviet command structures and party-military relations deserve note. These include John Erickson, *The Soviet High Command* (New York, 1962); Raymond Garthoff, *How Russia Makes War: Soviet Military Doctrine* (London, 1954); and Roman Kolkowicz, *The Soviet Military and the Communist Party* (Princeton, N.J., 1967). The impact of technological transfers from the West on the development of the Soviet air force before and during World War II receives attention in Anthony C. Sutton, *Western Technology and Soviet Economic Development, 1930–1945* (Stanford, Calif., 1969).

Articles on the Soviet air force during World War II appear frequently in the following aviation journals: *Aerospace Historian, Wings, Airpower, Air Enthusiast, Flying Review,* and *Air Classics.* These journals have published important information on the technical characteristics of Soviet aircraft. Much of these data have, however, been printed in one comprehensive volume, Jean Alexander's *Russian Aircraft since 1940* (London, 1975).

Although Western scholars of Soviet affairs have long noted the problems related to ideological bias, *partiinost',* and Soviet patriotism which affect Soviet historical literature, Soviet works on the history of World War II and the role of the Soviet air force in that conflict represent a most important resource. While Soviet works must be read critically, they cannot be ignored.

The Soviets have published two massive multivolume surveys of the Great Patriotic War: Piotr Pospelov et al., eds., *Istoriia velikoi otechestvennoi voiny sovetskogo soiuza 1941–1945,* six vols. (Moscow, 1960–1965), and A. A. Grechko, ed., *Istoriia Vtoroi Mirovoi voiny 1939–1945,* five vols. as of this date (Moscow, 1973–). Both these works present accounts of the war according to the official Soviet periodization of the hostilities. The Soviet Institute of Military History has also issued numerous books dealing with individual operations and the memoirs of outstanding commanders. These include A. I. Eremenko, *The Arduous Beginning* (Moscow, 1966); A. G. Federov, *Aviatsiia v bitve pod Moskvoi,* second ed. (Moscow, 1975); S. A. Krasovsky, *Zhizn' v aviatsii* (Moscow, 1968); A. A. Grechko, *Bitva za Kavkaz* (Moscow, 1967), and the latter's English-language version, *Battle for the Caucasus* (Moscow, 1971); I. S. Konev, *Year of Victory* (Moscow, 1969); N. Krylov, *Glory Eternal: Defense of Odessa, 1941* (Moscow, 1972); V. D. Lavrinenko, *Vozvrashchenie v nebo* (Moscow, 1974); K. A. Meretskov, *Serving the People* (Moscow, 1971); A. K. Nedbailo, *V gvardeiskoi sem'e* (Kiev, 1975); I. V. Parotkin, ed., *Kurskaia bitva* (Moscow, 1970), and the English-language version, *The Battle of Kursk* (Moscow, 1974); A. I. Pokryshkin, *Nebo voiny* (Moscow, 1975); G. K. Prussakov et al., *16-ia vozdushnaia: voenno-istoricheskii ocherk o boevom puti 16-i vozdushnoi armii, 1942–1945* (Moscow, 1973); K. K. Rokossovsky, *Soldatskii dolg* (Moscow, 1968), and the English-language version, *A Soldier's Duty* (Moscow, 1970); S. I. Rudenko et al., *Sovetskie voenno-vozdushnye sily v Velikoi Otechestvennoi voiny, 1941–1945* (Moscow, 1968), and the English-language version, *The Soviet Air Force in World War II,* ed. Ray Wagner and trans. Leland Fetzer (Garden City, N.Y., 1973); A. L. Shepelev, *V Nebe i na zemle* (Moscow, 1974); S. M. Shtemenko, *General'nyi shtab v gody voiny* (Moscow, 1968), and the English-language version, *The General Staff at War, 1941–1945* (Moscow, 1970); K. A. Vershinin, *Chetvertaia vozdushnaia* (Moscow, 1975); G. K. Zhukov, *Vospominaniia i razmyshlenia* (Moscow, 1969), and the English-language version, *The Memoirs of Marshal Zhukov* (Moscow, 1971); A. V. Vorozheikin, *Nad kurskoi dugoi* (Moscow, 1962); L. V. Zholudev, *Stal'naia eskadril'ia* (Moscow, 1972); and V. Zubakov, *The Final Assault* (Moscow, 1975).

The organization of the Soviet economy during the war is discussed in N. A. Voznesensky, *Voennaia ekonomika SSSR v period otechestvennoi voiny* (Moscow, 1947), and its English-language version, *The Economy of the USSR during World War II* (Washington, 1948); and I. A. Gladkov, *Sovetskaia ekonomika v period Velikoi Otechestvennoi voiny, 1941–1945* (Moscow, 1970). Both are important works.

In regard to the Soviet aircraft industry during the war, the following works deserve special mention: A. S. Yakovlev, *50-let sovetskogo samoletostroeniia* (Moscow, 1968), and its English-language version, *Fifty Years of Soviet Aircraft Construction* (Jerusalem, 1970), and *Tsel' zhizni* (Moscow, 1966), along with the latter's English-language version, *Aim of a Lifetime* (Moscow, 1972); P. Avdeenko, "Sovetskoe samoletostroenie v gody predvoennykh piatiletok, 1929–1940," *Voenno-istoricheskii zhurnal* 16, no. 7 (July 1974): 84-89; and A. I. Shakhurin, "Aviatsionnaia prom'yshlennost' v gody Velikoi Otechstvennoi voiny," *Voprosy istorii*, 1975, no. 3 (March), pp. 134–154, and no. 4 (April),

pp. 91–103.

Numerous articles on air operations and organization wirtten by Soviet military historians and former commanders of the Soviet air armies have appeared in *Voenno-istoricheskii zhurnal, Soviet Military Review*, and *Krasnaia zvezda*. Marshals P. S. Kutakhov, S. A. Krasovsky, and A. A. Novikov have contributed articles on air operations in various theaters, including Poland, Berlin, and Manchuria. Novikov's article on the struggle for air superiority (A. A. Novikov and M. Kozhevnikov, "Bor'ba za strategicheskoe gospodstvo v vozdukhe," *Voenno-istoricheskii zhurnal* 14, no. 3 (March 1972): 22–31, deserves serious attention.

The systematic study of recent Soviet publications in regard to the role of the Soviet air force in World War II has been rarely undertaken in the West. In spite of the fact that the wartime experiences of Soviet aviation have greatly shaped the posture and organization of the air force during the postwar period, Western scholarship on this aspect of Soviet military history is not well developed. The mass of books and articles published during the last decade has not been critically examined, although there are signs of progress. Maj. Gen. M. Kazhevnikov's "Rozhdenie vozdushnykh armii," originally published in *Voenno-istoricheskii zhurnal* 14, no. 9 (September 1972): 68-72, appeared in translation as "Birth of the Air Armies" in *Aerospace Historian* 22, no. 2 (June 1975): 73-76. Such efforts should be continued.

6

The Development of Naval
Aviation, 1908-1975

Jacob W. Kipp

When one is looking at the development of naval aviation in Russia and the Soviet Union, it is important to keep in mind the traditional patterns and problems of their naval forces. Western writers and naval officers have been inclined to think in Mahanic terms of a sea power which requires control of the seas in wartime. Since the birth of the Russian navy, geography has made such a doctrine almost impossible, since the state has had to maintain several separate fleets operating in isolated seas against a variety of enemies under diverse conditions. Moreover, limited resources and immense land frontiers caused the government time and again to downgrade naval demands in favor of the army. Though Russian admirals have frequently had a fair idea of what was desirable, their forces have hardly reflected their astuteness. Yet they have tried to educate their political superiors about the vital role naval forces must play in the successful defense of national interests. The rulers in

St. Petersburg and, later, Moscow have, however, tended to treat the navy as either an auxiliary to the army or a tool for obtaining diplomatic leverage in a particular situation. For the admirals, the Crimean War proved unfortunate; on the one hand it showed that Russia's navy was technologically backward, while on the other it demonstrated that the navy was unnecessary for the empire's defense even against a coalition of powers led by Britain and France. Consequently, the number of naval personnel was reduced by 75 percent to 28,000, with the result that Russia had lost her position as the world's third-ranking naval power by the end of the century. Thus, when the navy was called upon to defend the empire's far-eastern territories, its forces were numerically inadequate and technologically inferior—a fact brought home by the destruction of the Pacific and Baltic fleets by the Japanese in 1904–1905.

After this disaster, naval officers, statesmen, and nationalist politicians combined

Figure 39. Il-4 on a free-hunting mission near the Baltic. This plane has been modified to carry a torpedo.

to successfully lobby for a modern fleet. They failed, however, to give clear guidance as to what sort of force should be created. Should Russia build a battle fleet around dreadnoughts or a coastal defense force around minelayers and submarines? This was the same debate in which Alfred Thayer Mahan and champions of *guerre du course* had engaged before the turn of the century. The answer for each side depended upon the purpose for which the fleet was intended. Advocates of dreadnoughts in the Baltic understood completely that such crafts' range and firepower far exceeded the needs of coastal defense; that they perceived such a Baltic squadron as the foundation of a powerful battle fleet that would operate far from the Baltic is demonstrated by the Franco-Russian naval convention of 1913, which provided Russia with naval facilities in the Mediterranean, and the government's desire to control the Bosporus and the Dardanelles. On the other hand, advocates of a coastal defense force accepted the need to defend the Baltic from attack but pointed out that Russia lacked the resources to keep pace with the British or German construction programs. Further, they pointed out that, although Russia lacked overseas colonies and markets, she did require huge expenditures for the modernization of her army.

Ultimately, the argument that dreadnought construction would enhance national prestige carried the Duma. Mahan's theories never became the doctrinal foundation for the fleet-building program; instead, a compromise based on financial circumstances resulted in the construction of battleships and the neglect of essential light forces. When war broke out in 1914, the Russian navy was unprepared. The new dreadnoughts were not ready for service, and, like Britain, Russia had to embark upon a crash construction program for light forces under the most difficult financial and technical conditions.

The Birth of Naval Aviation

During the World War I period, naval aviation made its first appearance in Russia. Since 1910 the Naval Ministry and the Naval General Staff had conducted exercises using fixed-wing and lighter-than-air craft as a part of naval operations in the Baltic. By 1913 sufficient progress had been made to warrant the formation of the Naval Air Service. The building of airfields, hangars, and support facilities was authorized, along with a small training program for naval aviators. In 1914 Russia possessed an interest in naval aviation only as a reconnaissance tool and an organizational nucleus. Considered more a toy than a

Figure 40. Formation of Mig-17 Fresco fighters passing a Skory-*class destroyer. About 9,000 of these planes were built. Both ship and planes are typical of the Soviet navy before the nuclear-rocket revolution.*

weapon, the airplane fascinated some young officers, while their superiors looked on it with disdain. The fact that the Naval Ministry had no systematic procurement program before the war resulted in the ac-

cumulation of a diverse inventory that included foreign and domestic designs, seaplanes and land-based types, and even a nautical variant of Sikorsky's giant, four-engined Ilia Muromets. (The latter, how-

Figure 41. Firebar-A (Yak-28) light reconnaissance bombers in service with Soviet army tactical aviation. Later version is known as Brewer-D.

ever, crashed only days after the start of hostilities, and no replacement was ordered.) Like all air services during World War I, the Russian Naval Air Service grew rapidly from a harmless infant into a promising adolescent.

Because of the very different situations in the Baltic and Black Sea theaters, naval aviation evolved in two quite separate forms. In the Baltic, Adm. N. O. Essen, a brilliant officer and commander of the fleet from 1908 until his death in 1915, foresaw the effectiveness of naval aviation in combined-arms operations. With a small, outgunned force, Essen turned to minelaying activities to defend Russian coastal waters and disrupt German shipping operating from the Vistula estuary. Although hampered by interference from both the Ministry of War and the court, he scored a number of successes, which included the capture of the German naval codes. Thereafter, four elements became crucial to the Allied war effort in the Baltic: the mine, the submarine (particularly modern British boats operating from Russian bases), radio-transmission monitoring, and naval aviation. Aircraft carried out reconnaissance during the long northern

days and by 1915 were engaging in bombing and strafing operations—the latter without much effect, however. Although surface clashes occurred throughout the war, the new technological means of war determined the character of these confrontations: the Russians refused to battle against superior German forces; instead, combat usually erupted over the laying or clearing of minefields, particularly during the struggle for the Gulf of Riga which raged off and on after the summer of 1915.

In the Black Sea, war with the Ottoman empire began when the German battle cruiser *Goeben* and the light cruiser *Breslau* shelled Russian ports under the sultan's crescent. Although the presence of these modern German units gave the Turks a slight edge in warships, Russian sailors took the initiative. By 1916 the Black Sea Fleet, under the leadership of Rear Adm. A. V. Kolchak, could mount a mine offensive against the Bosporus. During these operations the Russians employed a strike force composed of three predreadnought battleships, destroyers, and two seaplane tenders. In addition to laying 2,500 mines, this force interdicted coastal shipping and bombarded

Figure 42. M-4 Bison accompanied by USN F-4 Phantom fighter. A contemporary of the B-52, it first appeared in 1954; by 1956 production was believed to be fifteen per month. With four 19,800-pound thrust engines, it had a range of 7,000 miles without refueling. The Bison-B, shown here, appeared in a reconnaissance version in 1964.

military objectives. Naval aviators scored their greatest success in January 1916, when fourteen planes attacked and sank a 7,000-ton Turkish transport in the port of Zonguldak. Naval aviators also bombed rail lines, military buildings, and troop centers, and conducted antisubmarine patrols as their part in the strike group's operations.

Although initially the Naval Ministry had sought new seaplanes abroad from the American firm of Glenn Curtiss, Russia's relative isolation forced the Naval Air Service to develop its own aircraft industry. Contracts for the design and production of airframes for seaplanes were given to the Shchetinin factory in Petrograd. In May 1915 the first trainer-reconnaissance type, the M-5, was produced. Experiments with new designs continued at the plant until the revolutionary situation in 1917 made further production impossible. Until then this firm, under the design leadership of D. P. Grigorovich, created twenty seaplane prototypes. These included the M-9, which went into production in mid-1916 and which had a 150-horsepower engine and an armament consisting of one machine gun, four 16kg bombs, and one 37mm cannon. In late 1916 a powerful seaplane fighter, the M-16, underwent flight tests, although few models were manufactured. The final collapse of the Russian war effort stopped work on a twin-engine, torpedo-carrying model, the MK. The progress in developing Russian airframes was not, however, matched in the design and construction of aircraft engines. Grigorovich and his associates either had to settle for inferior and underpowered domestic engines for their craft or gamble on the arrival of foreign engines. Thus, in spite of her successes in the domestic design of naval aircraft, Russia barely held her own in naval aviation during the first three years of the war.

Hand in hand with the struggle for aircraft production were the air service's efforts to train air crews and to construct support facilities. Only after a year's delay did the navy expand its training school near Petrograd. However, the severe climate, short daylight hours, and frozen gulf forced the closing of this facility during the long winter months. In 1915 a flight-training center was opened on the Black Sea. Initially, the student pilots and observers were drawn almost exclusively from the naval officer corps; however, the losses in air crews and the need to expand the air service during the struggle for the Gulf of Riga led to the enrollment of NCOs for pilot training, particularly those who had served as ground mechanics and had some appreciation of the aircraft as a machine. The number of sailors undergoing training fell rapidly after the February revolution. After the Bolsheviks seized power in October 1917 and civil war broke out in early 1918, few naval aviators proved loyal to the new revolutionary government.

Between 1914 and 1917 the Naval Air Service developed a formal organization. Two brigades, composed of three divisions each (18 first-line aircraft per division), operated in the Baltic. In addition to shore-based support depots, the Baltic Fleet employed the seaplane tender *Orlitsa,* a converted passenger liner. In early 1917 the Baltic Fleet listed 88 planes as ready for

duty. In the Black Sea, the Naval Air Service also included two brigades, but the number of combat aircraft was substantially higher—152 units in 1917. In addition, the Black Sea Fleet included three seaplane tenders and four small dirigibles. During the same period, more than twenty aircraft were assigned to flight-training schools. Altogether, more than 3,000 officers and men served in the Naval Air Service, although only about 300 of these were pilots. The number of aircraft available to the Naval Ministry just prior to the February revolution totaled 493, with engines being in short supply.

The role of naval aviation evolved gradually during the course of the war; only in 1917 did the Naval Ministry issue a general directive covering the operations of the Naval Air Service. This directive stipulated four primary missions: reconnaissance, air combat, bombardment, and artillery spotting. Air reconnaissance included three distinct activities: air surveillance at sea in support of fleet operations, air search operations against U-boats, and photographic reconnaissance of shore objects. Naval aviation had become valuable in both the Baltic and Black Sea fleets. Increasingly, reconnaissance had given way to other missions, including air defense and attack. Although the Naval Air Service had developed plans for bombers and torpedo planes that could attack even capital ships, the revolution interrupted these plans and, indeed, caused the near total destruction of the Naval Air Service.

Civil War

Throughout 1917 the Naval Air Service, like the rest of the tsarist forces, deteriorated. Class conflicts rent the brigade's ranks. Most of the sailors accepted the revolution and were violently hostile to their officers; the *Orlitsa's* sailor committee sided with the Bolsheviks during their seizure of power in October. Officer aviators, on the other hand,

Figure 43. Be-6 Madge piston-engined flying boat. The Beriev design bore a close resemblance to the Martin PBM.

opposed the decline in discipline within the fleet, and even planned to break the power of the Petrograd Soviet by bombing its headquarters at Smolny. When Lenin did finally seize power in the name of the Soviets, few fleet airmen supported him. These few, however, served in some of the first air units of the newly organized Red Army and were sent off to the Don to help fight the Cossack forces opposing the Bolsheviks. Other naval aviators joined the First Socialist Fighter Detachment when it was dispatched to the Ukraine in January 1918. While its personnel disintegrated into warring factions, the material bases of the Naval Air Service also collapsed in the wake of lockouts, strikes, demonstrations, and nationalization of plants. Replacements were not produced domestically, and supplies from allies could not be delivered. Between the October revolution and the signing of the treaty of Brest-Litovsk, the Naval Air Service vanished as a military organization. In the fires of civil war, a new service was created from the remnants of the imperial Naval Air Service.

Full-scale civil war began in the late spring and early summer of 1918, when the Allies decided to provide military assistance for the various anti-Bolshevik groups. Naval aviation took on a peculiar meaning in these struggles. Now, pilots and planes were fighting at lost distances from the sea in an essentially riverine war against the Whites. Seaplanes were thrown into the battle to retake Kazan in early August 1918. Four planes, two overworked pilots, and a leaky barge (romantically named *Commune* and optimistically classed as a tender) provided the only Red air cover for the retaking of the city in early September. Naval aviators conducted wide-ranging operations against Admiral Kolchak's flotilla on the Volga and Kama rivers until its final destruction. These improvised forces were the best that Lenin and Trotsky could assemble. On the first anniversary of the October revolution, Red naval aviation included fourteen seaplanes with the Baltic Fleet, seven craft on the Volga front, twenty-one planes based at Astrakhan and nineteen on the northern front, based at Petrozavodsk, Kiotlas, Sv. Plesetskaia, and Vologda—a total of sixty-one seaplanes in more or less working order. While this small force represented a disastrous decline from the forces that tsarism had deployed in the Baltic and Black seas during the world war, it did provide the Reds with air superiority in a number of theaters before the Whites began to receive assistance from the Allies.

In 1919 the British increased their air support to the Whites who for a time gained air superiority over Tsaritsyn on the Volga. Soviet airmen, including fliers from the Baltic Fleet, found the planes and pilots of No. 4 Squadron RFC to be formidable opponents. Night flying and the arrival of better aircraft at Soviet bases stabilized the situation, but Red airmen were not able to regain command of the skies until the British fliers were removed by their government. Likewise, Soviet aviators did little to disrupt British naval air operations against the remains of the Baltic Fleet at Kronstadt. Given the decline in Russian industrial production and the absence of any direct technological aid, the failure of Soviet aviation against the intervening powers is not surprising. During the entire period of the civil war, Soviet factories produced only 669 new aircraft and rebuilt 1,574 old airframes and 1,740 motors. Quite reasonably, the Soviets gave a low priority to naval aviation in allocating these scarce resources. The Soviet regime rapidly consumed Russia's industrial capital, maintaining only a minimum level of production in order to supply arms, clothing, and food to the growing Red Army. Lenin and Trotsky, realizing that the struggle with the Whites would be won only by a mass army equipped with the most basic instruments of war, sought to guarantee the production of such instruments, but they saw more advanced technology as being beyond their industrial capacity.

With the end of the civil war and the beginning of the NEP, the Soviet government faced the problem of reconstituting the Red Army as a permanent military force. Naturally, the lessons learned during the civil war served as the foundation. Two of these lessons were especially important:

First, the Soviet Union needed to develop its own technological and industrial base in order to support the Red Army with all types of weapons, including aviation. Although tsarist officers had already learned this lesson in the nineteenth century, the economic isolation of the civil-war period had drastically brought home this truth to the Soviets. On the other hand, the Soviets also learned that naval power was not a first priority of national defense. The great maritime powers—Britain, France, the United States, and Japan—had aided the Whites, but they had not been able to support offensives against Moscow in spite of their absolute command of the sea. This fact made naval development seem a secondary consideration to the Red Army in its mission of defending the socialist fatherland. Naval aviation, like the rest of the fleet, received scant recognition. In 1923 the Red Army had only thirty-six machines available. Although surface forces were gradually rebuilt during the NEP, no new construction was begun. Naval specialists were charged with developing a strategy that would make maximum use of the forces available. Because the Whites had been able to take a good portion of the old tsarist fleet with them when Wrangel abandoned the Crimea, in 1925 funds were approved for the construction of a new fleet of small submarines, motor-torpedo boats, and aircraft. Meanwhile, the Washington Naval Conference had halted the postwar naval race among the maritime powers and thereby reduced pressure for naval construction. Naval reconstruction and the development of naval aviation experienced a hiatus from the end of the civil war until the beginning of the First Five-Year Plan.

Birth of the Soviet Navy

The last years of the NEP saw a growing conflict between two irreconcilable military

Figure 44. Be-10 Mallow jet flying boat. This twin-engine model was produced in small numbers for Soviet naval aviation.

doctrines within the Commissariat of War. This conflict to a great degree reflected the larger struggle within the Communist party over the future course of the Soviet state: whether to seek a continuation of the NEP and of the class alliance between workers and peasants, with the prospect of slow long-term economic growth; or super-industrialization at the expense of the peasants, which would transform the USSR into a great industrial power within a generation. In military affairs this conflict can be found in the reports submitted by M.V. Frunze when he was commissar of war. On the one hand, he stressed that the Soviet citizen-soldier, guided by the Communist party, was the very foundation of the Red Army. This mass army could be counted upon to defend the interests of workers and peasants against foreign attack. But at the same time Frunze, recognizing that mere mass was not enough, called for the speedy modernization of the armed forces' technological base. In comparison with the bourgeois powers, the Red Army possessed obsolete weapons; without a major transformation of the Soviet Union's industrial plant, the Red Army would be dependent upon foreign technology. Frunze focused on aviation as one field that would require herculean efforts, warning: "The most important type of technological force which will play a large role on the fields of future battles is the air fleet." Although he noted the slow but steady progress in this area—the appearance of Soviet fliers on the world stage, the purchase of more than 700 planes from abroad between 1923 and 1925, and the construction of Soviet aircraft on the basis of domestic designs by 1925—the commissar of war wanted to end completely Soviet dependence upon foreign firms and designs. Such results could be achieved only with the radical transformation of the entire national economy. Aviation, a modern fleet, and mechanized armies subsequently became possible as a result of the forced-draft industrialization of the First Five-Year Plan. For all his errors and excesses, Stalin, more than any other man, was the father of the modern

Red Army, for it was he who categorically resolved the crisis of NEP in favor of industrialization.

The creation of a broad industrial base coincided with an ominous deterioration of the Soviet Union's strategic situation. Questions related to defense policy and particularly to the development of naval power were resolved in accordance with whatever immediate threats were perceived by Stalin and the Soviet elite. With the rise of hostile and expansionist regimes in Nazi Germany and imperial Japan, the Soviets faced strong potential enemies in Europe and Asia. The development of Soviet naval power depended upon the relative emphasis given to these threats. Initially, military planners opted for a gradual buildup of light forces in the four primary naval theaters: the Baltic, Black, Northern, and Pacific fleets. This buildup involved the construction of submarines, motor-torpedo boats, destroyers, and cruisers. New shipyards were established, the Belomore Canal linking the Baltic and Northern fleets was built, and naval aviation was expanded radically. Investment in naval aviation during the Second Five-Year Plan (1932–1937) increased by 510 percent. The lessons learned during World War I about mine warfare and the utility of light forces in protecting Russian coastal regions became basic naval doctrine. The wheeled aircraft rapidly replaced the seaplane as the basic tool of naval aviation.

By the end of the Second Five-Year Plan a serious split was apparent within the Soviet naval community over future development of four fleets. *Morskoi sbornik* (*Naval Digest*) repeatedly cited the developing naval race among the bourgeois states in calling for an implicit reappraisal of Soviet plans. The Anglo-German Naval Agreement was seen as the beginning of a German naval renaissance. Advocates of building a Soviet battle fleet cited German

plans and the existing Japanese fleet as reason enough for a massive ship-construction program. Articles describing Japanese carrier exercises and deployment were alternated with information about German decisions to build modern battleships and two 20,000-ton aircraft carriers. This naval "threat" did not go unanswered. Shortly before his death at Stalin's hands, Marshal Tukhachevsky used the pages of *Morskoi sbornik* to play down German naval rearmament, while pointing to the combination of tactical aviation and armored forces as constituting Germany's real threat to the Soviet Union. Tukhachevsky's supporters within the navy agreed with this analysis; they sought to defend the Baltic and Black seas from immediate attack through mine warfare, submarine attacks, and naval aviation operating from a well-developed net of airfields. Defensive in orientation, these officers considered this option as having been proven in World War I and as being the least costly in terms of men and resources. Capital ships could not hope to operate effectively in either the Baltic or Black sea and their assistance to other Soviet fleets would depend upon the attitudes of third powers. It also seemed unlikely to these officers that the Soviet Union could ever construct capital ships of the quality and quantity necessary to challenge the most likely opponents, Nazi Germany and imperial Japan.

Advocates of capital-ship construction stressed the utility of a battle fleet in war at sea. In Mahanic terms, they suggested that the best defense was a strong offense— a navy that could engage the enemy and gain command of the sea. While still emphasizing the battleship as the queen of war at sea, these officers recognized the utility of carrier-based aircraft. They pointed to the Japanese carrier group operating from Port Arthur as a balanced strike force and used articles in periodicals to

Figure 45. Be-12 Mail maritime reconnaissance plane. A turboprop version of the Be-6 developed for antisubmarine warfare, it made a series of altitude records in 1964 and in 1967 attained a closed-course speed of 351 mph.

discuss the role of carrier aviation in surprise attacks upon fleet bases. The strongest advocates of this approach were found in the naval academies and among the young officers of the Pacific Fleet. Unfortunately for the Soviet navy, Stalin accepted the idea of a modern battle fleet without endorsing the argument for carriers.

These debates among naval officers were in no way academic, for they transpired during Stalin's bloody purge of the military leadership. Between 1937 and 1939, command of the Soviet navy changed five times; Admirals Orlov, Viktorov, and Frinovsky all died by Stalin's order, apparently without trial. Adm. R. A. Muklevich, a former commander, old Bolshevik, and champion of light forces, was arrested in May 1937 and condemned to death as an ally of Marshal Tukhachevsky and an opponent of a powerful ocean navy. As was often the case, Stalin's paranoia had no basis in fact. In August of the same year, Axis warships began attacking Soviet mer-

chantmen who were crossing the Mediterranean with aid to Republican Spain. While England and France organized a maritime patrol to prevent such "pirate" attacks, there was little that the Soviet navy could do. Spain had proved the need for a battle fleet, as far as Stalin was concerned.

Naval officers did not, however, abandon their efforts to sell Stalin on the need for air power. V. Chernyshev, in an article on naval development since World War I, noted the technological advances in aviation and the recent carrier construction programs among the leading maritime powers. The carrier appeared to be a critical element in the struggle for command of the sea—the basic rationale for the construction of an ocean navy. But Chernyshev pointed out the reality of the Soviet situation: the carrier had only marginal utility in small bodies of water, over which land-based aviation could range freely. He implied that supporters of carrier construction in the Soviet Union emphasized the

Figure 46. Tu-95 Bear monitoring U.S. and NATO maneuvers in the Mediterranean. USN F-8 Crusader from CVA-38 Shangri-la *has intercepted the Bear.*

vulnerability of all surface ships to attack from the air without recognizing that the carrier was itself vulnerable. Further, the construction of large modern carriers demanded excessive capital investment of scarce resources. On the basis of Russia's experience during World War I, Chernyshev recommended the construction of small seaplane tenders (*aviatransporty*) in place of carriers. They would provide the necessary air cover beyond the range of shore aviation while being "less vulnerable and cheaper." The geographic position of the Baltic Fleet—which operated from bases at the end of a long, narrow gulf whose coasts were not controlled by the Soviet Union—certainly did not fit Chernyshev's assumptions. However, if he was concerned about building up the Black Sea Fleet, such tenders in the absence of carriers among the littoral states made some sense, especially if they were small enough to transit the straits under the terms of the Montreux Convention.

The debate over naval strategy was

drowned in two seas: the blood of the navy's leading cadres and the naive propaganda announcing the construction of an ocean navy. In January 1938 the commissar of the navy, Adm. P. A. Smirnov, declared that the new policy was above discussion. Repeating the line established by Stalin and Molotov, the admiral outlined the mission of this new force even before actual construction had begun:

> The duties of our navy are: to secure the impregnability of the maritime approaches to our sacred Soviet country, to guard the motherland from the attempts at invasion by fascist plunderers from the sea, and to secure the normal navigation of merchant ships under the Red Soviet Flag in any part of the world (P. Smirnov, *Morskoisbornik*, 1938, no. 1, p. 10).

Foreseeing the coming of a general war, Smirnov stressed the fact that conflict would occur on land, on sea, and in the air. Increased spending by other naval

Figure 47. Helicopter carrier/cruiser Moskva *off Naples in spring 1969. Note Hormone Ka-25 helicopters on the flight deck.*

powers made Soviet construction of capital ships imperative. But multiple threats in different theaters and disadvantageous geographic conditions made naval planning extremely difficult. While the construction of carriers was, on principle, accepted, the laying down of the keel of the first such unit was to be delayed until the end of the Third Five-Year Plan, according to Adm. N. G. Kuznetsov, commissar of the navy from April 1939 to January 1947. *Morskoi sbornik* published lengthy discussions of the carrier programs of other maritime powers, paying special attention to the French solution of the late 1930s. The advantages and disadvantages of attack carriers, medium carriers, escort carriers, and cruisers with flight decks astern were enumerated in *Morskoi sbornik*.

Western experts and Soviet critics alike have given Stalin very low marks for failing to build a carrier force during the Third Five-Year Plan. Robert W. Herrick, for example, asserted that Stalin committed four nearly fatal errors:

He destroyed almost all of the experienced and capable naval leaders; he prevented rather than promoted the construction of aircraft carriers; he overestimated the industrial capacity of the USSR to rush the warship construction program to completion; and he had an exaggerated opinion of his own ability, through diplomatic activity, to keep the USSR out of war for a prolonged period (*Soviet Naval Strategy,* 1968).

While Herrick may have been right on points one and three, points two and four seem ill-taken. To construct carriers, when fleet operations would have been hampered by hostile geographic circumstances, would have been criminal. It must be remembered that not until the middle of 1940 did the Soviet Union gain sufficient control of the Gulf of Finland or the Baltic coasts of the Estonian, Latvian, and Lithuanian republics to make possible the deployment of a Soviet battle fleet in the Baltic. Furthermore, the construction of carriers in the Black Sea, under the terms of the Montreux Convention and in the absence of a direct naval threat in that theater, would have been unjustified, especially in view of the enormous capital investment involved in carrier construction. Carriers became viable weapons for the Soviets only

Figure 48. USN Sea King and Soviet Ka-25 ASW helicopters. The Soviet Hormone helicopter operates from a Kresta-2 guided-missile cruiser.

after Stalin's diplomacy had gained the fleet the necessary room to maneuver in the Baltic.

In regard to point four, although Herrick may be correct about Stalin's "exaggerated opinion" of his own diplomatic ability, he nevertheless was able to keep the Soviet Union out of the European war long enough to begin modernizing his forces while improving defensive frontiers. For Soviet naval forces, his borrowed time was probably crucial, both for survival and to their ultimate victory after the German attack.

If Stalin erred, it was not in opposing carriers or in ultimately failing to keep the Soviet Union out of the European war. More critical were his failure to press for the modernization of Soviet armed forces and his decision to squander scarce resources on questionable weapons systems. In the case of the Soviet navy and naval aviation, these errors were particularly apparent. Although by June 21 the Soviets had developed a huge naval air arm in each of the four fleets—more than 2,581 aircraft in all—almost 90 percent of these planes were obsolete. Of the navy's fighters, the I-15*bis* had gone into series production in 1934, the I-153 in 1935, and the I-16 in 1938. The SB light bomber had entered service in 1934. All these aircraft were inferior to front-line types in Luftwaffe service. Only a few models of the Il-4, a modern torpedo bomber, had joined the fleet. Neither of the new fighters, the Mig-3 or the Yak-1, had been assigned by June 1941. Although Soviet naval doctrine

Figure 49. Ka-25 (Kamov) helicopter, photographed in the Mediterranean in 1972.

stressed the utility of naval aviation as an offensive weapon against enemy warships, shipping, and bases, less than 24 percent of the aircraft assigned to the fleets were bombers and torpedo planes. Of these, a full third were deployed with the Pacific Fleet on June 22, 1941. None of the new dive bombers (Pe-2s) or attack planes (Il-2 Shturmoviks) were in naval service. In addition, the bombers of the Northern Fleet lacked radio equipment and electronic navigational aids. In spite of territorial gains in the Baltic, the airfield net in the former republics was far from completed nor had any airfields or major naval bases been constructed in the Caucasus. Naval aviation was not, however, alone in its inadequacy; the navy, by Soviet admission, lacked ASW vessels, minesweepers, and support craft and had not even one specially designed landing craft. The army and air force also had serious technological problems. The new T-34 tanks were slow in

entering service, and the infantry did not have a first-rate antitank gun. The air force, although it had received modern aircraft earlier than the fleet, was also handicapped by obsolete machines. In these areas, more than in carriers or battleships, lay the real weaknesses of the Soviet armed forces.

The failures of Soviet armed forces during the first five months of the Great Patriotic War have led many Western historians to speak of the "bankruptcy" of Soviet strategy. In the case of the Soviet navy, this argument is based on the observation that, from the Arctic to the Black Sea, numerically superior Soviet naval forces had collapsed under the hammering attacks of the qualitatively superior German forces. (In spite of numerous shore-based naval aircraft and an absolute superiority in capital ships, the Soviet fleets lost command of the Arctic, Baltic, and Black seas.) This analysis, while generally correct, implies that the Soviets'

Figure 50. Il-38 May antisubmarine patrol aircraft. A derivative of the Il-18 transport, its wing is further forward because of its weight and the location of its electronic gear.

failure was due to superior German naval strategy, which was decidedly not the case. Indeed, Hitler and the OKW used Panzer divisions and the Luftwaffe in place of warships. The German battle fleet took no part in the initial offensive that cleared the Baltic ports; its best capital units were either blockaded in Brest, under construction, or in repair. No major German units were available to support the Rumanians in their battle with the Black Sea Fleet. If the Germans did score successes in their initial offensive, bottling up the Baltic Fleet in Kronstadt and Leningrad, they did not achieve their intended objective: the isolation of the Soviet fleet outside the Gulf of Finland and its capture or internment in Sweden. In their air operations in defense of the naval bases at Libau and Tallin, and in providing air cover for the Baltic Fleet on its desperate run to Kronstadt, Soviet naval airmen acquitted themselves well in spite of high losses.

In the Black Sea the Germans had even less reason for satisfaction with the results of their first offensive. Here the mere existence of the Soviet fleet and its naval air service performed a valuable role. With 673 aircraft and seven major airfields, Soviet naval aviation helped make the Black Sea Fleet seem a formidable threat to the southern flank of an advance through the Ukraine and to the Rumanian oil fields, Germany's chief source of petroleum. In addition, Hitler and the OKW considered the Black Sea the most direct route for Allied assistance to the Soviet Union. The Germans' deployment of substantial armored formations south of the Pripet Marshes and of aviation in Rumania proper was intended to offset Soviet naval superiority in this theater—Rumania, Hitler's only Black Sea ally, having no effective naval forces to speak of. Thus, although the Soviets proved unsuccessful in their attempts to use naval forces to attack

Figure 51. Yakovlev Freehand VTOL fighter, a prototype for testing VTOL technology.

strategic targets in Rumania (they did bomb and shell Konstanza, without effect), their very existence bled off valuable units from Army Group Center, then driving along the Smolensk road. Dogged Soviet resistance at Odessa, Perekop, and Sevastopol forced the Germans to commit badly needed units to what was only a secondary theater of operation. The net of airfields on the Crimean peninsula created a natural "carrier" that allowed the Soviets to support the reinforcement of Odessa and the evacuation of that city's industry and defenders. Only after the fall of Sevastopol, the result of an eight-month siege, did the Germans gain undisputed command of the air and seas around the Crimea in 1942. They were then able to attack and destroy isolated Soviet surface units operating in the sea of Azov and in the Kerch Straits.

Losses during the 1942 summer offensive were high because the Soviets lacked both the planes and the airfields to meet the German threat along the lower Don and in the northern Caucasus. When the Azov Sea Flotilla ran the straits in an attempt to escape total destruction, casualties proved extremely heavy: of 217 craft

that began the flight, only 144 reached the safety of Novorossiisk. The loss of the Crimea greatly reduced the effectiveness of Soviet naval aviation in its attacks upon German sea communications in 1942; navy pilots sank only 53 warships, transports, and light craft during the entire second half of that year.

After the victory at Stalingrad, the Soviets mounted a counteroffensive to clear the Black Sea coast and carry the war into Rumania. Soviet sailors and airmen provided valuable support to the Red Army. Sailors served at the front, carried army units forward in amphibious operations, and attacked the enemy at sea. The first combined blow—a classic, in terms of Soviet operations—came at Novorossiisk in September 1943, when air force and navy fliers bombed and strafed German positions while fighter units of the *front* command and fleet seized tactical control of the air.

By late 1943 the Germans could not afford the luxury of committing scarce aviation to every theater of operations. By Soviet estimates, the Germans had fewer than 150 planes in the Crimea when I. E.

Petrov's Fifty-sixth Army launched amphibious operations across the Kerch Straits. More than 1,000 Soviet aircraft supported the landings, among them 393 from the Black Sea Fleet. Superiority in numbers and the increased effectiveness of new Soviet aircraft and crews guaranteed command of the air over the battlefield in spite of stubborn German resistance.

In cooperation with submarines and motor-torpedo boats, the naval air service sought to interdict German sea communications with the Crimea. While the Red Army pressed the Germans back towards Sevastopol, naval air forces cut off resupply efforts and harassed evacuation. Attacking in mass formations, using torpedo bombers and dive bombers effectively, the naval air service bore the brunt of the attack, sinking more than eighty-six enemy craft. Neither submarines nor surface units were so effective. Indeed, in spite of Soviet air superiority, the Luftwaffe struck back effectively from its Crimean airfields when Soviet surface units offered targets of opportunity. In October 1943, eight Stuka dive bombers disabled the destroyer leader *Kharkov* about 100 miles off the Caucasian coast. A second attack sank the *Kharkov* and two escorting destroyers. By attempting to tow the disabled leader, the two destroyers had lost valuable time during which they might have withdrawn under naval aviation's cover. Under such circumstances the Black Sea Fleet Command was reluctant to risk using surface units as long as the enemy could rapidly transfer aircraft into the theater and thereby achieve even a temporary attack capability, such as had occurred October 3–6 in the Crimea.

Naval aviation adopted new tactics in its assault on German sea communications. In the second half of 1943, Red naval aviators abandoned the tactic of "free hunting" with torpedo planes in favor of coordinated mass attacks, launched in conjunction with frequent and intensive air reconnaissance. In these attacks, as many as 100 planes would assault a port or convoy in two or three waves; bombers, Shturmoviks, and torpedo planes attacked under heavy fighter cover. Against Operation Rowboat (the evacuation of the Crimea) in the spring of 1944, these attacks proved very effective; Soviet aviators claimed the destruction of 65 vessels and damage to another 55. As a result of such attacks and continuing pressure from the Red Army, Hitler was forced to abandon Sevastopol on May 13, 1944, in the face of grave political and military risks: that Turkey and other Balkan states might enter the Allied camp and that Soviet aviators based in the Crimea might mount powerful strikes against the Rumanian oil fields.

Soviet naval commanders came to consider the later operations in the Black Sea as the optimum utilization of "sea power" on the eastern front because the navy was assigned a prominent role in supporting the developing offensive. Naval aviation appeared to be a highly cost-efficient weapons system in support of tactical amphibious operations and for achieving sea denial. Defensively, it both augmented naval and land forces covering naval bases and provided a valuable reconnaissance capability. This conception of sea power became a part of Soviet postwar military doctrine. It should be noted that Admiral of the Fleet Sergei Gorshkov, commander in chief of the Soviet navy since 1955, served with distinction in the Black Sea Fleet throughout the war.

Naval operations in the Baltic failed to inspire any countervailing theories of naval strategy or doctrines for the use of aviation at sea. Because of the retreat of Soviet forces from the Baltic republics, the navy was confined to the Kronstadt-Leningrad region of the gulf from August 1941 to late 1944. During this period, the Baltic

Figure 52. Mil Mi-4 Hound ASW helicopter with chin-mounted radar. Magnetic anomaly detector (MAD) is mounted behind cabin.

Fleet and its air arm supported the defense of Leningrad. Offensive operations began in 1944 in support of Soviet troops on the Leningrad and Volkhov fronts in order to break the siege of the city. As this offensive developed momentum, more and more fleet aviation went into ground-attack missions. Only after the surrender of Finland and the destruction of the mine barrier across the gulf in late 1944 did the Baltic Fleet turn seriously to attacking German sea communications with Army Group "Kurland." As in the Black Sea, this mission fell to naval aviation in cooperation with submarines and MTBs. Given the numerical advantages enjoyed by Soviet capital units, the clear command of the air which the Soviets possessed during the last eight months of the war, and the numerous light craft and submarines that could have supported the large surface units, it is difficult to understand their reluctance to offer battle—particularly during the sieges of Kurland and Königsberg, when combined naval operations could have cut off German supply efforts and hampered the evacuation of troops, war materiels, and the civilian population. Undoubtedly the prolonged inaction of the Baltic Fleet, its losses to air attacks in 1941, and the continued threat of minefields discouraged a surface initiative, with the result that naval aviation assumed the responsibility for cutting sea communications.

Naval aviators destroyed the vast majority of enemy shipping sunk by the Soviets, while greatly improving the chances for success of submarine and MTB attacks.

According to Rear Adm. K. A. Stalbo, naval aviation accounted for 72.5 percent of all German shipping sunk by Soviet forces. (Mines accounted for 11.3 percent, MTBs for 7 percent, submarines for 5.7 percent, and shore artillery for 3.5 percent.) Three unusual characteristics of naval air operations in the Baltic were their greater reliance upon attack aircraft, the larger scale of the attacks on ports and convoys, and the increasing use of planes for minelaying. During the Baltic air offensive of late 1944 and early 1945, torpedo planes flew 1,887 sorties, bombers 915, and attack aircraft 7,054. The massive scale of Soviet attacks often called for two full air divisions and as many as 160 planes of various types. Thanks to their numbers and the absence of German air cover, the attackers were able to suppress antiaircraft fire and drive home their attacks with great success and low casualties. During this period, naval aviators dropped 938 mines. Weather conditions, operational problems, and enemy opposition made the precise placement of air-dropped mines very difficult, however, and more than 400 sorties by the converted torpedo bombers, flying alone or in pairs, were needed to achieve these modest results. Compared with similar operations undertaken by the Royal Air Force in the Baltic during the same period, the Soviets launched only a minor effort.

Of the Northern Fleet and its role in protecting Allied convoys on the Murmansk run, much has been written. Allied observers, German veterans, and Soviet naval historians agree that the Northern Fleet did not prove very effective in the defense of its own sea communications. However, while Western writers tend to blame technological backwardness and inexperienced personnel, the Soviets point to the geographic isolation of the theater, climatic conditions, and the vastness of the area of operations as being equally significant. In regard to naval aviation, Soviet military historians emphasize the slender resources available to the Northern Fleet in June 1941: 116 planes, most of them obsolete fighters. The first torpedo planes assigned to the fleet did not arrive until 1942. In 1941 just eight aircraft were equipped with radio compasses. Only gradually did the Northern Fleet develop a satisfactory air defense and an attack capability against German bases in Norway. Indeed, not until the systematic German offensive against Allied convoys began in March 1942 did it seem imperative to devote substantial resources to the Northern Fleet and its air service. Lacking both aircraft carriers and the capacity to construct them in the theater, the Soviets could not provide fighter cover beyond the range of their airfields ashore. Only in 1944 did the British dispatch carriers with the convoys in substantial numbers. By that time, however, German aviation in Norway had been greatly reduced. During the same period, the Soviets were able to employ American Catalina flying boats in long-range antisubmarine patrols. Soviet naval aviation, like other arms of the Northern Fleet, remained technologically inferior to that of the Germans throughout the war. Apparently the Soviets placed a low priority on the fleet and its oceanic missions. Naval aviators and marines were more effective ashore in wrestling the nickel mines at Petsamo from the Germans.

The brief campaign of August 1945 in the Far East suggested the outlines of Soviet naval doctrine in the immediate postwar period. Given overwhelming superiority in the theater of operations, the Soviets could employ naval power in combined-arms actions. When Marshal A. M. Vasilevsky struck the Japanese, he had more than 3,800 combat planes, 1.5 million men, more than 5,000 tanks and self-propelled guns, and 26,000 pieces of artillery. The

Figure 53. Soviet aircraft carrier Kiev *transiting the Mediterranean to the Northern Fleet in 1976.*

Pacific Fleet had 2 cruisers, 1 destroyer leader, 12 destroyers, 78 submarines, 19 guard craft, 10 minelayers, 52 minesweepers, 19 specially constructed landing craft, and 204 MTBs. By far the strongest element of the Pacific Fleet was its air arm, which included 1,549 planes. Naval aviators supported assaults across the Amur and landings on the North Korean coast, Sakhalin, and the Kurile islands. These attacks were well coordinated and successful. While the Soviets grossly exaggerate the importance of these operations in bringing about Japan's surrender, this distortion should not preclude a favorable evaluation of the scope or pace of this offensive. Its amphibious operations probably were the best conducted by the Soviets during World War II. By Soviet estimates, the Japanese lost 750 planes during the three-week campaign. Another 925 planes, 600 tanks, and more than 600,000 men were captured. The swift victories brought Manchuria, North Korea, southern Sakhalin,

and the Kurile islands within the Soviet sphere of influence.

World War II, the Great Patriotic War, was a crucible for the Soviet armed forces. As a life-and-death struggle testing the survival of the regime and imposing great human and material losses upon the population, it overshadowed the experiences of a generation. In terms of naval strategy, the war brought a multitude of changes. The intensive development of technology made possible weapons of greater speed, range, firepower, and accuracy. These developments had, in turn, made archaic the prevailing doctrines about the use of naval power. The battleship was gone; the airplane supreme. Submarine and antisubmarine warfare systems were in a deadly race. New weapons had appeared on the horizon which threatened to create even more profound changes: the jet engine, the rocket, and atomic weapons. In this context, naval officers the world over thereafter had to formulate naval doctrine on the basis of lessons learned during the war, while at the same time anticipating even more radical changes in the instruments for conducting war at sea. It is not surprising that naval elites in both the United States and the Soviet Union based postwar doctrine on their own experiences during World War II. Adm. Chester Nimitz spoke out forcefully in the *U.S. Naval Institute Proceedings* for establishing carrier task forces and amphibious capabilities that would make it possible for the United States to control the sea and seize bases close enough to the enemy so as to launch attacks with atomic bombers. Soviet naval officers opted for a sea denial force, a fortress fleet operating behind mine barriers in conjunction with naval aviation to prevent amphibious assaults upon the Soviet Union, and a submarine capability to attack enemy sea communications. Both naval elites had great difficulty in convincing their civilian counterparts about the value of their programs. In the United States, even the onset of the cold war did not create much support for naval modernization; the strategic bomber and the atomic bomb seemed to provide the most cost-efficient defense capability for the arsenal of democracy. Soviet naval officers had even more serious problems to contend with, since the destruction of the national economy during four years of war and occupation had made capital resources extremely scarce.

> In the mid-1950s, as a result of the revolution in military affairs, the Central Committee of our party determined the path of development of the navy and also its role in the country's system of defense forces. It took the course for the construction of an ocean navy capable of executing strategic missions of an offensive nature. Submarines and naval aviation equipped with nuclear rocket weapons occupied the most im-

portant place in this (Zakharov et al., 1969, pp. 561–562).

Lacking carriers and any real chance of developing a competitive carrier air arm, the Soviets adopted the cruise missile as the most cost-effective counter to the American carrier task group. These missiles were placed aboard nuclear and conventional submarines, surface ships, and navy medium- and long-range bombers. In the early 1960s the Soviets further rationalized their force disposition by removing fighter aviation from naval control and placing it under Soviet air defense forces (PVO *strany*), thus reducing naval aviation in size but allowing it to concentrate on certain vital missions: long-range air reconnaissance, anticarrier operations, and antisubmarine warfare.

Since 1961 the Soviet navy, under Admiral Gorshkov's leadership, has opted for a forward deployment of its forces in ocean areas from which strategic attacks against the Soviet Union could be launched, particularly the waters around Iceland, the eastern Mediterranean, and the Indian Ocean. These deployments became permanent stations during the last decade, and, in terms of ships and missions, the Soviet navy has become a worldwide force. What this has meant for naval air power is clear from Rear Admiral Stalbo's comments:

> Soviet naval aviation, as the most mobile type of naval force, is composed of aircraft and helicopters for different missions. In the first ten postwar years the mine-torpedo represented the basis of its attack power, and in the most recent period rocket-armed aircraft. These can find and destroy any ship or formation in the ocean in the face of all manners of defense. The basic weapon of aviation is various cruise missiles,

equipped with powerful warheads and systems of self-guidance that provide them with great accuracy against enemy surface warships. Rocket-armed aircraft can attack a naval adversary while remaining beyond the range of his SAMs, antiaircraft guns, and interceptors (Zakharov et al., 1969, p. 563).

Because of countermeasures by their likely opponents in defense of carrier task forces, the Soviets have come to stress two key ingredients in the successful use of naval aviation in its anticarrier role. The first ingredient is combined action with missile-armed surface ships and submarines to overwhelm the defense; the second is a strong emphasis upon a "first salvo" capability. (It should be noted that Soviet authors do not make a distinction between conventional and nuclear conflicts in this context.) The relative vulnerability of American carrier task forces to these Soviet countermeasures remains a highly debatable issue closely tied to questions of future naval posture. It is unlikely that the Soviets could effectively challenge carrier task forces far from land-based aviation and in a limited-war context. Most observers agree that, beyond the nuclear threshold, the task force remains quite vulnerable.

Such is not the case with the ballistic-missile submarine. In spite of early Soviet efforts to place part of their nuclear strike capability at sea, the United States and its allies gained a commanding superiority in this field with the deployment of the Polaris system in 1961. On the one hand, the Soviets sought to counter the Polaris threat by developing new classes of nuclear and conventional attack submarines and new forms of naval aviation. On the other, they devoted tremendous resources to the development of their own SSBN deterrent capability. Their search for effective ASW capability against American SSBNs has

been highly innovative but, as best as we can judge, hardly successful. Compare the tone of Rear Admiral Stalbo's statement on ASW operations with that of the one regarding anticarrier missions:

> As is well known, during World War II naval aviation recommended itself as a dread opponent of submarines. ASW aircraft possess not only long-range search capabilities but also the capacity to execute irresistible attacks upon submarines. These qualities of aviation have been taken into account in the development of Soviet ASW aviation, which incudes aircraft and helicopters equipped with modern means of search and destruction of submarines (Zakharov et al., 1969, p. 563).

Here are no ringing declarations about the vulnerability of the enemy or chances of success. Indeed, Admiral Gorshkov himself pointed out, in his series of articles on navies in war and peace, that successful ASW operations have traditionally involved a very heavy investment of men and resources—at his own calculation for Allied efforts versus German U-boats, a ratio of 100:1 *vis-à-vis* the enemy. In the case of the SSBN, the ratio must be even higher. Col. of Naval Aviation A. P. Anokhin made this point in a recent article for *Morskoi sbornik*:

> In future war, if the imperialists should unleash it, rocket-carrying submarines will present the gravest threat from the oceans and seas. Thus, it will be necessary to use practically all types of naval forces, including naval aviation, in the struggle with them (A. P. Anokhin, *Morskoi sbornik*, 1971, no. 6, pp. 35–36).

The Soviet response has been the construction of large ASW units. In 1967 the first class of surface ship with an anti-SSBN capability entered service with the Black Sea Fleet, the ASW cruiser *Moskva*. In the *Moskva* and her sister, *Leningrad*, the Soviets got their first afloat air capability; each displacing 18,000 tons, these ships were designed as rocket cruisers forward and helicopter carriers astern. An armament of twenty Ka-25 (Hormone) helicopters, variable-depth sonar, twin twelve-tube mortars, and single twin-mount ASW missile launcher gave each ship formidable strike capabilities. In cooperation with missile cruisers, modern destroyers, and nuclear attack submarines, they formed the first large ASW task force in the Soviet navy. For all the sophistication of its design, however, it does not appear that the Soviets found the *Moskva* a successful answer to their strategic ASW needs, since only two were built.

A major deficiency in the first generation of ASW cruisers probably resulted from the progress that had occurred in the U.S. Polaris-Poseidon system. With MIRV warheads and longer ranges, the same nuclear submarines could deliver more accurate attacks from much greater distances. By increasing the striking power and operational area of its submarine deterrence, the United States forced the Soviets to develop greater operational range for their own ASW fleet. Forced to operate far from their own bases and aware of the need for greater search capabilities and an effective endogenous air-defense system, the Soviets decided to invest in a second-generation ASW cruiser, the 39,000-ton *Kiev*. The rationale behind this investment hinged upon winning a nuclear war. As Capt. V. G. Efremenko observed in 1971, the SSBN represented a dangerous threat to the USSR. Neutralizing this threat would not depend upon

developing new weapons delivery systems; conventional depth charges, nuclear-armed ASW missiles, or torpedos would do if the target were precisely located. But target identification in the ocean presented a scientific and technical problem of great complexity. It was a vital issue, for ". . . victory will belong to him who will constantly known the location of the opposing side's submarines and deploy sufficient means to defeat them" (V. Efremenko, *Morskoi sbornik*, 1970, no. 10, pp. 20-21). With its angled deck and mixed complement of VTOL aircraft and helicopters, the *Kiev* represents the latest Soviet solution to this critical problem. It does not appear that the *Kiev* or her sister ship can effectively deal with Polaris. Indeed, given the development of intercontinental missiles for SSBNs—the new Delta class submarines armed with twelve tubes for the SSB-8 missile (range 4,000+ nm) and the planned Trident class—strategic ASW seems an insurmountable problem for both the Soviets and the U.S. under present technology.

In addition to cruiser-based aviation, the Soviets also deploy ASW patrol aircraft. Along with Japan, the USSR has the distinction of being one of the only two nations that maintain modern flying boats. About eighty Be-12 (Mail) turbo-prop planes are presently in service. In addition to a radome forward, the Mail has a magnetic anomaly detector (MAD) boom aft and a weapons bay. An adaptation of a four-engine turboprop cargo plane (Coot) has been also pressed into ASW patrol activities. The Il-38 (May) has been lengthened and fitted with a MAD boom, other electronic capabilities, and a weapons bay. About forty-five of the Il-38s are in service, operating from Baltic and Northern fleet bases as well as from Balkan fields and Egypt.

The great bulk of Soviet naval aviation

remains in its bomber forces. About 50 heavy bombers (Bear Ds) provide long-range oceanic reconnaissance, while another 50 Badgers and Blinder As provide medium-range surveillance capabilities. To improve her naval air reconnaissance, the Soviet Union has sought permission from other countries to use foreign fields for this purpose. Outside of her Warsaw Pact allies, these countries include Cuba, Libya, Iraq, and the Somali Republic. During Okean maneuvers, two Bear reconnaissance planes flew from a Northern Fleet base over Soviet ships operating near Iceland and then on to Cuba, a flight of 5,000 miles. Such reconnaissance missions support the approximately 300 Badgers armed with Kipper and Kelt standoff ASMs. At present, Soviet naval aviation has more than 1,250 fixed-wing aircraft and helicopters, making it the second-largest naval air arm in the world. In comparison, the United States deploys more than 5,500 aircraft. As suggested earlier, however, such comparative figures serve little purpose. Soviet naval aviation, in spite of rhetoric about balanced forces, remains a mission-specific force. Whatever its technological shortcomings, however, it has during the last two decades tried to make the transition from conventional war to the nuclear battlefield. Under the leadership of Admiral Gorshkov and the late Marshal Ivan I. Bozrov, it has become a force which both the military and civilian leadership consider very cost effective.

Conclusion

The long-range development of Soviet naval aviation shows a broad pattern of technological innovation. As was the case with other sectors of the Soviet military, its real growth began with the creation of an adequate economic-technological base during the early five-year plans. Because of the cost-efficiency of naval aviation in comparison with other forms of sea power and the peculiar geopolitical circumstances of Soviet naval policy, the Soviets have found it a valuable tool. Its composition and missions have changed over the years as the nature of the maritime threat to the USSR has changed. From a coastal defense force committed to support of the Red Army and sea denial during World War II, it has evolved into a strategic sea-denial force for the nuclear battlefield against carriers and missile submarines.

Because of the nature of the potential threat from the sea, Soviet naval air capabilities are crucial to the military posture of the USSR. In an age of détente, this fact is often overlooked by Western commentators, whether realists or alarmists. In the future, as in the past, the development of naval aviation will depend upon the threat perceived by the Soviet political elite. Because Marxism-Leninism sees war as "not an accidental event or fault, but the inevitable stage of capitalism," military preparedness must go forward in the USSR. As Rear Admiral Stalbo defined the threat to the Soviet Union, it comes from only one source: "American imperialism in every case strives to achieve its foreign policy objectives through reliance upon armed force. This policy has long since become the basic and now already long-standing traditional form of foreign policy action for the United States government." From this perspective, Soviet strategic forces have acted as a deterrent and "have cooled and continue to cool even the hottest heads on the shores of the Potomac, Thames, and Rhine." Naval spokesmen, including Admirals Gorshkov and Stalbo, continue to emphasize the Western threat to the USSR in spite of détente and SALT negotiations:

However, imperialism remains imperialism. Unconcerned with the lessons of history, it tries to rush forward in this imposed peace. . . . Making hypocritical statements concerning limiting strategic arms, American leaders simultaneously have worked out plans for a cardinal modernization of those arms and again recarved their strategy, adjusting it to the new material conditions of war (K. A. Stalbo, *Morskoi sbornik,*

1971, no. 8, p. 95).

So long as such a perception prevails within the Politburo, defense expenditures will remain high. Unless the next phase of the nuclear-weapons revolution should drastically reduce the effectiveness of aviation in war at sea—an unlikely prospect—naval air power will continue to be a very valuable instrument in the Soviet arsenal.

Research Notes

While in recent years there have been numerous publications on the Soviet navy, few authors have concentrated strictly on naval aviation. Asher Lee's *The Soviet Air Force* (London, 1961) and M. G. Saunders' *The Soviet Navy* (London, 1959) contain chapters on naval aviation during World War II and the first postwar decade. Neither has much to offer on the impact of the nuclear-rocket revolution, however. Some popular histories of Russian sea power give passing attention to naval aviation; others contain useful information on the composition and operations of the naval air service. These volumes include David Woodward's *The Russians at Sea: A History of the Russian Navy* (New York, 1965); Donald W. Mitchell's *A History of Russian and Soviet Sea Power* (New York, 1974); David Fairhall's *Russian Sea Power* (Boston, 1971); and E. M. Eller's *The Soviet Sea Challenge* (Chicago, 1971). Their perspectives range from an out-and-out lobbying effort for the USN, in the case of Eller, to semischolarly, in the case of Mitchell. All cling to rather ethnocentric visions of naval power and

have little of substance to say about the evolution of naval aviation.

Other works of a more analytical nature deserve mention. A pioneering work in this regard is Robert Waring Herrick's *Soviet Naval Strategy: Fifty Years of Theory and Practice* (Annapolis, Md., 1968). Based upon a careful reading of Soviet sources, especially *Morskoi sbornik,* this volume outlines the continuing debate over naval strategy in the USSR between the Old Mahanians and the young officers who advocate light forces. Herrick provides a thoughtful evaluation of the politics of naval policy. Recent works that have contributed to this approach include Wolfgang Höpker's *Weltmacht zur See: Die Sowjetunion auf allen Meeren* (Stuttgart, 1971); Norman Polmar's *Soviet Naval Power: Challenge for the 1970s* (New York, 1972); Siegfried Breyer's *Guide to the Soviet Navy* (Annapolis, Md., 1970); and Michael MccGwire's *Soviet Naval Developments: Capability and Context* (New York, 1973). To use Polmar's terms, these authors range from alarmists to realists in their assessments of Soviet naval developments. Some, like Herrick and MccGwire, see the Soviets as responding to Western developments, and play down the naval threat to the West. Polmar and Höpker, on the other hand, perceive a real shift in the naval balance of power. Each writer applies a strict analytical approach to the available data. But while MccGwire stresses an analysis of the process of weapons procurement and ship construction as the best guide to the evolution of Soviet policy, Polmar emphasizes hardware and Höpker the developing pattern of Soviet maneuvers. Under the leadership of MccGwire, analysts from NATO countries have assembled for the last three years at Dalhousie University to discuss recent trends in Soviet naval affairs. *Soviet Naval Developments,* under MccGwire's editorship, was one result. Another volume from Dalhousie is forthcoming.

If approached critically, Soviet publications can provide valuable information on naval developments. Important sources include *Morskoi sbornik, Kommunist vooruzhennykh sil, Voennaia mysl', Voennoistoricheskii zhurnal,* and *Krasnaia zvezda.* Works dealing with the development of the Soviet navy and sea power in general include Sergei Gorshkov, *Navies in War and Peace* (Annapolis, 1975), and S. E. Zakharov et al., *Istoriia voenno-morakogo iskusstva* (Moscow, 1969). The first is a translation of a series of articles which appeared in *Morskoi sbornik* in 1972 under Gorshov's signature. Adm. Elmo Zumwalt, responding to the series, asked if Gorshkov wasn't a "Twentieth-century Mahan" (*U.S. Naval Institute Proceedings,* November 1974, pp. 70-78). Interesting comments about the series have been made by Robert G. Wienland, Michael MccGwire, and James McConnell in *Admiral Gorshkov on "Navies in War and Peace,"* in CRC 257, U.S. Office of

Naval Research (Washington, 1974). (See also Comdr. Clyde A. Smith's analysis, "The Meaning and Significance of the Gorshkov Articles," *Naval War College Review,* March-April 1974.) Although few Western observers have commented on the Zakharov text, studying the very different emphases of these two works would seem a productive course. The leading authority on postwar naval developments in both the West and the Soviet Union is Rear Adm. K. A. Stalbo, who is also the Soviet navy's leading spokesman on U. S. military strategy and deterrence. For comments on Stalbo's contributions, see: Kenneth Hagan and Jacob Kipp, "U.S. and USSR Naval Strategy," *U.S. Naval Institute Proceedings,* November 1973.

Works dealing with the early period of Russian and Soviet naval aviation include K. F. Shatsillo, *Russkii imperializm i razvitie flota: Nakanune pervoi mirovoi voiny 1906-1914* (Moscow, 1968); S. Stoliarsky, "Iz boevogo proshlogo morskoi aviatsii voenno-morskogo flota SSSE" (*Morskoi sbornik,* April 1938); R. D. Layman and Boris P. Drashil, "Early Russian Shipboard Aviation" (*U.S. Naval Institute Proceedings,* April 1971); P. N. Mordvinov, *Kursom "Avrory": Formirovanie sovetskogo voenno-morskogo flota i nachalo ego boevoi deiatel'nosti* (Moscow, 1962); D. A. Kovalenko, *Obaronnaia promyshlennost' sovetskoi Rossii v 1918-1920* (Moscow, 1970); and M. V. Frunze, *Izbrannye proizvedeniia* (n.p., 1925). A necessary supplement to any of these works is John Erickson's *Soviet High Command: A Military Political History, 1918-1941* (London, 1962).

Although many works touch upon the expansion of naval aviation during the early five-year plans, few give it more than passing reference. Adm. N. G. Kuznetsov's *Nakanune* (Moscow, 1966) gives a none-too-candid view of decision making under

Stalin and the proposal for an oceangoing fleet. The general lines of the debate over the development of naval aviation can be found in various issues of *Morskoi sbornik,* although the question is usually discussed in terms of contemporary foreign developments. For the status of naval aviation with the young school, see V. Zof's "Mezhdunarodnoe polozhenie i zadachi morskoi oboroni SSSR" (*Morskoi sbornik,* May 1925). On the growth of Soviet war potential in the 1930s, see G. S. Kravchenko's *Voennaia ekonomiia SSSR* (Moscow, 1963) and A. M. Nekrich's *"June 22, 1941" Soviet Historians and the German Invasion* (Columbia, S. C., 1968). The latter work, edited by Vladimir Petrov, contains sharp criticism of Stalin's prewar efforts at military preparedness. (The attack was so sharp and telling that the Soviet edition was withdrawn from circulation.) On naval developments in specific fleets, consult their respective histories: G. Padlaka, *Krasnoznamennyi baltiiskii flot v velikoi otechestvennoi voine* (Moscow, 1949); S. E. Zakharov et al., *Krasnoznamennyi tikhockeanskii flot* (Moscow, 1973); P. Bolgari et al., *Chernomorskii flot: Istoricheskii ocherk* (Moscow, 1967); and I. A. Kozlov and V. S. Slomin, *Severnyi flot* (Moscow, 1966).

Regarding the Soviet navy and naval aviation in World War II, consult *Istoriia velikoi otechestvennoi voiny Sovetskogo Soiuza, 1941–1945,* six vols. (Moscow, 1960–1965); S. I. Rudenko et al., *Sovetskie voenno-vozdushnye sily v velikoi otechestvennoi voiny, 1941–1945* (Moscow, 1968); and V. I. Achkasov and N. B. Pavlovich, *Sovetskoe voenno-morskoe iskusstvo v velikoi otechestvennoi voiny* (Moscow, 1973). The Rudenko volume was translated by Leland Fetzer and appeared as Ray Wagner, ed., *The Soviet Air Force in World War II* (Garden City,

N.Y., 1973). The Achkasov and Pavlovich study treats Soviet naval theory and practice during World War II topically, with chapters devoted to the Soviet and German navies in the immediate prewar period, mine warfare, defense of naval bases, amphibious operations, artillery support of land forces, operations against sea communications, and the defense of Soviet sea communications. For those interested in the role of naval aviation on the eastern front, it is probably the best book available.

Soviet works on the nuclear-rocket revolution's impact on warfare include, in addition to the Gorshkov series and the Zakharov volume, V. D. Sokolovsky's *Voennaie strategiia* (Moscow, 1962–1963). A collection of essays has been edited and translated by W. R. Kintner and Harriet Fast Scott in *The Nuclear Revolution in Soviet Military Affairs* (Norman, Okla., 1968). For Western comments on Soviet responses, see Raymond L. Garthoff, *Soviet Military Policy* (New York, 1966); Thomas W. Wolfe, *Soviet Strategy at the Crossroads* (New York, 1965); John Erickson, "The Soviet Military, Soviet Policy, and Soviet Politics" (*Strategic Review,* Fall 1973); Leon Goure, Foy D. Kohler, and Mose L. Harvey, *The Role of Nuclear Forces in Current Soviet Strategy* (Miami, 1974); and S. W. B. Menaul et al., *The Soviet Union in Europe and the Near East: Her Capabilities and Intentions* (London, 1970).

Open data on Soviet warships and fleet composition can be found in the annual *Jane's Fighting Ships,* the biannual *Flottes de Combat,* and *Weyer's Warships of the World,* which is published by the U.S. Naval Institute in English and by J. F. Lehmanns Verlag in German in alternating years. Valuable data can also be found in the periodicals *Warship International* and *Soldat und Technik.*

With reference to the development of naval aviation under the tsarist regime and in the early Soviet republic, a major study of D. P. Grigorovich's career as a designer would be valuable. As do those of other specialists who served both regimes, his life provides an interesting focus for observing continuity and change in a revolutionary situation. Certainly attention should be paid to the development of naval aviation during the first two five-year plans, when it emerged as an integral, land-based weapon for the Red Navy. A careful survey of *Morskoi sbornik's* articles on naval aviation during the 1930s would be valuable. The hints about the possibility of building an oceangoing fleet during the third five-year plan, dropped by Admiral Kuznetsov in his memoirs, should also be explored more fully so as to determine the reasons why it was favored.

The history of naval aviation during World War II deserves serious study. Western authors have too frequently dismissed the Soviet navy's experience, but its failures and successes suggest much about the development of the navy during the war.

In the postwar period, probably the single most important topic is the impact of the Gorshkov era on naval aviation. How did the Soviets respond to the nuclear-rocket revolution? What is the relationship between Western (particularly American) weapons acquisition and deployment and Soviet developments? Admiral Gorshkov has dismissed out of hand the traditional techniques for evaluating the naval balance between the superpowers. Their asymmetric development deserves special attention, especially from observers interested in future trends in American development.

7

Soviet Civil Aviation
and Modernization, 1923-1976

Kendall E. Bailes

The history of Soviet civil aviation reflects in microcosm much of the history of Soviet society at large—its problems and its achievements. For these reasons it is of particular interest to a social historian. The thesis of this chapter is that Soviet civil aviation has played a modest but important role in the modernization efforts of the Soviet system (1) in strengthening the centralization of the regime, (2) in helping to legitimize Soviet rule in the eyes of various groups that make up Soviet society, and (3) in helping to modernize the economy and social structure. For an accurate evaluation, it is necessary to see the role of civil aviation in the proper framework of history, including aviation and transportation history as a whole, both in and outside Russia. This study is developed thematically, examining (1) the theory and organization of Soviet civil aviation in a historical perspective, (2) the development of Aeroflot's domestic passenger and freight services, and (3) the expansion of Aeroflot's international service. The conclusion attempts to relate civil aircraft and their many special uses to the modernization of the USSR during the first fifty years of its existence.

Theory and Organization of Soviet Civil Aviation

Soviet transportation theory since the 1920s has stressed the superiority of the Soviet system in developing a "unified transportation network" through central planning. What was once little more than a slogan has gradually taken on the outlines of a body of economic theory. Basically, this theory is that all forms of transportation in the Soviet Union should be complementary to each other and not wastefully competitive. Each form of transportation should be developed to do what it does best most efficiently, consonant with the overall Soviet goals of increasing material production and aiding national defense.

All forms of transportation are expected to contribute to these goals in the ways best suited to their particular modes. The best transportation network, in theory, is held to be one in which the least transportation is required. Therefore, the best transportation network is one so efficiently arranged that a minimum amount of time and other resources is spent on transportation. Thus, more energy can be allocated to material production and other tasks considered of higher priority. Economic planners and executives are expected to keep the relative factors of time and cost in mind when making transportation decisions.

The transportation planners, centered in Gosplan, the state planning agency in Moscow, work with planners in the various government organizations responsible for each type of transportation. They work under the general guidelines and supervision of the central organs of the Communist party and the USSR Council of Ministers. Since the late 1920s these planners have been faced with the enormous tasks of foreseeing the transportation needs of a country which covers one-sixth of the earth's surface and includes tens of millions of people, coordinating all modes of transportation, and structuring the availability and rates of each mode so as to encourage the most efficient use of the total transportation network. It is not surprising that in practice, reality has often fallen short of theory. Bottlenecks, breakdowns, competition for scarce capital resources, and controversy over transportation policies--all these problems have been endemic to the Soviet system; nonetheless, they should not be permitted to obscure its achievements.

How does Soviet civil aviation fit into transportation theory? Civil aviation is stressed in Soviet theory for many reasons. In a country with the size, climate, and distribution of resources, of the Soviet Union, aviation has a special role to play. It is part of a single system which includes river and sea transport, railroads, automotive and truck transport, and pipeline systems. According to Soviet theory, civil aviation should not try to duplicate what these other systems can do more effectively but should instead concentrate on its own unique advantages: particularly its speed and accessibility in serving remote areas and the low rate of capital investment it requires in comparison with roads, railroads, and pipelines. In defining those areas of advantage, Soviet transportation theorists emphasize history, geography, and climate in the development of Russian and Soviet transportation.

Traditionally, of course, the rivers of the Eurasian plain were the main highways of Russian history, and for centuries the history of Russian society was closely related to the trade which developed along these river routes and the overland portages between the main water highways. The advantages of water transport in this relatively simple economy were apparent: it was inexpensive, and it required relatively little expenditure of animal or human energy to develop and maintain.

For a large percentage of relatively imperishable items, such as coal, lumber, and grain, water transport may still have those advantages even in a modernizing economy. But with the economic development of Russia since the eighteenth century, water transport has become increasingly inadequate because it is both slow and periodic. The major river routes are frozen a good part of the year. The Volga, for example, which in 1960 handled sixty percent of all Soviet river traffic, is frozen 100–140 days a year; its northern tributary, the Kama, is frozen 170 days of the year. It may have been adequate for the Vikings and Slavs of the tenth century to ply their river flotillas only in the spring and summer, hibernating like bears the rest of the year to live off the fat of their trade and agriculture. But a modern industrial economy must keep functioning at a high level year-round in order to support its much larger population and higher standard of living.

While the rivers of Russia flow primarily north and south, her economy since the eighteenth century has become increasingly dependent on an east-west movement of material resources and population. The rich mineral resources of the Urals and Siberia have had to be exploited and shipped to the population centers of European Russia. The development of a modern economy has also involved the gradual redistribution of population from west to east. These east-west flows of people and material have required a major restructuring of the transportation network. Roads, and later railroads, pipelines, and air routes, have been developed to meet these needs.

In stressing the particular role of civil aviation, Soviet theorists have emphasized geographical and climatic factors that afford a distinct advantage to the regional use of air transportation. Many rivers and northern sea routes are frozen much of the year, with snow covering Siberia for 160–260 days annually and northern European Russia for 100–200 days. Forty-five percent of the entire USSR is covered by permafrost, at a depth ranging from several inches to three feet. During much of Russian and Soviet history, it was next to impossible to build viable roads and railroads over these permafrost areas. For example, if railroads had been constructed over frozen soil, engines, railroad cars, rails, and crossties might have disappeared during a brief thaw. Soviet scientists and engineers in recent years are said to have mastered some of the

problems of construction over permafrost, but the costs of such construction remain high in comparison with the amount of time and capital investment required to establish an air route in these areas, as well as in the vast stretches of swampy land in European Russia and the floodlands of the vast Siberian plains.

Given the distances, climate, and terrain of the USSR, Soviet theorists have stressed the increasing significance of civil aviation. They particularly emphasize its advantages for passenger service on long hauls and for relatively lightweight, high-value cargo. In tsarist times, it took a peasant family months to emigrate from European Russia to Siberia by oxcart, horse, or foot; and weeks for a letter from an official in Irkutsk, in central Siberia, to reach Moscow by the relatively well organized postal relays. In 1929, it took thirty-six hours for such a letter to reach Moscow by air and some six days by train. Today, conventional jets can make the trip in less than eight hours, and the new Soviet SST, which was scheduled to begin regular service on this route in 1975, can do it in less than three hours.

The capital investment required to establish an air route has been relatively low in comparison with other forms of transportation. In 1960, it cost only about 10,000 rubles per kilometer to establish an air route, against about 1.2 million rubles per kilometer for a rail route and about 800,000 rubles per kilometer for a highway. On the other hand, a major disadvantage of civil aviation has been its high cost of operation—the highest for any form of transportation. Another important disadvantage has been the difficulty of making air service reliable in all kinds of weather. Visibility is low or nonexistent in the greater part of the USSR for much of the year because of cloudiness, fog, rain, snow, or lack of daylight in the northern latitudes. Such obstacles to aviation have gradually been overcome during the past decade, as Soviet aviation advances in experience and technology. As the cost of operation decreases through the development of larger and more efficient aircraft and as reliability increases through the application of more sophisticated technology, Soviet theorists see a bright future for civil aviation.

In addition to the role of civil aviation in transporting passengers, mail, and cargo, Soviet theory assigns it a number of special roles. As defined by law, particularly in the Civil Air Code of August 7, 1935 (revised January 1, 1962), civil aviation was assigned three broad missions: (1) providing air transportation, (2) performing such special functions—more than sixty in all—as providing agricultural, geological surveying, forest firefighting, and air-ambulance services; and (3) supporting educational, athletic, and recreational activities; e.g., making propaganda flights and aiding aviation clubs. In most Western countries one would not expect such diverse duties to be united, but since the 1930s most of these activities in the Soviet Union have come under the monopoly of a single aviation conglomerate. Aeroflot is the common name for the organization which was officially known until 1964 as the Chief Administration of the Civil Air Fleet and subsequently as the Ministry of Civil Aviation. Although there has been a close relationship between civil aviation and the federal government in the United States since the 1920s, in that the government has regulated activity and promoted consolidation through the selective awarding of mail contracts, total monopoly and government ownership have been avoided; thus some competition has been maintained over major routes. The Soviet pattern more closely approximates that of government-owned airlines in Europe, although the re-

lationship in the USSR is perhaps closer and certainly broader. While information about its internal administration and personnel is sparse, it is known that Aeroflot in the 1960s contained fourteen central directorates with line functions, seven central departments with staff functions, and twenty-one territorial administrations. Aeroflot officials reported directly to the USSR Council of Ministers.

Besides the comprehensiveness of its activities, Aeroflot is different from most Western airlines in other basic respects. For example, Aeroflot's departments of sales and marketing are not separate divisions, and they absorb relatively little energy—in contrast to such departments in the competing airlines of the West. Second, the activity and importance of the Communist party in Soviet society is reflected in the organization of Aeroflot. The leading central directorate is the Political Directorate, which was established in 1933 after Aeroflot failed to fulfill its goals for the First Five-Year Plan. This directorate organized party cells and committees within all the divisions of Aeroflot and was responsible for ensuring that personnel were politically conscious and acting in conformity with the directives of the party. Analogous to the Political Administration in the Soviet army and to party organizations in other Soviet institutions, the Political Directorate is responsible for conducting regular courses in Marxism-Leninism, agitational meetings, investigations, and party purges. During the purges of the late 1930s, the Political Directorate of Aeroflot was responsible for the investigations which led to the dismissal and arrest of the top aide to the head of the airline, its construction chief, and at least twenty-two pilots, engineers, and technicians, according to the contemporary Soviet press. A third interesting feature of Aeroflot's organization is its responsibility for building and maintain-

Figure 54. Antonov An-10. Some 500 were built for the air force and Aeroflot. The plane cruised at 32,000 feet at speeds of up to 440 mph.

all airports and the traffic-control system for Soviet civil aviation. The Soviet government has centralized, in one superagency, functions which in the United States are carried out by a mixture of private and public authorities, including the commercial airlines, the Civil Aeronautics Board, the Federal Aviation Agency, and state and local governments.

The implications for efficiency and flight safety of combining all these functions in a single organization need to be considered. In the United States and other Western nations, it has been considered important to separate organizationally those who regulate and inspect (in the U.S., the Civil Aeronautics Board and Federal Aviation Agency) from those who actually fly. One might well wonder if Soviet complaints about the low labor productivity of Aeroflot and its poor safety record are not at least partly related to the practice of combining "pilot" and "check pilot" within the same organization. Some might see this practice as reflecting both the general lack of a "checks and balances" political philosophy in the Soviet Union and the monistic nature of Leninist theory and practice. The result of such monopolistic organization has been a growing bureaucratic structure, more comparable in size to a large government agency or major manufacturing corporation in the United States than to any single American transportation organization. Aeroflot grew from about 37,000 employees in 1948 to around 400,000 in 1973—approximately the size of the Ford Motor Company or International Telephone and Telegraph (ITT), two of the top ten corporations in the United States, which rank among the largest multinational business organizations in the world.

Given its monopolistic organization and function, Aeroflot can easily validate its claim to being the largest airline in the world, in terms not only of employment but also of length of air routes and transport volume. The largest U.S. airline, Pan Am, had about 45,000 persons on its payroll in 1973. However, when one adds all U.S. airlines together, as well as the CAB and FAA, civil aviation employment in the United States and in the USSR are roughly comparable, while the length of air routes and total volume of air traffic in the U.S. are considerably greater. (Together, all the airlines in the United States employed about 330,000 persons and the FAA and CAB accounted for about 55,000 employees in 1972.) However, while Aeroflot may be the largest single airline in the world, it is far from the most efficient—a fact the Soviet press has reported in detail for many years. Its labor productivity has been considerably lower than that of major Western airlines. The many levels of bureaucracy concomitant with its size and monopoly position tend to slow down service and stretch out the lead time for innovations.

Aeroflot's organization is also unusual in the composition of its top management. Since its origin, Soviet civil aviation has had an intimate relationship with military aviation in that many of its pilots and administrators were first trained as military aviators. At its birth in 1923, Aeroflot was established as the Inspectorate of Civil Aviation, directly under the Chief Administration of the Red Air Force. Although in 1930 it was separated administratively from the air force, it has maintained a very close relationship to military aviation.

In World War II Aeroflot was subordinated to the Ministry of Defense as an arm of military air transport, and its organization remains such that it can be quickly commandeered in a military emergency. Of course, U.S. airlines operated extensively as troop carriers in World War II and have aided the military effort in subsequent limited wars. But Aeroflot's ties to the Soviet military are more direct; since World War II, it has been headed by active Soviet air force officers. In 1948, its chief was Air Marshal Fedor Astakhov, and three of his key deputies were active air marshals and generals. From 1959 until 1970 Aeroflot was headed by a tough air force general, E. F. Loginov, who began his career as a military aviator in 1928, commanded a bomber squadron in World War II, and was chief of the Soviet tactical air forces until 1959. Loginov departed in May 1970 after Aeroflot received intense criticism in the Soviet press for breakdowns and inefficiency in its transport service. He was succeeded by his deputy, V. P. Bugaev, who was subsequently promoted to the rank of colonel general in the air force.

Bugaev's career is instructive of how to succeed in Soviet civil aviation. A graduate of the Higher Civil Aviation School, Bugaev combined a career in military aviation during World War II with civil aviation after the war. In the mid-1950s, he became one of the pioneers of Aeroflot's new jet airliner, the Tu-104. At this time he was selected to serve as a jet pilot in the "special air detachment" which is responsible for flying Soviet political leaders and which is directly subordinate to the State Security Organs (KGB). The contacts he made in flying such men as Andrei Gromyko to the United States probably played a part in his rise to commander of the special air detachment. During these years he was named an "Honored Pilot" and a "Hero of Socialist Labor." In 1963 he was awarded

Figure 55. An-12 Cub freight-carrying transport, in 1975 still the standard paratroop/ transport aircraft. Built to operate from unprepared fields, this 134,000-pound plane can get off the ground in 950 yards.

the Order of Lenin, the highest Soviet decoration (somewhat analogous to Knight of the Garter in the British system). Bugaev's career illustrates that the combination of a high degree of technical competence with a close relationship to the Soviet military, the Communist party, and the KGB is no hindrance to a pilot's rise in Soviet civil aviation. A member of the Communist party since 1946, Bugaev has held some of the highest positions in Soviet society. He has been a deputy to the Supreme Soviet and a delegate to the Twenty-fourth Party Congress, and has held membership in the party's central committee since 1970. In fact, his prestige and power—greater than those of any previous Aeroflot chief—are indicative of the rising status of his office.

By 1973 Aeroflot, although still plagued by a number of problems, was reported to be fulfilling its planned targets ahead of schedule. Under the new economic re-

forms, Aeroflot had been placed on a profitability basis—that is, its employees and executives were now rewarded primarily for their fulfillment of sales and profit goals, rather than on the basis of traffic volume per se or other production goals. Actually, according to Soviet sources, Aeroflot had been making a profit in its operational budget since 1952, although subsidies for such capital equipment as airplanes and new airports continued to come from the state budget. Since 1952, Aeroflot has been able to transfer part of its operational revenue into its capital budget, while at the same time substantially reducing Soviet air fares. As a result of the economic reforms of the 1960s (the so-called Lieberman reforms), sales and profitability became the principal goals of Aeroflot. In this respect, Soviet civil aviation seemed to be doing well under the management of Bugaev. Even Westerners and the Soviet press were impressed by his

Table 1. Freight Traffic (in billions of kilometer tons)

Year	All transport	Rail	Sea	River	Pipeline	Automotive*	Air
1913	114.5	65.7	19.9	28.5	0.3	0.1	—
1917	85.8	63.0	7.7	15.0	0.005	0.1	—
1928	119.5	93.4	9.3	15.9	0.7	0.2	0.0
1932	218.4	169.3	20.1	25.0	2.9	1.1	0.0
1937	434.4	354.8	36.8	33.3	3.6	5.9	0.02
1945	374.8	314.0	34.2	18.8	2.7	5.0	0.06
1950	713.3	602.3	39.7	46.2	4.9	20.1	0.14
1955	1165.0	970.9	68.9	67.7	14.7	42.5	0.25
1960	1885.7	1504.3	131.5	99.6	51.2	98.5	0.56
1970	3825.0	2494.6	655.2	174.0	281.6	217.7	1.89

*Includes truck and other automotive freight of all institutions, including collective farms.

Table 2. Passenger Traffic (in billions of passenger kilometers)

Year	All transport	Rail	Sea	River	Scheduled buses	Air
1913	27.6	25.2	1.0	1.4	—	—
1928	26.9	24.5	0.3	2.1	0.3	0.0
1932	89.9	83.7	1.0	4.5	0.7	0.01
1937	97.3	90.9	0.9	3.2	2.2	0.1
1945	69.8	65.9	0.6	2.3	0.5	0.5
1950	98.3	88.0	1.2	2.7	5.2	1.2
1955	170.2	141.4	1.5	3.6	20.9	2.8
1960	249.5	170.8	1.3	4.3	61.0	12.1
1970	548.9	265.4	1.6	5.4	198.3	78.2

Source: *Narodnoe Khoziastvo SSR v 1970*, Moscow, 1971.

poise, energy, and humor, and by the improvement they saw in Aeroflot's operations.

Development of Domestic Passenger and Freight Services

Several interesting patterns can be seen in the history of Soviet domestic air transport. Although the government had paid lip service to the concept of a unified transportation network prior to World War II, attention in these years was focused primarily on the railroads and waterways, to the relative neglect of intercity truck, bus, and air transport. The official Soviet figures cited in tables 1 and 2 convey some idea of Soviet transport patterns. Although civil aviation during the first fifty years enjoyed a very high growth rate, it had begun with a very low base; its proportion of total passenger and freight volume was minuscule until recent years.

Several factors determined the pattern indicated by the statistics in these two tables. For one, an extensive rail network in the central and most densely populated parts of the country already existed in 1917; the rail network merely needed to be rebuilt and expanded. A body of experienced personnel existed, both in railway transport itself and in the manufacturing industry which supplied it with equipment. By comparison, automotive and air transportation were still in their infancy, and the country had few sources of imports. The native industry required to supply these branches of transportation had to be built almost from scratch. Second, freight capacity, rather than passenger transportation, was given first priority during the rapid industrialization of the 1920s and 1930s. Railroads could be depended upon to perform yeoman service here, particularly in carrying large loads on medium and long hauls. Water and automotive transport were counted on to supplement the railroads in performing this function. But without an adequate highway system, most

Figure 56. Il-18 Coot turboprop. This one is in service with the Polish airline, LOT.

automotive production went into servicing short hauls, primarily local traffic in towns and on farms. Air freight was confined largely to mail, precious metals, medical supplies, precision instruments, breeding animals, and other relatively expensive and lightweight cargo. Such freight scarcely registered in the statistics.

Aeroflot, in fact, remained something of a Cinderella until a decade after World War II. While occasional compliments were paid to her potential beauty, most of the time she was somewhat neglected and had to subsist on leftovers. Most of Aeroflot's activity during these years was confined to carrying mail and other freight (85 percent of the airline's volume prior to 1939) and to flying officials from the central agencies of Moscow and other urban areas to the peripheries during emergencies. In these years the attention of Soviet civil aviation was deliberately centered on supplementing other forms of traffic—particularly in areas where the main linkage to the outside world had previously been supplied by dogsled, camel, horse, or donkey. Civil aviation also performed important services in keeping the borderlands, with their turbulent nationalities, in communication with the center. For example, in the early 1930s civil aviation played a role in the suppression of the *basmaki* rebels, Muslim nationalists who operated in remote areas near the borders of Persia, Afghanistan, and China. In the latter part of that decade, civil aviation was used to ferry troops to the Mongolian borderlands of the Far East, where the Red Army fought intrusions by the Japanese in 1938–1939. After 1928, Stalin had turned his attention to reviving the gold and other mining industries of the far north, as well as the fur trade in those areas, in order to provide some capital for industrialization. Civil aviation played an important role in linking that region to the rest of the country.

By 1939 the Soviet Union had surpassed the United States in air-freight volume, although that lead was lost after the war. Yet it remained far behind in passenger miles, as well as in the reliability, equipment, and comfort of airline service. For the most part, civil aviation was confined to good weather and daylight; much of it ceased during the winter months. In the development of traffic control and instrument flying, Soviet civil aviation remained far behind the West. The government proved to be generous with advice and criticism but niggardly in providing investment capital from the state budget.

Civil aviation was expected to supplement the meager capital allocated for its expansion with income from the sale of bonds to the general population. Here it was able to benefit from the "aviation mania" encouraged by the authorities through the press and through such voluntary organizations as the Air League (Osoaviakhim), a mass organization formed in 1923, the year Aeroflot was formed, to promote air clubs and aviation activities. (These activities included model-airplane building, sport flying, gliding, and sky diving.) Civil-defense activities, particularly among the young people, became increasingly important for this organization in the 1930s. The Air League had 15 million members by 1934, and it helped considerably to expand Aeroflot's fleet through the sale of bonds and other voluntary contributions. Some peasants reportedly were so impressed by the gallant fliers of Aeroflot that they contributed part of their crops—rye, oats, wheat, and even suckling pigs—to be converted into cash for flying machines.

While Aeroflot undoubtedly benefited from the air mania of the 1920s and 1930s, military and experimental aviation designed for propaganda purposes became the prime focus of popular interest. This pattern originated during the early years of the revolution and became increasingly apparent with the rise of Stalin and the threat from Japan and Germany in the 1930s. During the cold war after 1945, the military focus remained strong. The rapid expansion and modernization of civil aviation had to await the death of Stalin in 1953 and the gradual cooling of tensions with the West in the 1960s and 1970s.

In the early years of its existence, Aeroflot tried a number of interesting experiments to demonstrate its usefulness to the economy, although many of these failed. Their failure may, in fact, have impeded the development of civil aviation, giving the airline a reputation for harebrained schemes and spectacular fiascos. For example, in the 1930s gliders were the rage, not only for sport flying but also in attempts to create "air trains." From three to five gliders would be hooked up to a large prop plane in a V- or diamond-shaped formation and hauled into the air with a pilot and cargo in each glider. Before reaching their destination, they would be cut loose and would glide to a landing. Such air trains promised considerable savings in fuel but proved unreliable and uneconomical in practice. Even more extensive experiments were carried out with dirigibles. The first large Soviet dirigible was constructed in 1930. Despite several disasters with such airships, talk persisted throughout the 1930s of establishing regular dirigible routes between Moscow and outlying industrial areas. However, none of these experiments—which were designed to increase the freight capacity of Aeroflot and to compete with the railroads for capital funds—was effective during the 1930s and 1940s.

Given the economics of air transport, passenger service held the greatest promise for expansion. But here the most serious obstacles were not overcome until the 1960s. Several factors discouraged greater volume: Air fares remained very high until 1957. Flights were undependable and departed at odd hours so that destinations could be reached in time for daylight landings. Aeroflot did not have the best reputation for safety. If Aeroflot's safety record had been better than those of most Western airlines, Soviet media would more than likely have publicized that fact. However, no accident statistics have ever been published in the Soviet Union, as they are

Figure 57. Ka-26 multipurpose helicopter in demonstration maneuvers. The versatile Kamov design is widely used for agricultural and medical purposes.

regularly for Western airlines. Moreover, Aeroflot for many years lacked the reputation of providing comfort and reliability—a deficiency that reflected general Soviet policies during years when production in quantity was the main goal.

What it was like to fly on Aeroflot in its earlier days is illustrated by several surviving accounts, one of the most vivid being that of an Englishwoman who traveled in the Caucasus and Central Asia during the mid-1930s. Here, for example, is her description of a trip from Tiflis, the capital of Georgia, to Baku, the main oil-refining center of the Trans-Caucasus:

It was a good day for flying when we left Tiflis; the sun shone brilliantly, the sky was cloudless, there was no wind. We had, however, no real faith in there being a machine. We had at first been told that it left at eleven o'clock, then at twelve, and were quite prepared for it not to leave at all. When the car turned in at the airport there was no sign of any aeroplane. All we could see were empty fields, haystacks, byres. Chickens wandered about, and a woman was pegging out a line of washing between the ricks. The driver left the engine of the car running whilst he went into the airport building. He was gone for about fifteen minutes, and we feared the worst. There was no plane in sight, and there obviously wasn't going to be any plane. When the driver returned, Donia [the interpreter] asked him if anything was wrong. He said, No, only that two more places than existed had been booked on the machine; two of the passengers would have to be turned away. . . .

Nothing happened for some time, and then a number of men came out on the verandah of the building behind and stood watching, and a few minutes later mechanics appeared and began wheeling a machine out of a hangar.

"What," asked Donia, "will happen to the two passengers for whom there are no places? "

The driver shrugged. "They can go tomorrow. Or they can go by train."

"But it's disgraceful," I cried, when Donia had translated. "If such a thing happened in England another plane would be run."

We joined the small crowd of men standing by the plane. When the signal was given we mounted the steps and entered the narrow, claustrophobic confines of the machine. We seated ourselves; there appeared to be a place for everyone who had come aboard. Perhaps the two too many had been sent away? Anyhow, the door slammed, there was a roar of acceleration and we were off. . . .

The floor of the machine was covered with mail-bags. It would be impossible to step out into the aisle; one would have to crawl over the bags, and they were stacked up against the door of the lavatory at the tail of the machine. If the worst happened and one were sick there would be nothing for it but to be sick on the mail. Usually there are paper bags tucked into a pocket on the back of the seat front, but there were none in this machine. We concentrated on the scenery (Mannin, *South to Samarkand*, 1936).

Such grin-and-bear-it attitudes have had to suffice for many Aeroflot customers even in more recent times. As late as the 1960s, foreign travelers commented about the lack of oxygen masks, seat belts, life-jackets, and safety directions on domestic flights. Most flying was done at low altitudes so that pilots could keep landmarks in sight, making flights very choppy and uncomfortable at times.

The major expansion of Aeroflot and improvement in its service began around 1956 with the introduction of passenger jets and a lowering of air fares. Between 1957 and 1967, air fares were cut in half and became competitive with rail fares. In 1950, Aeroflot had carried only about 1.6 percent of all intercity passenger traffic in the USSR; by 1970 it was carrying 24.1 percent. On long hauls (over 1,500 kilometers), Aeroflot was carrying the majority of all domestic passengers by 1967. In fact, air transportation in the Soviet Union became so inexpensive that it was not uncommon for peasants 1,000 miles away to pack up a bag of fresh produce, such as fruit from Georgia, fly to Moscow, sell it in the market, and fly back with a handy profit. (The authorities tried to discourage this practice, not very successfully, by arresting a few such peasants for "speculation.")

The popularity of air travel in the Soviet Union is shown by the high percentage of seats filled. Whereas commercial U.S. airlines in 1969 flew with an average of only about 50 percent of their seats filled, Aeroflot flew with seventy-nine percent in the same year. These percentages remained fairly consistent for both countries during the last half of the 1960s. Of course, the U.S. capacity for air travel is much greater than that of the USSR. The more than forty U.S. airlines in 1970 flew more than twice as many passenger miles as Aeroflot— a gap which has increased in recent years despite the rapid expansion of Aeroflot. The United States has been a far more kinetic society, with fewer controls on travel and more money available for that purpose. The Soviet Union, however, has

Figure 58. Mi-12 heavy-lift helicopter. Aeroflot has ordered this design in small numbers for special work.

seemed to be moving in a similar direction. In the 1960s, Aeroflot began to actively advertise its services, although sales and marketing remained a minor part of the airline's organization. Posters, brochures, television commercials, and other devices were used to acquaint the traveling public with Aeroflot's services.

In 1960, a special project was carried out by the Young Communist League in an effort to popularize air travel. Teams of young people were sent into railway terminals to question travelers about their choice of transportation. A number of people who were traveling from Moscow to central Siberia by train expressed ignorance of the low airline fares and the extent of Aeroflot's services. Some even believed that airline service to their city virtually ceased in fall and winter months—a statement that had once been true.

The national campaign to sell air travel kept demand high and radically changed the traveling habits of Soviet citizens. By 1973, the Soviet Union seemed destined to become a more kinetic society. The political implications of this trend for increasing communication and sophistication

among the Soviet population, not to mention its potential effects on the physical environment, could easily be imagined. Whether or not the regime would take the next logical step and allow its citizens more freedom of travel outside their own borders remained uncertain; if so, the growing international network of Aeroflot would be there to serve the demand.

With the expansion of air passenger service inside the USSR, the airline's clientele became increasingly impatient about lapses in comfort and reliability. In the 1960s and early 1970s, Aeroflot remained from five to ten years behind Western airlines in computerizing its ticket services and automating its baggage handling. The line had expanded its fleet and cut its fares before it was ready to cope with the resulting huge increase in volume. This problem reflected the kind of uneven expansion that has been the general pattern of Soviet development. Lack of automation and other defects in organization kept labor productivity low, a situation that resulted in a major press campaign against Aeroflot by the Government newspaper, *Izvestiia,* and the labor-union organ, *Trud.* The spirit of this campaign was summed up in several comments that appeared in *Trud* in 1967: "Passengers who have long since become accustomed to traditional services are now demanding new conveniences. But, in point of fact, Aeroflot has offered nothing new for ten years." The labor newspaper went on to observe that the attitude of many Aeroflot employees toward public critics was that they could "love it or leave it." "As long as Aeroflot has no competitors," the Soviet newspaper added perceptively, "you may love the airline or may be outraged by it; but you can't avoid using it"—a complaint resembling American criticisms of large public-service monopolies. *Trud* concluded its attack with the following judgment: "Aeroflot has become a huge empire—powerful, strong and rich—one that should be able to show concern for its customers on the ground as well as provide maximum comfort in the air. But we come to the unhappy conclusion that our Aeroflot is not really concerned about its patrons and lacks elementary human warmth."

Although Aeroflot remained far from perfect, by 1973 there was evidence that it had begun to cope with some of the problems created by rapid and unbalanced growth. A computer center was established in Riga and began handling ticket services, while other research institutes planned automation in other areas of the airline's work. In late 1972, the Soviet Ministry of Civil Aviation announced a ten-year plan to rebuild the air traffic control system and bring it into line with the standards of the International Civil Aviation Organization (ICAO), which Aeroflot joined in 1970. Negotiations began with European and American companies to acquire the complex electronics systems which Soviet industry was not yet equipped to build. Faced with a projected tripling of traffic between 1970 and 1975,

Moscow's Central Airlines Agency introduced the Minsk-23 computer and planned the introduction of an even more advanced system, the Siren-1, which would be capable of handling reservations for all flights scheduled from Moscow airports over a thirty-day period—a minimum of 50,000 reservations per day. Such advances generally came first to Moscow and gradually filtered out to local airports.

Expansion of International Service

While the reasons for the expansion of Soviet domestic transport services are clear, the reasons for the rapid expansion of Aeroflot's international services in recent years are less obvious. Such expansion involved a radical change in Soviet policy. Before Aeroflot was established, the two pariahs of the Versailles Peace settlement of 1919 had formed a joint airline company, Deruluft, to provide service between Soviet Russia and Germany. Deruluft, which began service in 1921, provided highly efficient international mail and passenger service during the 1920s on a limited scale. Formed even before the 1922 Rapallo Pact between these two countries, Deruluft reflected the international alliances of the Weimar period and the broad range of cooperation that developed between Russia and Germany in those years. Once Lenin and the Soviet leadership had been disappointed in their hope of instigating a Soviet-style revolution in Germany, they had looked increasingly for peaceful ways of connecting the shattered Soviet economy with the industrial strength of a reviving Germany. Deruluft represented one such connection. While in theory it was jointly managed, in practice it was largely German-run, and it eventually fell victim to Stalinist centralization in Russia and the Nazi takeover in Germany. In general, Deruluft was an exception in Soviet civil

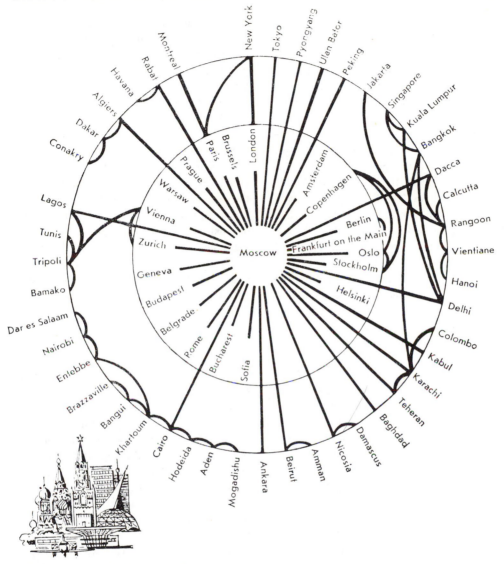

Figure 59. Aeroflot's international routes.

aviation.

As early as 1921, Lenin had declared in a government decree the principle of exclusive Soviet sovereignty over her air space. Throughout Stalin's long regime, isolationism remained the rule in Soviet civil aviation—as it did in Soviet foreign policy, with the exceptions of a short period during the 1930s and of the World War II years. In general, this policy meant the almost total exclusion of foreign aircraft from Soviet skies, and the converse for Soviet airliners. The few exceptions to that rule were usually made for political, not commercial, reasons.

An international division of Aeroflot was reportedly formed in 1937, during the period when Soviet foreign policy was attempting to create a united front against European fascism and Japanese imperialism.

At that time, civil air agreements were signed with Sweden, Czechoslovakia, Outer Mongolia, and the Chinese warlord of Sinkiang province in Central Asia. The primacy of politics has set the general pattern for Aeroflot's international service during most of its history.

International civil aviation was an issue in the cold war even before most people were aware of the growing conflict between the Soviet Union and the United States. In August 1944, well before Yalta and Potsdam, the United States called a conference in Chicago to establish new machinery for the conduct of international civil aviation. The Soviet Union sent a delegation of experts, who reached Canada before they were abruptly recalled. The official reason given for Soviet nonparticipation was the presence of delegates from such neutral countries as Spain, Portugal, Switzerland, and Sweden. The real reason is unknown. However, the United States clearly was in the strongest position to dominate international civil aviation after the war, with a greatly expanded aviation industry and the military and economic might to back it up. The United States stood for both a high degree of international regulation of air traffic and for major expansion of such traffic. Although the U.S. government did not advocate a complete "open skies" policy—i.e., freedom to navigate the planet's air space equivalent to the freedom of the open seas—the United States did want more openness and fewer barriers to international civil aviation, just as it wanted lower trade barriers and expanded international commerce. U.S. policy-makers believed strongly that nationalism—economic nationalism in particular—was the root cause of World War II. The key to a stable postwar world was seen in the lowering of international barriers and the development of institutions designed

to regulate conflict and to guide the development of an international community. Given the strength of America's position at the close of World War II, the United States seemed likely to play a dominant role in such institutions and to profit most from such openness.

The Soviet Union, with a war-shattered economy and distinctly different internal institutions, decided not to cooperate with America's civil aviation scheme. To the ever-suspicious Stalin and to a country long committed to isolation from and distrust of the West, American postwar plans signified a capitalist plot to dominate the world. One casualty of this attitude was Soviet participation in the International Civil Aviation Organization and the International Air Transport Association, which grew out of the talks begun at the 1944 Chicago conference. ICAO, which was eventually incorporated into the United Nations, became responsible for the establishment and enforcement of standards governing safety, navigational controls, airport services, and air charts. Unlike the ICAO, which is made up of representatives of the signatory governments, the IATA is a trade association composed of private and governmental airlines. The IATA has acquired some of the functions of a cartel, in that it helps regulate international air routes and attempts to prevent price wars by negotiating standard fares for its members. The Soviet Union had no use for either organization so long as Aeroflot remained primarily a domestic airline. During the height of the cold war, Aeroflot's international operations were confined largely to the satellites of Eastern Europe and to mainland China.

As the isolation of the Soviet Union began to break down after Stalin's death, Aeroflot followed the expansion of Soviet influence in the nations newly emerging

Figure 60. Iliushin Il-62. First flown in 1963, it did not go into service until three years later.

from the colonial empires and in the West. In 1956 Aeroflot had established only a handful of international routes outside the Soviet bloc; by 1973 bilateral civil aviation agreements had been signed with sixty-five nations, and Aeroflot served most of the world's major cities.

What were the reasons for this international expansion? Soviet goals in domestic air transport had been primarily economic: rational, in economic terms. Where it has not been seen as economically rational, domestic air service has not played a major transport role. However, political motives predominated in the international expansion of Aeroflot after 1956. The establishment of international air routes was analogous to the showing of the flag by the Soviet navy in foreign ports—an analogy that became increasingly apparent during the 1960s, when the flag-draped lines of Aeroflot served as an advertisement of Soviet power. Even though Western airliners had dominated the world's international air routes during the first decade after World War II, the proliferating presence of Aeroflot at major airports indicated that Soviet air power had come of age. This kind of technological advertising was especially important because all of Aeroflot's planes were Soviet-made. Except for the British, no other government insisted that its airlines buy the products of the home aircraft industry if foreign aircraft (usually those made in the U.S.) were more profitable.

Since 1935, Aeroflot has been obliged to fly Soviet-built craft. The first and second generation of Soviet jet transports were far from efficient by Western standards, being very heavy in relation to their capacity. Yet Aeroflot continued to fly them on international routes and even sought to sell them to other airlines, particularly those of the newly independent countries. This effort had met with little success by 1973; although the countries outside the Communist bloc which purchased Soviet craft (such as Mali, Guinea, and Ghana) received very attractive price and credit terms, they found the Soviet planes inefficient to operate, parts scarce, and maintenance difficult. Such other lines as Air India, after investigating Soviet craft, opted to buy Western planes. In the 1960s and early 1970s, Communist China increasingly turned from Soviet-made to Western planes, passing up the Tu-144 in order to take an option on six Franco-British SSTs. (In this case China's motives may have been political as well as economic since the relative merits of the Concorde and the Tu-144 were not yet fully known.)

It remains to be seen whether the next generation of Soviet commercial aircraft—particularly the giant Soviet airbus (Il-86), the Soviet SST, and the new Soviet jet-freighter (Il-76), all scheduled to go into service in the late 1970s and early 1980s—will prove to be competitive with the products of other aircraft industries. By 1973, despite fears expressed by some Western writers, the USSR had not posed a serious threat either in the sale of aircraft or in the competition for international air routes. Fears of Soviet price cutting in an attempt to gain strength in the market persisted, but seemed unrealistic. Aeroflot largely adhered to the rates established by IATA, while remaining outside that organization. By taking this position Aeroflot maintained its freedom to cut rates, although the pressures against doing so were strong. Aeroflot depended for its expansion abroad on bilateral agreements with other nations, most of which were represented in IATA. Such nations would certainly have disliked a rate war initiated by the Soviets.

In general, a spirit of cooperation marked Aeroflot's international expansion, which included a major effort to train the nationals of third-world countries in civil aviation. The Civil Aviation Institute in Kiev registered students from forty-nine foreign countries in 1972 as part of the USSR's overall foreign aid effort. While

remaining unattached to IATA, in 1970 the Soviet Union joined ICAO, which it had boycotted since that agency was founded in 1944. Fears of American domination of that organization had proved groundless, and the Soviet Union wanted to have a greater say in the regulation of international civil-aviation standards. Perhaps even more important in that decision was the desire to demonstrate that Aeroflot intended to be as safe and reliable on its international routes as were the other members of ICAO—an important factor, in view of both the uncertainty about Aeroflot abroad and its somewhat tarnished domestic reputation. In the early 1970s, Aeroflot embarked on a major revamping program in an effort to bring its services up to the standards of ICAO.

In 1973 the Soviets ratified the international treaty against skyjacking, with one important reservation: the Soviet government declared that it would not necessarily submit to the binding arbitration of the International Court of Justice in any dispute over interpretation or enforcement of the treaty—a reflection of the qualms it still had about potential interference with Soviet national sovereignty in aviation matters. Soviet concern about the problem of skyjacking had grown during the 1960s and early 1970s. Although statistics on such attempts have not been made public in the Soviet Union, seven attempted skyjackings have been publicized in the Soviet press since 1964, three of them in 1973 alone. All but one were foiled, and the crew members and passengers involved were decorated for their courage (at least one of them posthumously). The Soviet press describes skyjackers simply as "bandits." But more comprehensive reports of the seven known attempts indicate that some of the skyjackers were members of ethnic minorities—a

Figure 61. Tu-134. Close in size to the DC-9, it went into service in 1967. The bomber nose was replaced with a radome in the Tu-134A.

not-surprising finding, in view of the evidence about repressed ethnic unrest in the Soviet Union during this period. One of the attempts took place aboard an Armenian airliner, another aboard a Georgian craft; all the skyjackers attempted to force the crews to fly outside the Soviet bloc.

In June 1970, eleven persons, mostly Soviet Jews, attempted to skyjack an airliner in Leningrad. Their death sentences were commuted only after protests from abroad. In October 1970, a Lithuanian and his son successfully commandeered an Aeroflot liner and forced it to fly to Turkey, killing a young stewardess who tried to bar their way to the cockpit. Considering the fierce opposition of Soviet crews as publicized in the press, and the high-ranking decorations these crews later received, it would appear that Aeroflot personnel had orders to aggressively resist such attempts. The risk and difficulty entailed in obtaining small arms and other weapons in Soviet society made skyjacking attempts relatively uncommon, but they were common enough to cause concern among Soviet authorities and to encourage international cooperation in this area as well.

Its international service represented a vary small proportion of Aeroflot's traffic in 1972—only some 2 million of a total of 82 million passengers carried. As a latecomer to international civil aviation, the Soviet Union had an initial disadvantage; on the other hand, several factors worked in its favor. Although Aeroflot had little experience in this new environment, it could make the most of well established routes and traveling habits. Unused to any competition even domestically, it was forced to learn to operate in a new atmosphere characterized by intense competition for routes and traffic. Apparently unwilling to wage a price war, Aeroflot was required to compete for passengers by promoting novelty and high standards of service. This challenge represented a learning experience for Aeroflot; as a result, the line received moderately good marks from international air travelers but no extraordinary encomiums.

During the first five years of its New York–Moscow route, Aeroflot carried considerably more passengers than its American counterpart, Pan Am, which offered the same number of flights over this route. Pan Am later charged that Soviet citizens were required to fly Aeroflot, while American tourists and businessmen frequently chose Aeroflot because of its novelty. Pan Am officials further charged Intourist, the Soviet tourist agency, with playing dirty tricks in advising its customers that Pan Am was overbooked when such was not the case. The Soviet press countered with similar charges related to travel advice given by American consular officials. Whatever the truth of these various charges, traffic on the Moscow–New York route in all of 1972 amounted to only some 14,000 passengers, making it a very small factor in Aeroflot's overall international service. Because no data were available about Aeroflot's success on other routes, no definitive conclusions can be drawn.

In expanding its international traffic, Aeroflot had several aces up its sleeve. An obvious advantage, of course, was that it represented a superpower with a strong research and development sector in aviation and thus enjoyed all the concomitant leverage and prestige that reputation implied. Should the SST prove successful as a long-range aircraft, Aeroflot would be able to offer considerable savings in time to many international travelers. It also had the Siberian ace to play: transit rights across Soviet Siberia offered a shorter link between Europe and East Asia than the Middle Eastern–South Asian route. Soviet authorities dangled this bait, with mixed results, before other nations in its attempts to negotiate bilateral air agreements. The Siberian route

proved to be more attractive to Western European and Japanese airlines than to American carriers, which saw in it little potential advantage for themselves.

Despite the great expansion in air routes and in the volume of Aeroflot's international service, several factors seemed likely to limit this service for some time to come. Two of these factors were the stiff competition from other airlines and the limitations on freedom of travel for Soviet citizens. While tourism to the USSR promised to increase Aeroflot's volume, most tourists in 1972 continued to use other airlines in their travels to the Soviet Union. Tourism from the Soviet Union to countries outside the Soviet bloc was minimal; while some 50,000 Americans visited the USSR in 1972, only 256 Soviet tourists came to the United States. The figures for official Soviet delegations (including not only diplomats but athletes, journalists, musicians, etc.) were higher, but even when these trips were added the total volume of such traffic was small in comparison to that of other industrial countries. The most recent aggregate figures, from 1967, indicated that only 35,000 members of official Soviet delegations traveled abroad during that year. Nearly half of that number went to other socialist-bloc countries. While these figures were bound to increase, official travel scarcely provided a basis for a regularly scheduled international air service. Until the leaders of the Soviet system felt sufficiently secure to allow unrestricted travel by their citizens, Aeroflot would have to build its volume largely on the custom of foreign nationals. As a result, its international traffic seemed destined to remain small, in comparison with both its own domestic service and other international airlines, unless a spectacular breakthrough in service could be achieved.

Figure 62. Tu-154, designed to supersede the Tu-104 on high-density routes much as the Boeing 707 operates elsewhere.

Conclusion

One purpose of this chapter has been to demonstrate the role which Soviet civil aviation, in the first half-century of its existence, played in the modernization of the USSR. As one aspect of a modernizing society, what function has civil aviation served in that process? What can be learned about the wider society from a study of this one aspect?

At the risk of oversimplification, *modernization* can be defined as the process by which generally static, backward-looking, agrarian societies are transformed into largely urban and industrial societies oriented toward rapid change. Modernizing societies tend to make a virtual fetish of science and technology in their drive to dominate nature and boost the standard of living. Such theorists of modernization as Cyril Black and S. N. Eisenstadt have stressed the broad nature of the modernization process and the interrelatedness of the changes introduced in the political, intellectual, psychological, economic, and social dimensions of human life. They have also described the various forms modernization has taken in different societies. The development of Soviet civil aviation is richly illustrative of this process at work in Soviet society.

In the political realm, one prominent feature of modernization in the Soviet Union has been the extreme centralization and concentration of political power, a concentration even greater than that achieved under the tsars. Civil aviation has been both a symptom of and a spur to centralization. Its own organization represents a massive concentration of air power under the direct authority of the central government and the Communist party. As such, it is a symptom of the centralizing preferences of Soviet modernizers. As a spur to modernization, Aeroflot has provided means by which officials at the center can reach outlying regions of the country quickly, thus linking remote areas of the USSR into one close political entity.

Besides taking advantage of official travel opportunities which Aeroflot's domestic network expedited, Soviet modernizers exploited civil aviation politically. From the 1920s on, mats of the central government and party newspapers were flown from Moscow to other regions of the USSR, where large press runs could be distributed on the same day or the following day. This practice helped consolidate the information monopoly and propaganda goals of the center. Another interesting propaganda use of civil aviation was pioneered by the Soviets. In the 1930s, a special "propaganda squadron" was formed by Aeroflot to carry the message of the central government to the farthest corners of the land. Before it was disbanded on the eve of World War II, this squadron aided a number of mass campaigns, reaching more than 10 million people. Its planes, some thirty in number, were generally the largest and most modern in the Soviet fleet. They were equipped with loudspeakers, photo labs, movie projectors, and printing presses that could turn out some 8,000 leaflets an hour. Scattering messages bearing the names of contemporary Soviet political leaders, these planes brought concrete evidence of the power of the central leadership to even the most isolated villages. Where planes could not be landed, agitators would often be parachuted into remote areas with their messages. The squadron also aided in the annual spring sowing campaigns, in promoting literacy, in the drive for Stakhanovism, and in public health campaigns.

In another respect, civil aviation was used more consciously and extensively in the USSR than in many other countries to assert the political legitimacy of a modernizing regime. In traditional Russian society, the tsars had claimed that their

legitimacy came from God, from their role as Christ's representatives, protectors of the faithful, and defenders of the church. The religious rituals and ceremonial routines of the crown, from the anointing of the tsar during the coronation ceremony to the blessing placed by the church on imperial armies, served to reinforce this basis of tsarist legitimacy.

The Bolsheviks, on the other hand, appeared to many Russians as usurpers. They had seized power in the name of the working people and on the basis of their own alleged understanding of the "scientific laws of history." Not believing in God, they sought to legitimize their power in other ways. They claimed legitimacy in part on the basis of their ability to transform nature and society. But until they had done so, their legitimacy would be in doubt; to protect their position, they had to rely on a high level of coercion against those elements which viewed their power as illegitimate.

In his climb to power during the 1920s, Stalin had the further problem of legitimizing his personal ascendancy within the Bolshevik regime. Partly by distorting the historical record, he emphasized his close relationship to Lenin and his loyalty to the Bolshevik party as one basis of his legitimacy. But as he and his associates moved from their underground past into the rapid modernization of the 1930s, they increasingly emphasized accomplishments in science and technology. Aviation, both civil and military, was widely used in this effort to assert the legitimacy of Stalinism. Following precedents set in the West to publicize aviation (such as the Paris Air Show of the 1920s, the Hendon Air Show of the RAF, and the spectacular world-record feats of Western aviators), similar Soviet efforts were launched, but these were linked much more closely to the political leadership

Figure 63. The new Tu-144 supersonic transport landing in Tashkent.

than were those in the West.

In the 1930s, particular emphasis by Soviet pilots, many of them from Aeroflot, was placed on establishing world flying records. Having noted the publicity potential of such efforts in the West, including Lindbergh's dramatic flight in 1927, the USSR gave massive publicity to the efforts of its own airmen. By the end of that decade, Soviet spokesmen claimed to have set some sixty-two world records, including the longest, highest, and fastest flights, the first landing at the North Pole, and the first flight from the Soviet Union to the United States by a polar route. The holders of these records were called "Stalin's falcons," and Stalin was prominently featured in Soviet publicity about their flights. It was said that he had personally approved their plans and had mapped out some of their routes.

He was on hand to greet the successful when they returned and to award them some of the country's highest decorations. Photographs and posters of Stalin and his intimates greeting such aviation heroes as Chkalov, Baidukov, Vodopianov, and Papanin were given prominence during this period.

Much of this manufactured aviation excitement, which was publicized widely by the media, took place between 1935 and 1938, the period of the Stalinist purges. Indeed, it occupied the attention of the Soviet media perhaps even more than the purge trials themselves. As a countertheme to the purges, such publicity stressed the image of a creative, progressive leadership reaching new heights of achievement despite the efforts of the "renegades, bandits, and traitors" of the anti-Stalin opposition, which allegedly sought to undermine the Soviet system. Whether this coincidence of themes was accidental is impossible to document.

Beginning in 1933, every August 18 was declared Aviation Day; in Moscow, this became a day for ceremonial appearances by the Soviet leadership. Soviet leaders created a whole calendar of such events, including May Day, Navy Day, and the anniversary of the Bolshevik revolution. The similarity of this practice to the religious calendar of Russian orthodoxy and the ceremonial appearance of the tsar on important religious holidays is obvious. Revolutionary and technological celebrations are, to a modern regime, what the older religious holidays were to a traditional one. A description of the Aviation Day held on August 18, 1937, at the height of the purges, illustrates this analogy: As Stalin and members of the Politburo watched, a stratosphere balloon slowly raised a huge canvas image of Stalin above the tens of thousands of spectators. Dozens of planes flew overhead, changing formation to spell out L-e-n-i-n, S-t-a-l-i-n, and U-S-S-R and then to form the outline of a five-pointed star. With such dramatic displays of human organization and power over nature, one might say that the Soviet modernizers attempted to erase from the minds of their people the religious symbols of political legitimacy and substitute a different justification for political power. How successful they have been is debatable, but the attempt is fascinating. At any rate, such publicity provided a precedent for the political exploitation of aeronautics and space accomplishments in later decades, from Sputnik I to the Soviet SST.

Since the 1920s, aviation has enjoyed the glamour of modernity, especially for Soviet youth. Millions of them have participated in the Air League, which gave them an opportunity to learn about flying and aviation-related activities. In the 1930s, the Air League enrolled between 12 and 15 million members, most of them young people. In a society of 175 million people, this figure represented a significant proportion of the younger generation. The president of the Curtiss-Wright Corporation, T. A. Morgan, noted after an extensive visit to the USSR on business in 1934: "School children have hundreds of model airplane clubs or take training in parachute jumping. The press devotes what we would call a disproportionate share to aviation news of all kinds. . . . This country is not air-minded, but air-crazy!" Many of the Soviet air aces of the 1940s and cosmonauts of the 1960s and 1970s cited their experience in the Air League as being a formative influence in their choice of profession.

The Soviets were among the pioneers in special, nontransport uses of civil aviation. Light planes have been used by Aeroflot since the early 1920s for a variety of agricultural purposes, from crop spraying to the sowing of wheat, barley, rye, and oats. In Central Asia, an area devoted to raising such vital industrial crops as cotton, aircraft have been used to sow the saksaul tree, a desert plant which helps to hold the soil and prevents sand from drifting over irrigation ditches. In the far north, planes have not only carried supplies and passengers but also surveyed ice fields for northern shipping, spotted concentrations of fish and seals for state industries, and hunted down wolf packs that threatened reindeer and local villagers.

One of the major tasks of any modernizing regime is to map its territory and survey its geological resources. Aviation has played a vital role in rapidly increasing the Soviet Union's knowledge of its mineral resources and creating accurate maps of its territory. Another major aspect of modernization is to effect an increase in the quality of health services. Here, too, Aeroflot has played a role, by providing an extensive air-ambulance service and by facilitating visits by "air doctors" and paramedics to remote settlements in the USSR, in addition to regularly spraying large areas of malarial swamps.

Along with the more explicit uses which Soviet modernizers have made of civil aviation, it might be instructive to consider some of the general effects Aeroflot has had on the social and economic modernization of the USSR. Not only has it greatly increased the mobility of a once-stagnant society and contributed to its development by facilitating transfers of population and resources, it has also fostered such modernizing characteristics as sexual and racial equality of opportunity, interdependence and intergroup cooperation, accurate observation of nature, and technical competence. What matters when one takes to the air in the USSR is not the race or sex of the crew but its knowledge of aviation and its willingness to cooperate in achieving a high level of service. Racial and ethnic minorities, women, and young people have found opportunities in Aeroflot since the 1920s, as pilots as well as in a variety of other occupations. Many

Soviet aviation records registered with the Fédération Internationale Aéronautique in the 1930s were set by women pilots.

Civil aviation, like much of modern life, is generally a corporate enterprise. No individual person can hope to own and operate a major airline. Civil aviation requires a high level of specialization, the coordination of specialized labor in a corporate body that provides continuity to the enterprise, and the cooperation of that labor according to regulations that are clear and rational in terms of the airline's goals. Incompetence and arbitrary actions by individuals, whether they are managers, flight controllers, pilots, or ticket agents, can quickly lead to major tieups or, at worst, to disaster. Aeroflot, like many modern corporations, has performed less than perfectly in this respect, but it has helped to foster the trend in the direction of organizational efficiency.

To sum up, then, civil aviation has played a variety of roles in the modernization of the Soviet Union—some of them imaginative and unusual, some of them not very successful. Despite the tardiness in developing the potential of air transport during the first four decades of Soviet rule, civil aviation has begun to come into its own in the USSR. The steady expansion of Aeroflot now seems assured.

Research Notes

General Histories

The most comprehensive Soviet study, sponsored by Aeroflot on the fiftieth anniversary of the Bolshevik revolution, is *Grazhdanskaia aviatsiia SSSR 1917–1967* (Moscow, 1967). This work tends to promote Aeroflot, however, and thus omits many of the problems and difficulties which were discussed in the Soviet and Western aviation press over the years. Some of these problems were discussed rather frankly at a conference of Aeroflot workers held in 1968, the proceedings of which were published in *Bol'shoi sovet Aeroflota. Materialy soveshchaniia aktiva rabotnikov grazhdanskoi aviatsii SSSR* (Moscow, 1968).

A detailed overview of Aeroflot's development can be found in the pages of *Grazhdanskaiia aviatsiia,* the official magazine of Aeroflot, which was published between 1931 and 1941 and from 1955 to the present. Other articles from the Soviet press dealing with civil aviation can be found in *Samolet,* the journal of the Air League between 1923 and 1941, and the *Current Digest of the Soviet Press,* published in the United States from 1949 to the present. Among Western journals which have reported extensively on Soviet civil aviation are *The Aeroplane* (now incorporated into *Flight International*), *Aero Digest, Aviation Week and Space Technology, Interavia,* and the *New York Times.*

Soviet monographs of a general nature dealing with aviation include P. D. Duz, *Istoriia vozdukhoplavaniia i aviatsii v SSSR,* two vols. (Moscow, 1944, 1960); Rostislav Vinogradov, *Kratkii ocherk razvitiia samoletov v SSSR* (Moscow, 1956) and *Samolety SSSR* (Moscow, 1961); and A. S. Yakovlev, *50 let sovetskogo samoletostroeniia* (Moscow, 1968). Non-Soviet monographs and articles that deal with Soviet civil aviation include Janusz Babiejczuk, *Lotnictwo Kraju Radzieckego* (Warsaw, 1969); R. E. G. Davies, *A History of the World's Airlines* (London, 1964); Karl Heinz Eyermann, *Lufttransport* (Berlin, 1961); Heinz J. Nowarra, *Die Sowjetischen Flugzeugen 1941–1966* (Munich, 1967); Harriet E. Porch, "Aeroflot, The Soviet Airline—At

Home and Abroad" (*Journal of Air Law and Commerce,* Spring 1953). A somewhat dated but still useful bibliography is that of Bertha Kucherov, *Aeronautical Sciences and Aviation in the Soviet Union* (Washington, 1955). Arthur G. Renstrom, head of the Aeronautics Project, Science and Technology Division of the Library of Congress, and the library staff of the National Air and Space Museum, Smithsonian Institution, can be very helpful in locating sources.

Theory and Organization

In addition to some of the sources listed above, useful Soviet works on the theory and organization of civil aviation include Ruben E. Abramov, *Puti uluchsheniia organizatsii passazhirskikh aviaperevozok v tseliakh povysheniia ekonomiki obshchestvennogo vremeni* (Moscow, 1968); V. G. Bakaeva, ed., *Transport SSSR,* a textbook for higher education in the schools of the merchant marine and river transport (Moscow, 1960); V. M. Makarov, ed. *Ekonomika vozdushnogo transporta* (Moscow, 1971); Boris M. Parakhonsky, *Tekhniko-ekonomicheskie problemy vozdushnogo transporta* (Moscow, 1961) and *Transport SSSR: Itogi za piat'desiat let i perspektivy razvitiia* (Moscow, 1967); and D. P. Zagliadimov et al., *Razvitie edinoi transportnoi seti SSSR* (Moscow, 1963). A Western textbook on civil aviation, useful for comparison, is John H. Frederick's *Commercial Air Transportation* (Homewood, Ill., 1961). Western studies of Soviet transportation theory and organization include James H. Blackman, "Soviet Transport and the Process of Industrialization" (Columbia University Ph.D. dissertation, 1958); Holland Hunter, *Soviet Transport Experience: Its Lessons for Other Countries* (Washington, 1968) and *Soviet Transportation Policy* (Cambridge, Mass., 1957); George Kish, "Soviet

Air Transport" (*Geographical Review*, no. 36, 1958); Stephen Lee Sutton, "Geographical Factors in the Development of Civil Aviation in the USSR" (master's thesis, University of California at Los Angeles, 1964); and J. N. Westwood, *A History of Russian Railways* (London, 1964) and *Soviet Railways Today* (London, 1963).

Development of Domestic Passenger and Freight Service

Besides useful information in some of the sources above, relevant Soviet works include articles in the third edition of the *Bol'shaia sovetskaia entsiklopediia* (Moscow, 1970–); Viktor V. Gavrilenko, *Znakom'tes'—Aeroflot* (Moscow, 1968); Abram Z. Gol'tsman, *Grazhdanskaia aviatsiia* (Moscow, 1932); *Grazhdanskaia aviatsiia SSSR na poroge vtoroi piatiletki* (Moscow, 1933), and *Grazhdanskii vozdushnyi flot k VII vsesoiuznomu s'ezdu* (Moscow, 1935); Vsevolod P. Kliucharev, *Grazhdanskii flot SSSR; statistiko-ekonomicheskii spravochnik za 1923–1934* (Moscow, 1936) and *Grazhdanskaia aviatsiia* (Moscow, 1933); Anatolyi I. Langfang, ed., *Letchiki; sbornik rasskazov* (Moscow, 1938); V. S. Molokov, *Soviet Civil Aviation* (Moscow, 1939) and *Narodnoe khoziaistvo SSSR v 1970* (Moscow, 1971); V. F. Odintsova, *Ordena Lenina grazhdanskaia aviatsiia* (Moscow, 1967); Vartan S. Simoniants, *Aeroflot—vozdushnomu puteshestvenniku* (Moscow, 1967); Evgenii V. Sofronov, *V Vozdukhe—samolety Aeroflota* (Moscow, 1967); A Yegorov and V. Kliucharev, *Grazhdanskaia aviatsiia SSSR* (Moscow, 1937). Additional Western works of interest include John Grierson, *Through Russia by Air* (London, 1934); Ethel Mannin, *South to Samarkand* (London, 1936); Harriet E. Porch, *Russian Commercial Aviation—Friend or Foe?* (Denver, 1958); *World Aviation Annual* (Washington, 1948); *Jane's All the World's Aircraft*, published annually in London; and Jill Lion, *Long Distance Passenger Travel in the Soviet Union* (Cambridge, Mass., 1967).

International Service

Soviet and Western aviation periodicals have followed the expansion of Aeroflot abroad in great detail. In addition, these Western studies provide a useful framework: Hans Heymann, Jr., "The Soviet Role in International Civil Aviation" (*Journal of Air Law and Commerce*, Summer 1958); William E. O'Conner, *Economic Regulation of the World's Airlines: A Political Analysis* (New York, 1971); Robert L. Thornton, *International Aviation and Politics* (Ann Arbor, Mich., 1970); Stephen Wheatcroft, *The Economics of European Air Transport* (Manchester, 1956); and John Stroud, *The World's Airliners* (New York, 1973).

Conclusion

The theoretical and comparative framework for assessing the role of civil aviation in Soviet modernization efforts is provided by Cyril Black, *The Dynamics of Modernization* (New York, 1968); and S. N. Eisenstadt, *Modernization: Protest and Change* (New York, 1966); Richard J. Barber, *The American Corporation* (New York, 1970); Hugh Stephenson, *The Coming Clash: The Impact of the International Company and National State* (New York, 1972); and Maurice Zeitlin, ed., *American Society, Inc.* (New York, 1970).

Suggestions for Further Research

Controversies in the development of Soviet transportation theory, particularly in regard to civil aviation, deserve separate treatment, as do the history of Aeroflot's internal organization and the changes in the composition of its labor force. The bureaucratic structure of civil aviation, its relationship to other Soviet institutions, and what this relationship says about the society as a whole are still poorly understood. Of particular interest is the degree of autonomy granted to the individual sectors and territorial subdivisions of Aeroflot over the years, and the effects this policy has had on its performance. The relationship of those who regulate and inspect to those who actually fly, as compared to the Western system of inspection and certification, needs further study. The changing international role of Aeroflot in the Communist bloc and abroad, in the context of Soviet foreign policy and foreign aid programs, would make an interesting study. The activities of the Air League (Osoviakhim, later called Dosaaf) and its influence on the attitudes and career choices of the younger generation also merit greater attention. Finally, a comparative study of the special, nontransport uses of civil aviation in the USSR and abroad should be of interest to students of comparative modernization. This chapter only scratches the surface of these topics. If it raises as many questions as it answers and sparks the curiosity of other scholars, this effort will be judged a success by its author. The accompanying bibliography provides a starting point for further study.

8

The Lessons of World War II and the Cold War

Joseph P. Mastro

At the conclusion of World War II the Soviet Union found itself as one of the two remaining great powers in the world: Germany and Japan had been defeated, France's power had proven illusionary, and Great Britain had been nearly crippled, with its empire in the first stages of disintegration. Only the United States could have acted as a counterbalance to Soviet power, and the Americans were unwilling to assume such a role. Soviet armies were entrenched over half of Europe; the process of satellization of the Eastern European states had begun even before the end of the war; the United States had begun a rapid demobilization, leaving Europe to Britain; and the demarcation line between East and West was quickly taking form.

Although the physical costs of the war to the Soviet Union were incalculable in terms of both industrial capacity and people lost, the political benefits were quite substantial. The Soviet Union had

been able to achieve an international status of the first rank, the power to maintain that status, and a chain of client (puppet) states along its frontier. The key to this new position was the Soviet army, which had gained for the USSR what ideological rhetoric, propaganda, and the Comintern never could achieve.

The Soviet military had demonstrated its capacity to serve both Stalin and the Soviet state. It was at the same time a heralded force and a potentially dangerous one. The new international position of the Soviet state necessitated the latter's maintaining a substantial military force for purposes of international and domestic control as well as for the inevitable conflict with the Western capitalists. Because World War II had demonstrated the necessity and the value of a strong military, the continuation of such a force was assured as long as the ideology demanded a future war with the capitalists, now personified by the United States. The military was also needed as a defense against a possible attack. Even though the military was a valued institution, praise for all branches was by no means equal. The Soviet army received most of the praise and rewards after the war, with the air force and navy being placed in the background.

Throughout the war, the air force was viewed as a support unit of the army. Air power was considered essential not in a strategic sense but only in respect to what tactical support it could lend the army at the front. Even the air-defense system was neglected in favor of channeling resources into the harder-pressed ground forces. Although a few attempts were made by the air force to praise itself, such views brought reprimands from both the Soviet military command structure and the political leaders who were thinking "army" during and after the war.

While the victories of the Soviet army had been translated into political advantages in Eastern Europe, these advantages were by no means secure. The immediate postwar problem for the Soviet Union and Stalin was to consolidate the political advantages which had been gained through the war and occupation of the territory. The emphasis of Soviet policy thus became decidedly European in character. This policy choice was clearly in evidence through the Stalinist period and may even be considered the central interest of the Khrushchev period. The military, both army and air force, benefited from this European emphasis, at least those sectors of the military assigned to the European area. These forces were almost always the first to receive new weapons, to benefit from any new technology, and to be assigned more resources and manpower.

These decisions about policy and the military positions were clearly made by Stalin. The Soviet dictator apparently learned a great deal from World War II,

and he applied some of that knowledge in his decision making. It is equally clear, however, that some lessons were lost on the Supreme Commander. The avalanche of criticism directed at Stalin during the de-Stalinization campaign included attacks on his military decisions as well as on his cult of personality.

Anyone who reviews the lessons learned by political or military leaders as a result of war must first consider who the leaders were and when they were in a position to influence decision making. For these reasons consideration must be given to the various phases or periods of Soviet history between the termination of hostilities in 1945 and the present.

When one is discussing the lessons learned by Soviet leaders, it is important to note that leaders and the style of rule have changed, and that what is a lesson at one time perceived by one individual may not be viewed later in the same light. It is imperative that this caveat be clearly understood because of its implications for the military and military policy. With respect to Soviet leaders, one must first consider the inexorable Stalin, a perhaps more perceptive and certainly more flamboyant Khrushchev, and the more practical Brezhnev. It is a question not simply of what lessons were learned from a hot and a cold war but also of how information is perceived, utilized, and digested by different decision makers. For this reason, five distinct phases have been delineated for purposes of analysis: (1) immediate postwar, 1945-1948, (2) Stalinist cold war, 1948-1953, (3) reevaluation, 1953-1957, (4) Khrushchev's peaceful coexistence, 1957-1964, and (5) parity and search for détente, 1964–.

Phase 1: Immediate Postwar Period, 1945-1948

By the end of World War II, the Soviet

Union had gained a superior position in Eastern Europe but could not directly threaten the United States, which at the time possessed a monopoly on nuclear weapons and the capability to use these weapons against the Soviet state. The air-defense system was at best poor and in many areas almost totally nonexistent. The allocation of resources to air defense was not considered important during the war because the threat from German air power was considerably less than the threat from the German army.

Stalin apparently saw the need for a change in this policy almost immediately following the war. The military was assigned at least three fundamental tasks during the postwar period: (1) keep the European theater forces strong as a counterpoise to the United States (the possibility of a Soviet drive to the Atlantic was meant to deter the United States from using its nuclear weapons), (2) build Soviet air defenses as rapidly as possible, and (3) develop a nuclear capability.

The first of these tasks was largely operational at the end of the war. Soviet military forces were in control of Eastern Europe, and although their numbers had been significantly reduced (from 11 million to 3 million men), there was also a strong effort to modernize these remaining forces. Some serious problems could potentially have developed in the event of a conflict; air transport and resupplying over long distances were new to the Soviet military. The air force had neither the equipment nor the experience to carry out the massive resupplying of advanced Soviet troops. The Soviet leaders did recognize this as a potential problem, and some efforts were made to correct it.

Soviet fighter forces were also weak and could have done little to stop an air attack launched from bases around the Soviet Union or from aircraft carriers. The air-defense system as a whole (PVO) was virtually useless against high-altitude bombers or against an attack conducted in conditions of poor visibility. No radar network was available, and only limited visual warning stations were operational. Asher Lee estimated that half of the 15,000 combat aircraft in the Soviet Union at this time were assigned to air defense; however, this number appears more illusionary than real.

The air-defense system was the first to receive new jet fighters. The Mig-15 and later the Mig-17, both subsonic fighters, became the nucleus of the PVO forces during the Stalin years. The radar network was rapidly expanded and was eventually extended to the western edge of Eastern Europe. This development was a significant one because it not only increased Soviet security but also added a new dimension to the Soviet perception of Eastern Europe. Because the traditional route for land invasion of the Soviet homeland had been through these now "friendly" buffer states, the Soviets had apparently learned that any such invasion in the future would be of air–nuclear age dimensions, with attack from both land and air routes. Medium-range bombers equipped with nuclear weapons could easily strike the industrial heartland and population centers far behind the front lines. This perception resulted in the emphasis on air defenses, warning systems, and fighter planes. With this new emphasis upon air defense and the perceived need for such a system, offensive capability progressed at a faster pace than the defensive weapons needed to check them.

The third task assigned to the scientific and military communities by Stalin was the rapid development of a nuclear capability, a program apparently under way even before the end of the war. Stalin understood the significance of such a technological breakthrough and was determined not to allow the American nuclear monopoly to persist. If the Soviet Union were to retain the advantages won in the war, a nuclear force had to be added to the already impressive traditional armed forces. It is interesting, however, that neither aircraft carriers nor long-range bombers were developed in tandem with the dawning of the nuclear age in the Soviet Union.

The failure to develop a long-range bomber force was the result not of ignoring the idea of such a force, but rather perhaps of a lag in technology. This technology gap was demonstrated when the Soviets tried to copy Western aircraft after the war, building in the defects found in the samples. Another possible reason for the decision not to develop a strong strategic bomber force with long-range capability was the general thrust of Soviet policy, which centered on Europe. The strategy appeared to be to keep Europe as a "hostage" so that the United States would not attack the Soviet Union, which had the power to be a legitimate threat to Western Europe. While the long-range bomber force was not developed under Stalin, he did foresee the need for a delivery system for such time when the Soviet Union would possess nuclear weapons; thus the technological foundation for missiles probably was laid during this period.

During this early phase, however, the Soviet Union had neither the weapons nor the delivery system. Russia did not explode her first atomic device until 1949; her first thermonuclear device was tested just four years later. The quickness which characterized Soviet nuclear development indicates that Stalin had initiated a crash program even before the end of the war. This program was probably intensified after Potsdam, where Stalin learned of the successful American test. Even later, he did not seem impressed when President Truman told him of the American weapon. There is little doubt that Hiroshima left an impression on Stalin, forcing him to realize that the Soviet Union could never be a true world power without atomic weapons. What the Soviets did have in 1948 was a 3-million-man army, a series of hostage states in Eastern Europe, and a token bomber force; moreover, the USSR was on the threshold of becoming the world's second nuclear power. At the same time that Stalin recognized the new role and importance of the Soviet army, he could not tolerate an independent institution capable of challenging him personally. This phase thus witnessed considerable shuffling of military personnel. Marshals might be heroes in war but were considered to be threats in time of peace.

Phase 2: The Stalinist Cold War Phase, 1948–1953

By 1948 the Soviet Union had abandoned all pretenses of establishing a coalition of popular governments in Eastern Europe and had begun to consolidate its position. The Soviet buffer zone was composed of states whose governments were maintained in power with the aid of the Soviet military; they had in fact become true satellites. The military had filled a power vacuum in the immediate postwar phase, and nothing short of another war could have dislodged the Soviets from their forward positions. By this time the United States had returned to Europe with the announcement of the Truman Doctrine and the declared intention of forming the North Atlantic Treaty Organization. These actions made the development of a Soviet nuclear capacity even more of a necessity in the eyes of Stalin, although

Figure 64. Il-10, successor to the Il-2 Shturmovik of World War II. This plane was captured from the North Korean Air Force in 1950.

his military strategy remained essentially the same.

The experiences of World War II and the traditional focus of the Soviet military on the ground forces remained the cornerstone of Soviet doctrine. One can conclude that military strategy at the time of Stalin's death in 1953 was the same as it had been in 1945, despite the advent of the nuclear age. The air force was still viewed as a supporting arm of the large land army, which was superior to the Western forces. The object of war was to defeat the enemy's troops in the field and to capture territory—both of which the Soviet Army had done in World War II. Air power was a tactical necessity, not a strategic one. Because Stalin had seen the value of nuclear weapons, he fostered their development and also perceived some need for a delivery system and an air-defense system.

While some of the Soviet military memoirs published during the de-Stalinization campaigns of the late 1950s were critical of Stalin because he was rigid and old-fashioned in his military thinking, thereby hampering the development of new weapons systems, the facts indicate that Stalin was at least aware of new needs. If the programs and research on

new systems had not been started under Stalin, Sputnik probably would not have been launched in 1957. The lessons of the V-1 and V-2 rockets were learned in Moscow as well as in Washington. The Soviet Union was depending on a technological breakthrough that would enable it to catch and even surpass the Western powers. The decision not to develop a comparable long-range bomber force was made during this phase, one reason being the future development of missiles. This decision could also be indicative of an anti–air force feeling in the Soviet military high command and in Stalin. The preference for short- and medium-range bombers capable of reaching all European targets and the further development of tactical aircraft represent the thrust of Soviet air strategy in this phase. The air force was not designed to have a separate strike force but rather to act as a subsidiary of the army. What was good for the army was determined by what was good for the military and the Soviet Union, indicating a subordination of the military to political controls; in this case, the position of the army was in basic agreement with Stalin's military doctrine and strategy. Demands for an increased role for the air force would not have been viewed with great favor by Stalin; in fact, all suggestions for change stopped not long after the conclusion of the war. A further indication of the apparently subordinate role of the air force can be seen in its command structure, which was composed primarily of army men. Political and military rewards given by Stalin went to the army, a clear example being the composition of the Central Committee.

When the first party congress in thirteen years was called in 1952, a new Central Committee was selected. Stalin apparently wished to recognize the military for its performance in World War II; therefore, he added military men to the Central Committee, particularly at the candidate level. Twenty-seven military officers were chosen to serve on the committee; of this total, twenty-four were members for the first time. This number represented more than 11 percent of the total membership, a figure never to be surpassed by later committees. What is perhaps more significant is that nearly all of the committee members came from the Soviet army. Only the very top-level officers of the air force and navy were given the honor of Central Committee membership.

The morale of the Soviet armed forces was undoubtedly high throughout this phase. The position and stature of the military had never been higher; they had saved the Soviet fatherland from Hitler, Germany, and fascism. All branches gave themselves credit for winning the war and for maintaining the Soviet position. The rounds of congratulations, however, were not meant for the air force, which was sharply criticized for "inflating" its role in the Great Patriotic War and which was always reminded that it was supplementary to the ground forces. Whenever the role of strategic bombing in future war was discussed, it was nearly always in terms of how it would be related

to ground operations or how such bombing could aid the ground forces. Although a separate strategic role for the air force was advocated by some air force commanders, they were overwhelmed by the dominant voices in the army.

The few military men who hesitantly suggested changes in doctrine and strategy almost always submitted their ideas in the accepted context, camouflaged by much extraneous material. Some even tried a tangential approach, citing U.S. and British strategic air power and the role of the long-range bomber and strategic bombing in World War II. General Nikitin may have had just such an intention in mind when he wrote in 1949 that, in view of the United States' strategic bombing capability, the Soviet Union should consider the possibility of redistributing Soviet industrial plants. Both General Nikitin and Stalin were well aware of the destructive capacity of conventional bombing in Germany, Stalin having seen the ruins while at the Potsdam Conference.

Most of the military opinions during this phase continued to emphasize traditional ground forces and air defense. Conservative military doctrine was almost totally influenced by the successes of World War II; there was an assumption that a future war would be fought under similar conditions and with the same objectives. The Soviet military and political leaders at this time still viewed war in the context of ground-troop operations, with air power being used to supplement the power of the army. The military high command was critical of anyone who "exaggerates the role and significance of strategic aviation."

These views were being expressed at the same time that the Soviet Union was following a markedly risky foreign policy. While consolidating their own position in Eastern Europe, the Soviets were also

Figure 65. Il-28 Beagle light bomber. Revealed in May 1950, it is the equivalent of the Canberra.

encouraging and directing the French and Italian Communist parties and supporting both the Greek guerrillas and, to a lesser degree, the Chinese Communists. When one adds to these the Berlin Blockade, a coup in Czechoslovakia, a planned coup in Finland, some political and diplomatic pressure on Turkey, and finally the Korean conflict, the picture of an aggressive state is not difficult to imagine. Lacking a strategic nuclear capability, however, the Soviet military and

political leaders must have recognized the superiority of the United States. It was in this area of military strategy and thinking that significant change occurred almost immediately after Stalin's death.

Phase 3: Reevaluation, 1953–1957

Shortly after Stalin's death, Soviet military leaders began to discuss openly the need for some revision in military doctrine, at least as it affected strategic bombing and the possible use of nuclear weapons.

Military strategists began to talk of the
necessity of delivering devastating blows
to the enemy far to the rear of the front
and of developing a more powerful air
force. Some of these views had been
openly expressed in the immediate postwar
period, but such discussion had been
effectively stopped after 1948.

While the debate about such issues
had been cut off by Stalin, the ideas were
certainly not forgotten, and they arose
anew in the mid-1950s. The basic doctrine
did not change, in that the emphasis was
still placed on the army and on traditional
combat operations, but the new importance of nuclear weapons and means of
delivery was added to the doctrine, which
now included ". . . the combined efforts
of all arms of the armed forces. . . ." The
role of strategic air power was viewed
more in terms of its capability to destroy
military forces, bases, and other strategic
power than as the single means to achieve
military victory in time of war. This
latter role was the responsibility of the
army and its capacity to defeat enemy
military units and seize territory. The
destruction of an enemy's population
and industrial centers by strategic bombing
was considered to be secondary, although
it now assumed more importance than
it had during the Stalinist period. Striking
the enemy with nuclear weapons was
simply not an overriding consideration
in the development of military strategy.
There may be some justification for this
view in a situation where no country has
a nuclear monopoly. Questions were
then being asked even in the West about
whether the United States would use its
nuclear weapons if she were herself vulnerable to such weapons. With both sides
possessing a nuclear capability, do the
weapons not then become neutralized?
In the event that such thinking represented
an accurate appraisal of the conditions,

the burden in war would fall upon the
regular armed forces.

The Soviet Union sought to develop
both a nuclear capacity and delivery
system and an air-defense system which
could limit or stop a strategic nuclear
attack on the Soviet Union. By 1957,
the Soviets had attained both nuclear
capacity and the means of delivery. Their
air-defense system, which by now included
new all-weather jet interceptors, air-to-air
missiles, and the first generation of ground-
to-air missiles, was greatly improved but
still incapable of preventing an attack.

The new-found prestige of the air force
was reflected in the statements of various
military and political leaders, including
Marshal Zhukov. Development of the
air force did not include the notion that
such improvements should be at the
expense of the army, however. While
the position of the air force had been
upgraded by the time of the Twentieth
Party Congress, leaders hastened to place
this improvement in the context of coordinated military strategy and reliance
on air power.

Khrushchev's Twentieth Party Congress
speech raised some fundamental questions
about Soviet ideology, including the
inevitability-of-war doctrine. A change
in this doctrine was necessary, Khrushchev
reasoned, because of what a nuclear war
would do to both sides in such a conflict.
This did not mean that wars would end,
for there could still be limited wars; thus
the necessity of preparing for conflict
with conventional forces. Nuclear weapons
would therefore act as a deterrent, with
long-range strategic forces being necessary
to the deterrent—presumably, never to be
used. However, Khrushchev had a new
weapon in mind for the long-range delivery: the ICBM. Development of Soviet
superiority in such an area would benefit
Soviet policy in ways other than the

Figure 66. Mig-15, Po-2, and Mig-21 (foreground) on display at the Polish Air Museum in Warsaw.

potential for its ultimate use.

The development of such a delivery system was begun either near the end of the war or shortly after the war. At the same time that the response of the Soviet Union to the long-range strategic bombers of the United States was to build up, maintain, and modernize the ground forces and upgrade the air-defense system, all the while degrading the usefulness of strategic bombing, the development of long-range missiles was progressing. The launching of the first space satellite in 1957 and Khrushchev's subsequent boasts of Soviet superiority caused some alarm in the Western world. Such an accomplishment was certainly not expected at that time, at least by the general population. The official Western response was one of calm, while feverish work went on in an effort to launch an American satellite. Talk of "gaps" abounded—an education gap, an engineer gap, a technology gap,

a missile gap. A new round in the postwar arms race had begun. The Soviet response to American nuclear superiority, attained in World War II and maintained for twelve years, was to achieve at least the appearance of Soviet technological superiority.

The attainment of a workable ICBM gave the Soviet Union a temporary edge in the cold war, even though the supposed superiority was more imaginary than real. What is important is that Khrushchev began to act and to bellow as if the Soviet Union did possess a militarily superior position. The side effects of the Soviet ICBM were many: First, it caused an immediate speedup in the U.S. ICBM development; the Soviet challenge was being accepted. Second, it began to raise questions in Western Europe about the United States' resolution to protect that area, now that Soviet missiles could reach American cities. (Such questions hastened the French decision to develop their own nuclear force and prompted later calls from other countries for a share in nuclear weapons.) Finally, it stimulated a debate within the Soviet military and political leadership as to the value of a missile system, with some leaders advocating substantial cuts in the Soviet army.

Although this debate continued throughout the Khrushchev period, a few years passed before it emerged into full public view. Khrushchev—who had denounced Stalin, defeated the antiparty group, and abruptly changed Soviet foreign policy—initially had the full support of the military. He had aided Marshal Zhukov's rise to political importance. As minister of defense, member of the Central Committee, alternate Presidium member, and finally full member of the Presidium, Zhukov supported Khrushchev throughout this phase, even siding with the party secretary in the antiparty group struggle in 1957. Khrushchev's dependence on the military illustrates both the increased importance of the latter in Soviet politics and the new style of coalition politics: no single individual could survive without allies in powerful places. While Stalin was ever wary of popular and potentially powerful and influential military leaders, the new political leaders could not ignore them. There was no balancing institution to match the military, particularly after the degrading of the secret police in 1953. The fact that Zhukov was the first military officer to attain Presidium status is indicative of the new position of the military. World War II and the cold war rivalry with the United States had had its impact on Soviet politics.

Phase 4: Khrushchev's Peaceful Coexistence, 1957–1964

Khrushchev's emergence as the most powerful single individual in Soviet politics

ushered in a new era in state–military relations. While Marshal Zhukov's brief tenure on the party Presidium had brought increased stature to all branches of the military, his fall from power six months later clearly indicated that neither Zhukov's benefactor, Khrushchev, nor any other political leader was inclined to accept continued military influence on domestic politics. The goals of the Communist party began to shift toward the Soviet consumer and away from the long-standing emphasis on heavy industry and the military.

This shift in priorities was by no means made by unanimous agreement at the top of the party hierarchy. Khrushchev, who became the primary spokesman for the shift, and began his thrust by supporting the so-called modernist view in the military, which called for increased emphasis on technology, nuclear weapons, and missiles. The traditionalists, supported by some members of the Presidium, voiced more conservative views, emphasizing ground forces, tactical air power, and artillery. The traditionalists continued to support the conventional view of military preparedness, insisting that missiles and nuclear weapons were only a part of the whole. Military strategy could not be based, they reasoned, solely upon instruments of mass destruction. It should be noted that similar arguments being voiced in the United States during this time period were meeting with success in shifting the United States away from the Dulles doctrine of "massive retaliation." The Soviet traditionalists also argued for balance, warning against overreliance or dependence on any single weapon.

Khrushchev made many statements declaring his intention to trim the size of the standing army from 3.6 million to 2.4 million, his justification being that nuclear weapons and missiles more than compensated for such a cut. However, no evidence at the time suggested that Khrushchev's wishes represented Soviet policy. What he really accomplished was to heighten the debate over military strategy and the role of missiles and nuclear weapons. That he failed to achieve his objective is an indication that Khrushchev was being forced to compromise despite the fact that he held the two most important positions in the Soviet Union.

What Khrushchev may have desired was to present an image of strategic power without paying the costs of actually attaining such a position. If this image were to hold, it could be used by the Soviet Union to attain political advantages, particularly in Western Europe and Berlin. Questions about the United States' determination continued to be asked in Western European capitals: Would the United States commit itself to a conflict if the Soviet threat were directed only at Europe or if Soviet actions were aimed only at limited objectives? The United States tried to reassure its allies and renewed its determination not to allow the Soviets to gain a favorable strategic position. Khrushchev and his supporters, however, appeared interested not in strategic superiority but rather in a deterrent force, and seemed willing to settle for second place—at least for the time being. The military establishment actually suffered only minimal cuts in budget and in European-theater manpower. When the Cuban missile crisis occurred, the Soviet claims of superiority were clearly revealed to be little more than claims, as they quickly backed away from a direct challenge. The strategic balance which could have been altered by the missiles in Cuba reverted to imbalance; Khrushchev's gamble had not

paid off and had, in fact, weakened his power at home.

The European-theater forces remained essentially unchanged throughout this period. Although they were "nuclearized" with some tactical weapons, the basic organization, while supposedly modernized, resembled that of the army in World War II. This organization included several combined-arms and tank armies, a tactical air army, tactical missile units, an airborne formation, and a variety of support elements.

As in the past, the role of the air force was greatly limited; its brief strategic role was being phased out by the missile age. Even its tactical role was deemphasized in favor of tactical missiles, as Soviet leaders increased the number of medium-range bombers capable of striking European targets. They also developed a long-range bomber and established a small force of 150–200 aircraft, but this move appears to have been made only to fill the gap between the announcement of new Soviet policy and the development of sufficient long-range missiles to back it up. A commitment had been made to missile forces, particularly ICBM forces; and it became their responsibility to provide the deterrence to the United States.

This particular strategy did not appear to raise any serious controversy within the military leadership, which was dominated by army personnel with World War II experience. Reliance on strategic air power was not consistent with military doctrine nor with the historical role assigned to the military establishment. While, as noted earlier, some individuals had raised the question of developing a strong strategic air force before the advent of the missile age, there do not appear to have been discussions about such a course in the early 1960s; apparently, the modernists and the traditionalists did agree in this area. There also was apparent agreement about the need for improving the air-defense system on a continuing basis.

The PVO had been made a separate component of the military in the mid-1950s, and these forces were constantly being improved and modernized. They received the newest jet interceptors, and by 1962 had more than 4,000 of these planes. The SAM missiles were also operational, but these first-generation ground-to-air missiles were not fully effective. All these improvements in the air-defense system, however, did not alter Soviet vulnerability to attack from the air. Even military leaders openly recognized that defense against strategic air power would be, at best, difficult. Nevertheless, the Soviets continued to try new techniques, modifications, and new systems, including the antimissile missile, which Western observers felt was inadequate when it was first shown in 1963. While the Soviet air defenses had been considerably improved under Khrushchev, they were far from adequate to stop an attack from the United States.

It can be said that Khrushchev assigned more significance to air power, and that under him the armed forces and the development of military theory underwent some radical changes, primarily in regard to the deterrent power of nuclear weapons and the use of strategic missiles. The disputes between the traditionalists and the modernists did not result in a reduction of military expenditures; rather, they caused a shift in resource allocation from ground forces to strategic weapon systems. The Khrushchev years can be viewed as a period in which the Soviet Union came to recognize the importance of strategic nuclear weapons and the increased role that technology can play in military affairs.

Khrushchev continued to recognize the military as an important institutional group in Soviet politics. During his tenure as party secretary, the military achieved many of its objectives, which included attaining the preponderant position in the Ministry of Defense. (The precedent of choosing a marshal as minister of defense, set by Khrushchev, has only recently been broken, although this post had routinely gone to an army marshal.) The military was also given more representation on the Central Committee at the full (voting) level, as opposed to the candidate (nonvoting) level. The 1961 committee contained fourteen full members from the military as well as seventeen candidates, whereas the 1952 committee contained only six full members and the 1956 committee, eight. The 1961 group of full members included the heads of the air force and air defense forces. There is also some indication that military leaders from all branches (most of whom were full members) were routinely consulted about foreign-policy decisions. In all, the Soviet military attained a new prestige commensurate with the increased role of the Soviet Union in international affairs. This new-found stature of the military has not been altered in the post-Khrushchev period—indeed, it may have been enhanced.

Phase 5: Parity and the Search for Détente, 1964—

Debates over the nature and composition of Soviet military forces did not end with Khrushchev's fall in 1964, although there was a noticeable decline in the number of public statements containing contrasting views about military doctrine. The leadership seemed intent on concealing internal political and policy disputes. At this time, the Soviet Union was being challenged for leadership in the international

Figure 67. Mi-6 Hook general-purpose helicopter, 1973.

Communist movement by China; Khrushchev had not succeeded in bringing Yugoslavia back into even a loosened Eastern European community; Albania had defected to the Chinese side; and Rumania had become a most reluctant participant in Eastern European affairs, including the Warsaw Pact. To complicate matters for the new Soviet leaders, the United States had become deeply involved in Vietnam and had begun aerial bombing of the Communist state of North Vietnam. The new Soviet leadership quickly set about to undo some of Khrushchev's more radical domestic programs and to review his military strategy.

Apparently, little serious disagreement arose in regard to the Khrushchev changes; he had set the Soviet Union on a course upon which the new leaders agreed, although some concern was voiced about the state of both conventional and strategic forces. Where Khrushchev had sought to produce an image of strategic power, the new leaders sought to alter the actual strategic balance. This decision was made in tandem with the plan to improve the conventional forces. The size of the Soviet missile forces was increased rapidly in the mid-1960s, as was the number of missile-carrying submarines. Even though the long-range bomber was ignored, the air force as a whole was not.

Even before the Khrushchev period ended, the military had begun to question the decline of tactical air power. Although a shift had occurred in favor of the tactical missile forces, renewed interest in air support was now expressed—not by the air force, but rather by the marshals in the army. They reasoned that tactical bombing behind the front could be accomplished more effectively with fighter-bombers than with tactical missiles. This discussion probably contributed to the modernization of Soviet tactical air units in the mid-1960s. Older aircraft were replaced by new Mig-21 fighters, the Su-7s, and supersonic Yak-28 fighter-bombers. By 1967 the Soviet air force was proclaiming its superior tactical power. At the same time, the system began developing new fighters and bombers comparable to the best in the United States— as was demonstrated in the Middle Eastern War of 1973, in which the new Soviet aircraft were an equal match for Israel's U.S.-made planes.

A further role was assigned to the air force in the later 1960s, with new emphasis placed on airborne operations, air logistical support, and communications. These complemented a global policy, as the Soviet Union emerged from its traditional Eurasian viewpoint. Soviet interests were no longer confined to the Eurasian land mass, just as U.S. power had become global in the late 1940s and early 1950s. Given such a policy, the Soviets could no longer ignore long-range transports, communications, and logistical air support. At the same time, the Soviets could not allow the United States to maintain its strategic superiority. The rise of the Soviet navy and intimations about a significant amphibious landing force were also related to this new global outlook.

The United States had demonstrated many times during the cold war its use of the military both to indicate U.S. intentions (e.g., by sending the fleet to a troubled area) and to implement a foreign-policy decision in the event that other methods failed (as in the Dominican Republic and Vietnam). Although the Soviets never before possessed this capability outside the Eurasian area, it is clear that they are rapidly gaining it, as Soviet involvement in Angola demonstrates. Indeed, they may now have a deterrent force equal to that of the United States, and it appears that they are now striving to develop balanced armed forces to aid them in their newly found global interests. These global interests have not

obviated Soviet concerns in Eastern Europe, which remains an exclusive Soviet sphere of interest. The Brezhnev Doctrine, announced at the time of the Czechoslovakian intervention, served notice on Eastern Europe that the Soviets would tolerate no more Yugoslavias. The Czech invasion also demonstrated the value of the conventional military, including the Soviet airborne forces.

Brezhnev and Kosygin did little to alter the fundamental policy laid down by Khrushchev, who had set the course for significant change. The Soviet military is technologically oriented; it is fully missile-equipped, although not at the expense of the modernized ground forces; and it is rapidly becoming globally mobile.

Conclusions

After reviewing Soviet military strategy and doctrine over a period of more than twenty-five years, two general observations can be made. First, political and military leaders were greatly influenced until 1952 by the experiences of World War II and the traditional doctrine developed by Stalin. This attitude carried through the Khrushchev period, with changes noted only near the end of his tenure. At first, even whatever nuclear capability was developed was placed in a traditional context by the dominant faction in the military. The interests of the Soviet Union were largely confined to Europe and, to a lesser extent, the Far East. Second, the shortcomings of this land-based traditional policy were noted by some leaders throughout the years, and eventually the importance of strategic forces was recognized. Such a change in thinking facilitated the development of other sectors of the military and permitted the Soviets to pursue a global foreign policy, seek some accommodation with the United States, and maintain its position in Eastern Europe.

World War II had given the military the prestige of being a first-rank force that had demonstrated an ability to win a major war. The victories achieved in war became the lessons for the postwar world. Air power had been a secondary factor in the war and remained of secondary importance after the war. Challenges to Stalin's perceptions were not tolerated, and the development of a strategic air force with a long-range capability was effectively discouraged. (This was not the case with nuclear weapons, however, nor later, with the advent of missiles.)

By the late 1950s, the Soviets possessed the capability to launch both conventional and nuclear attacks on Western Europe. Air power was confined mostly to a tactical role after nuclear missiles were developed, and this role was further reduced in favor of missiles in the early 1960s. Only the air-defense forces were significantly and consistently improved. This branch of the armed forces did not lose status; in fact, it gained in prestige after the Soviet high command was reorganized.

In Soviet military thinking, the day of the strategic air force was a short one, terminated by the advent of missiles. The deterrent power of nuclear weapons could, theoretically, allow the Soviets to press for political advantages; the extension of Soviet influence now seemed possible even if the immediate results were negligible. The Soviets learned that there was more to possessing nuclear weapons than simply having the capacity to destroy the United States and other NATO countries. The development of the cold war—or the absence of hostilities, in a military sense—did not mean that no initiatives could be taken in foreign policy. While Khrushchev tried to advance Soviet influence, many of his policies

failed to produce the desired results—in part because of the Soviets' inferior strategic position. The post-Khrushchev leaders apparently learned much from the mistakes and misperceptions of the former leader.

Renewed emphasis was placed on building strategic power as well as on promoting the research and development necessary to produce new systems. The military supported these changes; in the late 1960s, military leaders made frequent references to the necessity of achieving technological superiority as well as developing new weapons systems that could change the balance between East and West. The post-Khrushchev leadership essentially supported the modernist view. A valuable lesson was learned from the cold war: the military cannot be permitted to remain in an inferior position or to become stagnant. Western technological advances had placed the Soviets at a disadvantage, and Soviet leaders were determined to close the gap. This was necessary for reasons beyond those involving status and prestige. As the Soviets approached a better strategic position, political leaders accelerated their efforts to normalize Soviet relations with Western Europe and the United States.

Although the post-Khrushchev leaders decided that they could pursue détente with the United States, this decision was not made in the kind of political or military context in which Khrushchev had tried to pursue his brand of rapprochement. The Soviet Union had attained a better strategic position in respect to the United States; at the same time, it was forced to recognize that the split with China had become permanent. Traditional military forces now had to contend with a potential adversary in the East. Even the search for détente with the West served to widen the gap between the Soviets and the Chinese and permit more flexibility in foreign policy for the states of Eastern Europe.

Even with the threat of conflict between the two global powers diminished, the Soviet military retains its preeminent position. The role of the military includes its function as protector of the Brezhnev Doctrine–defined "socialist commonwealth"; such a function requires emphasis on the traditional aspects of military power. The various responsibilities of the military dictates the maintenance of balanced forces, and Soviet forces are now better balanced than ever before in history. Soviet forces could now conceivably be used outside of Eastern Europe in much the same way that the United States has used its forces in the past. While the Soviets have always possessed this capability in Eastern Europe, they have acquired the capacity to move into areas outside the European theater. Their threat to intervene in the Middle East War of 1973 illustrates this improved capacity. The Soviet Union now possesses the kind of mobility that has long characterized the American military.

The rejuvenation of the Soviet air force was one factor in achieving mobile capability. After reaching a low point in the early 1960s, when it had lost both its limited strategic role and many of its tactical assignments to missile forces, the air force is now in a good position. While the primary strategic role remains with the missile forces, the tactical, support, and supply roles of the air force have been enhanced. These roles would become critically important in the event of either a conflict on the Sino-Soviet border or a broader conflict with China. The new Soviet air force would also be a valuable asset if the Soviet Union became involved in some area that was not contiguous to the Communist world. Soviet airlift capability—an area of air power to which the United States had possessed almost exclusive rights—has been greatly improved during the past few years. This new Soviet capacity was clearly demonstrated in the quick resupplying of the Arab states in 1973. While the Soviet air force has little strategic responsibility and cannot be considered equal to Western forces, it is clear that it has been vastly improved and expanded to meet the needs of the Soviet Union and its foreign policy.

Research Notes

Of the numerous sources of information about the Soviet military, few have been concerned specifically with the Soviet air force. Two exceptions are Asher Lee's *Soviet Air Force* (New York, 1962) and Robert A. Kilmarx' *History of Soviet Air Power* (New York, 1962). However, both of these works, while of some value, are quite dated. For views of the lessons learned as a result of both World War II and the cold war, the best sources are to be found in *Krasnaia zvezda* (Red Star) and in scattered articles in both *Pravda* and *Izvestiia* during the immediate postwar and de-Stalinization period. Also of value are the military memoirs published during de-Stalinization found in Serwyn Bialer, *Stalin and His Generals* (New York, 1969).

Of specific interest here are the memoirs of Marshal Rokossovsky, *"Dorogoi bor' by i slavy"*; S. A. Kalinin, *"Razmyshliaia o minuvshem"*; and S. D. Lugansky, *"Na glubokikh virazhakh,"* all of which contain military views of political leaders' decisions.

Reports of discussions about military doctrine and strategy can be found in the newspapers *Red Star* and *Kommunist vooruzhennykh sil* [Communist of the Armed Forces] as well as in the published speeches of Soviet political and military leaders. The most valuable American sources are to be found in numerous Rand Corporation publications, specifically those by Thomas Wolfe and Roman Kolkowicz. See, for example, Thomas Wolfe, *Impact of Khrushchev's Downfall on Soviet Military Policy and Détente* (Santa Monica, Calif., 1964) and *Soviet Military Policy Trends under the Brezhnev-Kosygin Regime* (Santa Monica, Calif., 1967) or Roman Kolkowicz, *Soviet Party-Military Relations: Contained Conflict* (Santa Monica, Calif., 1966) and *Political Controls in the Red Army: Professional Autonomy versus Political Integration* (Santa Monica, Calif., 1966). Wolfe's book *Soviet Power in Europe, 1945-1970* (Baltimore, 1970) contains much of his

Rand work, with some important additional material on Stalin, Eastern Europe, and Brezhnev-Kosygin.

Of more general interest on various aspects of Soviet military policy and the Soviet air force are Michael P. Gehlen's *Politics of Coexistence* (Bloomington, Ind., 1967) and Raymond Garthoff's *Soviet Military Policy* (New York, 1966) and *Soviet Strategy in the Nuclear Age* (New York, 1958). Garthoff has written numerous journal articles on the same theme, some of which are to be found in *Military Review*, a periodical which examines American military affairs and regularly publishes articles dealing with the Soviet military. Other books of general interest include William Kintner and Harriet Fast Scott, *The Nuclear Revolution in Soviet Military Affairs* (Norman, Okla., 1968), which contains a collection of speeches and articles from Soviet sources on military policy and doctrine.

Because it is impossible to discuss the role of the Soviet air force without understanding the position and role of the Soviet army, Michel Garder's brief work *A History of the Soviet Army* (London, 1966) is useful, as is Herbert Dinnerstein's *War and the Soviet Union* (New York, 1962).

9

The Soviet Strategic Air Force and Civil Defense

Alfred L. Monks

With the advent of the nuclear age in the 1950s, many Soviet and Western military authorities predicted the early demise of the manned bomber as a useful weapon. The vastly improved ABM and antiaircraft capabilities achieved by both superpowers in the early 1960s seemed to seal the fate of the manned bomber. Yet both superpowers still cling to the long-range and medium-range bombers, and each has continued to perfect its air defenses against them.

Without neglecting the strategic air force (Dal'naia aviatsiia, or DA), Soviet military and political leaders since 1961 have directed their strategic thinking toward rocket forces and a nuclear-armed navy. This was one of the most crucial policy choices faced by the post-Khrushchev leadership. The evidence suggests that Khrushchev's policy of reducing the Soviet heavy bomber inventory while upgrading the medium-range bomber capability of the DA, was basically followed by his successors. This posture enabled the Soviets to combine a modest intercontinental strategic capability, aimed primarily at the United States, with a larger medium-range bomber capability directed at Europe.

This chapter will discuss the origins of the Soviet weapons posture in the context of the development of the DA and the related role of civil defense in the USSR. The development of air-force equipment, the possible role of the DA in a future war, and Soviet air defense forces deserve special emphasis. While Soviet reactions to U.S. technological innovations are neither automatic nor predictable, an action-reaction mode of analysis seems to offer an appropriate framework for studying Soviet behavior. This is not to argue that such other factors as national institutional biases are irrelevant in an assessment of Soviet strategic choices. Nor do we maintain that Soviet military planners responded to every U.S.

strategic initiative in a reactive manner. We are convinced, however, that there is substantial evidence of Soviet responsiveness to U.S. strategic initiatives, and vice versa.

Origin of the Soviet Strategic Air Force

The Soviet strategic air force has neither the long tradition nor the prestige that other branches of the Soviet military possess. One reason for its lack of prestige was the subordinate role of the tsarist air fleet during World War I. Another was the economic chaos caused by the Russian civil war, which retarded development of Russia's four-engined bomber force. In the late 1920s and early 1930s, aided by the industrial growth that occurred during the First Five-Year Plan, Soviet leaders made successful efforts to improve the quality of the air force. The Soviet air force added a series of heavy bomber squadrons, the TB-1s and TB-2s, to its inventory, and in 1932 the USSR became the first post-1918 air force to fly a substantial force of four-engined, all-metal, long-range bombers: the TB-3 squadron.

Conflicting trends are evident in pre–World War II Soviet strategic air policies. On the one hand, many Soviet military thinkers belittled the importance of long-range bombing. On the other, the status of the DA was elevated in 1935–1936 by the creation of a separate command for long-range bombers under the direct control of air force headquarters in Moscow. Soviet medium and heavy bombers were organized into a separate unit in 1937. By that time, the Soviet bomber command consisted of several hundred TB-3s, the largest long-range bomber force in the world. However, by the late 1930s, a decline of Soviet interest in long-range bombers was evident. Several factors were possible: Stalin's purges, which had eliminated many advocates; the failure of Soviet aircraft designer Andrei Tupolev to design a

worthy successor to the obsolete TBs; and the need of Soviet industry to expand its production of tactical aircraft because of their lower costs and the imminence of war.

Soviet belief in the value of strategic bombing must have been persistent, because in April 1942 the DA (called ADD at that time) was established. The idea of a separate long-range bomber command was based on the Soviet conviction that bombers could be employed for tactical as well as strategic missions—a novel concept, and one which predated similar U.S. developments by several years. Yet, during World War II, Soviet planners gave preference to tactical air power; thus most of the Red Air Force's medium bombers consisted of Lend-Lease U.S. B-25s and short-range Iliushin DB-3Fs. Because the role of the Soviet strategic air force during the war was modest, the Soviet long-range bomber, the Pe-B, never constituted more than 10 percent of the total Soviet air inventory. Poor navigational equipment, absence of substantial fighter escorts, shortages of supplies, inadequate training, and the need to use the ADD for tactical support and air-transport missions reduced its importance. By the end of 1944, the ADD had become one of the Soviet's tactical air armies.

In the early postwar period the significance of long-range air attack was upgraded by Soviet planners. A key factor responsible for this was the deep impression made on Stalin by the heavy damage caused by Western bombing of German cities and the bombing of Hiroshima and Nagasaki. In 1946, one year before the U.S. Air Force became a separate service, the Soviet strategic air force (renamed DA) became a separate branch of the armed forces. By 1947 the Soviets had produced the Tu-4, their own version of the U.S. B-29, based on Soviet redesigns of four B-29s which had been forced to land in Soviet territory

Figure 68. Il-28 Beagle light bombers in formation.

in 1944. In the period 1946–1948, Soviet-built long-range bombers were very similar to several contemporary Royal Air Force and USAF bombers. By the end of 1946, the Tu-4 was in series production, but the Korean War revealed the vulnerability of the B-29 to Soviet Mig-15 fighters.

By 1953 the DA consisted of three air armies with a total strength of about 100 Tu-4s. In the period of 1953–1960, the Soviets began to close the gap between the DA and the U.S. Strategic Air Command. Recognition of the growing importance of strategic bombing in Soviet military doctrine may have been a contributing factor. Toward the end of 1954 the Tu-16 twin jet medium bomber began to enter service. This aircraft compared favorably with SAC's B-47, but its range was restricted because it had no forward bases from which to penetrate North American targets. Greater threats to the West were the turboprop Tupolev Tu-95 (NATO designa-

tion Bear) and the turbojet Myasischev M-4 (Bison), which entered service in the mid-1950s and replaced the older Tu-4s.

Conflicts of Personality and Budgetary Squabbles

In the Soviet Union, as in all states, conflicts over budgetary matters exist; indeed, the scope and intensity of such struggles are presumably more severe in the USSR than in the West because available resources are more limited. Yet very little direct evidence about such matters exists, because official Soviet doctrine denies the existence of factionalism. Clues to internal disputes are revealed by analyzing specific salient issues.

One contentious issue was the possible role of the DA in a future war. Three factions were discernible in the USSR over this issue: (1) an air-force group led by Lt. Gen. N. Sbytov, Col. Gen. I. Moroz, and Marshal A. A. Grechko, who argued that the DA, in conjunction with the strategic rocket forces and the nuclear-powered navy, could achieve the main strategic goals in a future war; (2) an air-force group led by the commander of the Soviet air forces, Marshal P. S. Kutakhov, who maintained that the role of the DA had expanded and that it still must be considered the main means of destroying strategic targets in a future war; and (3) a faction apparently led by Maj. Gen. A. Kravchenko, who insisted that the goals of the air force should remain modest and should include only the destruction of such relatively small mobile targets as enemy subs, aircraft carriers, and troop movements. Except for the years 1968 and 1970, the views of the first group held the upper hand in Soviet military circles.

Soviet leaders are continuously faced with the problem of how to allocate limited funds. Given the tautness of their economy, this question assumes commanding importance. The Twenty-third Party Congress in 1966 decided to upgrade the strategic rocket forces (SRF), the navy, and the air force. In 1968, however, Soviet military leaders made ambiguous statements about the respective roles to be assigned to the SRF, navy, and air force in a future war, probably because of debate within the military establishment about priorities. One related question concerned intrabranch priorities: Would the tactical air force, including the new generation of fighters, and the new STOL (short takeoff and landing) technology be pushed, or would the emphasis be placed on the development of a strategic bomber force to replace the aging Bear and Bison bombers? The dominance of the Kutakhov and Grechko school since 1970 may have been due to the successful development of both a new Soviet medium-range bomber with a standoff missile capability and a new supersonic bomber, Backfire, which was first

reported in the West in 1969 and which became operational in 1974.

Long-Range Bombers

During Khrushchev's period of power, a modest force of some 150–200 long-range bombers (Bisons and Bears) had been introduced and maintained in the DA. There was a sizable gap between the Soviet long-range and medium-range bomber programs; thus less than 10 percent of the Soviet strategic bomber procurement program during that time period was devoted to heavy bombers. In late 1961, the Soviet bomber inventory consisted of 190 aircraft: fewer than 70 turboprop Bears and 120 four-jet Bisons. Some 50 of that total were utilized as tankers for in-flight refueling. By the fall of 1973, the Soviets had reduced this component of their air arm to 140−100 Bears and 40 Bisons—with an additional 50 Bison tankers. By the fall of 1975 this figure had dropped to 135−100 Bears and 35 Bisons. By comparison, the U.S. forces in late 1961 included about 1,500 long-range bombers, a total which dropped to 516 in late 1973 and to 463 in late 1975.

The Bisons and Bears have been the backbone of the Soviet long-range heavy bomber force since they became operational in 1956, when the U.S. B-52s were entering SAC. In 1960 the total Soviet strategic bomber strength was about 1,500 aircraft; the SAC total was then about 1,800. The Bear had a lower speed and a greater range than the Bison; both were equipped for aerial refueling. The Bear carried a single 1,000-mile-range winged Kangaroo ASM (air-to-surface missile), giving it a maximum weapon load twice that of the Bison. In terms of range, speed, weapon load, combat ceiling, warhead total, and penetration capability, both the Bears and Bisons were vastly inferior to their closest U.S. counterpart, the B-52.

Figure 69. Tu-20 Bear-C over the North Pacific. Between 100 and 300 strategic bomber versions were built; many were converted in the early 1960s to reconnaissance aircraft.

While some high USAF officials talked about the necessity of building a replacement for the B-52, the consensus of top Defense Department (DOD) officials was that the U.S. still maintained a sizable lead over the USSR bomber force. During the past decade, the size of the Soviet long-range bomber force has not exceeded one-third that of the U.S. Strategic Air Command's B-52 force; in late 1973, DA strength was slightly more than one-fourth that of SAC. By equipping the B-52 with standoff supersonic missiles (SRAMS), which were deployed in 1974–1975, the gap widened between U.S. and Soviet long-range bomber forces.

Soviet leaders did not abandon the long-range bomber as a useful weapon. After much Western speculation, the four-jet M-52 (Bounder), a new Soviet long-range bomber, was unveiled in Moscow in mid-1961. Many

Western oberservers declared that this was the replacement for the aging Soviet Bison. This development may have been one of the determining factors in the decision to allocate funds for producing more B-52s and B-58s in mid-1961. But the Soviet Bounder never attained operational status; the prototypes were utilized only as research aircraft in connection with the USSR's supersonic airliner program.

The Soviet abandonment of the Bounder as a long-range bomber was related to several U.S. developments. First, in late 1961, the U.S. decided to cut back on its original plan for expansion of its B-52 force. This decision was based on the conviction that U.S. strategic retaliatory forces, including long-range bombers, were sufficient and would remain so for a period of years. Therefore, SAC resumed its phasedown of the B-47 long-range bomber inventory in mid-

1962, and by 1966 all B-47s had been officially retired. Moreover, production of the B-52 series was terminated in October 1962. In January 1963, the Defense Department ordered the immediate phaseout of the B-52's new air-to-ground Skybolt missile because of repeated failures. Finally, the USAF's XB-70, launched in mid-1963, was plagued with technical problems; after more than $1 billion had been spent, only two aircraft had been constructed. These development problems were widely publicized in a leading Soviet air-force periodical, *Aviatsiia i kosmonavtika.*

The most dramatic Soviet development following the unveiling of the Bounder was the appearance in 1969 of a new swing-wing strategic bomber, designated Backfire by NATO cataloguers. Its appearance surprised Western officials, who had assumed that the USSR had ceased further development of her long-range strategic bomber fleet. Mystery surrounded this new aircraft. While some of its performance specifications were known to the West (e.g., that its maximum speed exceeded 1,500 mph), controversy abounded concerning its maximum range, intended targets, and current status. Was it simply a prototype aircraft like the Bounder, or was it currently in series production? Some Western observers contended that the Backfire was limited to prototype testing and that its relatively limited range (about 3,000 miles) severely restricted its utility as a replacement for the 140 long-range Soviet bombers then in service. The inference was that the Backfire was designed solely for targets in Eurasia.

Other Western observers asserted that the Backfire had been test-flown and could be operational in substantial numbers by the mid-1970s. In fact, two squadrons did become operational by late 1974, and deployment continued in 1975–1976. With a range reputed to be nearly equal to that of the Bison and inflight refueling capability, a later

version, the Backfire B, was seen as an intercontinental attack aircraft able to challenge the USAF's B-52, as well as the prototype B-1, and to reach virtually all U.S. targets. It would be shortsighted to overlook the importance attached to this aircraft in Soviet air-force circles. Beginning in mid-1969, Soviet officials began to make vague but frequent references to their new "variable-wing" bomber with its "long-range capability" and its capacity to deliver "all types of modern weapons." According to recent reports, some Soviet Backfire bombers, using air-to-air refueling and operating from bases near Murmansk, are conducting maritime reconnaissance flights, including some flights over U.S. installations in the Azores. Backfire B was scheduled to be deployed in some numbers in East Germany in 1976.

The appearance of the Soviet Backfire and other indications of stepped-up Soviet bomber production can be associated with U.S. developments during this period. The Pentagon announced in December 1965 the planned replacement of a sizable portion of its B-52 bomber force by a substantial number of smaller and speedier FB-111 aircraft. Key features of the supersonic FB-111 were to be the SRAM missile and a new radar system. About $225 million was earmarked for the development and procurement of this plane during 1966–1967. Plans were announced in early 1966 for the FB-111 to enter the U.S. operational inventory by 1969; all 210 aircraft purchased were to be deployed by 1971. In addition, the USAF planned to continue its efforts to obtain the interceptor F-12, arguing that the USSR would continue to develop its advanced bomber projects. Procurement plans for this aircraft, killed in an earlier DOD decision, suddenly acquired increased congressional support. In early 1967, the DOD announced plans to study the feasibility of developing two aircraft to replace its aging Air Command interceptors, presumably because of the new Soviet bomber program. Prospects for these two planes hinged on an airborne warning and control system (AWACS), which would be utilized to detect and track enemy aircraft operating beyond the range of existing air-defense radars. Its success in turn depended on the ability to develop reliable airborne radars; tests of five such systems began in 1967. These developments continued into 1968, when the USAF requested $502 million for the first major procurement of the FB-111 bomber; in 1969 the USAF requested $550 million to purchase 75 FB-111s. At that time, plans were announced to modify the F-106 so as to make it capable of coping with advanced Soviet bombers.

The development of the B-1, a new long-range bomber to replace the B-52, was first reported in late 1969. This plane, which carries about twice the payload of a Boeing B-52 but is only two-thirds the size, was designed to penetrate an enemy's antiaircraft defense and was to be armed with the new ASMs. Congress allotted $448 million for this bomber in fiscal year 1973, reversing an earlier Senate reduction of $100 million for the plane. The B-1 had its initial prototype flight in April 1974 and began a two-year flight-test program in December 1974. Delivery to SAC was scheduled for January 1978.

U.S. interceptor aircraft lacked a "look down, shoot down" radar capability against such low-flying bombers as the Soviet Backfire. That top USAF officials acknowledged this weakness provided a final incentive for the Soviets to proceed with new bomber designs. Another possible clue to improved Soviet capabilities was the appearance of a new U.S. surface-to-air missile system, the SAM-D, in the summer of 1973. This system, based on the track-via-missile guidance principle, was expected to be more effective than the older Hawk in countering increased Soviet bomber defense-suppression tactics.

In summary, it can be argued that U.S.

developments influenced the Soviet decisions to abandon the long-range Bounder in the early 1960s and to develop the Backfire in the late 1970s. It is also possible that such factors as the wind-down of the Vietnam War prompted the acceleration of certain U.S. programs.

The Medium-Range Bomber

The Soviets consistently maintained their medium-range bomber force in a high state of readiness and modernization. The workhorse of the Soviet medium-bomber fleet has been the Tu-16, bearing the NATO code name Badger, which became operational in mid-1959. Equipped with a single missile, the Badger has a range of about 4,000 miles and a maximum speed of about 600 mph.

At the Tushino air show in 1961, the Soviets unveiled a new twin-engine supersonic medium bomber, the Tu-22 (Blinder), to replace the Badger. Beginning in 1963, the Badger began to be gradually phased out with the introduction of the Blinder. By late 1972, 200 Blinders had been introduced into the Soviet air arm, and by late 1974 another 55 were operating with the Soviet naval air force. During 1975, however, the number of Soviet Blinders in service dropped to 170. Four versions of this aircraft are in service, the latest of which—the maritime reconnaissance version—is fitted with windows for six cameras in the weapons-bay door. The Blinder was intended as a strike and reconnaissance aircraft, mainly for the European theater.

The Soviets still hold the Badger in high regard. Although the overall number of Badgers in the Soviet air arm was reduced from about 1,000 in 1962 to 500 in late 1973 and to 475 in late 1975, six versions remain in service. About 400 Badgers were transferred to the Soviet navy for ship attack and ASW as well as for naval reconnaissance. In 1969, about half the Badger fleet was outfitted with advanced Kelt or Kennel missiles. A few Badger bombers were delivered to Egypt, where they were used to launch a number of Kelt missiles at Israeli targets.

There is little doubt that the Soviet medium-range bomber force was superior to its U.S. counterpart. It is true that the United States had aircraft similar to the Soviet Blinder: the B-58 Hustler, introduced in 1960, and the FB-111, which became operational in 1969. However, the latest version of the Blinder—with its 4,000-mile range, reputed standoff missile capability, new refueling probe, and larger engines—was clearly superior to the Hustler, which was withdrawn from SAC in 1969. Although the FB-111 appeared to be superior to the Soviet Blinder on paper, technical and financial problems continued to plague the U.S. bomber. While in 1975 there were about 170 Blinders in the Soviet air force, Western intelligence reported only 66 FB-111s in the U.S. active inventory, and funding for the FB-111's ASM capability had been slashed.

In summary, Khrushchev's strategic concept of allowing the long-range fleet to dwindle while continuing to upgrade the medium-range bomber force has been adhered to by Soviet military officials. However, we have only limited insight into the status and performance features of the newest addition to the Soviet long-range bomber fleet, the Backfire. If the Backfire is indeed intended to be an eventual replacement for the long-range Bisons and Bears, this summation will require some revision.

The West knows relatively little about Soviet strategic air bases. What is known is that such bases are grouped in three main areas: western Russia, the central Ukraine, and the (Russian) Far East. About 75 percent of the Soviet long-range and medium bombers are based in European Russia; most of the remainder are located in the east. Airfields are also maintained on the Arctic islands of Novaia Zemlia, Severnaia Zemlia, and Franz Josef Land and on the Talmar

and Kola peninsulas for training, dispersal, and staging purposes. In addition, approximately 475 Soviet Badger and 170 Blinder medium bombers and 50 long-range Bears are based near the northwest and Black Sea coasts of the USSR. The probable reason for the Soviet distribution of air bases is the relatively restricted range of Soviet long-range bombers. However, with increased aerial refueling capability and a new long-range bomber, the USSR could disperse its bomber bases inland, as the U.S. did with SAC bases during the 1960s.

Future Role of the Strategic Air Force

Controversy has existed within Soviet military circles concerning the specific role of the strategic air force in a future nuclear war. Such controversy is not new to Soviet military thinkers, although the role of the DA has not been as seriously debated as have those of the other Soviet military branches. Until early 1964 the Khrushchev doctrine, which postulated that the strategic rocket forces (SRF) constituted the main branch of the Soviet military and would independently achieve the main strategic goals of any future war, dominated Soviet military thinking. But the ouster of Krushchev in late 1964 precipitated spirited debate within Soviet military circles. Studies of Soviet military writings during 1965-1969 indicate the existence of factionalism within the Soviet military establishment. The outcome represented a compromise: while the decisive role of the SRF during the initial stages of a future conflict was retained, the other branches were recognized as having sizable roles in achieving final victory. This "combined arms" concept, vigorously advanced by Soviet traditionalists during the 1965–1969 period, became prevalent in Soviet military thinking. But two serious questions arose from this concept: (1) What were the strongest features purportedly possessed by the Soviet DA? (2) What specific role would

Figure 70. Experimental M-52 in flight. An unsuccessful design, it may have been influenced by the B-58. Though the plane was capable of reaching speeds of up to 1,240 mph, only two were built.

the air force play in a future war, and what would its relationship be with the other branches of the Soviet military? The attribute most consistently stressed by Soviet air-force officials was the capability of the long-range air force to deliver missiles to enemy targets without entering the enemy's antimissile system. This standoff capability claim was first advanced in mid-1963, soon after Soviet bombers were equipped with ASM, and continued to be heard in 1974-1976. A second strategic claim, first made in 1969, asserted that Soviet strategic bombers could reach "virtually any point on the globe."

What specific tasks were assigned in 1975–1976 to the long-range air force? Some dissent was evident in Soviet military thinking on this issue. Some argued that the DA could perform strategic operations in a future war independently of the other branches; i.e., it could destroy the enemy's

military-industrial potential, his state and military administration, and his means of nuclear attack, as well as his large military, air, and naval forces. Others asserted that the DA could accomplish those tasks only in close cooperation with the SRF and the nuclear-armed navy. Still others maintained that only the SRF and the navy could achieve these strategic goals. In 1968, the Soviet High Command itself was divided as to which formula was the most expedient. By 1973 a compromise had been adopted: the Soviet air force would conduct strategic operations independently as well as in cooperation with the other branches. This "combined-arms" formula, which was prevalent in 1975–1976, might serve as an indication to the Chinese of enhanced Soviet strategic air flexibility.

How realistic were these strategic goals in terms of 1975–1976 Soviet aircraft capabilities and inventories? The answer is directly linked to Soviet strategic claims. If the Soviet long-range bombers had a striking potential that allowed them to be based great distances from their intended targets, they could operate outside the combat envelope of the enemy's interceptor aircraft; they would then be capable of accomplishing their assigned strategic tasks.

In late 1975 the Soviets had 100 long-range Bear and 35 Bison bombers in their strategic inventory, with about two-thirds of the former armed with standoff Kangaroo missiles. They also had about 25 supersonic Backfire bombers capable of inflight refueling. Several factors had to be considered in assessing the Soviets' standoff capability. First, the Soviet Bears, while they were capable of striking North American targets over the polar regions and returning home without refueling, were propeller-driven. Their relatively slow speed presumably made them totally inadequate against the retaliatory capability of the NORAD interceptors. Second, the payload of the Soviet long-range bomber fleet was reportedly about 4.8 million pounds, while that of the U.S. fleet was about 30.5 million pounds. In theory, these figures indicated that the Soviet bombers could carry a total of about 420 weapons over U.S. targets, while the B-52s could carry 2,000 weapons to Soviet targets. Moreover, since the U.S. finished equipping its bomber force with SRAM weapons (short-range attack missiles) in 1974–1975 the latter figure has increased to about 7,000 weapons.

Finally, SAC's high-performance B-1 bomber was expected to enter the U.S. inventory by the end of this decade or the early 1980s. Armed with thirty-two SRAMs, this bomber was reported to have a payload double that of the B-52s in addition to a greater penetration capability, a reduced radar cross-section, and a more rapid reaction time to enemy first strikes. Moreover, the USAF was developing a 1,750-mile-range cruise missile for the B-1, along with a version capable of being launched from surface vessels and submarines in order to better penetrate Soviet air defenses.

PVO Forces

The air defense forces (PVO) were for a long time the weakest component of Soviet military power. Until the end of World War II, this weakness had no serious consequences. Although Soviet cities came under German air attack, the Luftwaffe's strategic air threat to the USSR was minimal. Hence Soviet air defenses were virtually untested at the war's end. The total absence of a radar warning system was probably the most glaring weakness. The strongest component of the PVO forces was the artillery. The fighter interceptor force was weak, presumably because the Soviets, with their vast land mass, felt no need to build up this force. Soviet interceptor forces consisted of roughly one fighter division during both the prewar and wartime periods. By the war's end, however, Soviet political and military leaders realized that it was imperative to build up their air defenses.

Foremost was the need to develop an effective early-warning radar system. The Soviets were able to exploit German radar technology abandoned by retreating German armies, as well as captured German radar technicians and engineers. By the end of 1946 the Soviets had built a rudimentary radar system, and by June 1950 this system extended from the East Baltic to the Black Sea and the Far East. As the U.S. strategic stockpile of atomic weapons was expanded, so was the Soviet radar system. But no evidence exists that the Soviets adapted and produced an airborne radar for use during the Korean War, nor that any ground-to-air or air-to-air missiles were developed by the Germans in 1944–1945.

Soviet jet interceptor aircraft development was impressive in the decade after

Figure 71. Tu-22 Blinder-C bomber. The supersonic twin-jet craft first appeared at Tushino in 1961; the "C" version does photoreconnaissance.

World War II. In 1944, a fighter command (IA-PVO) was established in the PVO forces. Soviet leaders pressed jet-propulsion experimentation and development with the aid of captured German technology and purchased British engines. In early 1946, the first two Soviet jet fighters were test-flown; one was the Mig-9, said to be powered by the German BMW-003 A engine. The new Soviet jets appeared to be on a par with the U.S. F-80 and the British Vampire.

Even though, in 1944–1948, the Soviets began to develop swept-wing jet fighters, the Soviet failure to develop jet engines comparable to those of the West impeded progress. In 1947 and 1948 the Soviets purchased from England twenty-five turbojet engines in an effort to improve their interceptor force. On the eve of the Korean War, the So-

viet IA-PVO forces, numbering about 2,000 aircraft, were well equipped with Mig-15s, which compared favorably with the U.S. F-86 except for the absence of airborne radar and radar gunsights. However, Soviet aircraft designers should not be underrated during this period, because Western imports probably did little more than accelerate Soviet programs. Since the Korean War, and coincident with the buildup of SAC, the Soviet interceptor arm has continued to improve.

Beginning in 1955–1956, Soviet air advances narrowed the gap separating the USSR from the more advanced West. Soviet developments included radar gunsights on the newer jets, experimental use of air-to-air missiles, radar-controlled SAM guided missiles, and an early warning system. Also, two new aircraft—the supersonic Mig-19, the Soviet counterpart of the USAF F-100 Super Sabre, and the all-weather Yak-25—made their appearance.

Shortly after the Korean War, a separate branch was established for Soviet air-defense forces. In 1975–1976 this branch, under the command of Marshal P. F. Batitsky, included fighter-interceptor aircraft, surface-to-air missiles (SAMs), anti-aircraft artillery, and an airborne warning and control system (AWACS). About 500,000 men were assigned to the Soviet PVO forces, while the U.S. Air Defense Command was composed of only about 80,000 men. The USSR had spent roughly two-and-one-half times what the U.S. had spent on antiaircraft defense since World War II.

In 1975–1976, Soviet PVO forces had about 2,550 fighters, a total which had steadily declined since 1965 yet was substantially higher than that of the 374 interceptors in the U.S. inventory. There is little doubt that the USSR has upgraded its fighter inventory. In the years 1958–1975, the USSR built more than twenty different types of fighter aircraft, eight of which were operational in 1975. Then, more than 50 percent of the Soviet jet interceptor component consisted of newer planes, including the Su-11 (Fishpot C), the Su-15 (Flagon), the improved Tu-28P (Fiddler), the all-weather Yak-28P (Firebar), and the speedy Mig-25 (Foxbat). Soviet emphasis on advanced interceptor aircraft was demonstrated at the Domodedovo air show in 1967. Of the seven fighters shown, five were interceptors, four of which demonstrated STOL or VTOL capability.

The strong Soviet support for development of STOL (short takeoff and landing) and VTOL (vertical takeoff and landing) technologies alarmed some DOD officials, who pointed out the sharp contrast between the Soviet emphasis and the U.S. apparent lack of concern. In 1968, high U.S. military officials expressed increasing anxiety about the new generation of advanced Soviet interceptors, suggesting that the United States must keep pace with the Soviets. These developments pushed the DOD toward approval of several long-delayed air force programs, just as navy and air force officials were encouraging the development of new aircraft for their services. In September 1968, the Senate recommended appropriating $130 million for the navy's new aircraft, the F-14, and in December 1968 the navy ordered 463 of these planes. The new air force plane, the F-15, was supposed to be more maneuverable and armed with enough missiles to ensure Western air superiority over the new generation of Soviet Migs.

In early 1969 both navy and air force requests for funds increased sharply. While the navy's requirement of $239 million was aimed at restoring some of the capability lost when the F-111B program was killed in Congress, it might be argued that it was also associated with Soviet technological advances. In addition, the navy initiated procurement for the fiscal year 1970 of a new electronic countermeasures aircraft (ECM), presumably to oppose improved Soviet SAMs.

The USSR by 1969 had also expanded its fighter inventory, which consisted of eleven versions of the Mig, five versions of the Sukhoi, and two versions of the Yak. Of the Mig aircraft, the most challenging to the West was the speedy (more than 2,000 mph) Mig-23 Flogger, which had a service ceiling of 80,000 feet and STOL capability. The evidence shows that it was ordered into production shortly after the U.S. began work on the now-aborted B-70 bomber. Two new Sukhoi interceptors, whose primary task was

Figure 72. Tu-28 Fiddler long-range interceptor. First seen in 1961, it is designed for all-weather operations against the Anglo–U.S. bomber threat. The later version does not have the ventral fins visible here.

defense against low-level penetration, also entered the Soviet inventory.

Meanwhile, the United States responded to these developments. The USAF announced in late 1969 that its new SRAM system, designed chiefly as a short-range air-to-surface missile, was expected to enter production in mid-1970. U.S. officials claimed that the F-15 would surpass the Soviet Flogger in all respects except speed. Construction of the first F-14A was to begin in 1971 and that of the F-15 in 1972. In January 1970, the USAF requested authority to buy 700 F-15s to meet the Soviet strategic challenge. USAF development and funding continued to shift from missiles and astronautics into new aircraft programs, especially for fighters and bombers. Funding requests for SCAD systems for use on the B-52 and B-1 rose sharply in early 1970. The USAF received $100 million for the B-1 in fiscal year 1970 and requested the same amount in 1971. This figure was halved by Con-

gress, largely because the projected service of the B-52 had been extended into the 1980s.

Two other details of the 1970 U.S. budget can be associated with Soviet strategic developments: First, funding was increased for the SRAM, the proposed offensive countermeasure to growing Soviet air defenses, which was scheduled to be adapted to the B-52 and FB-111 bombers. Second, $58 million was allocated for an improved Hawk SAM system.

In 1970, two strategic developments occurred in the USSR which clearly demonstrated continued Soviet efforts to upgrade its fighter aircraft: First, the USSR phased out its older Mig-17 in favor of the much faster Mig-21. Second, three squadrons of the Mig-23 Flogger, which was equipped with a down-looking radar capability against low-flying bombers, were put into service.

The Soviets continued their push for better fighters. In 1971 they began producing fifteen new Sukhoi (Su-11, or Fishpot C) aircraft each month as replacements for the Mig-21s. Also, they continued to improve the performance capabilities of their Tu-28 Fiddler for high-altitude long-range interceptions.

In early 1973, an aircraft which had been identified by the West in 1965 as the E-266 was reclassified as the high-speed Mig-25 interceptor (Foxbat). Some Western observers claimed that the Foxbat—capable of flying at speeds of well over 2,000 mph and of over Mach 3 at 77,000 feet, armed with four advanced air-to-air missiles, and equipped with a down-looking radar against low-flying bombers—was superior to the best fighter interceptors in the U.S. inventory, because both the naval F-14 and the air force F-15 had experienced numerous technical and funding problems and were not yet operational. The Foxbat, able to perform both interceptor and reconnaissance roles, operated off the Israeli coastline and over the Sinai in 1971–1972 without hindrance. The interceptor version is armed with four new air-to-air missiles, while the reconnaissance version is equipped with cameras located in the nose cone. In May 1975, an aircraft believed to be the Mig-25 Foxbat recaptured two time-to-height records and earned a new climb record for the Soviets. At the end of 1975, the trainer version of the Mig-25—similar to the combat version but with a new nose—became known to the West, and in September 1976 a Mig-25 landed in Japan.

Finally, an air-superiority version of the Mig-23 entered service in 1973 to complement the ground-attack version of this plane, which was introduced in 1970–1971. There were also indications in 1975–1976 that the Flogger might be introduced into the Soviet PVO force.

U.S. Responses

The United States responded vigorously to the Soviet technological advances in the period 1973–1976. By early 1974 it seemed that both the navy's F-14 and the USAF's F-15 air-superiority fighter had cleared their major funding and technical hurdles; moreover, both had demonstrated in-flight capability for attacking and defeating such a plane as the Soviet Foxbat. The navy had two squadrons of the F-14 in service by late 1974—although it appeared that the F-15, which was also built for a ground-attack role, might not be operational until 1975–1976, inasmuch as it was still experiencing technical problems related to engine stalls. Top DOD officials, concerned because the Soviets reportedly had about 150 Mig-25s in service, secured congressional approval for a fiscal-year 1977 appropriation for 108 F-15s and for an inventory objective of 729 fighters by 1982.

The prototype testing in 1974 of two new lightweight interceptors, the YF-16 and the YF-17, as possible complements to the F-15 and F-14, was another indication of the U.S. response to Soviet aircraft advances. In 1975 the F-16 air combat fighter was adopted as a future complement to the F-15, and the navy selected the F-18, a derivative of the YF-17, as its air combat fighter. Other indications of the Western response to Soviet developments were the testing of a new hypersonic air-defense aircraft capable of speeds in the Mach 5-6 area and the continued testing of the A-10 close-support aircraft, scheduled to enter operation in 1976.

Israel's request in mid-1974 for American F-14 or F-15 jet fighters, in addition to F-16s or F-17s to cope with the Mig-23 Floggers possessed by Syria,

Figure 73. Tu-126 Moss airborne early-warning aircraft. This plane was developed from the TU-114 transport, itself a derivative of the Tu-95 Bear (whose engine it shares). It became known to the West through a 1968 film, and preceded the USAF AWACS 707 derivative by nearly nine years. This photograph was taken from a fighter based on the HMS Ark Royal *during a NATO exercise.*

will certainly be a factor compelling the Soviets to perfect newer aircraft. The Senate's ratification in 1976 of the five-year U.S.–Spain treaty of cooperation (which commits the United States to provide Spain with four complete F-16 squadrons of eighteen aircraft each) and the decision to sell F-14s to Iran may also push the Soviets to develop new aircraft.

The U.S. Navy's efforts, in conjunction with NASA, to push the development of lift-fan studies in an attempt to meet military needs for VTOL aircraft and its work to develop the prototype XFV-12A VTO aircraft could be related to the appearance of a new Soviet fighter which was test-flown from a helicopter

carrier deck in 1973 and which was to be produced for operation both from helicopters and from the new series of Soviet aircraft carriers. In July 1976 this new fighter, the Yak-36 VTOL, was spotted on the flight deck of the Soviet aircraft carrier *Kiev.*

U.S. efforts in 1974–1976 to develop improved cruise missiles, capable of being launched from aircraft as well as from surface vessels and submarines, are clearly related to Soviet technological advances. In arguing for such a program, top Pentagon officials declared that the United States would have to counter an improved Soviet air-defense system built around an AWACS-Foxbat network by employing new penetration devices, including cruise missiles. Examination by U.S. intelligence officials of a Mig-25 which was flown to Japan by a defecting Soviet air-force pilot should facilitate this endeavor, which, in turn, will probably compel the Soviets to further improve their air-defense system.

Surface-to-Air Missiles (SAMs)

The Soviets have devoted a great deal of attention to improving their SAM capabilities. As early as 1959 a leading observer, Asher Lee, noted that Soviet antiaircraft weapons did not operate effectively against low-altitude penetrators—a grave weakness, in view of the fact that the new supersonic aircraft in the West were designed to fly at very low altitudes. As a result, the Soviets strove to strengthen their SAM forces. By mid-1967, an extensive system of SAMs had been perfected which included an improved version of the SA-2, the two-stage medium-altitude SA-3, and the triple-mounted mobile SA-6. One impetus for this development may have been the increased effectiveness, after initial failures, of the USAF's jamming devices and of other ECM against the Soviet-built SA-2s in North Vietnam.

The USSR installed an elaborate air-defense system in the Mideast, dominated by SA-2s, and SA-3s, and the mobile SA-6 (by far the most devastating new Soviet missile, effective from treetop level up to about 70,000 feet). This last weapon, which shot down most of the Israeli aircraft lost during the early days of the Yom Kippur War of 1973, demonstrated Soviet progress in applying an advanced weapons technology called integral-ramjet propulsion. Maj. Gen. Benyamin Peled, the Israeli air force commander, stated that the greatest impact of Soviet SAM systems in the 1973 war was their capability of reducing pilots' loiter time over target zones in order to acquire "eyeball

intelligence" of ground targets.

The most recent addition to the Soviet SAM inventory in the Mideast was the shoulder-fired SA-7, first used in North Vietnam in 1972. After effective ECM were introduced, the Soviets mounted the SA-7 on a vehicle and fired it in salvos, complicating the ECM. In the Yom Kippur War, the SA-7 was able to avoid decoy flares.

The SA-8, a new short-range all-weather surface-to-air missile system, was first publicly displayed at Moscow's Red Square Parade in November 1975. The SA-8, which can be airlifted by Soviet training aircraft, is said to be in its first service-evaluation stage. The Soviets have also displayed the SA-9, an improved version of the SA-7. The SA-9, like the SA-7, is mounted on a vehicle, but it fires a missile with a larger warhead. In early 1975 the Soviets were developing a new high-acceleration surface-to-air missile capable of intercepting SRAM missiles carried by B-52s. These various developments demonstrated the importance of SAM mobility.

In 1974 the U.S. DOD began to upgrade the mobility of its SAM-D system, and by mid-1975 three successful test firings of the system had been completed. The army was expected to complete in 1975 sixteen proof-of-principle tests demonstrating the capability of the SAM-D system. In addition, a new weapon, the Stinger, which appears to be similar to the SA-7, was under development.

AWACS (Airborne Warning and Control System)

The USSR learned from the Korean War that ground radar protection and interceptor squadrons were insufficient to protect a country from air attack; hence they pushed the development of an airborne radar system. Captured electronic equipment, including airborne radar and advanced gunsights acquired from downed U.S. interceptors in Korea, aided their endeavor. Moreover, the Soviets may have captured the all-weather F-94 interceptor and may even have flown captured U.S. jet fighters.

Beginning in 1955, the USSR introduced its own airborne radar on a growing scale. Soviet progress in tracking, guidance, and control received a powerful boost from its early successes in space-flight research during 1957–1962. Yet Soviet airborne intercept radars were mediocre by Western standards, and this situation persisted until 1968. Since then, Soviet progress has been impressive. In 1968, two years before Boeing was named prime contractor for the USAF's AWACS program, the Soviet Union flew its first AWACS aircraft. Given the NATO name Moss, the Soviet aircraft was based on the airframe of the Tu-114 airliner, which itself had evolved from the Tu-95 Bear strategic bomber. In 1975 ten of these aircraft—whose primary tasks are to provide early warning of approaching enemy aircraft at any level down to sea level and to direct interceptors toward intruding enemy aircraft—were in service. Two interceptors were supplied with guidance and airborne-intercept radar, and Soviet bombers were equipped with radar tail-warning sets.

The United States was reticent to acquire an AWACS capability because of its conviction that enemy missiles, not long-range bombers, were the overriding defensive objective. Another factor was the uncertainty among Pentagon scientists about the ability of airborne radar to detect and track low-flying targets in the presence of ground clutter. In 1968, after successful AWACS flight tests, the USAF decided to convert the F-106 to an AWACS aircraft, and by December

the DOD had authorized the USAF to proceed slowly with AWACS. USAF funding requests in 1970 increased sharply, even though resistance to an expanded AWACS was still strong.

Although the U.S. 1971 fiscal-year budget included $87 million for AWACS aircraft development, only $5.3 million was allocated for an early-warning radar system, and Congress refused the USAF's request for funds to modernize the F-106 and to buy a small number of F-12s in order to convert them to AWACS aircraft. Nonetheless, by late 1973 the U.S. had four AWACS aircraft under development, including the Boeing E-3A (a converted 707 jet) and the E-4A, which was based on the Boeing 747 airframe. Although doubts about the operational capability of the Boeing E-3A persisted in Congress and there was some talk about the demise of the program in 1974–1975, the USAF obtained release of production funding that had been held up by Congress. What may have helped the AWACS cause was the successful performance of the E-3A aircraft over NATO land and sea environments in early 1975. Production of the AWACS aircraft began in mid-April 1975, and delivery of the first six production aircraft was scheduled for November 1976.

These developments can be traced to Soviet technological advances. Early U.S. interest in AWACS was linked to Soviet aircraft technologies unveiled at the 1967 Domodedovo air show—especially the new version of the medium-range Blinder bomber, with its aerial refueling probe and new standoff missile. In late 1969 the Soviets began testing their new Mach 2 Backfire bomber, which was capable of making supersonic penetrations from both high and low altitudes. A new Soviet ASM, capable of being launched 2,000 miles from target, was also under development. The appearance of two squadrons of Backfire bombers provided another strong stimulus for AWACS supporters in the United States. The Yom Kippur War of 1973 may also have influenced the growing U.S. awareness of AWACS importance; that conflict demonstrated that an effective Israeli AWACS capability could have ascertained from a safe distance of hundreds of miles when Arab aircraft had left their hangars.

Radar Equipment

At least four types of tracking and control radars for the SA-2 (Fan Song) were built and widely used in North Vietnam and Egypt. This radar, which can track six targets and guide three missiles simultaneously, was credited with downing B-52s over Vietnam in late 1972, causing SAC to modify the planes' ECM antennas in early 1973. The influence of U.S. scientific advances is revealed in the Fan Song radar, in that its tracking system is based on a scanning concept invented by a U.S. scientist, Dr. Willard D. Lewis, in the early 1950s. In an attempt to duplicate Fan Song, the USAF and USN utilized for training purposes a number of Lewis scanners as mimics of Soviet emitters. Several high-performance variations of the land-based SA-3 radar units (Low Blow) were also developed. The radar system of the SA-6 missile posed the greatest threat in Vietnam. Until December 1973, lack of precise knowledge of its features precluded the U.S. from taking effective evasive measures. Also, the Soviets deviated from their practice and used higher missile-command frequencies, which are more difficult to jam.

The USAF and the USN launched crash programs in an effort to develop effective radar warning and jamming technology to counter the SA-6 threat. The origin of these developments can probably be set at around 1968, when

the USAF requested about $150 million for modifying its B-52Hs to carry SRAMs in order to provide them with standoff capability against advanced Soviet air-defense systems. As a result of the detection of highly effective Soviet-built radar systems in Vietnam, ECM and electronic reconnaissance began to receive attention in USAF funding requests beginning in early 1969. The Soviet SA-2s and SA-3s encountered in the Mideast in 1970 provided the model for the new ECM equipment in which the navy and USAF began to invest heavily in early 1972.

Developments in 1973 demonstrated the United States' vigorous reaction to Soviet radar advances and also revealed some frustrations. Successes in blunting the SA-2 radar system during the late stages of the Vietnam War appeared to be of dubious value in countering newer Soviet-built radar systems. One example of U.S. frustration followed the discovery of considerable amounts of unintentional energy leakage in the SA-2 radars in Vietnam. To exploit this weakness, the navy sought to incorporate in its latest antiradar missiles a radar-emission detection capability. But the Soviets, aware of this shortcoming, had built into their newer radars an improved counter-ECM capability designed to reduce such leakage.

The USAF had planned to produce several prototypes of a new subsonic cruise armed decoy (SCAD) system in an effort to ensure that its B-52s and FB-111s could reach their targets by confusing hostile radar defenses. Although this missile was cancelled by the DOD in July 1973, the success of the SA-6 in the Yom Kippur War caused some DOD officials to reexamine SCAD's capability. Enthusiasm was generated within USAF circles in 1973–1974 for developing a multipurpose missile based on advanced ramjet technology as a defense

Figure 74. Backfire bomber, first flown in 1969. Probably derived from the Tu-22, it has variable-geometry wings. Its normal range is estimated at 3,000 miles; with inflight refueling it can fly about ten hours after being topped up. This is probably a drawing.

against increasingly sophisticated Soviet antiaircraft (A/A) threats. The paucity of effective SA-6 jammers complicated the problem. While the navy and air force had such systems under development, they would not be operational, as a result of funding restraints, until the 1980s. Pending perfection of new ECM, aircraft-dispensed chaff supplied by the United States and rushed to Israel in mid-October 1973 provided the major ECM used by Israel. The higher frequencies of the SA-6 radar system necessitated that USAF and navy aircraft be retrofitted with new expanded-frequency airborne-launch warning devices; in fiscal year 1974 the navy received $45 million to complete this program. But there were indications that neither these devices nor the B-52's new ECM were adequate to cope with the SA-6, and in late October 1973 both services acknowledged that they possessed, at best, a questionable capability to detect the SA-6 missile launch in order to generate the necessary pilot warning and to introduce jamming.

In early November 1973 six Soviet-built SA-6 systems, including their radar

vans, were captured by the Israelis and flown to the United States for analysis. While DOD specialists praised the missile for its simplicity and effectiveness, they insisted that U.S. systems under development were superior—yet they acknowledged that it would require about $100 million and several years of work to duplicate the SA-6's performance. At the same time, the Pentagon was moving quickly to develop a new series of ECMs to counter the SA-6. One option under consideration was the use of an expanded-capability navy aircraft, the Grumman EA-GB, with the USAF's EF-111 fighter-bomber. Other options being considered in 1974–1975 included a distance-measuring guided weapon which, when linked with an electronic intelligence system, would allow a missile to be guided to target without visual or radar acquisition.

Antiaircraft Artillery

The antiaircraft artillery performs a vital function in Soviet air defense. Nonetheless, Soviet military leaders acknowledged the paramount importance of SAMs in their air-defense system by phasing out, between

1967 and mid-1970, most guns in their A/A artillery larger than 57mm. What were retained were guns effective against low-flying aircraft—which, until recently, could penetrate below radar and SAMs. The larger guns fired too slowly and could not track the supersonic jet and strategic bombers rapidly enough; yet in 1973 the authoritative Institute of Strategic Studies in London reported the reappearance of 85mm, 100mm, and 130mm guns in the Soviet A/A inventory. This surprising development might be related to the Soviet perception of an enhanced Chinese land threat, or it could be related to the new lease on life for larger guns provided by the Yom Kippur War of 1973. Given the partial neutralization of the fighter-bomber threat by SAMs in that conflict, military analysts felt that greater stress must henceforth be placed on precision targeting by surface-to-surface missiles and the artillery. The most nearly perfected Soviet A/A weapon, the ZSU-234, which consisted of 23mm four-barreled guns mounted on a tank or weapons-carrier chassis, was used in the Mideast in 1970 and again in the most recent Mideast war in order to protect the mobile SA-6 sites at low and medium altitudes. This deadly weapon, with its broad-band, high-frequency radar director (called Gun Dish by NATO), took a heavy toll of Israeli attack planes in the Yom Kippur War. In late 1973 the West still had no active ECM to counter its radar system, but vigorous efforts were made in 1974–1975 to correct this deficiency.

Civil Defense

In the USSR, civil defense (CD) holds very high priority. The immediate past CD chief was a Soviet marshal, and the present head holds the important position of deputy minister of defense. Another indication of the importance attached to CD is the massive annual drive sponsored by Soviet officials to increase the public's awareness of the need for improved CD techniques. Corollary with this trend is the sharply increased role of the Communist party as the nation's chief coordinating agency. Soviet attitudes on CD can probably be linked to World War II, when the Soviet Union carried out large-scale evacuations of people and industries to the Urals and Siberia. Such attitudes have also been shaped by the conviction that civilians represented a second line of defense in that conflict, and that post-attack mobilization was crucial to Soviet World War II successes. The political unity of stressing an external threat to the masses should not be discounted.

Soviet CD doctrine can be understood only by examining Soviet military doctrine, because Soviet officials have consistently subordinated their thinking about CD to their doctrinal views about future warfare. Beginning around 1960, most Soviet military writers argued that if a new war were to occur it would be global, a confrontation between the capitalist and socialist systems.

While ruling out the exclusive use of nuclear weapons in such a conflict, Soviet theorists have asserted that the main weapons would be nuclear in character. In addition to troop formations, the industries, communication networks, energy resources, urban and military centers, and agricultural areas would be exposed to enemy attack. Even in rural areas, the population (as well as animals and plants) would be subjected to radioactive fallout and nuclear contamination. In short, no populated areas would be invulnerable to nuclear attack. Thus, they argued, victory in a future war would be impossible without protecting the major sectors of the population and economy. The scattered locations of Soviet cities, the planned nature of the Soviet economy—which allows for more effective dispersal and coordination of industries—and the high "moral-political" unity of the Soviet people—all these factors presumably would reduce population and production losses, thus allowing a CD program to be effective.

Several assumptions can be derived from these doctrinal tenets. First, Soviet officials assert that protective measures against a possible nuclear attack must be carried out in each city, village, and factory throughout the country. Second, it is assumed that local antiaircraft and antimissile units will be unable to adequately protect the population. Third, CD thinkers maintain that only a massive and highly organized effort under party and government guidance can adequately train the population in peacetime and safeguard them during and after an attack. This assumption has been shaped by the Soviet experience in enforcing discipline on the population and in controlling their actions through the centralized and bureaucratized apparatus of the CPSU.

Soviet CD doctrine holds that the population can be protected from nuclear attack through (1) blast and fallout shelters and (2) evacuation and dispersal of the population. "Evacuation" applies to children, the elderly, and the ill, while "dispersal" applies to the working segments. Until the early 1960s, the main emphasis was on shelter construction, in both the urban and rural areas. Beginning in the period 1960–1966, however, dispersal and evacuation began to be emphasized, on the ground that it was more economical to evacuate and disperse the population into adjacent areas than to protect them in shelters in the main cities.

Nonetheless, shelter construction continues to be of no small importance in Soviet CD programs. It is acknowledged that evacuation has not yet reached the desired state of readiness because of transportation problems; hence blast shelters must be provided for those people who remain behind in the urban areas. Furthermore, even after the population has been evacuated from the cities to the rural areas, fallout shelters would have to be provided for them as well as for the animals.

Current Soviet CD literature mentions three types of shelters: built-in, free-standing, and radiation-protective dugouts. The first two types, which can hold up to forty persons, are designed to provide protection from direct blast waves, from thermal and radioactive radiation, and from poisonous substances and bacterial agents. The dugouts are designed primarily for protection against radioactive fallout in the rural areas. In addition, the subways in Moscow, Leningrad, Kiev, Tiflis, and Baku have been adapted to shelter large groups of people by equipping them with blast doors and high-speed escalators. Similar subways are being built in Tashkent and Kharkov.

The available evidence indicates that the Soviet CD program is a massive effort directed by the CPSU and that it involves all Soviet communication media. Training the population in proper procedures, in part by providing compulsory instruction in Soviet schools, occupies a key role. Yet we know little about the Soviet public's reactions to CD, although some evidence of alleged shortcomings, ranging from bureaucratic mishandling to public apathy, does exist. There have been some reports of featherbedding in CD sections in Moscow and Leningrad staffed by retired field-grade army and air-force officers. On the other hand, the efforts of the people have on occasion been praised. It seems reasonable to suggest that, while the people's attitudes may leave something to be desired, some progress in enlisting their enthusiasm has been made.

Conclusions

Soviet leaders in general have continued Khrushchev's policy of limiting their long-range bomber fleet while maintaining a sizable medium-range bomber force. While a neat pattern of offensive-defensive interactions is not always discernible, the evidence strongly suggests that Soviet weapons development had a powerful impact on U.S. technologies and vice versa. This action-reaction pattern may occur either as an offset choice (i.e., a defensive development by one superpower provokes an offensive countermeasure by the other) or as an equivalent development (i.e., a new generation of Soviet interceptors accelerates the development of similar U.S. aircraft). Soviet stress on air defenses probably has had the greatest impact on U.S. weapon technologies, while Soviet fears of U.S. and Chinese nuclear attacks have made both authorities and the general public take civil defense seriously.

The Soviets probably will continue to rely on a mixed-offensive-weapons concept of heavy and medium bombers. The number of long-range bombers may be limited or reduced under future SALT agreements. The number of Soviet Backfire bombers may be reduced if a mutually acceptable agreement can be reached on the sensitive question of whether to include the Backfire and U.S. cruise missiles in the new launcher ceilings established at the November 1974 Vladivostok summit conference. The Ford administration, reversing its previous position, insisted in 1975–1976 that the Soviet Backfire be included within these ceilings, since the latest U.S. intelligence suggested

that the latest Backfire version, with its in-flight refueling, possessed a two-way mission capability against North American targets. At the same time, the United States argued that only its air-launched missiles with ranges exceeding 600 km (375 miles), not its cruise missiles, were intended to be included in the Vladivostok ceilings. Conversely, the Soviets insisted that the U.S. cruise missile should be included in the ceilings, and that their Backfire bomber was not a strategic weapon.

There were indications in 1975–1976 of some progress in resolving this issue, in that the Soviets proposed to lower the Vladivostok ceilings (from 2,400 offensive systems to 2,100–2,200, a figure which could be increased to the original 2,400 level in order to include Backfire bombers added to the Soviet inventory). However, recent reports indicate a hardening of the Soviet position on the issue of U.S. cruise missiles.

Even if the heavy-bomber component is not reduced, the most vital responsibilities of the DA will probably be air strikes and naval reconnaissance support. The number of Soviet long-range bombers may dwindle if the United States reduces its present bomber force by converting to the B-1 bomber by the end of the 1970s. If, however, the Soviets perceive that the B-1 and the new U.S. cruise missile represent an attempt to achieve limited strategic superiority, the continued development of these weapons could sharply accelerate a corresponding Soviet bomber program and/or air-defense system. Withdrawing support for the B-1, or even scrapping it, would presumably have the opposite effect. But total abandonment of the B-1 is unlikely, despite reports that the Soviets would agree to limit production and mounting of their MIRVs if the United States scrapped

Figure 75. Tu-95 Bear, photographed in October 1973 during NATO maneuvers in the North Atlantic.

its B-1 bomber and other strategic programs, as General Secretary Brezhnev suggested at the Twenty-fifth Party Congress.

There is little doubt that Soviet leaders will continue to place the highest priority on their air-defense forces, especially interceptors and the prototype development of newer aircraft. The USAF's decision to give top budget priority to its B-1 and to such new penetration devices and techniques as cruise missiles, bomber defense missiles, and improved ECM was a contributing factor. As the United States perfects its new lightweight interceptors, the USSR will be under pressure to keep pace, especially if these aircraft are given to Israel or other states in considerable numbers. If the USAF develops a relatively inexpensive remote-controlled

reconnaissance and attack plane, as they plan to do, the Soviets will concentrate on this area as well.

A major factor associated with Soviet emphasis on air-defense programs—the presence of U.S. forward base systems (FBS) and carrier-based aircraft in Europe—might be amenable to a future SALT agreement. While neither SALT 1 nor SALT 2 answered the question of whether such aircraft are "strategic," this problem may eventually be resolved; SALT 1 at least laid the foundation for a shift in emphasis from weapons capability to intent in regard to the definition of "strategic." Thus U.S. strategic planners might be able to convince the Soviets that tactical aircraft deployed in Europe are not "credibly" intended to reach the

USSR. One incentive for Soviet agreement to this principle is that their 645 medium-range Tu-16 and Tu-22 bombers as well as their new longer-range Backfire bombers, have the capability of reaching U.S. targets, although the Soviets claim they are not intended to do so. Furthermore, there was some evidence of modest progress in negotiating mutual force reductions, including forward-based aircraft, in 1975–1976. While neither Soviet nor Western proposals managed to break the deadlock which had plagued the talks since they began in late 1973, they did seem to represent a constructive advance in superpower dialogue. If this issue were resolved, the perceived threat to the Soviets from Europe could be allayed and a corresponding deemphasis on air defenses might follow; or they might maintain their present PVO force levels but refocus their defensive aircraft on China.

Soviet stress on effective CD preparations as a deterrent to nuclear attack challenges the West's doctrine of "mutual assured destruction" (MAD), which postulates that the best route to nuclear peace and security is through exposing the civilian populations in both countries to attack. Thus, stability and deterrence, in the Western view, are said to reside in high population hostage levels and in limits on ABM systems such as those imposed by both SALT 1 and SALT 2. Correlatively, civil defense, according to many in the West, is not a valid defense measure because it is purportedly ineffective against nuclear weapons and too time-consuming. If the Soviets could evacuate their cities, and thus reduce the vulnerability of their population to fire damage and fallout, before a nuclear attack (or even possibly during an attack), the hostage level would drop sharply and the MAD doctrine would lose credibility. The West's deterrent, based on the threat to the Soviet urban population, would be degraded. Defense Secretary James Schlesinger's call for new strategic planning, based on the retargeting of U.S. missiles on Soviet military sites rather than on cities, may have reflected Western acknowledgement of Soviet war-survival capabilities and programs. Finally, the hardened Soviet bargaining posture evident at SALT 2—while clearly related to enhanced nuclear capability—was perhaps buttressed by the perception of a growing Soviet war-survival capability and an eroding U.S. deterrent. While evacuation procedures and civil-defense training in the USSR may still leave much to be desired, the Soviets have compelling reasons for devoting so much effort to improving them.

Research Notes

Relatively little has been written in the West about the Soviet air force. The three basic books in the field are Asher Lee's two works, *The Soviet Air and Rocket Forces* (New York, 1959), and *The Soviet Air Force* (New York, rev. ed., 1961), and Robert Kilmarx' *History of Soviet Air Power* (New York, 1962). In his first book, Lee as volume editor devoted four chapters to the period 1917–

1945 and the remaining chapters to Soviet air defense, the strategic air force, jet fighters and fighter-bombers, and airborne troops. The Soviets' dependence on Western air advances up to 1955 and their air-defense weaknesses were stressed in order to show that insecurity made Soviet foreign policy cautious. In his second book, Lee stated that Soviet PVO forces became technically, numerically, and politically stronger than the air-defense forces in the United States but militarily and tactically weaker, largely because of the growing IRBM and ICBM threat. The author introduced the latest Soviet missile advances but was hesitant to dismiss the manned bomber as a weapons system. Lee also noted the similarities in the weapons systems, military policies, and long-range planning of the two superpowers, especially in such areas as strategic bombers, military air transport, and radar. His chapter on Communist party influence on Soviet air power was a new attempt to assess the significance to the military of party controls and of political factors in general. Kilmarx' book deals with the period 1910–1945 in four of its seven chapters. Kilmarx also stressed Soviet dependence on Western states for aircraft design, engines, and factories in the prewar period, and concurred with Lee that the role of the Soviet air force was minimal in World War II.

In *Soviet Strategy in the Nuclear Age* (New York, 1958), Raymond Garthoff described the evolution of Soviet air doctrine under Stalin and after Stalin within the framework of Soviet military doctrine and strategy. Garthoff analyzed the Soviet strategic concept of long-range bombing and concluded that it is more flexible than its U.S. counterpart. Herbert Dinerstein, in his *War and the Soviet Union* (New York, 1959), focused on the impact of the nuclear revolution on Soviet military and political thought. He argued that the role of the DA had been upgraded around 1955, but was later downgraded by Khrushchev with the advent of missiles in the late 1950s.

In his chapter "The Future of Manned Aircraft" in John Erickson, ed., *The Military Technical Revolution* (New York, 1966), Martin Edmonds argued that the future of manned aircraft is shaped by the defense and foreign policies of the two superpowers. He was pessimistic about the future of the strategic bomber, but optimistic about tactical aircraft. Edmonds asserted that, with a few exceptions, parallel trends are discernible in the USSR and the United States; e.g., development of multipurpose aircraft, stress on long-range transport, and low priority afforded VTOL and STOL aircraft.

Why ARM?, ed. Johan Holst and W. Schneider (New York, 1969), offered a bureaucratic interpretation for certain anomalies in the Soviet air defense posture, among them its emphasis on tube-fired antiaircraft artillery, day interceptors, and SAMs. *The Red Falcons*, by Robert Jackson (London, 1970), was a non-scholarly account of Soviet air force battles from 1919 to 1969. Michel Garder, in *A History of the Soviet Army* (London, 1966) devoted about thirty pages to the Soviet air force, primarily to Soviet military strategy and doctrine. His treatment of the PVO and DA forces is sketchy.

The two foremost U.S. specialists on Soviet civil defense are Leon Gouré and Joanne Gailer of the Oak Ridge National Laboratory. Gouré has concentrated on Soviet CD doctrine and views on dispersal and evacuation. Gailer, writing in the CD journal *Survive*, focused on the survival gap purportedly existing between upgraded Soviet CD programs and downgraded U.S. programs, and on the role of CD in Soviet society.

Much more research is needed in several key areas. First, there is a paucity of works on the structure of Soviet decision making, especially in regard to strategic-weapon procurement policies and policy determinants. We also need more in-depth studies on Soviet military policy debates and on the impact of such recent conflicts as the Vietnam and Mideast wars on Soviet air defense and defense policy. An analysis of Soviet views about the use of air power as an instrument of Soviet foreign policy would be important. Another neglected topic is the extent of Communist party control over the Soviet air force. An examination of technocrat-traditionalist cleavages within the Soviet air force would also be valuable. More research is needed on the scope and intensity of Soviet CD evacuation and dispersal exercises, shelter construction, and the organization of CD programs—specifically, the web of inter-relationships between the party and other CD agencies. Probably our most serious research gap pertains to the Soviet public's attitudes on CD. Pending a further cooling of ideological passions in both the United States and the USSR, with a concomitant lowering of mutual distrust, this gap will undoubtedly persist.

10

Strategic Missile Forces and Cosmic Research

Phillip A. Petersen

Soviet strategic missile forces and cosmic research are of great importance in the context of Soviet military power, for they have given the Soviets strategic parity *vis-à-vis* the United States. That parity, of course, has tremendous military and political implications. Militarily, it provides the Soviets with a strategic situation in which their superiority in conventional forces becomes of greater value. Politically, it provides evidence to the world that the Soviets must be granted a coequal role in resolving international problems.

The Ballistic Missile and the Space Race

With the conclusion of World War II, the Soviet Union gained control of a number of German rocket research and test facilities. It is not difficult to understand, therefore, that the Soviet Union obtained a great deal of German research which, when combined with native Soviet efforts and skills, provided a unique opportunity

for breakthroughs in ballistic missile technology. The Soviets centralized these resources in the Office of Special Weapons. This agency, the headquarters of which was located in Moscow, was directed by Gen. A. S. Yakovlev.

The first Soviet ballistic missiles were launched before 1950. By 1957 the Soviets had orbited the first earth satellite, and they displayed medium-range ballistic missiles during the celebrations honoring the fortieth anniversary of the October revolution. Those missiles (NATO code-named Shyster, now obsolete) were developed from the German V-2 bombardment missile in two stages, producing missiles known as Scunner (in reality a Soviet-built V-2) and Sibling. By 1959, the Soviets had begun to deploy the SS-4 Sandal (see figure 76), an improved version of the SS-3 Shyster. While engaged in deploying these missiles, the Soviets undoubtedly devoted much thought to the development of organization and role; for

Figure 76. SS-4 Sandal MRBM on display in Red Square. The Soviets have deployed more than 500 of these missiles since 1959. Sandal's range is approximately 1,200 miles and it carries a one-megaton warhead. This was the MRBM system deployed in Cuba in 1962.

within the Soviet military, the ballistic missile was perceived as merely an extension of army artillery.

The postwar Soviet concept of "hostage Europe" had grown out of a lack of capability to match U.S. nuclear strength. Partly out of necessity, therefore, the USSR had emphasized the preparation of its armed forces for an invasion and occupation of Western Europe. Both Stalin's public depreciation of the military and political significance of nuclear weapons and his vaunting of large conventional forces must be understood within the context of his need to make the Soviet strategy credible at least until such time as the Soviet nuclear-weapons program produced a deterrent. Thus, the struggle between 1953 and 1960 to free Soviet military thinking from "Stalinist doctrine" and to adjust to the military-technological revolution was founded in the rising state of Soviet weapons technology—developments for which credit, in no small way, is due to Stalin.

The evolving state of Soviet weapons technology, in addition to economic considerations, made a military reformer out of Khrushchev and led him to attempt to drag a traditionally conservative military establishment into the space age. He worked out a concept of substituting "firepower for manpower," and in January 1960 laid out a plan for a shortcut to military parity with the United States. Had his ideas been fully implemented, there would have been a total transformation of Soviet military strategy and force structure: in his report to the Supreme Soviet, he proposed cutting the Soviet armed forces by approximately one-third. Khrushchev stated that he felt that this reduction in force could be achieved without sacrificing Soviet security because the military-technological revolution had made it possible to increase the firepower of the armed forces by equipping them with rockets and nuclear weapons. He stressed that these would be the principal element in any future war, and that the nation's defensive capability was no longer determined by mere numbers of soldiers under arms.

When he made his report, Khrushchev claimed to have consulted the military and the General Staff concerning his proposed strategy and force structure. Furthermore, he implied that they agreed that Soviet defense would be "quite adequate" under his plan. Yet, in fact, he did not have the concurrence of the Soviet military establishment, most of whom opposed Khrushchev's proposed shortcut to achieving military parity with the United States.

By bluff and bluster, Khrushchev attempted to make his newborn ballistic missile force seem an equitable counterforce to the entire nuclear arsenal of the United States. He arranged for the new missiles to be displayed in Red Square and openly tested progressively larger and more powerful warheads for them. At the same time, however, he proposed nuclear disarmament —clearly hoping in this manner to obtain U.S. assistance in reaching nuclear parity.

Several developments provided Khrushchev's opponents with the opportunity to prevent implementation of his shortcut program. They used one such incident, the downing of an American U-2 reconnaissance aircraft in May 1960, to demonstrate U.S. awareness of the paucity of Soviet missile strength. In fact, the military had been aware of these incursions into Soviet air space long before the Powers flight. Partly as a result of these reconnaissance flights and partly as a result of corroborating evidence obtained from Col. Oleg Penkovsky and from satellite reconnaissance, the United States had indeed reappraised Soviet nuclear-missile strength downward. This reappraisal occurred at a time when the United States was expanding its Minuteman and Polaris programs. Khrushchev took the gamble that he could negate both trends and restore credibility

to the Soviet nuclear deterrent by introducing ballistic missiles into Cuba. The crisis which developed as a result of stiff U.S. resistance ended in an embarrassing capitulation.

While the 1962 Cuban crisis helped convince the Soviets of the need for a flexible military strategy and force structure, it also demonstrated their glaring inadequacy in missile strength. In July 1962 the United States had 294 intercontinental ballistic missiles (ICBMs) and 144 submarine-launched ballistic missiles (SLBMs), while the Soviets only had 75 ICBMs and a small number of SLBMs. It is not surprising, therefore, that before the end of 1965 the post-Khrushchev leadership acquiesced to the military establishment's demand for a military buildup that included an accelerated strategic missile development program.

Along with an offensive missile program, the Soviets were developing an anti-ballistic missile program. In November 1963 they paraded in Red Square the surface-to-air missile known as Griffon, which they claimed was capable of destroying missiles. Although the Soviets began to deploy Griffon (a SAM primarily designed for bomber defense, though capable of providing some limited ABM protection) around Leningrad in 1962, the first operational Soviet ABM system was Galosh, which was deployed around Moscow. The Galosh missile first appeared in public during a November 1964 Red Square parade. It is a multistage missile with a range in excess of 200 miles and carries a nuclear warhead in the megaton range. In the case of both the Griffon and the Galosh, however, Soviet claims exceeded the capabilities of the systems.

The growth of Soviet ICBM forces between 1965 and 1975 was extremely impressive. The number of ICBM launchers jumped from some 224 in 1965 to approxi-

Figure 77. Mitrofan I. Nedelin.

mately 1,618 in 1975. In contrast, the U.S. land-based missile force expanded slowly from a 1965 total of 854 to 1,054 ICBMs in 1967, a figure which has remained static since that time. By 1971 the Soviets had achieved their goal of strategic numerical equality; from then on they merely attempted to offset the qualitative superiority of the U.S. force.

To the impressive Soviet ICBM strength must be added the SLBMs carried by the Soviet ballistic-missile submarines. The 1968 introduction of a genuine strategic missile-launching system in the Y-class submarine, each of which carried sixteen SS-N6 missiles with a 1,500–1,750-mile range, assured the Soviets of a "post-exchange balance" that might be described as a capability to deter an opponent from a follow-up strike. Since then, the Soviets have deployed newer D-class submarines, some of which carry twelve and other

sixteen SS-N8 missiles with a range of 4,800 miles.

Clearly, the buildup in Soviet missile strength has created a situation in which Soviet conventional superiority assumes greater importance. Besides the political value of nuclear-missile parity with the United States, the Soviets can now less easily be intimidated from utilizing their ever-growing, increasingly flexible and sophisticated conventional/general-purpose forces. Ironically, however, just at the time when the Soviet Union had finally obtained nuclear parity with the United States, the armed forces of the Soviet Union and those of the People's Republic of China began to square off.

The Chinese had perceived the Soviets as possessing strategic superiority over the United States in the late 1950s. The Soviet missile and Sputnik launchings of 1957 and Khrushchev's accompanying bluff and bluster had convinced the Chinese, as well as the West, that the so-called missile gap was real. In view of his perceptions, Mao pressed Khrushchev to assume greater risks *vis-à-vis* the United States. Khrushchev, of course, knew the true measure of Soviet strategic gains. Now that the Soviets indeed do possess at least nuclear-missile parity with the United States, both China and the U.S. are confronted with the reality of what was once merely a projection.

Soviet missile and space activity has remained at a high and essentially constant level. In regard to missile developments, the Soviets continue to strive for improvements in quality as well as quantity. Even after an upper limit to the number of missile launchers was frozen by the 1972 and 1974 Strategic Arms Limitation Agreements, the Soviets continued their effort to achieve qualitative improvements. The total Soviet space effort

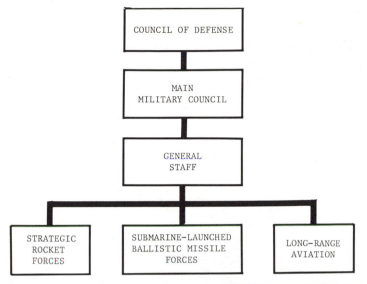

Figure 78. Chain of operational control of the Soviet strategic forces.

now exceeds that of the United States, at least in terms of dollars expended and spacecraft launched.

Strategic Rocket Forces

As part of Khrushchev's proposed military strategy and force structure, the strategic rocket forces were created in 1960, with Chief Marshal of Artillery Mitrofan I. Nedelin (see figure 77) as commander in chief. As such, Nedelin—already a candidate member of the CPSU Central Committee and a deputy to the Supreme Soviet—also became a deputy minister of defense. At this juncture it might be appropriate to take a look at the operational chain of control of Soviet strategic forces (see figure 78).

Essentially three bodies constitute the Soviet high command: the Council of Defense, the Main Military Council, and the General Staff. The Council of Defense unifies the military and civilian leadership so as to insure centralized political direction of the economy and military operations. The military-political tasks arrived at

by the Council of Defense fall to the strategic direction and leadership of the Main Military Council which insures that the strategic policy decisions of the Council of Defense that do not come down to the Main Military Council as specific directives are transformed into such directives for the armed forces. The contribution of the General Staff is to insure the development and exercise of a unified military strategy for the operational commands. In exercising its responsibilities for the Ministry of Defense, the General Staff would possess operational control of Soviet strategic forces.

Soviet strategic forces consist of both defensive and offensive forces. As Marshal V. D. Sokolovski's book *Military Strategy* set out the defensive function of *PVO Strany*, the mission is to prevent penetration by enemy means of attack into the airspace of the country and to prevent his nuclear attacks against the most important regions of the country and elements of the armed forces. Offensively, Soviet strategic forces consist of long-range aviation, the

Figure 79. Kirill S. Moskalenko.

submarine-launched ballistic missile force, and the strategic rocket forces. Long-range aviation consists of long- and medium-range bombers utilized in strategic roles. The submarine-launched ballistic missile force consists of strategic missile-launching submarines armed with missiles of different ranges. The strategic rocket forces constitute the main strategic force of the Soviet Union. Their arsenal consists of medium-, intermediate-, and intercontinental-range ballistic missiles.

The Soviets have split the strategic rocket troops into two distinct forces. One, an intercontinental ballistic missile force, is aimed at deterring the United States. The other, a force including both intermediate- and medium-range ballistic missiles, is concerned primarily with European, Chinese, and Japanese targets. Using typical Soviet organizational charts and the relative strength of the ICBM and IRBM/MRBM forces, it is not difficult to construct the most likely organization of these two forces. The ICBM force probably consists

of several armies composed of several divisions each. The IRBM/MRBM force probably consists of two or three armies, each with several divisions. In both forces the organization could be taken down through regiment and battalion level to a battery consisting of a single ICBM or IRBM/MRBM launcher.

Inasmuch as the Soviet Ministry of Defense is a unified ministry, it can be assumed that the operations of the strategic rocket force are integrated with those of the naval forces' ballistic-missile submarines and the air forces' long-range aviation component. Thus, while it constitutes the main strategic force of the Soviet Union, the strategic rocket force is only one arm of a three-pronged nuclear deterrent. Its mission, like that of the other two components of the Soviet strategic nuclear force, is to destroy the enemy's means of nuclear attack and its main governmental, military, and economic centers.

The struggle to obtain the capability of accomplishing its mission was not so easy as the mere creation of the strategic rocket forces. In October 1960, Marshal Nedelin was listed as a victim of an "aviation catastrophe." The informant Penkovsky, however, insisted that Nedelin was one of more than 300 people killed when a missile exploded during a test launch, apparently prematurely scheduled in an attempt to back up Khrushchev's claims of Soviet supremacy in the nuclear-missile field. That time, at least, Khrushchev's boasting propaganda tactic proved to be rather costly. At any rate, late in 1960 Marshal Kirill S. Moskalenko (see figure 79), commander of the Moscow Military District, assumed the position of commander in chief of the strategic rocket forces.

Under Moskalenko the arsenal of the strategic rocket forces grew to include several missiles with various ranges. The SS-5 Skean (see figure 80), the Soviets' first

Figure 80. SS-5 Skean IRBM, first operational in 1961. Its range is 2,300 miles. Only about 100 have been deployed.

intermediate-range ballistic missile, was deployed in 1961. In 1976 the SS-5 and the earlier-mentioned medium-range SS-4 Sandal still dominated the Soviet IRBM/MRBM force. Also included in the inventory of the strategic rocket forces when Moskalenko took over were the SS-6 Sapwood and SS-7 Saddler ICBMs.

In 1962 Moskalenko was promoted to chief inspector of the Ministry of Defense. He was succeeded by Marshal Sergei S. Biryuzov (see figure 81) as commander in chief of the strategic rocket forces. Biryuzov, who had been commander in chief of the Soviet Union's antiaircraft defenses, likewise did not remain in the position long. In March 1963 he was promoted to chief of the General Staff. His replacement as commander in chief of the strategic rocket forces was Marshal Nikolai I. Krylov (see figure 82).

Krylov was to break the pattern of his three predecessors' short tours, remaining

Figure 81. Sergei S. Biryuzov.

Figure 82. Nikolai I. Krylov.

as commander in chief for almost a decade. Under him, the strategic rocket forces' ICBM deployment surpassed the U.S. ICBM force in number of launchers. In their drive for strategic "parity," the Soviets deployed four new ICBMs. The SS-8 Sasin was deployed in 1963, followed in 1965 by the SS-9 Scarp (see figure 83), which became perhaps the best known of the Soviet missiles. The following year saw the deployment of the SS-11 Sego, and by 1968 the Soviets had begun to deploy the SS-13 Savage. Thus, the strategic rocket forces' operational inventory had grown to include one MRBM system, one IRBM system, and five ICBM systems (the SS-6 had long since become obsolete as a strategic weapons system) by the time Krylov died in February 1972.

Krylov was succeeded by army Gen. Vladimir F. Tolubko (see figure 84), who had been first deputy commander in chief of the strategic rocket forces from their creation in 1960 until the spring of 1968. At that time he had been made commander of the Siberian Military District in accordance with the traditional practice of shifting senior officers from headquarters to important field commands after a number of years. In mid-1969, however, he was reassigned to be commander of the Far Eastern Military District, probably because of events along the Sino-Soviet border. While Tolubko's record and length of service

Figure 83. SS-9 Scarp ICBM, first deployed in 1965. This system carries a warhead of up to twenty-five megatons and has a range of 7,500 miles. A later modification carries three MRV warheads.

alone may have garnered him his new assignment, his eight years as second in command of the strategic rocket forces, during which he probably was a central figure because of the frequent turnover in commanders, certainly stood him well also. Under Tolubko, in 1975 the strategic rocket forces began to phase out the SS-7 and SS-8 missiles (these were replaced by SS-N-8 missiles aboard D-class submarines), replace the SS-9 with the SS-18, and replace the SS-11 with the SS-17 and SS-19. The SS-18 is a two-stage liquid-fueled missile capable of carrying up to eight warheads. The SS-17 is a two-stage liquid-fueled missile capable of carrying four sub-

Figure 84. Vladimir F. Tolubko.

stantially smaller warheads. The SS-19 is a liquid-fueled ICBM capable of carrying six warheads.

NAME	DATES
MITROFAN I. NEDELIN	1960
KIRILL S. MOSKALENKO	1960-1962
SERGEI S. BIRYUZOV	1962-1963
NIKOLAI I. KRYLOV	1963-1972
VLADIMIR F. TOLUBKO	1972-

Figure 85. Commanders of the Soviet strategic rocket forces since 1960.

Table 1. Soviet Missiles—Rocket Identifications

U.S. numerical designation	NATO code name	Range category
SS-1	Scunner	SRBM
SS-1b	Scud A	SRBM
SS-1c	Scud B	SRBM
SS-2	Sibling	SRBM
SS-3	Shyster	MRBM
SS-4	Sandal	MRBM
SS-5	Skean	IRBM
SS-6	Sapwood	ICBM
SS-7	Saddler	ICBM
SS-8	Sasin	ICBM
SS-9	Scarp	ICBM
SS-10	Scrag	ICBM
SS-11	Sego	ICBM
SS-12	Scaleboard	Mobile SRBM
SS-13	Savage	ICBM
SS-14	Scapegoat (Scamp, when mounted)	Mobile MRBM
SS-15	Scrooge	Mobile IRBM
SS-16	(A replacement for the SS-13)	ICBM
SS-17	(A replacement for the SS-11)	ICBM
SS-18	(A replacement for the SS-9)	ICBM
SS-19	(A replacement for the SS-11)	ICBM
SS-20	(Utilizes two stages of the SS-16 and is designed as a replacement for the SS-4 and SS-5)	IRBM

In mid-1976 the strategic rocket forces consisted of 375,000 personnel and an inventory of approximately 1,527 ICBMs and 600 medium- and intermediate-range ballistic missiles. (See table 1 for a list of Soviet missiles.) The ICBM inventory broke down into about 159 SS-7 and SS-8, 252 SS-9, 900 SS-11, 60 SS-13, 20 SS-17, 36 SS-18, and 100 SS-19 missiles. It should be noted, however, that about 100 of the SS-11s were located within IRBM/MRBM launch fields. The IRBM/MRBM inventory broke down into about 100 SS-5 intermediate-range and 500 SS-4 medium-range missiles. Of the IRBM/MRBM force, the majority were deployed near the western border of the USSR, targeted against Western Europe. Some of the missiles in these fields, however, were programmed for targets in the Middle East. The remainder of the IRBM/MRBM force was deployed east of the Urals and was mostly targeted against China and Japan. As for the personnel, the majority of the enlisted men of the strategic rocket forces had received their training through what is referred to as the cadre system, in which experienced unit personnel teach acquired skills to the recruits. A number of the enlisted men had attended engineering and artillery schools and training centers for short courses in various specialized tech-

Figure 86. SS-12 Scaleboard mobile SRBM. It entered service in 1969 and has a range of 450 miles. It is seen here on an MAZ 543 carrier.

nical fields. As for officers, the higher command-engineering schools and command-technical schools probably provide the bulk.

Despite the Soviet attainment of strategic parity with the United States, a permanent ongoing research and development program has continued to produce new and more sophisticated equipment and techniques for the strategic rocket forces. Soviet design teams continue to produce ever-more-advanced ballistic missiles. While the SS-17, SS-18, and SS-19 had already become operational by mid-1975, the Soviets continued to test the SS-16, a three-stage solid-fueled missile that has about twice the throw weight of the SS-13. Furthermore, the Soviets have been testing the SS-20, which utilizes two stages of the SS-16, for use in both silos and in a mobile mode.

The Soviet Union has also developed what has been called a pop-up technique for launching some of its new ICBMs. This new launch technique is a "cold-launch" method similar to that utilized in the undersea launches of the U.S. Trident fleet missiles. It consists of an ejection system that uses compressed air and gas to expel the missile from its silo before ignition of the missile's engine. Since the propulsion system ignites after the missile is aloft, the Soviets have been able to remove the silo shielding which is required to permit the silo to withstand the high temperatures of expanding gases during "hot launches." With this new cold-launch technique, the Soviets are therefore able both to place some of the new and larger missiles in existing silos and to more rapidly reuse silos.

Another direction in which Soviet design teams have moved in their effort to qualitatively improve the strategic rocket forces' weapons inventory has been toward the area of mobile weapons systems. While

Figure 87. SS-14 Scapegoat mobile IRBM, first deployed in 1968. Powered by a solid-fuel rocket engine, it carries a one-megaton warhead and has a range of 2,500 miles.

the Soviets had a spinoff from the SS-1 Scunner, known as the Scud missile series, in 1969 they deployed a short-range ballistic missile (SRBM) whose range of 500 miles bordered on that of a medium-range ballistic missile. The latter missile, the SS-12 Scaleboard (see figure 86), was to be only one step in an orderly and progressive series of mobile missile developments. By 1976 a missile known as the SS-14 Scapegoat (see figure 87) had been mounted on a transporter-erector-launcher system referred to as Scamp (see figure 88) and displayed and tested, but had not yet been operationally deployed. This mobile system apparently has the range of an IRBM. Still another mobile system is the SS-15 Scrooge (see figure 89), an IRBM which had also been displayed and tested but not yet operationally deployed in 1976. Considering that

the Soviets had progressed through the developmental series from SRBM to IRBM, it should have come as no surprise when it was discovered that the SS-16 was being tested as part of a mobile ICBM system. Whether the Soviets will seek to deploy mobile ICBMs remains to be seen. (Table 1 lists Soviet missiles and their NATO code names.)

In essence, the strategic rocket forces have represented the vanguard of the Soviet drive for strategic nuclear parity with the United States. Under five commanders, the strategic rocket force has striven to achieve credibility as a deterrent for the Soviet state. Although it has achieved its goal—and partly as a result of that success—it should not be surprising if the strategic rocket force is increasingly required to share center stage with the navy's submarine-launched

Figure 88. Scamp mobile IRBM in May Day parade. The Scamp has a range of 2,500 miles. Many have been deployed near the Chinese border.

ballistic missile force.

Antiballistic Missile Systems

Although almost any sophisticated air-defense missile system could be employed in a ballistic-missile defense role with some success, the most striking difference between antiaircraft and antimissile defense systems is the extremely complex combination of specialized technical support equipment required by the latter. The countering of a large-scale sophisticated missile attack would require equipment capable of handling massive quantities of data within the seven or eight minutes that would elapse between the early tracking of incoming missiles and the launching of the first interceptors. Theoretically, a sophisticated surface-to-air missile (such as the two-stage SA-5 Griffon) could intercept some ballistic missiles if appropriately launched and controlled. The reason that the Griffon

is not considered useful as an antiballistic missile interceptor is that the large complex of support equipment which would be required for its effective utilization in that role is not deployed with it. Such support equipment would be difficult to hide, if only because of its size: the Soviet radar arrays are presently about 1,000 feet in length.

In the mid-1960s, the Soviet Union began to deploy its first truly antimissile defense system. In mid-1976 that system consisted of sixty-four Galosh long-range missile launchers deployed at four sites located in the Moscow area. Phased-array Hen House radar, located along the borders of the Soviet Union, provides early warning for the system. Target acquisition and tracking are by phased-array Dog House radar, which turns the targets over to Try Add engagement radar when they come into range.

On May 26, 1972, the United States

Figure 89. SS-15 Scrooge mobile IRBM, deployed in 1970. Solid fueled, it has a range of 3,360 miles and carries either a single one-megaton warhead or three MRVs.

and the Soviet Union signed a formal treaty limiting antiballistic missile systems. This treaty is of unlimited duration but is subject to review every five years. The facts that the Soviets had one such system already operational and located so as to protect their capital and that the United States had under construction two such systems to protect its ICBM force were dealt with by limiting each country to two ABM "deployment areas." According to the treaty, one deployment area could be located to defend the capital and the other to defend the ICBM force. Each deployment area could have a 94-mile radius, but their center points must be at least 810 miles apart. Both launch areas were restricted to 100 ABM launchers and 100 ABM interceptor missiles. In 1974 it was further agreed to limit each country to a single ABM area. In accor-

dance with the terms of the agreements with the United States, the Soviets have resumed construction of the Moscow deployment area. While by mid-1976 the Soviets had not yet expanded to the maximum 100 launchers presently allowed, they were known to be continuing the development of a more advanced ABM interceptor. (See table 2 for a comparison of U.S. and Soviet strategic missile complements from 1959 to 1976.)

The Space Program

The Soviet space program grew out of Russia's intensive postwar drive to develop ballistic-missile technology. Unlike the American space program, the Soviet program is not managed by a single directing agency. The Soviet space program consists of many different organizations, although most of its activities are centrally

Table 2. U.S. and Soviet Strategic Missile Forces
A comparison by year

Year	ICBMs		SLBMs	
	U.S.	USSR	U.S.	USSR
1959	0	some	0	0
1960	18	35	32	0
1961	63	50	96	some
1962	294	75	144	some
1963	424	90	224	107
1964	834	190	416	107
1965	854	224	496	107
1966	904	292	592	107
1967	1,054	570	656	107
1968	1,054	858	656	121
1969	1,054	1,028	656	196
1970	1,054	1,299	656	304
1971	1,054	1,513	656	448
1972	1,054	1,527	656	500
1973	1,054	1,527	656	628
1974	1,054	1,575	656	720
1975	1,054	1,618	656	784
1976	1,054	1,527	656	845

Note: Figures are for the middle of the years indicated.

coordinated by the Commission on the Exploration and Use of Space. This commission, whose members represent various agencies, is within the organizational structure of the Academy of Sciences of the USSR. In general, the Academy of Sciences directs the scientific program, while the Ministry of Defense controls the military program.

Within the Academy of Sciences are several organizations specifically devoted to the space program. High-level space-program policy planning within the academy is performed by the Commission on the Exploration and Use of Space. The academy's Institute of Space Research, however, is in charge on the operational level, supervising the scientific research program and the design and con-

struction of both manned and unmanned spacecraft. The institute is also responsible for training the cosmonauts, although this is done with the help of the Soviet air force. Training is conducted at Zvezdnyi Gorodok (Star Village), which is in suburban Moscow. The president of the academy and the director of the Institute of Space Research generally serve as public spokesmen for the nonmilitary aspects of the Soviet space program and conduct foreign negotiations affecting the program. The academy also manages the tracking stations within the USSR, the tracking ships assigned to the space program, and the main deep-space tracking station at Evpatoriia in the Crimea.

The design and construction of most

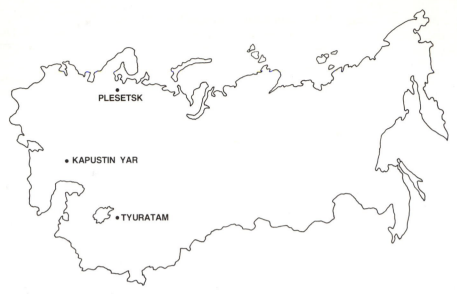

PLESETSK

KAPUSTIN YAR

TYURATAM

Figure 90. Space launch sites in the USSR.

of the launch vehicles utilized in the Soviet space program are accomplished by a group of defense-related industrial ministries referred to collectively as the Machine Building and Metal Working Enterprises, or, more simply, the Machine Building Industry. Khrushchev referred to them as the "metal eaters" because they receive such a disproportionate share of investments and resources that the growth rate of the rest of the economy lags. The heads of these ministries have a great deal of political clout and, therefore, a significant voice in the formation of space-program policy.

Despite criticisms to the contrary, the Soviet space program has developed in an orderly fashion according to a rather conservative, step-by-step plan oriented toward science and its practical application. As early as July 30, 1955, the Soviets had announced their intention to put a payload into orbit as part of the coming International Geophysical Year. Still, the West was shocked when, on October 4, 1957, the Soviets sent up the 184-pound Sputnik 1. This first satellite was launched from near Tyuratam (located at about 45.6° N latitude, 63.4° E longitude) in Kazakhstan, an area which the Soviets refer to as the Baikonur Cosmodrome (see figure 90 for a map of Soviet rocket test sites). The launch vehicle was a version of the Soviets' first ICBM, the SS-6. While Sputnik 1 was rather simple, the 1,121-pound Sputnik 2, launched in November, carried a dog whose biological data was relayed to Earth. This experiment provided the Soviets with much of the basic information required for manned flights. Furthermore, the record for total weight in orbit set by Sputnik 2 was not matched by the United States until the mid-1960s.

After a third impressive Sputnik launch in 1958, the Soviets added an additional stage to their launch vehicle and on January 2, 1959, utilized it in an unsuccessful attempt to strike the moon. The Soviets were eventually successful, however, when Luna 2 did impact upon the moon and when, later, Luna 3 relayed back to Earth photos of its far side.

Meanwhile, the Soviets were practicing recovery techniques with dogs launched from their test site near Kapustin Yar (located at about 48.4° N lattitude, 45.8° E longitude) on the Volga River east of the city of Volgograd.

On May 15, 1960, the Soviets announced the beginning of precursor flights to a manned flight program and, on the same day, sent up Korabl Sputnik 1 (weighing about 10,011 pounds). This satellite carried an instrumented dummy that was apparently supposed to be returned to Earth; but when commanded to return, the cabin separated and ascended into a higher orbit from which it took five years to decay. When the test was run a second time, two dogs were successfully returned. Thus the first living creatures were returned from orbit on August 19, 1960—just eight days after the United States had managed to recover its first payload from orbit, a data capsule dropped into the Pacific by Discoverer 13. During a third Soviet flight in December, two dogs were lost in the recovery phase. The precursor flights ended in the successful recovery of a single dog aboard each of the Korabl Sputniks 4 and 5 during March 1961.

When, on April 12, 1961, Yuri Gagarin in Vostok 1 became the first man to make a space flight and to orbit the Earth, the West was again shocked, but the Soviets had laid the groundwork for this flight far better than the United States was to do for John Glenn's three orbits in February 1962. The Soviets had acquired some eighty orbits of experience with their program of precursor flights before Gagarin's success, while the United States had flown only three orbits with biological payloads before Glenn's launch. Thus it is quite apparent that Soviet concern for safety does not warrant much of the criticism it has received from some observers in

the United States.

By August 1962 the Soviets had orbited two ships, Vostok 3 and 4, only one day apart and so timed as to cause them to draw within four miles of each other during their scissorslike orbit patterns. The Soviets by this time were so confident about their system that they allowed a relatively untrained former factory worker to become the first woman in space during June 1963, when Vostok 5 and 6 were launched two days apart. At the conclusion of her flight, Valentina Tereshkova's forty-eight orbits had given her more time in space than that of all the United States astronauts combined.

After a precursor flight in October 1964, Kosmos 47, the Soviets orbited Voskhod 1, carrying three men. (The Voskhod was essentially a modified Vostok, probably developed in an attempt to get the most milieage out of a vehicle production run.) After another precursor flight in February 1965, the Soviets orbited Voskhod 2, which traded the weight of a third crew member for a collapsible airlock through which Alexei Leonov became the first man to perform extravehicular movements outside a spacecraft. However, the Soviets had difficulty in recovering Voskhod 2. Because of a malfunction, manual override had to be used for reentry, and the ship ended up in the snowbound taiga of Siberia. Upon landing, the crew had to remain in the capsule for protection from wolves until rescuers could locate the ship and open a path through the evergreen forest. Eventually the crew was brought out on skis.

After five precursor flights that seemed aimed at working toward linkups and an eventual lunar landing, the Soviets launched Soiuz 1 on April 23, 1967. This spacecraft, whose name means "Union," was manned only by Vladimir Komarov, who had captained Voskhod 1. While a linkup with a second ship had been predicted by observers, no second spacecraft was launched. Whatever the original Soviet plan, Komarov began a descent after eighteen orbits. This decision was unusual, given the pattern of Soviet flights; the implication is that Komarov came down at that point because of the same problems that had caused the cancellation of a second flight—problems which apparently prevented him from descending during the sixteenth or seventeenth orbits, when his craft would have been lined up with the normal recovery area. During his return from orbit the lines from the ship's parachute became tangled, and as a result Komarov and his spacecraft plunged to the ground.

Komarov's tragic death dealt a staggering blow to the Soviets. A board of investigation was appointed to look into the troubled Soiuz program, and the Soviet space effort lost the initiative in the race to land men on the moon. No more manned flights were attempted by the Soviets until October 1968, when, with design problems apparently corrected, Georgi Beregovoi in Soiuz 3 rendezvoused with the unmanned Soiuz 2. In January 1969, Soiuz 4 and 5 accomplished both the first docking of two manned spacecraft and the first transfer of crew members from one craft to another. Apparently the Soviets had opted for a program involving the construction of manned orbital space stations, around which Soviet space exploration would center. They had mastered the techniques of rendezvous and docking, and they continued their efforts to develop new rocket engines capable of delivering the thrust necessary to send manned flights beyond Earth's orbit.

As the United States rushed forward with a lunar orbit in May 1969 and the landing on the moon in July, the Soviets continued their conservative step-by-step

program. In October they launched three spacecraft on three consecutive days. The Soiuz 6, 7, and 8 carried a total of seven men, the greatest number of men and spacecraft ever assembled together in orbit. In June 1970 Soiuz 9 carried two men into orbit in an effort to test man's ability to withstand sustained periods of weightlessness.

The Soviets began to move toward their goal of creating a permanent Earth-orbiting space station. On April 19, 1971, they launched the space station Saliut 1. This was followed three days later by Soiuz 10, which linked up with the orbiting space station. In June the Soviets sent up Soiuz 11, which, like Soiuz 10, carried a crew of three. It, too, linked up with Saliut 1, but the Soviet space program was again to suffer tragedy: the crew of Soiuz 11 died just before reentry because of a loss of pressurization in the spacecraft. These deaths signaled another halt to Soviet manned space missions. The remainder of 1971 and all of 1972 passed without a single Soviet manned flight. Late 1972 and early 1973 saw the sixth and last U.S. manned lunar landing in the Apollo program and the launching, assembly, and manning of the Skylab Earth-orbiting space station. It began to appear that the United States was opening up a significant lead in another direction.

As part of the Brezhnev-Nixon détente, the Soviet Union and the United States agreed to plan an Earth-orbit rendezvous, docking, and exchange of crew members in 1975. Some in the West, however, began to have doubts about the ability of the Soviet Union to participate because of the problems that plagued the Soviet space program. In September 1973, after a two-year hiatus in manned flights, the Soviets launched Soiuz 12 in an effort to check out a modification designed to prevent the kind of tragedy which had occurred to the

Figure 91. SS-10 Scrag ICBM.

crew of the Soiuz 11 spacecraft. This flight was followed by the launching of Soiuz 13 in December. Its mission was to check out another modification that would allow the Soiuz spacecraft to dock with the American Apollo spacecraft during the agreed-upon 1975 joint mission. Then followed Soiuz 14, 15, 16, 17, and 18, all of which docked with Saliut 4 with the exception of Soiuz 15, which overshot the space station but returned to earth safely. These successes were capped in July 1975 by the Soviet's participation in the world's first international manned rendezvous and docking in space. The Soviet manned space program was not dead; it had just been "retooling" before taking another slow and deliberate step forward.

As a result of the overlapping times involved in the various Soviet space programs, they have not been considered in this chapter in chronological order. Moreover, a chronological presentation would have been further complicated by the fact that some of the Soviet space launches have used the same name designation (for example, Kosmos) for different programs, launch sites, and launch vehicles.

While the Soviets strove to advance their manned program, they also pursued an equally aggressive program aimed at launching unmanned flights to the moon and the planets, as well as providing satellite coverage of the Earth for various purposes. One of the projects in this unmanned program which held a special potential for disaster was a Mars mission attempted on October 24, 1962. During launch the vehicle broke into many pieces, and the debris flew toward the United States' ballistic missile early-warning system in Alaska. Occurring as it did during the height of the Cuban crisis, this accident might easily have been misread as an ICBM attack. Fortunately, panic was not the response when the debris appeared on American radar screens, and a few moments of tracking indicated that the flying debris was not a missile attack.

Soviet unmanned spacecraft have been launched from an area near Plesetsk (located at about 62.9° N latitude, 40.1° E longitude), which lies between Archangel and Moscow, as well as from the previously mentioned Tyuratam and Kapustin Yar launch areas. The Plesetsk complex has been routinely utilized to launch military observation satellites. Beginning with Kosmos 112 on March 17, 1966, military observation satellites have been sent up from Plesetsk to cover the airfields of northern Norway and all of Alaska, and to provide a slant view of Thule, Greenland. This clear connection between the military and scientific missions of the Soviet space program is not unusual; the strategic rocket forces conduct the actual launches of all the Soviet space programs and control even strictly scientific space missions until ten minutes after launch, when control is passed to the command complex operated by the Academy of Sciences in Kaliningrad, on the outskirts of Moscow. In conducting the launches, the strategic rocket forces often utilize versions of military missiles, a practice which provides the Soviets with an excuse for the near-total secrecy maintained in their space program.

From the outset, military missiles have been the principal source for most of the first stages of Soviet space-launch vehicles. The standard Soviet launch vehicle is an adaptation of the SS-6 Sapwood ICBM and is sent up from Tyuratam or Plesetsk. While the SS-3 Shyster was utilized for vertical-probe launches and biological flights during the late 1950s, an adaptation of the SS-4 Sandal MRBM has become the small utility launch vehicle for the Soviets. The primary test site for the SS-3 and SS-4, Kapustin Yar, came into use as a launch site in March 1962. Presently, the SS-4 is launched from both Plesetsk and Kapustin Yar. The Soviets began launching a flexible intermediate launch vehicle (an adaptation of the SS-5 Skean IRBM) from Tyuratam in 1964 and from Plesetsk in 1967. The Soviets had undoubtedly intended the SS-10 Scrag (see figure 91) for use as a military combat space-launch vehicle; for some reason, however, they turned to the

SS-9 Scarp instead. The latter is an adaptation of the SS-9 which has been launched from Tyuratam to test fractional orbital bombardment systems and what appears to be a satellite inspector/destructor system. When the weight of payloads began to exceed that which existing varieties of military missiles could launch, the Soviets turned to a nonmilitary vehicle, the Proton, the first launch of which occurred in 1965. This, as well as all successive launches, took place at Tyuratam. The Soviet development of a very heavy launch vehicle apparently received a major setback when a test of this type of vehicle ended in its explosion during an attempted launch from Tyuratam in the summer of 1969.

The early lead in powerful engines enjoyed by the Soviet space program was due to the fact that the first Soviet ICBM was designed before the thermonuclear breakthrough; hence it possessed, out of necessity, a large lift capacity. As more lift capacity was needed, the Soviets adopted the simple solution of clustering engines so as to provide the necessary thrust. Thus the conservative step-by-step Soviet program, in which more than a decade of constant effort had gone into developing the ICBM, simply failed to develop the more powerful engines required to keep pace with the less conservative American program. This is not to say, however, that the Soviet space program is hopelessly behind the American program—although the view of the U.S. Central Intelligence Agency in early 1976 was that the Soviet space program was "in a shambles," and that Soviet science had lagged in applying advanced technology.

Political maneuverings undoubtedly will continue to affect both programs. One can be sure that the political "sparks" were flying in the USSR after the deaths of the Soviet cosmonauts, particularly those that occurred after the Soviet Union had lost the race to the moon. On the other hand, the political mood in the United States has changed since the first moon landing. While the Soviets continue to work on new rocket engines with increased booster power and to investigate the use of such high-energy fuels as liquid hydrogen and nuclear-powered rockets with plasma motors, the United States has slowed its space program substantially without quieting demands for its further reduction.

The Military in Space

While the Soviets have long been on public record as being in favor of the peaceful uses of space, they have also engaged in a rather extensive exploration of the military uses of space. They have investigated, in turn, satellite reconnaissance, fractional orbital bombardment systems (FOBS), satellite-destroying satellites, and a worldwide satellite defense communications system. In the spring of 1962 the Soviets began launching reconnaissance satellites, and as early as the fall of 1966, they ran a full-scale FOBS test. A satellite-destroying satellite may have been tested in orbit as early as 1968. Although they have been utilizing less advanced communications satellites since 1965, the Soviets orbited their first synchronous equatorial satellite only in March 1974. (The U.S. has been successfully orbiting such satellites since 1963.) The importance of such an achievement is that it eliminates the need for a series of satellites in order to ensure continuous coverage over a particular location on the globe.

The Soviets originally conducted vociferous attacks against U.S. proposals and programs for spaceborne reconnaissance because they regarded secrecy as one of their greatest military assets. However, they eventually discovered that their secrecy and boasting resulted in inflated U.S. intelligence estimates of Soviet strength. This in turn created pressures for

a U.S. military buildup with the result that the Soviets had difficulty keeping pace with consequent American advances—advances predicated by misconceptions of what the Soviets possessed in terms of weapons and weapon technology.

Then, in February 1961, the U.S. secretary of defense released the information that there was no evidence of a "missile gap." Reconnaissance satellite photos undoubtedly had something to do with this reappraisal, because they had been in use before he made his statement. Thus, not only had Soviet secrecy helped promote a military buildup by the United States, but the later breach in secrecy helped President John F. Kennedy to use that buildup to obtain increased political leverage.

The Soviet moon photos of October 1959 demonstrated not only that the Soviets possessed the equipment and techniques required for spaceborne observation but also that they had the ability to electronically transmit spaceborne photography. In the spring of 1962 they began a program of reconnaissance from space. By the fall of 1963 the Soviets had begun to alter their official opposition to the use of space for reconnaissance purposes. Apparently, having lost their secrecy, the Soviets themselves had found the application of space technology advantageous to a military Earth observation program.

While Soviet observation satellites perform essentially the same functions as do those of the United States, there are some differences. Most Soviet satellites are placed in orbit for a relatively short time. Unlike their American counterparts, they do not eject recoverable capsules but instead return to Earth by parachute; thus they must carry explosive charges to enable them to self-destruct in the event of non-Soviet recovery. Unfortunately for the Soviets, sending up a satellite in order to obtain data necessitates its early recall if those data are urgently needed. The other alternative, of course, is to utilize a radio-transmission satellite. One problem with this type, however, is that the data transmitted can be received or intercepted by anyone. Essentially, Soviet observation satellites are less sophisticated than those of the United States, but the Soviets make up for their lack of sophistication by placing more of them in orbit.

When the Soviets began their satellite reconnaissance program, they undoubtedly wanted to ensure that all Western strategic facilities were identified and all targets pinpointed so as to be able to preprogram their missiles. This identification effort probably will eventually include an attempt to "fix," or locate, Western submarines capable of launching ballistic missiles against the territory of the Soviet Union. The general military situation is continually monitored, and special-mission satellites have been launched whenever a particular situation warrants such a move.

While Soviet satellite reconnaissance was originally directed against the West, it soon found application against the People's Republic of China. Indeed, there appears to be a definite correlation between the frequency of Soviet observation satellite launches and changes in Sino-Soviet relations. For example, 1969 was a particularly active period of reconnaissance activity. That year the Soviets launched thirty-three recoverable satellites, while the previous year they had launched twenty-five. The explanation for this accelerated activity apparently was related to worsening Sino-Soviet relations. Ten recoverable observation satellites were launched between February 25 and April 23, a period which corresponds to the build-up of tensions and the outbreak of fighting over Damansky Island in the Ussuri River of the Soviet Union's eastern Maritime Territory. Another five recoverable

observation satellites were launched between June 15 and July 22, approximating a period of armed conflict near the western Mongolian border. Still another period of increased observation satellite launch activity was set off by the outbreat of hostilities along the Mongolian border on August 13.

During 1965 the Soviet Union displayed a large three-stage ICBM, the SS-10 Scrag, at Moscow parades in May and November. Moscow Radio described the SS-10 as an orbital weapons system. On September 17 and November 2, 1966, the Soviets ran their first orbital flight of a fractional orbital bombardment system. Both flights, which were unannounced by the Soviets, appear to have been failures. By the time the testing was continued on January 25, 1967, the Soviets had changed their policy and announced the flights, although not as FOBS tests. Eight more FOBS tests were conducted before the U.S. secretary of defense announced on November 3, 1967, that they were probably FOBS tests. During the fiftieth anniversary Moscow parade on November 7, 1967, the Scrags displayed were not called orbital weapons; however, a new missile, the SS-9 Scarp, was described as an orbital weapons system. Conjecture yields two possible conclusions: first, the two first full-scale FOBS tests, which were failures, were conducted with the SS-10, and the later successes were achieved with the SS-9; second, the Soviets might have reasoned that, as long as the SS-9 could handle the FOBS function of the SS-10, it would be less expensive to expand the serial production of the SS-9 than to produce the SS-10 solely to fulfill the FOBS function. Whatever the true explanation, the Soviet fractional orbital bombardment system is apparently operational, utilizing the SS-9. Since 1967 the Soviets have utilized the FOBS only occasionally, which would be consistent with troop training and minor modification tests. Warheads from the Soviet FOBS would take only about six minutes to reach their target, when ordered down from orbit. Thus, militarily the FOBS poses a great threat to an enemy's population and to any strategic air forces that would be caught on the ground.

The FOBS can be considered a space weapon because it attains orbital velocity and, depending on its altitude, can remain in orbit like a satellite. The concept is that a warhead package placed in orbit can be retrofired so as to reduce the velocity of the package and cause it to fall on a target. Since it can approach from any direction and be called down on short notice, the defense cannot determine its target until it has already begun to drop. This, along with the fact that its orbital flight path would be lower than that of the ballistic trajectory of an ICBM, makes the FOBS a weapons system of interesting potential.

While the United States recognizes the value of the FOBS as a first-strike weapon, DOD leaders have not believed that the cost of opting for the smaller warhead size of an orbital package is worth the element of surprise gained, because the fractional orbital bombardment system necessitates the use of smaller and less-accurate warheads. Besides, unless the FOBS is utilized on its first orbit, the large number required to make a difference in the outcome of a nuclear exchange would give away any element of surprise. The U.S. government, however, does not regard the Soviet Union's FOBS or her tests as a violation of the January 27, 1967, Treaty on Principles Governing the Activities of States in the Exploration and Use of Outer Space, including the Moon and Other Celestial Bodies. While the treaty specifically prohibits any party to the treaty from placing "in orbit around the Earth any objects carrying nuclear weapons or any other kind of weapons of mass destruction," none of the Soviet FOBS tests flew a complete orbit and in all likelihood none carried a nuclear warhead.

Undeniably, satellite reconnaissance has played a significant role in preventing a nuclear holocaust, and both the U.S. and the USSR recognize this fact. Yet, should a war between the two nations ever occur, having an opponent's reconnaissance satellites overhead would be a severe liability. The ability to destroy another nation's satellites becomes, therefore, part of a nation's security capability. Communication satellites would be another target of strategic importance; thus both the United States and the Soviet Union have investigated the possibility of a "satellite destroyer." Although the United States eventually abandoned the project, it appears that the Soviets have perfected such a system. In the mid 1960s the United States depended upon the use of either the air force's Thor intermediate-range ballistic missile or the Army's Nike-Zeus antiballistic-missile missile with nuclear warheads, which would have been fired from an island in the Pacific as a satellite passed overhead should a antisatellite capability have been required. That system, however, is no longer operational.

In October and November of 1968 the Soviets ran tests in which one satellite was maneuvered near another. As the two satellites later moved apart, one was destroyed. The unanswered question is, which satellite possessed the destructor capability? The inspecting craft may have been detonated upon sensing the other as "hostile," but in the vacuum of space there are no shock waves from an explosion; thus the inspecting satellite would have had to have been close enough to destroy the target satellite with shrapnel from the explosion. In the early Soviet tests, the inspected satellite was not destroyed by the destruction of the other. It seems, therefore, that the inspected satellite must have possessed a satellite destructor capability in the form of some sort of antiinspection defensive missile system. Should this in fact be the case, it could portend a Soviet capability, even if not the intention, to ensure the secrecy of a nuclear force stationed in space. Whether these space warfare developments will bring the PKO (antisatellite) elements of PVO *Strany* into a revised relationship with the strategic rocket forces remains to be seen.

The year 1976 saw several Soviet "hunter-killer" satellite tests, and late in the year both the U.S. Defense and State departments found it necessary to deny that the Soviet Union had used high-powered laser beams sent up from a site in Siberia to blind an American early-warning satellite stationed over the Indian Ocean. However, the Defense Department did say that it had been concerned about the survivability of its satellite systems, and that it was launching aggressive basic technology research efforts in order to protect its satellites from this potential threat. Such research was, at that time, concentrated on methods for "hardening" satellites and their instruments against either lasers that might be carried by a hostile satellite or the potentially destructive burst of X rays that would be triggered as a result of a nuclear explosion in space.

As the Soviet navy expanded its operations in its effort to become a truly global navy, it came to require a satellite communication system that could provide the command-and-control communication links that were simply unavailable otherwise. Thus, in the mid-1960s the Soviet Union began to deploy satellites as part of an operational data relay network for its military forces. Since then, the Soviets have deployed a series of satellites with a single launch vehicle that releases the satellites one by one in such a manner as to string them out at more-or-less regular intervals around the Earth so as to form a continuous worldwide communication link. Although there is a theoretical basis for assuming that the system fulfills its purpose, the eccentric orbits of the satellites result in communication "gaps." The eventual deployment of a synchronous satellite communication system will assure uninterrupted coverage and eliminate the necessity for continuous tracking of moving satellites by surface stations.

The Soviet attitude toward the use of space cannot be understood solely in terms of military space activities. The Soviets have attempted, and probably will continue to attempt, to apply the utilization of space to many facets of life. However, it can be expected that the Soviets will actively pursue as wide a range of goals as possible in an orderly fashion. It must be understood that this approach can be translated into a well-funded Soviet military space effort because of the nature of the Soviet system, which is geared to interpreting space activities in terms of their ideologically perceived practical needs.

Expectations and Projections

In the future, the military and political significance of Soviet efforts in the areas of ballistic missilery and cosmic research will to some degree depend upon the political mood in the United States. During the first three-quarters of this decade, American public opinion was not prepared to support increases in the funding of such programs. There was a great deal of pressure applied—in some cases successfully—to reduce expenditures in these areas.

The Soviets have their own budgetary difficulties. For, although the Soviet government does not have to contend with public opinion in the way that the U.S.

government does, it is faced with the difficulty of stretching resources adequately to fund all the areas requiring investment. It is certain, however, that Soviet design teams will continue their efforts to improve present hardware and techniques for their military and space efforts. The importance of these future developments to the United States will depend upon whether the United States keeps pace with them. To the Soviets, the status quo is the unimpeded expansion of their program and progress toward their goals.

The other major rival of the Soviet Union, the People's Republic of China, constitutes a major complicating factor in making any projection about the future. The inability of the Soviet Union and China to subjugate their divergent national interests is reflected in the fact that the number of Soviet ground forces stationed along the Sino-Soviet border area jumped from fifteen divisions in 1968 to forty-three divisions in 1976. The Soviets have several times even considered a preemptive strike against their former ally; they have approached and been rejected by the United States with requests for either a joint strike or U.S. neutrality. The Soviets have since lost their chance to strike China before she developed a nuclear-missile retaliatory capability against Moscow; by mid-1973 the People's Republic of China had produced about fifty medium-range missiles capable of striking targets in Soviet Asia and fifteen to twenty intermediate-range ballistic missiles capable of reaching Moscow. The Soviets simply do not possess the sophistication required to preempt the Chinese ballistic missile forces, which in many cases have been deployed in silos, caves, and narrow mountain valleys. Exactly how these developments will affect the Soviet missile and space programs cannot be known.

Research Notes

Some of the best books about the evolution of Soviet military strategy are by Thomas W. Wolfe; these include *Soviet Strategy at the Crossroads* (Cambridge, Mass., 1964), *The Soviet Military Scene: Institutional and Defense Policy Considerations* (Santa Monica, Calif., 1966), and *Soviet Power in Europe, 1945–1970* (Baltimore, 1970). Another excellent investigation of Soviet military strategy was reported by John Erickson in *Soviet Military Power* (London, 1971). An updated version of this book appeared as an additional section in the Spring 1973 issue of *Strategic Review*, published by the U.S. Strategic Institute. All the latest figures concerning the Soviet military came from *The Military Balance*, published annually by the London-based International Institute for Strategic Studies.

For research on the strategic rocket forces, good sources are difficult to find. *The Military Balance* does, however, provide data about some of the missiles utilized by the Soviets. Data about the strategic rocket forces per se must be compiled from numerous sources. Even when such Soviet materials as *Soviet Rocket Forces,* by P. T. Astashenkov, are available, they have been so sanitized by Soviet censors that they are of relatively little value. Thus in this area data must be painstakingly gathered from sundry sources.

The (now International) Institute for Strategic Studies is a good source of data on Soviet antiballistic missile defenses. Each year *The Military Balance* contains the latest data on Soviet ABM interceptors and their assorted radars. Missile defense in the strategic balance between the United States and the Soviet Union is a topic in the appendix of *The Military Balance, 1972-1973.* ABM systems is also a topic in the institute's *Strategic Survey, 1971.*

For information about the space programs of the Soviet Union, the staff reports prepared by the Library of Congress for the U.S. Senate Committee on Aeronautical and Space Sciences are a key source of data. See, for example, *Soviet Space Programs: Organization, Plans, Goals, and International Implications* (May 1962), *Soviet Space Programs, 1962-1965* (Decem-

ber 1966), *Review of the Soviet Space Program* (1967), *Soviet Space Programs, 1966-1970* (December 1971), *Soviet Space Programs, 1971* (April 1972) and *Soviet Space Programs, 1971-1975,* volumes 1 and 2 (August 1976).

Another sound work is Charles S. Sheldon II, *Review of the Soviet Space Program* (New York, 1968). The main body of Sheldon's book was derived from a 1967 study for the U.S. House of Representatives Committee on Science and Astronautics. Other recent works of interest include Robert Salkeld's *War and Space* (Englewood Cliffs, N.J., 1970) and Peter L. Smolders' *Soviets in Space* (New York, 1973).

Further research on the strategic rocket forces and Soviet space efforts will, of necessity, be based largely on Congressional studies and reports, inasmuch as the Soviet propensity for secrecy causes Western governmental sources to take on an unusual importance. The finest nongovernmental source will probably continue to be the International Institute for Strategic Studies. Such periodicals as *Aviation Week and Space Technology* and the *New York Times* have been, in the past, the best source for the most recent developments.

11

Patterns in the Soviet Aircraft Industry

Otto Preston Chaney, Jr.,
and John T. Greenwood

The Soviet aircraft industry differs from that of other countries in that its design establishment consists almost exclusively of team leaders who graduated from one school (the TsAGI) following World War I. It also differs from such industries in the West, not only because it is exclusively state-owned, but also because it is divided into three independent parts—design bureaus, testing facilities, and manufacturing plants. In many respects this is an ideal situation in that designers are free from certain (notably financial) pressures. As aircraft have become more specialized and complex each bureau has tended to concentrate on one general type—just as, in the United States, Grumman has specialized in naval fighters. With a domestic production which has never lacked stimulation (the Soviets produced 5,000 machines a year in 1975), the industry has not had to compete or even to seek export sales. However, the Soviet policy of maintaining full employ-ment of facilities may necessitate greater attention to outside sales.

In general, the history of the Soviet aircraft industry can be broken into several stages: the *ab initio,* which lasted from the development of flying through 1917, the civil war, the First Five-Year Plan, World War II, and the postwar period.

About 1922, a true domestic aircraft industry began to emerge, feeling its way, still relying heavily on foreign designs. The real takeoff point came with the First Five-Year Plan, when small teams of Russian designers began to make progress and production was accelerated. Subsequent growth and development placed the Soviets in the forefront of world aviation until 1941. During the war, the physical shifting of the entire industry to the east and the amalgamation of design bureaus and factories under the pressure to achieve maximum aircraft production benefited the designers by giving them practical experience in mass production.

These developments also created new factories which had to be kept productive after 1945.

From 1945 to 1953 the Soviets were influenced by foreign material captured or borrowed from the Americans, the British, and, especially, the Germans. Thereafter, Soviet teams specialized and developed their own designs. Two patterns remain evident: first, Soviet aircraft have generally been less sophisticated, though not necessarily less effective, than foreign designs; second, the long tradition of licensing or copying Western designs and the avid reading of Western technical literature have influenced some significant Russian designs, such as the Il-62 and the Tu-144, which bear strong resemblance to contemporary Western machines.

The leaders of the design bureaus, whose names grace the aircraft built in the USSR, have generally been a generation younger than those who founded and long dominated the industry in Britain. They resemble the British design leaders, however, in that they are a close-knit, homogeneous group. A small clique of designers dominated the Soviet aircraft industry from the late 1920s to the mid-1970s. Their personalities remain obscure; however, except for Yakovlev, they seem to have been somewhat colorless characters whose individual traits are best reflected in the evolution of their designs.

Throughout its history, the Russian and Soviet aircraft industry has been closely attuned to and has borrowed heavily from foreign sources. Such transfers of technology, however, have been given a uniquely Soviet shape and orientation, in accordance with the tactical needs of both Aeroflot and the air forces.

Early History

The man whom Lenin called the "father of Russian aviation," Nikolai Yegorovich Zhukovsky (see figure 7, chapter 2), was born in 1847, took his degree in applied mathematics at Moscow University in 1868, wrote his master's thesis on "liquid kinematics," and received a doctorate in applied mathematics in 1882. In 1885 he became a professor of theoretical mechanics at Moscow University. In 1902 he set up one of the first wind tunnels in Europe at Moscow University. In 1904 he founded the Institute of Aerodynamics in the village of Kuchino, near Moscow, and by 1913 was teaching courses for officer pilots. In addition, Zhukovsky carried out extensive research on lifting capacity, wing contours, propellors, hydraulics, hydrodynamics, astronomy, and mathematics. During World War I he worked on bombing techniques, artillery ballistics, and navigation, while continuing his theoretical mechanics. After the revolution in Russia, in December 1918, Zhukovsky helped create and headed the Central Aerodynamic Institute (TsAGI). Zhukovsky established a course of instruction for military pilots which became the basis for the Institute of Engineers of the Red Air Fleet in 1920. Following his death in 1921, the institute was renamed the N. Ye. Zhukovsky Military Air Engineer Academy.

The first Russian aviation enterprises emerged in the period 1910–1913. Soon fifteen plants and workshops employing a total of 10,000 workers were turning out aircraft and engines. The majority were of foreign design (principally French), made according to Western blueprints or assembled from parts purchased abroad. The only factory engaged in turning out heavy aircraft of Russian design was the Russo-Baltic railway car plant in St. Petersburg, where Igor Ivanovich Sikorsky built his Ilia Muromets, the first multi-engined heavy aircraft in the world.

Sikorsky, born in 1889, was graduated from the Naval Academy in St. Petersburg in 1906. He became one of the few greats who not only designed aircraft but also tested them. In 1912-1913, he built a biplane, the Russian Knight (more commonly known as the Grand, because with a wingspan of twenty-eight meters [ninety-one feet] and an overall length of twenty meters [sixty-five feet] it was by far the largest heavier-than-air craft built up to that time). It was the world's first airworthy four-engine plane and the first to have an enclosed passenger cabin.

In January 1914 Sikorsky brought out his Ilia Muromets, an improved version of the Grand. During World War I some twenty-five Ilia Muromets planes participated in battles on the eastern front. The Ilia Muromets boasted a speed of 135 kilometers per hour and a ceiling of 4,000 meters (13,000 feet) and accommodated a seven-man crew; each plane could carry almost a ton of bombs and was armed with seven machine guns for protection against German fighters. In 1919 Sikorsky left Soviet Russia; he became an American citizen in 1928.

World War I greatly stimulated the Russian aircraft industry. In 1914 only 250 planes were available to the military command. By 1917, the Duks plant in Moscow alone was producing 75 to 100 planes per month. The Shchetinin plant in Petrograd produced, in addition to a variety of aircraft of French design, about 200 of D. P. Grigorovich's M-5 and M-9 hydroplanes for the Russian navy. Despite the rapid growth of the Russian aircraft industry during the war years, the bulk of Russia's aircraft and engines was imported. Only 10 to 15 percent of the aircraft engines used by the Soviets were produced by Russian factories and workshops.

Soon after the October revolution in 1917, the Bolshevik Defense Commissariat created an aviation board, whose task was to reorganize aviation and collect from every corner aircraft, engines, and spare parts for the defense of the fledgling Soviet regime. The start of the civil war provided new impetus for creating a military air force. In May 1918, the Main Administration of the Workers' and Peasants' Red Air Fleet was formed, and on June 28, the Soviet government issued a decree nationalizing aircraft factories and workshops.

Toward the end of 1918 a special center for the management of the aviation industry, the Glavkoavia, was established within the Supreme Council of the National Economy. Almost simultaneously the TsAGI was set up. As more and more young people became interested in aviation, the Moscow Higher Technical College began to offer aerodynamics; a number of design personnel graduated from this school.

During the civil war, the Reds scraped together about 350 aircraft, organized into thirty-three aviation detachments. These new Soviet air units did not distingush themselves during the first two years of the civil war; their resources were dissipated on too many battle fronts, and many of the best tsarist pilots either supported the Whites or had emigrated. The Bolsheviks in these years had only five small factories engaged in the manufacture and assembly of aircraft; these produced less than 700 new planes during the civil war.

After the Red victory in 1921, the Soviets turned to rebuilding the economy and the defense of the country. Completely surrounded by hostile neighbors, the Bolsheviks undertook a program to build a strong military air arm. Soviet historians readily admit that during the years following the civil war the Soviets still depended upon foreign suppliers. In

1922–1923 they purchased Fokker D-7 fighters from Holland, Martinyside fighters from England, Ansaldo reconnaissance aircraft from Italy, and Junkers Ju-13 passenger planes from Germany. Aircraft left behind by the Allies during the period of intervention were carefully copied. While the Duks and Aviarabotnik plants in Moscow began turning out the De-Havilland 4, 9, and 9A, the Krasny Letchik (Red Flier) plant in Petrograd began producing the Avro 504, copied from a White plane shot down in 1919. In some cases, licenses were obtained for production of such aircraft as the Fokker D-11. In 1922, however, 90 percent of all Soviet aircraft were purchased abroad.

During this period, clandestine military collaboration between the Germans and the Soviets began; the Reichswehr circumvented restrictions laid down by the Versailles peace agreements by training its pilots and tank crews in Russia, and the Soviets sent Red Army officers to Germany for schooling in modern tactics and doctrine. Agreements in 1922–1923 led to the signing of a contract granting the Junkers corporation concessions for the manufacture of aircraft engines at the Fili plant near Moscow. Junkers produced the Ju-21 and assembled the Ju-13 passenger plane in Fili.

At Lipetsk, approximately 300 kilometers southeast of Moscow, the Germans laid the basis for their own future air force. A steady stream of aircraft, engines, spare parts, and technicians secretly entered the Soviet Union by way of Leningrad. Many of the "civilians" traveling to Lipetsk were, in fact, German officers carrying forged passports. In Lipetsk these officers were assigned to the "Fourth Squadron, Red Air Force." Security was strict; to contribute to the deception, the Soviets positioned a few old Russian planes around the air base.

The "Society for Promotion of Industrial Enterprises" handled the movement of the contraband material within Russia. Fokker fighters, ammunition, and bombs came in by sea, while certain aircraft were flown in. As a variety of experimental aircraft arrived at Lipetsk for testing, at least 120 German fighter pilots and another 450 fliers, including reconnaissance and dive-bomber pilots, were trained there. Russian pilots and technicians were, in turn, educated by the Germans. Soviet engineers worked closely with the Germans in developing and testing aircraft and sharing plans and designs. Thus, both nations benefited from this clandestine cooperation. (The Soviets have recorded almost nothing of this period of collaboration, which lasted nearly to Hitler's accession and even included the founding of a German-Soviet joint-stock company, Bersol, for the manufacture of poison gases.)

Soviet design and development efforts went hand in hand with this foreign collaboration, with the intention of becoming self-sufficient in the future. Much hope was placed in a young generation of Soviet engineers and designers. One of these was Alexander Sergeevich Yakovlev (see figure 92), author of the highly readable memoirs *Tales of an Aeronautical Engineer* (1957) and *The Aim of a Lifetime* (1972). Born in 1906, he soon demonstrated an interest in mechanical objects. After completing secondary school at the age of seventeen, Yakovlev decided to be an aircraft designer. His first step was to obtain a job as an ordinary worker in the carpentry shop at the Aeronautical Academy. Then, to get even closer to the planes, he took a job as a mechanic's helper in the academy's flight-training unit and eventually worked his way up to engine mechanic. In 1926, when several amateur groups were building light sport planes,

Figure 92. A. S. Yakovlev.

Yakovlev built his own two-seater AIR-1 biplane powered by an English Cirrus engine. Yakovlev and his test pilot, Piontkovsky, flew the plane from Moscow to Sevastopol, a distance of 1,500 kilometers, in ten hours and thirty minutes. His successful designing of this aircraft gained Yakovlev admission to the Aeronautical Academy and opened a long and rewarding career.

"Copying foreign models was a necessary evil," confesses Yakovlev. However, Soviet aircraft designers were beginning to produce some original items. In 1920, the Soviets produced the first 200-horsepower Soviet engine. In 1922, the first whole aircraft, the light sports plane ANT-1 designed by Andrei N. Tupolev, took to the skies. At about the same time a three-seater passenger plane, the AK-1, was produced. This plane flew the first air route from Moscow to Nizhni Novgorod in 1924 and later participated in a flight from Moscow to Peking. N. N. Polikarpov built the single-seater I-1 fighter plane in 1923, while his colleague in the Duks design office, Grigorovich, put the finishing touches on his similar I-2.

In 1924, the Soviets built a 400-horsepower engine, the M-5. In the same year they also made an impressive flight from Tashkent to Kabul across the Hindu Kush peaks at an altitude—according to Soviet sources—of over 8,000 meters (26,000 feet), though Yakovlev reported that this flight only reached about 5,000 meters (16,000 feet). Also in 1924, the first Soviet all-metal plane, Tupolev's ANT-2, made its test flight. In 1925, Tupolev built the all-metal two-seater ANT-3 (R-3) reconnaissance plane; in November of the same year he produced the twin-engine heavy bomber ANT-4 (TB-1), 216 of which were built from 1926 to 1932. After being phased out of the bomber units, they were redesignated G-1s and used for cargo.

The aerodynamic laboratory of the Moscow Higher Technical College soon found its quarters too small, and in May 1924 a new laboratory, named for the engineer S. A. Chaplygin, was founded. Other laboratories were established for research on aircraft materials and engines. Meanwhile, on March 8, 1923, the Society of Friends of the Air Fleet (ODVF) was founded; its mission was to propagandize Soviet aviation, solicit financial support from Soviet citizens, and offer practical assistance in the creation of a native aviation industry. In June 1924, this society presented the Thirteenth Party Congress with the first of several squadrons of planes and also organized a number of endurance flights to test men and materiel. In August 1927, an R-3 was flown from Moscow to Tokyo and back, a distance of about 22,000 kilometers, in 153 hours.

Nikolai Nikolayevich Polikarpov, the son of a priest, was born in Orel in 1892. In 1916 he graduated from the Petrograd Polytechnical Institute and began his engineer work with the air-navigation department of the Russo-Baltic plant in Petrograd. After 1918 he was the director of a number of aircraft plants, and in 1923 he designed and built his first fighter.

One of Zhukovsky's brighter students was Andrei Nikolaevich Tupolev, who was born in 1888 to a middle-class provincial family. While attending the Moscow Higher Technical College, he developed an interest in aviation. Working with Zhukovsky, Tupolev, while still a student, helped design the first Russian wind tunnels. Tupolev also designed and built training gliders, one of which he piloted. Graduating from the college in 1918, he became a cofounder of the TsAGI with Zhukovsky and was assistant director from 1918 to 1935. Imprisoned during the purges, he developed his own design team, and through his successes gained his freedom just prior to World War II. Tupolev built many successful aircraft during and after World War II and finally developed the Tu-144 SST.

In 1929 a ten-passenger, three-engine Tupolev ANT-9 with a complement of Moscow correspondents carried out a flight to Berlin, Paris, Rome, London, and Warsaw, a distance of 9,000 kilometers, at an average speed of 180 kilometers per hour. After this flight the plane was put into serial production for the emerging civil air fleet. In the fall of 1929, two Soviet pilots (Shestakov and Bolotov), a navigator (Sterligov), and a flight engineer (Fufaev), flew an ANT-4 from Moscow to New York. This 21,500-kilometer flight required more than a month, because much of the journey was over the ocean and considerable time was needed to replace wheels with floats. In Yakovlev's memoirs, he boasts that "this was the first flight of Soviet fliers in a Soviet plane with a Soviet engine to America . . . an outstanding achievement"—only two years after Lindbergh.

The Impact of the Five-Year Plans

In 1928 Stalin announced the first of his five-year plans, the goals of which were very impressive: total industrial output was to be increased by 250 percent, heavy industry by 330 percent, pig-iron production tripled, coal output doubled, and electric power quadrupled. The next year the original quotas were revised upward, and a decision was made to complete the First Five-Year Plan in four years. Although not all of the plan was fulfilled, its actual achievements were tremendous. Capital invested in industry jumped from 2 billion to more than 9 billion rubles, allowing the USSR to proceed with a vast industrial expansion. One of the important goals of the First Five-Year Plan had been for the Soviet aircraft industry to "rid itself finally of foreign dependence." Although this goal was overambitious (the Soviets would lean heavily upon Western designs and technical information for the next several decades), a native aviation industry began to take definite shape and to produce planes in quantity. In January 1933 Stalin, describing the accomplishments of the First Five-Year Plan, declared: "We had no aviation industry. Now we have one." During the First Five-Year Plan many new aircraft and engine factories were built, and annual production reached 2,000 planes by the end of 1932. Even greater successes were achieved by the aviation industry under the Second Five-Year Plan from 1933 to 1938, as the volume again increased. New aviation factories were equipped with modern equipment, and emphasis was placed on increasing the productivity of labor. The result was, according to Soviet histories, that "in 1938, mass production of a two-engine plane required only 47 percent of the time needed in 1937."

Figure 93. V. M. Miasishchev.

At the beginning of the First Five-Year Plan there were two large design centers in the Soviet Union: the Central Aerodynamic Institute (TsAGI), headed by Tupolev, and the Design Bureau, headed by Polikarpov. In the early 1930s, Tupolev's office was spun off from TsAGI and established as an independent experimental and design organization. The institute continued with scientific research, leaving Tupolev and his associates to develop new types of aircraft, especially multi-engined bombers and planes. Tupolev attracted and trained a number of outstanding individuals, including A. A. Arkhangelsky, V. M. Miasishchev (see figure 93), V. M. Petliakov, A. I. Putilov, and P. O. Sukhoi (see figure 94). Polikarpov's design office was assigned to the development of new fighter aircraft. For about ten years Soviet fighter units were equipped almost exclusively with Polikarpov planes—including the I-5, which was designed in prison. Then came a series of failures, followed by Polikarpov's death in 1944. Smaller design offices were managed by other designers. D. P. Grigorovich, who was also placed in a labor camp, worked on fighter engines and airplanes. K. A. Kalinin, who designed the K-5 passenger plane, worked with Yakovlev for a time of the development of low-performance aircraft.

Yakovlev and his associates established their own small design bureau in a bed factory near Moscow. The head of the aircraft industry division, who had grudgingly supplied the premises, informed Yakovlev that the bed factory was to carry on as before. "No one ever thought at the time," Yakovlev later noted, "that this little shop was destined to turn into a leading aircraft plant. . . ."

By 1930 the Soviets had tested and adopted a series of their own planes. The air fleet received small numbers of Polikarpov I-3 fighters and R-5 reconnaissance planes and Tupolev TB-1 bombers. About 400 I-3s, wooden biplanes with speeds of 280 kilometers an hour and two mounted machine guns, were produced.

Figure 94. P. O. Sukhoi.

The I-5, also a biplane, was a follow-up to the I-3; it could reach speeds of 286 kilometers an hour (180 mph). About 800 K-5s were manufactured. Widely used for many years, the K-5 saw service in World War II. It was eventually replaced by another excellent Polikarpov aircraft, the U-2 (Po-2).

Tupolev's TB-1 (ANT-4) bomber was one of the largest planes built in the 1920s.

An all-metal monoplane powered by two water-cooled engines in the wings, the TB-1 could carry a payload of three-and-a-half tons. With a ton of bombs, the plane had a range of 1,350 kilometers (850 miles) and a speed of about 200 kilometers an hour. The TB-1 was the first plane to be equipped with boosters which reduced takeoff distance. Its successor, the TB-3 (ANT-6) a four-engine bomber first built in 1930 which was in series production from 1932 to 1937, could carry five tons of bombs; reducing the load to two tons provided a range of almost 2,500 kilometers. With a crew of eight, the TB-3 defended itself with eight machine guns. During the ten years preceding World War II, Soviet factories provided the air fleet with 216 TB-1 and 818 TB-3 bombers.

A giant plane designed by Tupolev, the ANT-20, or Maxim Gorky, was described by Soviet historians as an agitation and propaganda aircraft intended to popularize the regime. This eight-engine craft, which made its first flight in June 1934, could carry eighty passengers at a speed of 280 kph. Weighing forty tons, it had a radio station, printing press, photo laboratory, telephone switchboard, telegraph office, and motion-picture projectors. In 1935, it collided with another plane in midair, killing thirty-five persons.

In 1933–1934, Polikarpov designed and built the biplane I-15 fighter, with a maximum speed of 360 kph, and the I-16, a monoplane fighter with a retractable landing gear which could achieve speeds up to 454 kph (285 mph). Both planes were powered by a 715-horsepower air-cooled radial engine with a controllable-pitch propeller. For the first time, armor plate was installed behind the pilot. Armament consisted of two synchronized 7.62mm machine guns. These two planes entered service at about the same time. Soviet air tactics then involved the use of the less

maneuverable but speedier monoplane to catch up with the enemy and locate him so that the biplane could make the kill. In actual combat in Spain (1936–1938) and Khalkhin-Gol (1939), the Soviets found that these tactics were not practical, so they determined to improve the maneuverability of monoplanes and to phase out biplanes. Meanwhile, more than 6,500 of each type of aircraft had been supplied to the air fleet, representing the bulk of the fighter force. The I-15's maneuverability was outstanding; it required only eight seconds to execute a turn and six minutes to climb to 5,000 meters (16,500 feet). Its service ceiling was more than 9,000 meters. Several modifications improved its speed and upgraded its armament. The I-153, for example, built in 1938, attained speeds up to 443 kph (278 mph) because of its streamlining and retractable landing gear (it was the only Soviet biplane so equipped). At Khalkhin-Gol in 1939 the I-153, mounting four machine guns and rockets, proved to be an outstanding fighter.

Polikarpov's I-16 also was continually improved over the years. Eventually the plane was fitted with a movable canopy; its engine was continually upgraded until it had developed 1,000 horsepower, giving the aircraft a speed of 525 kph (330 mph). The I-16 was the first monoplane with retractable landing gear and controllable-pitch propeller to be accepted by the Soviet air force. After several years the various modifications, including additional armor plate, became a problem: the takeoff weight and wing loading had been increased by 30 percent, hampering the plane's maneuverability. Soviet historians admit that the plane was difficult to control and required "highly skilled" pilots. The I-16 saw service in the Spanish civil war, at Khalkhin-Gol, and throughout World War II.

In 1938, Soviet operational fighters

Figure 95. Aviation design leaders of World War II. From left, S. A. Lavochkin, A. N. Tupolev, A. S. Yakovlev, A. I. Mikoian.

were well ahead of those of the USAAC or the USN. Bombers were being produced simultaneously with fighters. The first Soviet ground-support bomber to be put in series production was Tupolev's SB. Manufacture began in 1934, and eventually 6,656 SBs came off the assembly line. Its two 860-horsepower engines gave the SB a speed of 420 kph, a range of 1,000 kilometers, and a bomb load of 500 kilograms (1,100 lbs). Unlike earler Tupolev aircraft, which had corrugated skins, the SB was made completely of smooth duralumin.

Sergei Vladimirovich Iliushin, born in 1894 to a peasant family from the Vologda province, was twenty years old when he saw his first plane at the St. Petersburg Aerodrome. In 1914 he was called into the army, and in 1916 he became involved with military aviation—first as a workman in a hangar, then as an engine mechanic. In 1917 he passed his pilot's examinations. When the Red Army was created, he enlisted, and in 1921 he was sent to the TsAGI, where he designed and built training gliders. Iliushin graduated from the academy in 1926, and from 1931 on has been fully engaged in aircraft design, with the four-jet Il-62 being a recent product.

Iliushin's DB-3 twin-engine bomber appeared in 1935. Continually modified, the DB-3, renamed the Il-4, became the main Soviet long-range bomber of World War II. Almost 6,800 were built. The basic characteristics are shown in the accompanying table. During World War II, when shortages developed, Tupolev replaced some of the metal with wood.

	DB-3	Il-4
Engines	765 hp	1,100 hp
Speed	253 mph	276 mph
Bomb load	2,000 lbs	3,307 lbs
(to 4,000 kilometers)		(7,700 max.)

Tupolev's ANT-25 (also known as the RD) was produced in 1933. This all-metal monoplane with a very large wing span gained fame in the summer of 1937 when Chkalov, Baidukov, and Belyakov flew it for sixty-three hours nonstop from Moscow to the United States, a distance of more than 9,000 kilometers (5,650 miles). Initially designed as a long-range bomber, its low speed (200 kph) ruled out such employment.

Yakovlev, in his history of Soviet aircraft construction, states that certain serious mistakes were made before World War II: too few light bombers and reconnaissance aircraft were produced; in fighter design, speed and firepower took second place to maneuverability; and the Soviets became smug and boastful after the successes of their fighters in the Spanish civil war. The Germans, on the other hand, had profited by their Spanish experiences and began taking urgent steps to improve their aircraft.

The Soviet air establishment suffered for another reason: Stalin's bloody purges of 1937 and 1938 decapitated the armed forces. The total consequences of the purges are difficult to estimate.

The air force suffered from the purge of aeronautical engineers and designers. Sergei A. Chaplygin, head of the Central Aerodynamic Institute, had lost his post to Kharlamov, who had little to offer but was considered by Stalin to be politically reliable. Thousands employed in the aircraft industry were dismissed. K. A. Kalinin, who was responsible for the advanced swept-wing aircraft designs, was shot after four Communist party members were killed in a crash of one of his experimental aircraft. The outstanding designer Tupolev, accused of sabotage and espionage after a visit to the United States and Germany in 1936, was arrested in 1937 or 1938. He was sentenced to a five-year

imprisonment and his "ANT" planes were rechristened. While serving his term, however, he designed the Tu-2 dive bomber, using a team of prisoners. Fortunately, for a number of those imprisoned, the threat of war in Europe won them their freedom. Following Tupolev's release, he returned to work with orders to create a new Soviet combat aircraft.

World War II and the Evacuation of Industry

As the war clouds gathered over Europe, the Soviets became increasingly concerned about the capabilities of their aircraft, compared with those of potential enemies. Sobering lessons learned during the last year of air combat in Spain contributed to this anxiety. Front-line Soviet aircraft of the 1935–1937 class were hard pressed to match the newer German aircraft: the Bf-109s, He-111s, Dornier 17s, and Junker 87s of the Condor Legion. The Messerschmitt Bf-109s presented the most serious problem because they could outfly the I-15 and I-16 fighters while handily shooting down the SB-2 and SB-2*bis* fast bombers. Responding to this situation, in early 1938 the Central Committee of the CPSU (Communist Party of the Soviet Union) and the government jointly called a conference of leading aviation personalities, including designers, inventors, plant managers, scientists, engineers, and air-force pilots. The stars of Soviet aviation attended—engineers V. Ya. Klimov, A. A. Mikulin, A. D. Shvetsov, A. A. Arkhangelsky, and M. N. Shulzhenko, and the design-bureau chiefs Yakovlev, Polikarpov, and Iliushin. While not arriving at any final recommendations for overcoming the backwardness of Soviet aviation, this conference did set the stage for similar meetings later the same year. Attention was focused upon the rapid procurement of the latest design types. Fortunately for the program initiated at these meetings, the Soviet aircraft industry received considerable attention in the Second Five-Year Plan (1932–1937). The Third Five-Year Plan (1938–42) envisioned extensive use of this existing capacity, plus a significant expansion in both airframe and aeroengine production for increased output of military aircraft.

In 1939, the Commissariat of Defense Industry was split up and a separate Commissariat of Aviation Industry (Narodnoi komissariat aviatsionnoi promyshlennosti, Narkomavprom) was established under M. M. Kaganovich in an effort to improve the organization and management of aircraft production. The new commissariat immediately ordered further assembly and engine plant construction, and nine aircraft and seven engine plants were added in 1939 alone. A. I. Shakurin, who replaced Kaganovich early in 1940, directed further expansion and the conversion of seven civilian industrial plants to aircraft production. Much of this expansion was ticketed for the more secure regions of Siberia, Central Asia, and the Urals because of the two-front threat posed by Japan in the Far East and Germany in Europe. By 1941, forty-six aircraft and fifteen engine plants were already at work as a direct result of these actions. More important, the new aircraft plants—built in such places as Tashkent, Omsk, Irkutsk, and Komsomolsk —were producing nearly half the output of the older Western factories.

Paralleling the enlargement of the aircraft industry was the movement toward greater decentralization in aircraft development. Until the late 1930s, only two major design bureaus existed for military aircraft: N. N. Polikarpov's office for fighters and A. N. Tupolev's bureau for bombers and multiengine aircraft. Realizing the increasing inadequacy of this arrangement, the Soviet government encouraged the leading designers in each bureau to form their own teams. Thus a number of talented designers were able to answer the Central Committee's call for new fighters when it was issued at the 1939 Kremlin conference (see figure 95).

A. S. Yakovlev, A. I. Mikoian and M. I. Gurevich, and S. A. Lavochkin, assisted by M. I. Gudkov and V. P. Gorbunov, submitted new single-engine fighter designs. All three were soon approved for prototype development and flight testing prior to state acceptance trials that would determine their suitability for full-scale production and deployment to the air services. Yakovlev's I-26 fighter, redesignated the Yak-1 in 1940, completed its state tests early and went into series production. The Lavochkin-Gudkov-Gorbunov effort, the I-22 (later Lagg-1), first flew on March 30, 1940. An aircraft built of resin-impregnated birch and plywood sheathing, the Lagg-1 was considered of such great importance that it was rushed into series production on the basis of the initial flight test report. Problems with the original Lagg-1 required such significant reworking, however (including a new M-105PF engine of 1,210 horsepower and changes on the Taganrog production line), that the aircraft was redesignated the Lagg-3.

While the Yak-1 and Laggs were air-superiority fighters destined for tactical use, the I-61 of Mikoian and Gurevich was primarily intended as a high-speed, high-altitude interceptor for air defense. The I-61 (later Mig-1) first flew early in April 1940, but, as with the other two new fighters, all was not well with the Mig-1. The aircraft was difficult to handle for any but an expert pilot. It had poor range and high-wing loading, and tended to be unstable at landing speeds. Consequently, it underwent a series of tests and changes emerged as the Mig-3 (I-200) with improved range and stability. Production of the Mig-3 began after the last of 100 Mig-1s was completed early in 1941.

Artem Ivanovich Mikoian, born in 1905, grew up in a remote Trans-Caucasian village and graduated from the Zhukovsky Academy in 1936. His close associate, Mikhail Iosifovich Gurevich (Mig aircraft bear their initials, the "i" standing for the word "and"), born in 1892, studied physics and mathematics for two years at Kharkov University. During the revolution he emigrated to France but returned in 1921 to study at the Kharkov Institute of Technology, graduating in 1925. As did other Soviet aviation personalities, he spent several years working on various types of gliders. In 1929 he joined the aircraft industry.

Work was already under way on new-model ground-attack and bomber aircraft when the Kremlin conference met in 1939. S. V. Iliushin and P. O. Sukhoi worked on suitable ground-attack aircraft in an effort to satisfy the air forces' requirements for a new armored tactical aircraft. Iliushin's TsKB-55 was completed first and flew, albeit somewhat indifferently, in 1939. Military officials were not pleased with the sluggish performance of the two-seat prototype, and it was reengined with the more powerful A. A. Mikulin AM-38 engine (1,600 hp) and redesigned into a single-seat aircraft without defensive protection. This new version, the TsKB-57 (Il-2), began flight testing in 1940 and successfully completed state trials in March 1941. Later known as the Shturmovik or Iliushka, the heavily armed and armored Il-2 was already in limited production and slated to replace the I model fighters that had been pressed into temporary service and the Su-2s then in the ground-attack units. P. O. Sukhoi's Su-6 missed the deadline in the design competition with the Il-2. Although it was possibly a better aircraft, the Su-6 was not built in quantity because the Il-2 was by

then performing satisfactorily and headed toward full production.

During 1938 Iliushin modified his DB-3 twin-engine bomber, which had entered service in 1937, improving range, bomb load, and overall performance. The new DB-3F, subsequently redesignated the Il-4, went into production in 1939 and formed the backbone of the VVS and naval air force (VVS/VMF) medium-bomber units throughout the war.

The replacement for Tupolev's now-obsolescent SB series of fast, light bombers came from the drawing boards of V. M. Petlyakov's design bureau. Originally developed as a high-altitude fighter, Petlyakov's twin-engine aircraft (the VI-100) completed its first flight tests in 1939. It was then converted into a dive bomber, the PB-100, before entering production in late 1940 as the Pe-2 light bomber. An extremely versatile aircraft that served as a dive or horizontal bomber as well as a fighter or fighter-bomber, the Pe-2 became the mainstay of the tactical bomber force, at times accounting for as much as 75 percent of the Soviet twin-engine bomber force.

Tupolev also designed and built an excellent twin-engine tactical bomber, the Tu-2, as a replacement for his SB, but it appeared in 1941—too late to compete with the Pe-2, which was already in full production. Hindered by the need to convert to M-82 radial engines, the former craft did not see combat until 1944. Only 1,100 Tu-2s were built from 1942 to 1945, representing barely 10 percent of the 11,426 Pe-2s of all varieties produced before and during the war.

While these new Soviet aircraft were crude by contemporary Western standards, they were tailored to Soviet needs and resources—simple in design, rugged in construction, economical and easy to build in large numbers, and easy to maintain. All

Soviet combat aircraft were designed and built to operate in the primitive conditions and severe winter weather found in many parts of the Soviet Union. Compared to Western aircraft, they were underpowered—the result of lagging Soviet engine development. For this reason, the performance of the aircraft was generally inferior to that of the comparable German Bf-109E/F or the British Spitfire. Indeed, this deficiency holds true for most Soviet aircraft of the time, because the Soviet aircraft engine industry continued to be heavily dependent upon older Western designs and had yet to develop sufficiently powerful new engines. The chief engine designers, A. D. Shvetsov, A. A. Mikulin, and V. Ya. Klimov, worked to correct this shortcoming, and a series of improved and more powerful engines emerged from their efforts during the war years. However, deficiencies in engine production limited the output of the entire aircraft industry.

During 1940–1941, the Soviet aircraft industry began building modern planes that had been designed and approved for series production in 1939–1940. Tooling up and establishing production lines took precious time, while the aircraft suffered the inevitable problems associated with the hasty commitment of prototypes to production before all defects have been detected by thorough testing. Considering the critical two-front threat facing the VVS in 1940, however, the decision to move quickly into full-scale production was the only one possible. Production of the new military aircraft was quite small in 1940, numbering only 86 out of the 10,565 built; however, production jumped to 2,653 in January–June 1941 as more plants came on the line and technical problems were resolved.

Between January 1, 1939, and June 22, 1941, the total production of newer models, including the Il-4, represented only 3,719 of the 17,745 combat aircraft built. The vast majority of the aircraft turned out were such obsolescent types as the I-153 and I-16 fighters, whose production ceased only in 1940 when the new types came on line. On the positive side, the Soviet aircraft industry had clearly been gearing for war during the last years of peace. From 5,469 aircraft built in 1939, output increased to 10,565 in 1940 and reached 15,735 in 1941 despite severe disruptions during the opening months of the war.

Aircraft output greatly benefited from a concentration on single-engine fighters and attack planes and from a rationalization program that limited production to a few basic models of engines and combat aircraft so as to take full advantage of standardization and mass production. This approach, which characterized most Soviet armament programs of the period, simplified the persistent Soviet spare-parts problem as well as facilitating maintenance and training. Once the production lines were operating at full capacity, ample aircraft became avaliable to reequip the existing air regiments and to outfit new units added in the expansion of the VVS.

One of the younger of the Soviet designers who had attained some success before World War II was Oleg Konstantinovich Antonov (see figure 96), born in 1906 in the village of Troitsa in Moscow province. He completed his training at the Kalinin Polytechnical Institute in Leningrad in 1930. Already active in gliders and sport flying, he was immediately appointed chief engineer at the Moscow Glider Factory and rose to be its chief designer before it was closed in 1938. He then joined the Yakovlev team and was placed in charge of Yak-3 development. At the end of the war he was ordered to create his own design bureau and produce a utility airplane with a 730-hp engine. The resulting AN-2 biplane won him a Stalin

Prize in 1952. Since then he has concentrated on large turbine-powered transports.

Figure 96. O. K. Antonov.

Design and Production in Wartime

The heavy attrition in June and July of 1941, along with the evacuations, spurred further rationalization of Soviet aircraft production. The VVS decided to concentrate almost exclusively on the fighter and attack air arms, and production plans followed suit. The unnecessary duplication of types was eliminated; production was narrowed to a few types with frozen designs, so as to facilitate large-scale output. As a stopgap measure until relocation had been completed and newer aircraft were ready for service, I-16 and I-153 production was briefly resumed during 1941 in order to provide some replacement aircraft for use at the front. Their production was soon halted, however, as plants were transferred and industrial space was converted to the building of newer types.

The result of this policy was a sharp decline in the anticipated growth of aircraft production in the July–December 1941 period because most of the existing aircraft assembly and engine plants were located west of the Volga. Although output was maintained at respectable levels through October, November production (627) dipped to 27 percent of the Septem-

ber level (2,329). This precipitous drop denied the VVS sufficient planes to recoup its continuing heavy losses.

The combination of front-line demands and limited production capacity led to the discontinuation of a number of aircraft and engine models, so that valuable plant space could be devoted to a few essential aircraft until the evacuated plants were back in operation and new ones had been built. Engine production was restricted to four basic air-cooled types and three liquid-cooled power plants. Shvetsov's ASh-82 (M-82), Klimov's VK-107 (M-107), and Mikulin's AM-38 engines (in their improved 1,600–1,850 hp variants) were used in most Soviet combat aircraft—in all Yak and Lavochkin fighters as well as the Pe-2 and Il-2 series.

Superfluous aircraft models were quickly dropped. Sukhoi's excellent Su-6 attack aircraft was discontinued; available plant capacity could not support building two types of attack aircraft, and Iliushin's Il-2 was already in production and operational. The Pe-8 four-motored bomber was dropped so that more Pe-2 light bombers could be built. Except for forty-eight aircraft built in 1942, Mig-3 production ended in November 1941 when its Mikulin AM-35A 1,350-hp engine was terminated in favor of expanded production of the 1,600-hp AM-38 engine for the Il-2.

The termination of Mig-3 production was accepted as necessary in order to satisfy the more urgent demand for Shturmoviks. Although Mikoian's fighter was an excellent high-altitude interceptor, it was little needed in the tactical air war. When pressed into service as a frontal fighter during the summer, it had performed poorly in this entirely foreign low-altitude role. Its inadequate armament and maneuverability made the Mig-3 no match for German fighters. Accordingly, losses were heavy throughout the year. The Mig saw service simply because more Mig-3s were built during 1941 than other modern fighters. As the Lagg-3 and Yak-1 became available in numbers, the Migs were progressively withdrawn from frontal service and were transferred to IA/PVO units, where they remained until 1943–1944. From July 1941 until the end of production in November 1941, 2,013 Mig-3s were completed, bringing total output to 3,222 for its production life (excluding 100 Mig-1s).

That the production of the Yak-1 was the smallest of those of the three fighters accepted in 1940 was due in part to plant evacuations. Only 1,354 of these planes were built in 1941. During that year, 3,222 Mig-3s and 2,463 Lagg-3s were built. The Yak-1 was probably the best of the three and became the forerunner of the exceptional series of Yakovlev fighter aircraft developed during the war.

Refinements introduced in the Yak-7B and the Yak-7DI long-range fighter became the basis for the initial Yak-9s, which were produced in the fall of 1942 and which first saw action with Guards units at Stalingrad in December of that year. This aircraft was the progenitor of an entire family of multipurpose Yak-9 fighters built after 1942. The basic Yak-9 had a ceiling of 33,000 feet and a maximum speed of nearly 370 mph at 10,000 feet, was armed with one 20mm ShVAK cannon and a 12.7mm UBS machine gun, and had a range of approximately 600 miles.

Although not as hard-hit as that of other planes, Lagg-3 production was seriously dislocated during the late summer of 1941 as the German forces neared Taganrog, prompting the relocation of equipment and personnel to five factories in Tiflis, Georgia. Despite this interruption, Lagg-3 output reached 2,141 in July–December 1941 and totalled 2,463 for the year.

The relocation difficulties were minor compared to those affecting the aircraft itself. The decision to emphasize mass output locked defects into the Lagg-3 that proved to be difficult to remedy. In this case, as in others, pressures caused by evacuation and pressing demands of the front combined to exaggerate technical deficiencies already in the aircraft. Frontline units equipped with Lavochkin fighters encountered so much trouble that the designer, an engineering team, and test pilots had to be sent to investigate the problems and devise solutions. The earlier efforts in 1940–1941 to improve the original Lagg-1 design had failed to correct its weak undercarriage and inadequate armament. The aircraft lacked maneuverability and was unwieldy in the air because its engine lacked the power to compensate for its weight of more than three tons. The Lagg-3, although comparable to the Yak-1 in overall performance (307 mph at sea level, 354 mph at 13,000 feet), was less maneuverable than Yakovlev's aircraft. Despite these problems, 1,766 Lagg-3s were built in the first half of 1942 before output dropped to 970 as Lavochkin's new fighters entered production.

In an effort to solve basic problems and improve performance, Lavochkin and Gorbunov substituted Shvetsov's 1,570-hp ASh-82 air-cooled radial engine (and later the 1,600-hp ASh-82A) for the Klimov VK-105PF (1,210 hp) engine and made other changes that resulted in the Lag-5. Redesignated the La-5 after Gorbunov left the team, the new fighter entered production in the summer of 1942, and 1,129 were completed during that year. The La-5 went into action in August 1942 with the 287th FAD in the defensive fighting at Stalingrad. Its maximum speed of 388 mph at 10,000 feet and its range of 390 miles quickly made the new fighter a mainstay of the VVS fighter force. The introduction of the Shvetsov radial engine lessened the aircraft's vulnerability, especially to engine fires, and other improvements made the La-5 easy to control and to maneuver.

The most important addition to the VVS in 1941 was Iliushin's single-seat Il-2 Shturmovik. Although it was a rugged aircraft with good armament of two 7.62mm Shkas machine guns, two 20mm ShVAK cannon, and excellent armor protection, the early version of the Il-2 was sluggish because of its maximum takeoff weight of over 11,000 pounds. Intended to replace the Su-2 and I-model fighters, the Shturmovik was gradually introduced into combat, while the obsolete Su-2 had to remain in service during 1941–1942 despite crippling losses. Only 249 Il-2s had been completed by the time the war started. Production rose slowly to 1,293 for July–December 1941 but fell far short of meeting the incessant demands of the front.

The first Il-2 units were dispatched to the front in late June (Fourth GAAR) and early July (Sixty-First GAAR) 1941. The appearance of the Iliushins in numbers in August indicated the VVS' recovery. Moreover, it marked a milestone in the development of Soviet ground-attack aviation (*shturmovaia aviatsiia*), whose principal function was providing close support for infantry and armored forces. Shturmoviks—or the "Black Death," as German troops came to call the Il-2s—were pressed into action in direct battlefield support of the Red Army before they were available in large numbers. The aircraft performed well during the summer of 1941, demonstrating more-than-adequate loiter time, weapons load, and armament. Being a slow, single-seat aircraft, however, it was highly vulnerable to rear attacks by fighters, even though its armor made it difficult to bring down. Yet the appearance of the Il-2s over the front lines provided a much-needed boost to the ground troops' morale as the

war progressed and the Il-2 came to dominate the battlefield.

During 1941–1942 the Il-2 played a key role in VVS air operations, although numerous weaknesses required correction. A series of conferences between pilots and designers delineated the need for a defensive rear gunner, a better engine, and heavier armament, especially for use against German tanks. The direct result was the Il-2m2, in which the 1,750-hp AM-38F engine had been optimized for operation under 5,000 feet and the two 20mm ShVAK cannon had been replaced by two VYa 23mm cannon. In the fall of 1942, Il-2m2s were supplied to the air regiments. However, the basic problem of defense against rear attacks had not yet been solved.

Acting on their own in the summer of 1942, VVS units of the Northwestern Front and the Sixteenth Air Army at Stalingrad further modified their Il-2s by adding a rear gunner. Because machine gunners were not included in personnel allocations, mechanics, technicians, and armament specialists began flying as gunners in addition to performing their normal duties. Finally, in November 1942, the first of the two-seat Il-2m3 Shturmoviks armed with 12.7mm machine guns in the rear gunners' position began arriving at the front—a development which came as a nasty surprise to many German fighter pilots. With minor modifications, particularly in armament, the Il-2m3 remained the basic Soviet ground-attack aircraft for the rest of the war. Il-2 production more than doubled during 1942, increasing from 2,629 in the first six months to 5,596 in July–December. The total 1942 output of 8,225 such planes was nearly six times that of 1941 (1,542), an increase which contributed to the growth of the ground-attack air arm.

The Pe-2 lighter bomber was a well-constructed twin engine aircraft, superior in speed, armament, and flight characteristics to other Soviet bombers. Although the speed and defensive firepower of the Pe-2 made it a match for the Bf-109E, in early 1942 the subsequent introduction in the east of the Bf-109F, the FW-190A, and the Bf-109G forced the Pe-2 into an increasingly unfavorable operational environment and a consequent loss of bombing effectiveness. While Pe-2 output had suffered from the dislocations of the last half of 1941, 1,405 were built and turned over to VVS units during that period, bringing production for the year to 1,863.

By June 1942, Pe-2 units were suffering such heavy losses from German fighters that the aircraft were field-modified by front-line engineering teams. Their efforts to improve the plane's defensive armor and firepower by replacing the 7.62mm guns with dorsal and ventral 12.7mm Beresin UBT machine guns had the effect of increasing its weight appreciably while reducing its performance; hence the more-powerful 1,210-hp VK-105RF engine was substituted for the 1,100-hp M-105R. The Pe-2, equipped with a Klimov engine, began coming off the production lines in February 1943. Its maximum speed of 360 mph at 16,000 feet represented an improvement over the previous 335 mph maximum, and its cruise speed was nearly 300 mph—an increase of 35 mph. Range was improved by nearly 200 miles, from 900 to 1,100 miles.

Despite their catastrophic early losses of men, materiel, and territory, the Soviets had preserved their basic aircraft-manufacturing facilities, training schools, and rear services—the ingredients necessary for the painstaking rehabilitation of the VVS. Aircraft production keyed the recovery of the VVS. Excluding naval aircraft, production in 1941 totaled 15,735, of which 10,731 (68.2 percent) were new-model

aircraft introduced in 1940–1941. From July through December, Pe-2, Yak-1, Lagg-3, Mig-3, and Il-2 production reached 8,078 aircraft, more than half of the annual output and triple the January–June total.

By early 1942, most aircraft factories had been relocated and series production engines and planes had been resumed. Production expanded greatly during the year, and total output reached 25,436—21,577 being military aircraft. New and improved aircraft, the La-5, Yak-7B, Yak-9, and Il-2m3, entered production and combat before the close of the year.

The continuing development of the Soviet aircraft industry provided the means for the VVS' seizure of air supremacy in 1943 and its retention during 1944–1945. Safe from German interference, Soviet aircraft enterprises profited from factory expansions and refinement of mass-production techniques. The average monthly output was increased from 2,100 aircraft in 1942 to more than 3,350 in 1944 and to 3,480 for January–June 1945.

These large yearly increases in production allowed the Red Air Force not only to make up for its heavy combat losses but also to add new air units and more aircraft to the existing regiments. The fighter and attack regiments, which had been increased to 32 aircraft each late in 1942, jumped to 40 planes in 1943, while bomber regiments were expanded to 32 aircraft in three 10-plane squadrons during that year. The growth in numbers and in front-line combat strength was the result of the industry's concentration on building combat aircraft. In 1944, when 40,300 aircraft were produced, 17,872 (44.4 percent) were fighters, 10,719 (26.6 percent) were attack planes, 4,039 (10 percent) were frontal and long-range bombers, and the rest (19 percent) were transports and trainers. Thus, 32,630 aircraft, or 81 percent, of total output were combat planes. Significantly, the combat aircraft built after 1942 were predominantly of good design and quality, easily equal or even superior to German models. All told, the USSR produced about 130,000 aircraft in World War II.

The most significant improvements in aircraft came in the VVS fighter force. Older models, such as the Lagg-3 and Yak-1, gave way to reengined, upgunned, and aerodynamically refined versions of the same types. The La-5, La-5FN, and La-7 replaced the Lagg-3. The basic Yak spawned an infinite variety of ever-improving offspring, culminating in the Yak-3 of 1943 and the Yak-9U in 1944. These aircraft had greater range and firepower in order to support the offensive operations of the Red Army. The standard 7.62mm machine gun of 1941–1942 was replaced by harder-hitting 12.7mm machine guns and later by 20mm cannon. Eventually 37mm and 45mm cannon were installed in such planes as the Il-2m3M (modified) and Yak-9T in order to make them deadly tank killers. The Yak-3, Yak-9U, and La-7 were equal to, if not better than, the standard German Bf 109G-6 and FW 190A-8 fighters in speed and maneuverability, especially below 10,000 feet, but were generally inferior in firepower.

Yakovlev's fighter aircraft were by far the most numerous in the VVS fighter arm. From 1941 to 1945, a total of 36,737 Yak fighters of all varieties were built—26.7 percent of all aircraft produced—while 22,200 Lavochkin fighters were completed.

The vast qualitative improvements distinguishing the Soviet fighter arm after 1942 were not effected in the lesser-priority ground-attack and bomber branches. However, the VVS ground-attack regiments were equipped with the finest aircraft of its type in any air force—the Il-2m3 Shturmovik. With the attainment of air superiority, and with such fighters as

the La-5FN and Yak-3 providing cover, the Il-2s operated in ever-larger swarms with great effect against German infantry and armored units. For more effective antitank operations, in May 1943 the GKO ordered Il-2s equipped with two wing-mounted NS-37 37mm cannon. This new Il-2m3M (modified) version made its combat debut in the Kursk, fighting with telling effect. The Shturmoviks contributed substantially to the Soviet air and ground effort and remained in series production from 1941 through 1944; total output of the Il-2s reached 36,163, representing 26.3 percent of all aircraft built during the war.

The VVS bomber arm was the proverbial poor relative when compared with either the fighter or attack branches. As a result of both doctrinal emphasis and tactical demands, bomber development lagged behind. The improved Pe-2FT version of Petliakov's basic tactical bomber entered service in 1943, a year after the designer's death in an air crash. An excellent light bomber, the FT remained the mainstay of the frontal bomber forces for the rest of the war.

After the new Tupolev aircraft Tu-2 began frontal service in 1943, it proved to be better than the Petlyakovs and vastly superior to the Il-4 medium bombers. Iliushin's aging bomber was phased out of production during 1944 after a total of 5,256 had been built. Despite its wartime assignment to ADD, the Il-4 medium bomber had seen considerable tactical duty, especially during major offensive operations.

Lend-Lease, Captures, and Purchases

In general, Soviet sources discount the impact of Lend-Lease; however, deliveries from England and America were nevertheless significant to the air war. The first U.S. planes, 195 Curtiss Tomahawk P-40C fighters, were shipped over the Arctic route in October 1941. In 1942, the improved P-40E was sent; however, a number of aircraft were lost to German submarine attacks. As the northern route became increasingly dangerous, many planes were shipped around Africa to Iran, where they were assembled for delivery to the Soviet Union. Other aircraft were ferried by air through Alaska and Siberia.

Of 14,798 American aircraft allocated to the Soviet Union, 14,018 were delivered. Almost 11,000 of these American planes were shipped prior to mid-1944. The British sent their first contribution in September 1941, within three months after Hitler's invasion, and eventually supplied 2,952 Hurricanes, 143 Spitfires, and about 30 other aircraft.

It is true that the 18,000 aircraft provided by Lend-Lease did not represent a large proportion of the 130,000 USSR production during World War II. What is often overlooked, however, is that the program contributed $500 million in machine tools and factories (including an aluminum rolling mill) in addition to 2.25 million tons of steel, 400,000 tons of copper, and 250,000 tons of aluminum (the latter equalling two years' Soviet production at 1945 rates). All of this material permitted the changeover from wooden to metal aircraft late in the war.

As the war ended, the Soviet Union urgently set about studying captured and interned aircraft of both friend and foe. In 1944 three American B-29 bombers landed in the Soviet far east, forced down by combat damage or lack of fuel. The Soviets interned the crews and dismantled the B-29s, and a Tupolev team copied each component (high-horsepower engines and electronics, remote-controlled guns). In 1946, the Soviets tried to buy tires, wheels, and other parts from the United States. Finally, the Soviet copy of the B-29—designated Tu-4 by the Soviets—appeared at the Tushino air show in 1947; a civilian version, the Tu-70 airliner, was also built.

The Soviets also began a high-priority examination of German jet aircraft. (The Soviet Union was the only major power which had not produced a jet fighter by the end of World War II.) In 1945 a Soviet team headed by Mikoian went to East Germany to study wartime jet aircraft designs. The Me-262 especially interested them. First flown in 1942, the Me-262 was flight-tested in 1942 and 1943 and was then put into series production. Powered by two 850-kg (1,870 lb.) thrust turbojet engines, the Me-262 had a maximum speed of almost 900 kph (565 mph) at about 6,700 meters. With a service ceiling of about 13,000 meters (43,000 feet), it was the world's first jet-propelled fighter to go into squadron service.

The Soviets were naturally eager to exploit German technology. Although they resisted the temptation to build an exact copy of the Me-262, they nevertheless copied its Junkers Jumo-004 engine. They also used the captured MBW-003 engine, which had a thrust of 800 kg. Asher Lee pointed out that the Soviets found in defeated Germany perhaps the largest and most advanced pool of scientific and engineering skills that any victorious nation has ever acquired in modern war. Nearly four-fifths of Germany's aircraft production centers fell into Soviet hands, including the Junkers plant at Dessau, the Siebel plant at Halle, and the Heinkel plants at Oranienburg and Warnemunde. In addition, the Soviets carted off hundreds of aviation and rocket specialists to the USSR.

With this foundation, they turned to British engines for their aircraft. Mikoian had studied jet technology in England, and the Soviets soon adopted two British engines for their own use: the Rolls-Royce Derwent, with a thrust of 1,600 kg, and the Nene, with a thrust of 2,200 kg (5,000 lbs). German engines were used for the Yak-15 and Mig-9, while British engines were installed in the single-engine fighters Mig-15, La-15, and Yak-23 and a twin-engine tactical bomber, the Il-28. The design offices of V. Ya. Klimov, A. A. Mikulin, and A. M. Lyulka conducted the work on the Soviet engines.

Jet propulsion brought Soviet designers many headaches in addition to the problem of where to locate the engines. However, in the Yak-19 of 1949 they adopted the standard straight-through jet fuselage design. Undercarriages were redesigned to fit into fuselages instead of inside the new slim, swept wings; the delta wing was investigated and tailplanes were redesigned. Facilitating this process was the Soviet tradition that the minister in charge must be a recognized expert in the field; therefore, decisions were approved by men with the necessary technical expertise.

The Road to Supersonic Aircraft

The Mig-15 was produced in large numbers and proved to be a superior fighter. Its design included swept wings, tricycle landing gear, and an ejection seat. It was armed with one 37mm and two 23mm cannon. This impressive fighter was followed by others of the Mikoian and Gurevich family, the Migs-17, 19, 21, 23, and 25.

Yakovlev and Sukhoi also designed and produced a number of jet fighters. Among them were several aircraft in the current inventory, including Yakovlev's all-weather Yak-25, his tactical general purpose Yak-28, and Sukhoi's Su-7, Su-9, and Su-11. Yakovlev also built a vertical takeoff aircraft, the Yak-36, which, like the Hawker Harrier, uses vectored thrust. In 1976, Yak-36s began to appear on the new carrier *Kiev* in the Soviet fleet. In addition, Tupolev built a family of impressive jet bombers: his twin-engine Tu-16, seen in numbers in 1954 and still in service; and

the Tu-22 and Tu-28, both shown at Tushino in 1961.

Bomber technology created a fleet of civil aircraft. In the mid-1930s the license for production of the twenty-four-passenger Douglas DC-3 was purchased in the United States and put into production in the Soviet Union, where it was renamed the Li-2 after B. P. Lisunov, the chief engineer who organized its production. In late 1943, unsuccessful consideration was given to converting a bomber into a transport and passenger plane. One of the main contenders was V. G. Ermolaev's Er-2 bomber, which designers felt could be modified to carry twelve passengers; however, it was rejected because of the radical fuselage changes that would have been necessary to ensure passenger comfort. Iliushin began working on his twin-engine Il-12, which appeared in 1947, followed by the twin-engine Il-14 in 1950 and the four-engine Il-18 in 1957. Meanwhile, Western nations had begun operating turbine aircraft in commercial fleets; the Soviet Union felt itself seriously lagging behind. Therefore, the government turned again to its bomber-design bureaus with orders to produce a jet passenger plane.

Tupolev had already converted the Tu-4 into the 72-seat Tu-70. It was found that the Tu-16 could be quickly adapted for passenger use; the modified craft was dubbed the Tu-104. Tupolev's second jet airliner, the Tu-114, carried 170 passengers and was powered by four turboprop engines which gave it a speed of about 900 kph. The Tu-124, appearing in 1960, was powered with two five-ton D-20P engines and resembled a scaled-down Tu-104. Radically modified, with its engines relocated to the tail section, the plane was designated Tu-134. In 1967, the 186-passenger transcontinental Il-62, which closely resembled the British VC-10, joined the Aeroflot inventory. Powered by four aft-mounted NK-8 jet engines of 10.5 tons thrust each, this sleek Iliushin plane has in recent years been plagued by fatal air crashes. The competitor to the Concorde, the Tu-144, was also cursed with bad luck when its pilot exceeded the plane's limitations at the Paris Air Show in June 1973 and crashed before horrified spectators.

Until what might be called the fourth German invasion in 1946, Russian designers were generally hampered by lack of sufficient horsepower; thus their designs have emphasized such essentials as cleanness, singleness of purpose, maintainability, and the necessity of volume production. As a result, Soviet designers have produced aircraft which are highly suited to both their operational climate and their air crews and which are, in the long run, much less wasteful than comparable British, American, or French designs. While it might be argued that the Russian system of designing competitive prototypes is wasteful, such a system ensures success through permitting comparison at independent testing establishments of real, not paper, machines.

The Russian procurement procedure possesses many advantages over Western systems. By allowing each designer to develop his own specialty rather than forcing designers to compete for arbitrary operational-requirements aircraft, the Soviets can push the best basic design to the limit of the art and then adapt it along the lines of Sir Geoffrey de Havilland's Mosquito approach. The present system also has the advantage of allowing jigs and tools to be adapted progressively, thus reducing costs, while the generally simpler aircraft produced cost less per copy and are easier to maintain in the field.

One of the problems for Soviet aircraft designers is that since 1945 the Red Air Force has not officially been involved in war. Thus operational feedback is limited to the use of Soviet planes by satellites and by such other countries as North Korea, North Vietnam, Egypt, and Syria.

Most writers outside Russia feel that the Soviet procurement process is a mystery and are puzzled by the decline of competition between the design bureaus. The reason for the latter trend can be understood by looking at recent procurement patterns in Britain and by considering the complexity and consequent manpower demands of modern aircraft designs. The Tu-2, for instance, weighed 28,000 pounds fully loaded, while the Tu-144 takes off at 396,000 pounds and operates in a far more aerodynamically demanding environment. Given such conditions, it is natural that, except for cases of "insurance" aircraft, Soviet design teams will become more and more specialized and undertake fewer and fewer projects, with a small percentage ever coming to fruition.

This pattern is likely to be reinforced by the narrow, technical nature of Soviet education, by the lack of commercial pressure to develop aircraft which can be sold to operators all over the world, and by the gradual imposition of financial and cost restraints. Already there is evidence of the impending conversion of some aircraft factories to production of such consumer items as radios, television sets, and automobiles. On the average, seven of the twelve members of the Council of Ministers have been engineers, whereas in the West top policymakers are more likely to be lawyers, journalists, or other nontechnical persons.

In summary, the Soviet military has been the main recipient of the labors of the Russian aviation industry; this fact remains true today. The Soviets have not been averse to copying foreign models. Moreover, though their historians have little to say on the subject, the Soviets have never hesitated to use engines of Western manufacture when it suits their purpose, a practice that was still prevalent in the 1960s. Nevertheless, it must be acknowledged that the USSR has produced both a group of outstanding designers—Yakovlev, Tupolev, Iliushin, and others—and the industrial-technical base which enabled them to produce a fleet of impressive aircraft.

Research Notes

In the preparation of this chapter, we relied heavily on recent Soviet source material. This material included two works by the outstanding designer Alexander S. Yakovlev. *50 let Sovetskogo samoletostroeniia* [Fifty Years of Soviet Aircraft Construction] (Moscow, 1968) was subsequently translated into English and published for the U.S. National Aeronautics and Space Administration and the National Science Foundation by the Israel Program for Scientific Translations (Jerusalem, 1970). The second Yakovlev volume, *The Aim of a Lifetime,* was published in Moscow in 1972. Also useful are articles on "aviatsiia" in volume 1 of the *Bolshaia Sovetskaia entsiklopediia,* in both the second (1949) and third (1970) editions. Regrettably, when using such sources, one must wade through a certain amount of propaganda. The second edition of the encyclopedia, for example, is replete with references to Stalin's personal influence in virtually every development.

Another useful Soviet source is the monthly magazine *Aviatsiia i kosmonavtika* [Aviation and Cosmonautics], which has been published since 1918. In June 1973 its editors began presenting a series of articles on aircraft of the Soviet Union, starting with the earliest models. This journal contains considerable historical information, although current data are lacking because of the Soviets' reluctance to publish anything which borders on the "classified." The series on Soviet aircraft is being drawn out; issue no. 4 of 1974 had only reached the year 1935.

Another valuable source is the official history of tthe Soviet air forces in World War II. We recommend the English translation by Leland Fetzer, with its excellent editorial comments by Ray Wagner, *The Soviet Air Force in World War II* (Garden City, N.Y., 1973). Two useful works dealing with Soviet military aviation published by the USSR Ministry of Defense are the six-volume *Istoriia Velikoi Otechestvennoi voiny Sovetskogo Soiuza, 1941-1945* [History of the Great Patriotic War of the Soviet Union] (Moscow, 1960–1965) and *50 let vooruzhennykh sil SSSR* [Fifty Years of the Armed Forces of the USSR] (Moscow, 1968). Both works were compiled from articles by a number of authors. Another interesting work is Lev Ekonomov's *Poiski Kryl'ev* [Searching for Wings] (Moscow, 1969).

In addition to these general studies, the following specific materials—both Soviet and Western—were consulted: for individuals, Michael T. Florinsky, ed., *McGraw-Hill Encyclopedia of Russia and the Soviet Union* (New York, 1961); for Sikorsky's early aircraft, John W. R. Taylor, ed., *Jane's 100 Significant Aircraft* (London, 1969); for German-Soviet collaboration after World War I, Peter Townsend, *Duel of Eagles* (New York, 1971), and Gustav Hilger and Alfred G. Meyer, *The Incompatible Allies* (New York, 1953); for the purges, Otto P. Chaney's *Zhukov* (Norman, Okla., 1971), Asher Lee, *The Soviet Air Force* (New York, 1962), and Robert Conquest, *The Great Terror* (New York, 1968); for prewar and wartime aircraft production, S. M. Shtemenko, *The Soviet General Staff at War, 1941–1945* (Moscow, 1970), and Yakovlev's *Aim of a Lifetime,* already cited; for Lend-Lease, Robert Huhn Jones, *The Roads to Russia* (Norman, Okla., 1969), and Fetzer and Wagner's *The Soviet Air Force,* already cited; for exploitation of captured German aircraft, Asher Lee's outstanding book, already cited, and Yakovlev's *Aim of a Lifetime;* for the "copycat bomber" and recent Soviet developments, Colin Munro, *Soviet Air Forces* (New York, 1972), John Batchelor and Bryan Cooper, *Fighter* (New York, 1968), *Jane's All the World's Aircraft,* Jean Alexander, *Russian Aircraft since 1940* (London, 1975), John Stroud, *Soviet Transport Aircraft since 1945* (New York, 1968), and Jerzy B. Cynk, *Polish Aircraft, 1893–1939* (London, 1971).

Also useful are Abram Bergson, *The Economics of Soviet Planning* (New Haven, Conn., 1964), and Alec Nove, *An Economic History of the USSR* (Baltimore, 1972). Especially interesting are three works by Anthony C. Sutton, *Western Technology and Soviet Economic Development, 1917–1930* (Stanford, Calif., 1968), *Western Technology . . . 1930–1945* (Stanford, 1971), and *Western Technology . . . 1945–1965* (Stanford, 1973); and I. A. Gladkov, *Sovetskaia ekonomika v period velikoi otechestvennoi voiny, 1941–1945* (Moscow, 1971).

For those who read Russian, in addition to those materials cited above, individual entries in the *Bolshaia Sovetskaia entsiklopediia* are a good beginning for further research, keeping in mind its propagandizing propensities. For information about newer models of aircraft, it is often more profitable to consult Western aviation journals or *Jane's All the World's Aircraft* (London, annual). The reader is cautioned, when using Soviet materials, to be on guard for untruths or deceptive statements. (For example, Yakovlev reported that Il-4 bombers were the first to raid Berlin in August 1941. He may have meant that they were the first *Soviet* bombers; the British had already been bombing Berlin for some time before the Soviets entered World War II.)

More study needs to be devoted to Soviet aircraft design, research, and production establishments in comparison with those in other countries as well as to the personalities involved and relations with satellite states. In the future, as the old men of Soviet aviation step down, it will be interesting to see how aircraft design organizations change and how factories are adjusted so as to maintain full employment.

12

The Peacetime Air Force
at Home and Abroad, 1945-1976

Kenneth R. Whiting

At the end of World War II, the military power of the Soviet Union rested upon its enormous ground forces, which were armed with tanks, artillery, and tactical aircraft. The United States also had large ground forces, but in addition possessed the world's biggest navy, large numbers of what were then long-range aircraft, and a monopoly on the atomic bomb. The United States, unlike its Soviet ally, had made its main contribution to the defeat of the Axis by seizing control of the seas and using strategic air power. In short, because the Americans fought the war on a global scale, they had to develop the weapons and strategy for such a war. The Soviets contributed to the defeat of the common enemy by trading huge land masses for the time necessary to organize and deploy a superiority in manpower, artillery, tanks, and close-support aircraft. From the global strategic point of view, the Soviets fought a local war using battering-ram tactics. In any appraisal of the respec-tive military strengths of the two powers in the immediate postwar years, the United States had the edge.

During this period the Americans, in their role as peacemakers, relied on two forces: their own monopoly of the atomic bomb, which was tied to the world's largest strategic air force, and the United Nations. There was some justification for their reliance on the first force, but very little for their faith in the second. Almost from the beginning, it was evident that, although the United Nations could do many things—some of them even well—it alone could not keep the peace in a world dominated by two superpowers, the United States and the Soviet Union. In retrospect, however, one may legitimately wonder whether SAC and "the bomb" could have effectively defeated the Soviet Union in the 1946–1950 period. U.S. strength during the first five or six years after the war was probably far less than was commonly thought at the time. For one thing, the Soviet Union had absorbed far more devastation at the hands of the Germans in 1941 than SAC could have dealt in the late 1940s, and the very awesomeness of the new weapon restricted its use against anything short of a Soviet attack on Western Europe.

Considering the Soviets' inability to match the United States in strategic weapons systems, it is not surprising that military theorists echoed Stalin's glorification of the infantry, artillery, and tactical air forces. The nuclear weapon was denigrated, if it was mentioned at all. But in spite of their obeisance to the artillery as the god of war, with air power considered only one of the handmaidens, Soviet military leaders must have suffered some agonizing moments when they contemplated the idea of American B-29s loaded with atomic bombs. Although they may have felt relatively safe from a mortal blow, they were sitting under SAC's bombsights—a position likely to make them feel somewhat nervous. Furthermore, behind the facade of their conventional military doctrine, the Russians were desperately striving for the very weapons they decried in their public statements. Enormous amounts of scarce resources and even scarcer technical personnel were expended on the research and development of weapons to match the American strategic wallop. The highest priority, next to that of acquiring a nuclear capability, was the establishment of an air-defense system— which, in that period, meant the development of jet fighters, radar networks, and antiaircraft artillery.

These three elements—interceptors, antiaircraft artillery, and early-warning networks—were the responsibility of the Air Defense Command, or PVO (Protivo-vozduzhnaya oborona). Although PVO's record during the war had been somewhat spotty against the sporadic strategic bombing of the Luftwaffe, the name of the

game in the early postwar years was bomber interception; thus the PVO had to be improved drastically, especially its interceptor element, or IA/PVO (Istrebitel'naya aviatsiia/PVO). Soviet designers of jet aircraft were handicapped at first by being restricted to the use of captured German turbojet engines, the relatively low-powered Jumo-004 and BMW-003. But in 1947 the Soviets were able to purchase twenty-five Rolls-Royce Nene and thirty Derwent centrifugal-flow turbojet engines, an acquisition that helped considerably in placing their jet-engine development on a solid footing. The Mig-15 jet fighter, a product of the design team of Artem I. Mikoian and Mikhail I. Gurevich, was the followup to their Mig-9, one of the first Soviet jet fighters to go into squadron service. The Mig-15, which was equipped with the Soviet version of the Rolls-Royce Nene engine, the RD-45, had a 5,000-pound thrust that enabled it to attain a speed of 660 miles per hour. The aircraft began to appear in squadron service in 1949, and by late 1950 Mig-15s were coming off the assembly lines at the rate of several hundred a month. Before being replaced by the Mig-17 in 1953, some 15,000 Mig-15s were produced.

Because of Stalin's adulation of artillery, rather substantial numbers of antiaircraft weapons were on hand in 1945, although Soviet antiaircraft capabilities had not been severely tested during the conflict. But antiaircraft guns and interceptors were bound to be ineffective without an efficient early-warning radar system, something the Soviets lacked at the end of the war. Building on acquired samples of German radar and using captured Luftwaffe technicians, the Soviets were able to extend their early-warning network to the periphery of the USSR by 1950.

The Korean War gave the Soviets an opportunity to test their aviation, radar,

Figure 97. Mig-15 on display at the USAF Museum at Wright-Patterson AFB in Ohio. This plane was flown to Kimpo USAF base by a North Korean pilot on September 21, 1953, and was later tested by U.S. pilots on Okinawa.

and antiaircraft weapons under combat conditions. The North Korean Air Force (NKAF), created by the Soviets, was more than adequate to handle the almost non-existent South Korean Air Force, but turned out to be woefully incapable of standing up against the U.S. Far Eastern Air Force. The NKAF went into the war with some 150 obsolete Soviet planes, mostly Yak-7s and Il-10s; in addition, the North Korean pilots were extremely short on flying experience and had no combat expertise. The result was sheer disaster: by early August 1950 the NKAF had only 35 operational aircraft. Because the United Nations air forces were able to roam the Korean skies without hindrance, aircraft carriers were able to operate close to shore.

Furthermore, the obsolescence of the North Korean aircraft meant that the U.N. air forces could still use piston aircraft effectively during the first months of the war.

Apparently, the Soviets either did not anticipate the intervention of the U.S. Air Force in Korea or felt it was impossible to provide North Korea with an indigenous air force capable of standing up to the USAF. Certainly the generous supply of armament for the North Korean ground forces was incomparably greater than the meager equipment doled out to the NKAF.

The U.N. breakout from the Pusan perimeter in mid-September, combined with the almost simultaneous Inchon landing, caught the North Koreans between

MacArthur's "hammer and anvil," with the result that their armies had ceased to be viable military forces by the end of September. The U.N. forces crossed the 38th Parallel and headed for the Yalu, an action that brought the Chinese into the war.

The Chinese People's Air Force was a Johnny-come-lately, dating only from 1948, when the first aviation training school was established in Manchuria. In 1949, Liu Ya-lou, then chief of staff of Lin Piao's Fourth Army, was made head of the new air force, which had a total strength of around 100 decrepit aircraft. This was indeed a modest beginning—a nonflying commander in chief and a mixed bag of antique planes. The deterioration of the situation in Korea, however, left the Soviets with the unpalatable options of either building up the Chinese air capabilities or supplying air cover in Korea themselves, and they chose the first alternative. In late 1950, an all-weather airfield and a radar warning network at Antung, in Manchuria, plus a steadily increasing flow of Mig-15s to the Chinese, created a whole new ball game in the air war over Korea.

There was no American fighter in the Far East which could cope with the Mig-15 when it first appeared over the Yalu in November. But the F-86A Sabre-equipped Fourth Fighter-Interceptor Wing arrived in Korea in mid-December 1950, and on December 17 the first Mig-15 was destroyed in combat by a Sabre. The Sabre pilots soon realized that the Mig-15 was an even match as a machine, and that only superior piloting and tactics would enable them to keep control of the air. The chief defect of the Mig-15 was its instability at high speeds and its inferior armament.

By early 1951, Liu Ya-lou had more than 1,000 combat aircraft, including over 400 Mig-15s, a complex of airfields in Manchuria, and a forward fighter base at Antung on the Chinese side of the Yalu.

Against these assets were some liabilities. If he succeeded in really hurting the U.N. forces, would he be allowed to retain his sanctuary in Manchuria? This sobering thought was always with the Chinese leaders, and probably also with their Soviet mentors; as a result, there was a good deal of backing and filling in the implementation of their air strategy. Furthermore, General Liu's best aircraft, the Mig-15, was short on range; and from its Manchurian bases, it could attack only targets within a hundred miles of the Yalu. Most important, his pilots needed further training before they could hope to match their opponents in flying skill and shooting ability.

After an unsuccessful attempt to construct forward airfields in North Korea, the Mig-15s were restricted to operations in northwestern Korea—the famed "Mig alley." American pilots began to recognize certain of their opponents in Mig alley as being much more proficient than the run-of-the-mill fighter jockeys they had previously engaged. These "honcho" pilots were probably Soviet and Chinese instructors, flying combat in order to help the morale of their students and to learn at first hand the tactics of their opponents. After the beginning of the armistice negotiations in July 1951, the air war in Korea was a constant struggle to gain control of the air north of Pyongyang. The Chinese, with nearly 600 Mig-15s, put the Sabre pilots to the test in Mig alley—a test that became even more challenging when the Chinese got a better machine, the Mig-15*bis*, with a 6,000-pound-thrust engine designed by Klimov. In December the air war over northwest Korea was fast and furious, with the laurels going almost exclusively to the Sabre pilots. By late December the Chinese had given up any serious attempt to wrest air superiority from the U.N. and began to follow a cyclical pattern of air opera-

Figure 98. Yak-25 Flashlight-A light bombers in formation at the Moscow Air Show in June 1956.

tions obviously aimed at providing combat training for as many pilots as possible. Each "class" began by flying high and avoiding combat. As the class became more proficient, it also became more belligerent. Then the class graduated and the cycle was repeated.

By mid-1952, the Chinese People's Air Force had nearly 2,000 planes, including more than 1,000 jet fighters; moreover, the Chinese had constructed four more airfields in the Antung complex, thus ensuring their ability to keep hundreds of Migs just beyond the Yalu. The U.S. F-86F, which arrived in the Far East in June 1952, was a match for the Mig-15*bis*. In the fall of 1952 the ratio of Mig kills was eight to one: 123 Migs were shot down in three months. As Mig alley was again becoming Sabre alley, the Chinese pilots lost their belligerency. Even more to the point in the overall context of the cold war, the Soviet leaders were being made conscious of the danger of tackling the U.S. Air Force in other arenas of potential conflict, as well of as being hit in their pocketbook as the toll of Migs mounted.

The Soviets, however, realized some gains from the Korean War: they were able to blood some of their pilots; they were able to gain first-hand experience in coping with U.S. tactics and strategy in air warfare; and they were able to test their aircraft and early-warning systems under combat conditions. The loss of approximately 3,000 aircraft, some 2,000 of which were Migs, was the price paid—but the bill went to the Chinese, who later revealed that they were charged by the Soviets for the war materiel provided them.

While testing their air-defense systems in the Korean War, the Soviets simultaneously

Figure 99. Mig-17 Fagot jet fighters taxiing for takeoff.

pushed ahead in the acquisition of long-range offensive weapons systems, especially long-range bombers. They tested their first nuclear device in 1949 and in August 1953 came up with a thermonuclear bomb. The main problem, however, was how to deliver this new weapon of mass destruction to an opponent located thousands of miles away. The Soviet long-range air force (Dal'naya aviatsiia, or DA) had played a very modest role in World War II, and only a small percentage of its bombers were four-engine Petlyakov Pe-8s. Fortunately for the Soviets, the forced landing of three B-29s in the Soviet far east had provided them with a ready-made model for a long-range aircraft. Tupolev was able to produce a Soviet copy, the Tu-4, or Bull, in record time, and it was in mass production by 1948. By 1953 the DA had three air armies of Tu-4s, consisting of some 1,000 aircraft. But even with in-flight refueling and operating through Arctic bases, the Tu-4 could fly only a one-way mission to most targets on the North American continent. Furthermore, the reluctance of the U.S. B-29s to operate in daylight against Mig-15s in the Korean conflict must have been discouraging for Golovanov and his DA, because the Tu-4s lacked the radar bombsights and the long-range navigational gear necessary for carrying out night attacks. As a vehicle for strategic bombing,

the Tu-4 was obsolete by the end of the Korean War.

The lack of powerful jet engines was holding back Soviet development of long-range bombers. Not until 1953 did Mikulin begin to produce a 10,000-pound-thrust turbojet, which was increased to 15,000 pounds the following year. The Myashishchev M-4, Bison, a four-engine heavy long-range bomber, was built in 1953 and was flown over Moscow on May Day in 1954. In that same year, the two-engine Tu-16 Badger was unveiled, and in July 1955 about fifty flew over Moscow on Aviation Day. In 1955, the Tu-20 (Bear) made its appearance at the Tushino air show. This was a four-engine turboprop long-range aircraft with a relatively slow speed but an extremely long range, more than 7,000 miles. Then Marshal V. A. Sudets, who took over the DA in 1953, put pressure on the plane designers to get cracking with something to match SAC. As a result, by 1955 the DA was getting aircraft with the range, the speed, and the load to constitute a viable strategic force. But even with the three new bombers, it was not until the late 1950s that Sudets had enough in his inventory to pose a real threat to the American continent.

It would seem in retrospect that during the 1955–1957 period Khrushchev was only bluffing about an effective Soviet stra-

Figure 100. Mig-19 Farmer, the first Mikoian design to achieve supersonic speed in level flight using twin jets instead of a single engine. First in service in 1955, the planes were still being built in China in 1975.

tegic capability, and that the Soviets' publicity about their ability to mount a preemptive strike to thwart any U.S. strategic attack was sheer bravado—it is extremely unlikely that the Soviet air force could have inflicted unacceptable damage on the United States during that period. Until the fall of 1957, the Soviets were simply responding to an American lead in strategic weapons. Even geography was against them. Their advanced air bases on the northern rim of Siberia and in the Arctic islands (Severnaia Zemlia, Novaia Zemlia, and Franz Josef Land) were more than offset by the U.S. bases ringing the Soviet Union. Their inventory of long-range bombers, although somewhat similar to that of the United States in types, was very inferior in numbers. A doctrine of preemption may have been a measure of desperation, but it was the only doctrine feasible at the time. If the Soviets had too little to preempt with, they certainly had far too little to retaliate with after an American attack.

By the late 1950s, Khrushchev was becoming enamored of a new strategic delivery vehicle, the ICBM, which was first tested in the late summer of 1957. The new ICBM, combined with the successful launching of Sputnik in the fall of that year, had a miraculous effect on the Soviet attitude toward strategic balance *vis-à-vis* the United States, and Khrushchev began to make noises about a Soviet superiority in strategic delivery vehicles. Early in 1957 he verbally relegated bombers to museums and seemed determined to make ICBMs the be-all and end-all of the Soviet strategic posture. As one looks back at this display of cockiness, it is difficult to see it as anything other than a bold gamble in an attempt to gain a psychological advantage. The West was in a mild state of shock, and Khrushchev was cashing in on the situation. Of course, the Soviets had achieved a military "first"—a weapon that was not merely a duplication of some other na-

Figure 101. Sukhoi Su-7B Fitter-A ground-attack aircraft. These are standard equipment not only in the Soviet air forces but also in those of the Czechs, Poles, East Germans, Hungarians, North Vietnamese, Egyptians, Syrians, and Indians.

tion's "first."

Khrushchev brandished his new ICBMs as an implicit backup to his Berlin ultimatum in November 1958 but was reluctant to allow Mao Tse-tung to draw him into an actual confrontation with the United States in the Taiwan Straits crisis. The wind might be blowing from the east, in Mao's opinion, but Khrushchev was more aware of how little force there was behind that wind.

Why did not the Soviets maintain their lead in ICBMs? Probably for the same reason that they did not produce Bisons at the rate American intelligence judged them capable of: namely, their limited economic resources. As early as the Malenkov-Khrushchev duel for power in 1954, it is evident in retrospect, Malenkov realized that something had to give if the Soviet economy was not to be seriously overstrained. But Khrushchev, seeking the support of the military and of the conservative majority of the party leadership, gambled on the traditional bias toward heavy industry and military production; the period after 1955 saw an unusually heavy commitment to military hardware, research and development, and manpower. By 1958, however, Khrushchev realized how overextended he was in his "races" with the

United States. He was racing the United States in space, in armaments, and in economic aid to the third world, and he was promising to overtake and surpass the U.S. in per-capita production—all of this on half the American GNP. At this point, Khrushchev tried to back off a bit. He began to seek a détente with the West (which led eventually to Camp David in late 1959) and to try to renege on his military commitments.

Given the tight economic situation, Khrushchev was unwilling to put up the wherewithal necessary to push ICBMs off the production line like "sausages," as he once put it. Furthermore, the liquid-fueled ICBM of that period was an extremely expensive and complicated gadget, not adaptable to hardened sites and thereby vulnerable to American attack. Whatever their reasons may have been, the Soviets did not produce their new ICBMs as fast as Western intelligence estimated.

Khrushchev, in a famous speech to the Supreme Soviet on January 14, 1960, challenged the military leadership by stating that it was necessary to cut conventional forces in the interests of economy. He justified this policy by bragging that the Soviet deterrent force was capable of keeping the West at bay. He went on to state

Figure 102. Su-11 Fishpot-C at the Tushino Air Show in 1961. This photo shows the modified Su-9 design that first flew in 1956. In 1975 the Su-9 and Su-11 still comprised 25 percent of the USSR's 2,500-fighter force.

that new developments in military technology had made military aviation and a surface navy relatively unimportant. Because military aviation was being almost entirely replaced by missiles, the production of bombers would be drastically reduced. Needless to say, his proposed cuts in manpower and his derogatory observations about conventional weapons, especially aircraft, were not enthusiastically received by the military leadership.

While Nikita Khrushchev downgraded the role of conventional weapons in the Soviet armed forces, he simultaneously expanded Soviet commitments in the third world. Moscow, ever more involved in the global arena, played quartermaster for a

number of client states in the Middle East, in Southeast Asia, and even in the Western hemisphere after 1960.

The breakthrough in Soviet penetration of the third world came in 1955 with the so-called arms-for-cotton deal with Egypt. Nasser, upset by the key role given his rival in Iraq, Nuri al-Said, in the new Baghdad Pact, turned to the Russians as a source of support. The Russians, who regarded the new alliance of Turkey, Iraq, Iran, and Pakistan under U.S.-U.K. auspices with alarm, were delighted to leapfrog the barrier and get into the heart of the Middle East via Nasser. In September 1955, an agreement was signed with Czechoslovakia which provided for $250 million in arms for Egypt, a deal which included Mig-15s and Il-28s along with naval craft, tanks, and artillery. Egyptian personnel were sent to Eastern Europe for training, and Soviet military advisers and technicians arrived in Egypt. In the following year, 1956, Syria asked for and got military aid from the Soviet bloc, a development which led Yemen, which was interested in ousting the British from Aden, to apply successfully for Soviet largesse in military equipment. Prague acted as a cover in all three deals.

Over the next decade, Soviet arms deliveries to Middle Eastern and North African client states were continually increased, amounting to about $2.5 billion in monetary terms. The lion's share (around $1.5 billion) went to Egypt, with Iraq, Syria, and Algeria the other major recipients. Yemen, Iran, Cyprus, and Morocco received smaller quotas. The quality of the armaments also improved over time: Egypt and Iraq got Mig-21s in 1962, followed by Tu-16 bombers; SA-2 missiles went to Egypt in 1963, and other countries got them shortly thereafter. On the eve of the June war in 1967, the Egyptian air force had around 350 jet fighters, including 160 Mig-21s and more than 50 Su-7 fighter-bombers; the Syrian and Iraqi air forces also had large numbers of Migs, including some Mig-21s, as well as Il-28 light bombers. However, the Soviet air force faced a major task in providing the training needed to make sophisticated pilots and technicians of the Arabs in their client states.

The Soviets began giving military aid to South Asia as early as 1956, when they shipped a dozen Mig-15s and a couple of helicopters to Afghanistan, where they also built some airstrips. By 1960 the government in Kabul had received more than $100 million in Soviet military assistance. Then the simultaneous development of the

Sino-Soviet split and deterioration of Sino-Indian relations caused the Soviets to look toward New Delhi for a potential ally in the containment of China. In the summer of 1962, Moscow promised the Indians some Mig-21s as well as aid in building plants to manufacture them. The Sino-Indian conflict in October 1962 put the Russians in a bind: how could they, in good conscience, supply aircraft to a nation fighting a Communist country? By December, however, the Russians had shelved any ideological doubt, and they went through with the Indian Mig deal. In late 1966 the Indians received some 170 Soviet aircraft, including 60 Mig-21s, and the Mig plants were under construction.

Another major recipient of Soviet military aid in the early 1960s was Indonesia. In an effort to support Sukarno's campaign to oust the Dutch from West Irian, the Soviets came through with $1 billion in military equipment. Although heavily biased toward naval units, this complement included more than 100 Migs, including some Mig-21s, the first of that type of aircraft sent to a nonbloc country. In the decade between 1956 and 1965, the Soviets expended nearly $2 billion on military aid to Afghanistan, Indonesia, and India. Much of this consisted of aircraft, including well over 300 Migs.

While the Soviets were distributing their military largesse to a coterie of client or potential client states in the Middle East, South Asia, and Southeast Asia during the late 1950s and early 1960s, their relations with the United States vacillated from the euphoria of the Geneva Conference in 1955 through the depths of the 1956 crisis to another euphoric episode in 1959. But in spite of Khrushchev's posturing and speech making, the United States was troubled by its inability to get hard intelligence about Soviet air and missile capabilities. The decision to build an aircraft

Figure 103. Fiddler interceptor in flight. Note air-to-air missiles mounted under the wings.

capable of overflying Russian territory with impunity coincided with the Soviet rejection of Eisenhower's "open skies" proposal at Geneva in July 1955. C. L. "Kelly" Johnson of Lockheed had begun work on the U-2 in December 1954, and it was ready for service by 1956. Because it was very light, with wings twice the length of its fuselage, the aircraft could get to 70,000 feet, putting it out of the range of Soviet interceptors. U-2 flights along the Soviet borders began in September 1956, and by November the U-2s were penetrating USSR air space. Soon there were U-2 bases ringing the Soviet Union: Incirlik at Adana in Turkey, Bodö in Norway, Giebelstadt in Germany, Atsugi in Japan, and Lahore and Peshawar in Pakistan. The Russians were soon aware of the overflights, but they could do nothing about them between 1956 and early 1960, and the information being obtained by the U.S. was making it difficult for Khrushchev to sustain his boasts about missiles coming off the production lines like sausages. Finally, on May 1, 1960, Francis Gary Powers made his ill-fated flight from Peshawar with the intention of landing at Bodö in Norway; he was shot down by a SAM missile at 68,000 feet over Sverdlovsk. Powers, who was unable to trigger the destruct mechanism, landed safely; and Khrushchev had what he needed to wreck the Paris summit conference: the wreckage

of the U-2 and its pilot alive and talking. But the U-2 flights had demonstrated the limited capabilities of the Soviet air defenses, that the location and numbers of its missiles could not be concealed, and that, once revealed, the unhardened launching sites were vulnerable.

Although Khrushchev would have nothing more to do with Eisenhower, he did agree to meet with the new president, Kennedy, in June 1961 in Vienna. Apparently Khrushchev misjudged the young president egregiously. He came up with an ultimatum on Berlin which in turn led Kennedy to call up the reserves and generally beef up the American military posture. The Soviets responded in kind by retaining on active duty Soviet servicemen scheduled to be released in 1961. To make matters worse, in Khrushchev's view, the Americans had revised their estimate of the Soviet-American ICBM balance and were trumpeting to the world that Russia was now low man on the totem pole.

Khrushchev, looking around for some way to redress the strategic balance and also to enhance his sagging image as a diplomat—preferably through an inexpensive "quick fix"—decided to use the newest addition to the socialist camp, Cuba, as a base for Soviet MRBMs and IRBMs as well as for Il-28 light bombers. These weapons systems, which lacked the range to be effective while stationed in the Soviet Union,

Figure 104. Mig-19 Fresco, in service with the Polish Air Force. With its wing fences, drop tanks, and tail chute, this plane is typical of Soviet aircraft built under license in Poland and other satellite countries.

would be the equivalent of ICBMs and long-range aircraft if positioned in Cuba, ninety miles from the American mainland.

Castro, who had come to power at the very end of 1958, had begun almost immediately to expropriate U.S. property, and he accompanied this action with an ever-more-venomous stream of anti-American diatribes. The Soviets lost no time in cultivating Castro; Mikoian was in Havana as early as February 1960. Between July and November 1960, Cuba received some 30,000 tons of Soviet arms, including some Migs. Cuban-American tensions rose steadily, and in January 1961 President Eisenhower broke relations with Castro. The new president, John F. Kennedy, had scarcely settled in office when the Bay of Pigs fiasco exacerbated relations still further. Castro responded by declaring

Cuba a "socialist republic" in May and in December proclaimed himself a Marxist-Leninist. The Organization of American States, except for Mexico, isolated Cuba in February 1962. In the spring of that year, Soviet military aid was escalated and included fifty to seventy-five Migs, with the Soviets training Cuban pilots. Raúl Castro, the Cuban minister of defense, conferred with Malinovsky in Moscow and got still more arms, and by September some 3,500 Soviet military advisers and technicians were in Cuba.

On September 28, American intelligence reported that crated Il-28s were being shipped to Cuba. Sen. Kenneth Keating throughout September had maintained that his own sources of information were reporting the building of intermediate-range missile sites in Cuba, although U-2 flights

Figure 105. Polish U-Mig-21 Mongol two-seat trainer. The Soviets used this type of plane to establish the women's height record (79,725 feet) in May 1966.

were unable to spot them. Finally, on October 14, two air force majors photographed MRBM and IRBM launching sites in advanced stages of construction near San Cristóbal. Reconnaissance the next day revealed missiles being hauled to the sites under tarpaulins. President Kennedy, upon seeing the photographs, immediately set up an executive committee of the National Security Council to deal with the crisis. The committee saw U.S. options as ranging from doing nothing—that is, accepting the presence of Soviet offensive missiles in Cuba as a *fait accompli*—to attacking Cuba, either by launching an invasion or by destroying the missiles with bombs. The committee also saw the Soviet Union, not Cuba, as constituting the real danger. After a week of deliberations, it was decided to make the following responses simultaneously: institute a naval quarantine of Cuba to prevent further deliveries of offensive weapons, publicly expose the Soviet action, present the case to the OAS, and proceed with the total mobilization of the U.S. military forces.

On October 22 President Kennedy described the situation to the nation on television and radio, stating clearly that any nuclear attack from Cuba would lead to retaliation upon the Soviet Union. The gauntlet being down, Khrushchev had only two options: back down or risk a nuclear war. Meanwhile, the United States was busy presenting its case far and wide: Dean Acheson to the NATO powers, Dean Rusk to the OAS, and Adlai Stevenson to the U.N. The rapid U.S. mobilization, especially of SAC and of conventional forces in Florida, and the rumors that an invasion of Cuba was imminent left Khrushchev little time to react. On October 25 he wrote to Bertrand Russell stating that the Soviet Union was willing to deal with the Cuban crisis at a summit meeting, and on the following day he sent a letter to Kennedy in which he agreed in principle to remove the missiles. Some ten letters passed between the two during the next few days, the net result of which was the Soviet removal of the offensive missiles and Il-28s. By November 12 the Soviets had withdrawn all forty-two missiles and begun the destruction of the launching sites, and in early December they brought home more than forty Il-28s.

Khrushchev had lost prestige in the eyes of his marshals. They had been told by the new authority on strategy in 1960 that the Soviet Union could afford to reduce its conventional forces because, from now on, intercontinental missiles with nuclear warheads were the new order of firepower and the decisive factor in the course and outcome of war. But when the chips were down in Cuba in October 1962, the Soviets were forced to back off. In addition to being on the short end of the new order of firepower, the Soviets had neither the naval power nor the air support necessary to protect their installations in Cuba. Khrushchev's "minimum deterrence" limited the Soviet Union to a single option—nuclear war. And that option had no credibility.

For a number of reasons, one of which was the growing estrangement from his military leaders, Khrushchev was ousted in October 1964. His successors, Brezhnev and Kosygin, apparently realized that, if they were to continue their predecessor's policy of competing with the United States in the third world while simultaneously avoiding a nuclear war through deterrence and maintaining a strong military posture against NATO and China within the Eurasian continent, they would have to gain more credibility in the eyes of the potential opponents. Moreover, unless this new team intended to back down in pursuit of the Khrushchevian global objectives, it would have to provide better means for implementing them. Khrushchev, committed to expand Soviet influence throughout the globe, had gone beyond Stalin's "continental" strategy, a strategy concerned primarily with the defense of the Soviet Union and its satellites. But Khrushchev's ambitions had outrun Soviet capabilities, as the Cuban episode clearly demonstrated in late 1962, and the new team had to face the fact that only the rapid augmentation of Soviet strategic weapons, plus a buildup of conventional forces in order to exert military pressure beyond the Eurasian continent, would make the Kremlin's global pretensions credible. Over the next few years, the new team concentrated enormous efforts in building up the military punch lacking during the Khrushchev decade. ICBMs, ABMs, SLBMs, naval vessels, and aircraft poured out of Soviet plants at a rate calculated to make "parity" with the United States a reality, not a dream.

The new regime had barely taken over when it was involved in an indirect confrontation with the United States over the bombing of North Vietnam in February 1965, while Kosygin and a Soviet military mission were visiting Hanoi. Apparently, the Soviet leadership had decided to involve itself in Southeast Asia—a reversal of Khrushchev's policy of staying out of that area after his mild involvement in Laos. This new turn in Kremlin policy coincided with the American escalation of the conflict in Vietnam. Soviet military and economic aid to North Vietnam increased precipitously in the 1965–1968 period, but the military assistance was confined to materiel and technicians. Air defense in North Vietnam was rapidly augmented, and by the late spring of 1965 Hanoi had 70 Mig-15s and Mig-17s as well as SA-2 surface-to-air missiles. The SAM sites came to around 60 by the end of the year and were increased to 150 by the end of 1966. Furthermore, delta-wing supersonic Mig-21s were fed into North Vietnam in 1966. Although the American pilots were much more than a match for the Migs, the SAMs exacted a heavy toll of American aircraft.

Figure 106. Su-7 Fitters taking off from a Polish air base. Designed on the basis of Korean War experience, these fighters were also supplied to Egypt.

The new leadership was also faced with a nasty problem much nearer home—the ever increasing hostility of the People's Republic of China. The so-called Communist bloc, probably never so monolithic as Western observers were wont to describe it in the 1950s, came apart at the seams in the late 1950s and early 1960s. Khrushchev's "new doctrines" enunciated at the Twentieth Party Congress in 1956, his failure to back Mao in the Taiwan Strait crisis of 1958, his wooing of Eisenhower at Camp David at what Mao felt was China's expense, his unilateral abrogation of the Sino-Soviet nuclear assistance pact, the withdrawal of Soviet economic aid and technicians in 1960, and his ambivalent posture in the Sino-Indian clashes of 1959 and 1962—all helped widen the split. Mao retaliated

by hinting, in 1964, that China would someday present her claim to the territories "stolen" by tsarist Russia in the "unequal treaties" of 1858, 1860, and 1881. Although the new regime in the Kremlin tried to smooth Mao's ruffled feathers, by late November 1964 the Chinese were again publishing anti-Soviet diatribes and defining the new Soviet leadership as "Khrushchevism without Khrushchev." This growing Chinese hostility was another reason for reversing Khrushchev's curtailment of Soviet conventional capabilities. His "minimum deterrence" was not suitable for the guarding of the extremely long Sino-Soviet borders.

At the other end of the Soviet Union were the satellite nations, which, although they had been incorporated into the overall

Soviet defense system through the mechanism of the Warsaw Pact, had to be pressured into compliance with Moscow directives by the threat of Soviet military might. Missiles with nuclear warheads were awkward tools when it came to repressing recalcitrant satellites, as had been demonstrated in Hungary in 1956 and was later to be proved true in Czechoslovakia in 1968. Tank and motorized rifle divisions covered by close air support were the only feasible tools for dealing with such troubles.

Thus the Brezhnev-Kosygin regime faced the formidable tasks of gaining strategic parity with the United States, maintaining adequate conventional forces on the Chinese border and *vis-à-vis* the European satellites, and building up the necessary naval and airlift capabilities to extend the Soviet reach beyond continental limits—all these to be done in an economy whose growth rate was slowing and with the Soviet populace clamoring for a better shake in consumer goods, especially for a better diet.

The Soviet air force was well endowed with fighters, fighter-bombers, and interceptors, as well as light bombers, before Khrushchev left in late 1964. Both tactical aviation and the fighter segment of PVO had large inventories of Mig-17s, 19s, and 21s, as well as Su-7 (Fitter) ground-attack fighters, Su-9 (Fishpot) all-weather fighters, and Yak-25 (Flashlight) all-weather interceptors. The Tu-22 (Blinder), a supersonic twin-jet light bomber first seen in 1961, was obviously intended to replace some of the slower Il-28s. The introduction of ICBMs, however, had evidently taken the pressure off the development of long-range bombers—the DA was still operating with an inventory of Badgers, Bisons, and Bears. Because the new regime continued to invest heavily in aeronautical research and development,

during the next few years new fighters and interceptors were developed, among them the Su-11 (Flagon-A), a twin-jet tactical fighter, the YAK-28P (Firebar) interceptor, and the Mig-25 (Foxbat) high-altitude all-weather interceptor. There was, and still is, a good deal of effort put into the development of STOL (short takeoff and landing) and VTOL (vertical takeoff and landing) aircraft. As early as 1967, Western observers were identifying the efforts of the Mikoian design group in its STOL versions of the Mig-21, the Fishbed-G and the Faithless, the Sukhoi team's Su-11 (Flagon-B), and the Yak Freehand. There were also the variable geometry versions of the Su-7 and the Mig-23 Flogger. Even the Tu-114 (Cleat) civilian transport was converted to a military version in order to carry an airborne warning and control system (AWACS), known in NATO parlance as the Tu-114 (Moss).

The Soviet aviation industry, in addition to its main task of producing the machines needed for the defense of the Soviet Union and its satellites, was also acting as the major source of aircraft for an ever-growing number of client states. The Israeli clobbering of Egypt and Syria in the six-day war of June 1967 left both Arab states almost bereft of aircraft. The Soviets began immediately to replace the losses and then some. By mid-1972, Egypt had more than 600 combat aircraft, including Mig-17s, Mig-21s, and Su-7s, in addition to almost 200 helicopters and about 100 transports, all of Soviet origin. Iraq received almost 200 Mig-17s, Mig-21s, and Su-7s, while Syria was into the Soviets for more than 300 combat aircraft, 200 of which were Mig-21s. The Arab clients were proving expensive in aircraft, let alone the SAMs, tanks, and artillery the Soviets were feeding into the Middle East.

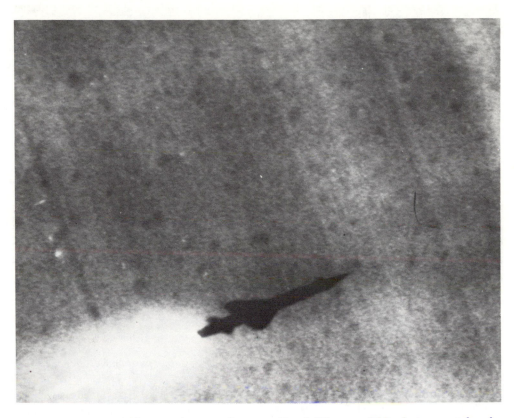

Figure 107. Soviet-built SAM in operation over North Vietnam. This photo was taken by a USAF RF-101 Voodoo pilot in 1967.

The Six-Day War was followed in the autumn of 1968 by an Egyptian bombardment of the Israeli positions on the east bank of the Suez Canal, an attempt by the Egyptians to parlay their superiority in artillery into an Israeli withdrawal. The Israelis responded by using their superior weapon, the aircraft. The so-called War of Attrition was under way, and the edge soon went to Israel because the Egyptian pilots were still unable to match their Israeli counterparts. By late 1969 Israeli planes, now including F-4 Phantoms, were penetrating deep inside Egypt, and they had reached Cairo itself by January 1970. At this point Nasser went to Moscow to plead for help, and subsequently the Soviets took over the air defense of Egypt. A belt of high-altitude SA-2s and low-altitude SA-3s along the Suez Canal provided a twenty-five-mile-wide block to Israeli penetration by air. The standoff gave U.S. Secretary of State William Rogers a chance to persuade both sides to agree to a cease-fire, although the Egyptians and their Soviet advisers took advantage of the hiatus to push their SAMs forward. Until their expulsion in July 1972, the Soviets provided the technical skills needed to man the SAM sites, flew reconnaissance along the Suez in Mig-25s with Soviet pilots, and used Egyptian airfields for Tu-16 reconnaissance over the U.S. Sixth Fleet.

In the Yom Kippur War of October

Figure 108. Mig-17 flown to Homestead AFB, Florida, by a Cuban pilot on October 5, 1969.

1973, the performance of the Egyptian and Syrian air forces was hardly a fair test of the capabilities of their Soviet-supplied aircraft. Of the slightly more than 100 Israeli aircraft lost in combat, less than 10 percent were shot down by Arab pilots, while better than 400 Arab planes were lost in air-to-air combat. The Soviet-supplied Egyptian air force, some 600 aircraft, was never fully committed to battle. The Russian-supplied ground-to-air missiles, however, were another story entirely. Large numbers of SA-6 (Gainful) missiles with a twenty-mile range and both radar and infrared guidance proved nearly impervious to the Israeli electronic countermeasure equipment (ECM). The SA-7 (Grail), mounted on an armored carrier, was lethal at short range. Thus an Israeli pilot who was able to avoid the SA-6 by flying low was likely to get hit by an SA-7. If he dodged both, there were still the older

SA-2s and SA-3s to be avoided as well as accurate antiaircraft guns. The Soviet air-defense weapons proved to be extremely effective against skilled Israeli pilots flying first-class machines.

During the post-Khrushchev decade (1965–1975), Soviet military capabilities were increased tremendously. For example, on late 1964 the Soviets had only about 200 ICBMs versus more than 800 American Minuteman missiles. By 1975 the Soviets had more than 1,600 ICBMs, while the United States had frozen its level at 1,054. During this period, the Soviet navy made its great leap forward: both submarines and surface ships were produced in ever-increasing numbers, and the new vessels included two helicopter carriers (the *Moskva* and the *Leningrad*) for ASW operations and an aircraft carrier, the *Kiev*. Two more *Kiev*-class aircraft carriers were being constructed. The Soviet air

Figure 109. Tu-16 Badger, since 1954 the standard Soviet medium reconnaissance bomber. Of the 2,000 Badgers built, 280 were still in service with the Naval air force in 1976.

force came up with a dozen new types of aircraft and went in for quality as well as quantity. The ground forces now had a veritable cloud of close air support, and the interceptor arm of PVO was equipped with highly sophisticated machines.

Partly for geriatric reasons and partly because of a changed outlook, the high command of the Soviet armed forces began to get an infusion of younger blood in the late 1960s. The army-dominated command, in the saddle since the Great Patriotic War, was finally being phased out as a result of death or senility, and younger officers were reaching the top. Kulikov (b. 1922) replaced the aged Zakharov (b. 1898) as chief of the General Staff; Kutakhov (b. 1920) replaced Vershinin (b. 1900) as commander in chief of the air force, and Okunev (b. 1920) took over as first deputy commander of PVO

from Shcheglov (b. 1910).

Since March 1953 the Soviet military forces have operated under a single Ministry of Defense, headed at present by Dmitry F. Ustinov, who succeeded Marshal Grechko upon the latter's death in April 1976. Although Ustinov is a civilian, he has played a leading role in Soviet military production since 1941 and is a full member of the Politburo. The minister is advised by the General Staff, whose chief is now Gen. Viktor G. Kulikov. The minister also receives advice and assistance from a council made up of three first deputy ministers of defense (Kulikov; Yakubovsky, commander in chief of the Warsaw Pact forces; and Sokolov) and ten deputy ministers of defense, the chiefs of the various services. These top commanders plus Ustinov represent the core of authority in the Soviet armed forces.

Figure 110. Tu-16 Badger in Egyptian markings, flown by a Soviet pilot. This 1969 photo shows the plane being intercepted by an F-8 Crusader during NATO maneuvers over the Mediterranean.

The Soviet Union proper is divided into sixteen military districts: Baltic, Leningrad, Moscow, Byelorussia, Carpathia, Kiev, Odessa, North Caucasus, Volga, Urals, Transcaucasus, Turkestan, Central Asia, TransBaykalia, Siberia, and the Far East.* The four major fleet commands—Baltic, Black Sea, Northern and Pacific—are equivalent military districts. Each military district is semiautonomous, responsible only to the minister of defense, and has operational control of the military forces in its area except for those directly under the Ministry of Defense, such as the PVO and the Long-Range Air Force units. The commander of the military district is usually a top general; with his chief of staff and his chief political officer, commonly a general,

he administers the military district. The number and quality of the forces under him depend upon the strategic importance of his district.

The minister of defense is also directly in charge of the four "groups" of forces outside the USSR: the Group of Soviet Forces in Germany, with twenty divisions; the Northern Group of Forces in Poland, with three divisions; the Southern Group of Forces in Hungary, with four divisions; and the Central Group of Forces in Czechoslovakia, with six divisions—a total of thirty-one divisions. These forces provide the backbone of the Warsaw Pact forces, commanded by Marshal Ivan I. Yakubovsky—who, in turn, is subordinate to Ustinov. Thus, for all intents and purposes, the pact forces are an integral part of the Soviet armed forces.

The Main Directorate of the air force (Voenno-vozdushnye sily, or VVS) has been headed since 1969 by Marshal of Aviation Pavel S. Kutakhov, who was only

---

*In the fall of 1969, the old Turkestan Military District was split in two: the Turkestan Military District and the new Central Asian Military District (Kazakhstan, Khirghizia, and Tadzhikistan) so as to cope more effectively with the growing Chinese threat.

Figure 111. Mig-21 Fishbed short-range delta-wing interceptor. This plane, in service with the Yugoslav air force, was photographed at Rota AFB in Spain.

forty-nine when he took over. The VVS has more than .5 million men and an inventory of nearly 10,000 combat aircraft and about 3,500 transports and helicopters. The VVS has the following components: the tactical air force (called Frontal Aviation by the Soviets), Fighter Aviation/ PVO, Long-Range Aviation, Air Transport Command, and Naval Aviation. Marshal Kutakhov represents all the branches of the air force in his capacity as commander in chief of the VVS and deputy minister of defense on the Military Council. He is responsible for procurement, training, and other housekeeping activities for all the components of VVS. Operational control of Frontal Aviation is in the hands of the the various ground-force commanders to whom the units are assigned. Fighter Aviation/PVO, headed by Col. Gen. A. Borovykh since Kadonitsev's death in 1969, is subordinate operationally to the commander in chief of the PVO, Marshal P. F. Batitsky, Long-Range Aviation, under Col. Gen. Vasili Reshetnikov, is directly responsible to the Ministry of Defense, and part of Air Transport Command's planes are assigned to the airborne forces. Although navy pilots wear VVS uniforms and have air force ranks, Naval Aviation units are under the operational command of the naval force to which they are assigned. In short, Marshal Kutakhov has administrative responsibility for all, but operational control over little.

Frontal Aviation, the tactical air force, has around 4,500 combat aircraft. Frontal air armies are assigned to military districts under the operational control of ground-forces commanders.* New types of aircraft have been entering the tactical air force in recent years, allowing the phasing out of the obsolescent Mig-17 (Fresco) and Mig-19 (Farmer). They are being replaced with the high-performance, all-weather Mig-21 (Fishbed) and Mig-23 (Flogger). The Sukhoi Su-9 (Fishpot), a single-engine all-weather fighter; the Su-17 (Fitter-C); the Su-19 (Fencer); the Tu-28 (Fiddler), a Mach 1.75 twin jet; and the Yak-28 (Brewer), a two-seat tactical

---

*An air army is the largest unit in the VVS. In Frontal Aviation, an air army consists of three corps, and each corps of three divisions. Each division has three regiments, and a regiment, in turn, is composed of three squadrons.

Figure 112. Mig-25 Foxbat high-altitude interceptor. Designed to counter the B-70, the Foxbat is the fastest fighter in the Soviet inventory.

attack aircraft, are also in service in Frontal Aviation. Kutakhov is pushing hard for more training in STOL aircraft.

Fighter Aviation/PVO has about 2,500 aircraft, mostly the same types used by Frontal Aviation. The Mig-25, Su-11, Tu-28, and Yak-28P (Firebar, an all-weather interceptor) are the best, but the older Mig-19, Mig-21, and Su-9 are still in service in large numbers. A variety of infrared and radar-homing air-to-air missiles (Alkali, Anab, Ash, Atoll, and Awl) gives the PVO interceptors a real wallop.

Long-Range Aviation consists of three air armies, two deployed in European Russia and the third in the Soviet far east. Of a total of somewhat more than 800 aircraft, there are approximately 35 Bisons, 100 Bears, 475 Badgers, about 170 Blinders, and probably 50 Tupolev Backfires. Only the Bisons, Bears, and Backfires could reach the continental United States without refueling. The Bisons, Bears, and Badgers, first flown in the mid-1950s, are now outdated and somewhat obsolescent. The Tu-22 Blinder,

however, a medium-range bomber (2,600 nautical miles) with a supersonic dash speed of Mach 2, carries the high-speed Kitchen air-to-surface missile. The Mach-2.5 bomber Backfire is in production and some 50 are in service.

Air Transport Command has around 1,500 aircraft, approximately half of which are An-12s (Cubs) and Il-18s (Coots) with ranges in the neighborhood of 2,000 nautical miles. The largest transport is the An-22 (Cock), called the Anteus by the Russians. The Anteus has a maximum range of almost 6,000 nautical miles and can carry a payload of 176,000 pounds over a range of 2,500 nautical miles. In addition, Air Transport Command can call upon Aeroflot, Soviet civil aviation, for assistance. Actually, Aeroflot is a military force on loan to the civil authorities. Aeroflot has a very respectable fleet of medium- and long-range transports as can be seen from the accompanying table. The supersonic Tu-144 went into service in late 1975 and a 350-passenger "airbus" is in the works. All in all, Aeroflot's 300 or so long- and

Large Aeroflot Transports

Type	Engine component	Passenger load	Range (in nautical miles)
An-10	4-engine turboprop	100	650
An-24	2-engine turboprop	50	1,400
Il-18	4-engine turboprop	110	2,000
Il-62	4-engine turbofan	185	4,000
Tu-104	4-engine jet	100	2,000
Tu-114	4-engine turboprop	200	3,300
Tu-124	2-engine turbofan	60	650
Tu-134	2-engine turbofan	80	1,100
Tu-154	3-engine turbofan	150	4,000

medium-range transports constitute a valuable backup for the Air Transport Command and could be an integral part in making the seven airborne divisions a viable force.

The invasion of Czechoslovakia in August 1968 demonstrated the value of an airlift capability, as did the various airlifts to Egypt, Yemen, and the Sudan in recent years. With a force of fast transport aircraft and a large number of helicopters at its disposal, the VVS has increased its airlift capability tremendously, as evidenced by its successful replenishment of arms to the Arabs in the Middle East wars of 1967 and 1973.

Naval Aviation is part of the VVS, and its aircraft are mostly air force types—few of its planes are specifically designed for naval work, except for a few amphibians. Of a total of about 1,200 planes and helicopters, about 600 are bomber types (280 Tu-16 Badgers, 60 Tu-22 Blinders, 10 Il-28 Beagles, and 55 Bears), mostly used for reconnaissance and ASW work. In addition, there are some 50 Il-38 May reconnaissance planes, 250 Mi-4 and Ka-25 ASW helicopters, and 200 transports. There is a close connection between Naval Aviation and Long-Range Aviation because the latter has provided the Tu-16s and Tu-95s for long-range

reconnaissance. The Tu-16s and Tu-22s, assigned to attack roles, are equipped with Kipper, Kelt, and Kitchen air-to-surface missiles. Approximately 200 Tu-16s and Tu-22s are specifically equipped for reconnaissance, and the Tu-95s have radar reconnaissance gear for tracking carrier forces. The two helicopter carriers now in service and the recently launched carrier for fixed-wing aircraft are indications of a serious intent to augment the capabilities of the naval air arm.

The air-defense system of the entire Warsaw Pact area is centered in Moscow and is closely controlled by the commander in chief of the Soviet PVO. Furthermore, the various air forces of the Warsaw Pact nations are tightly integrated with the Soviet VVS. There are also contingents of Soviet Frontal Aviation assigned to the Soviet forces in the German Democratic Republic (DDR), Hungary, Poland, and Czechoslovakia.

The air forces of the six non-Soviet members of the Warsaw Pact combined have more than 2,000 combat aircraft, plus some 500 transports and helicopters. Bulgaria has approximately 250 combat aircraft, mostly Mig-17s, 19s, and 21s. Czechoslovakia has 500 combat aircraft—mostly Migs, in addition to a few Su-7s and some Il-28s for reconnaissance. The

DDR, with slightly more than 300 Migs of its own, is more than adequately backed by the air components attached to the twenty Soviet divisions stationed in East Germany. Hungary has the smallest of the air forces, only 100 or so Migs, while Poland has the largest—some 700 combat planes, including Migs, Su-7s, and Il-28s. Finally, Rumania has 20 squadrons of Migs, ranging from 15s to 21s, plus a few Il-28s, for a total of 250 combat aircraft.

Even this cursory review of the Soviet developments in air power over the last two decades should be sufficient to establish the probability that the VVS will continue to get new and better machines in the coming years. To some extent this amplification of Soviet air power will consist, as in the past, of improvements to aircraft already in the inventory. For example, the Mig-21 was continually modified over the years from a light fighter with a 9,000-pound thrust engine to the Mig-21 MF (Fishbed-J), with a 14,500-pound thrust engine and vastly improved armament. The Mig-25 (Foxbat) is a much heavier and improved interceptor, and the Mig-23 (Flogger) is an excellent combat fighter and attack aircraft. A new twin-jet variable-geometry air superiority fight-

er, the Fearless, is now being tested. The Backfire, equipped with engines similar to the Tu-144 supersonic transport and partially variable-geometry wings, has a range of 4,000 nautical miles and, with in-flight refueling or flying from Arctic bases, could reach most points in the United States. There are reports that some 50 Backfires are now flying. The VVS does not seem to have slackened its pace of modernization and seems very much interested in better interceptors, ground-attack aircraft, bombers, and improved transports. As John Erickson has pointed out, while the world has been awed by the rapid growth of the Soviet navy, it has tended to ignore the equally rapid augmentation of the Soviet air force, especially its advances in flexibility and mobility. The VVS, with its more than 10,000 aircraft, is augmented by the 2,000 combat planes in the air forces of its Warsaw Pact associates; moreover, Soviet Migs, Sukhois, and Il-28s provide the guts of the air forces of a series of client states around the globe. The VVS and the Soviet Ministry of Aviation Industry have indeed grown into an awesome combination during the last quarter-century.

Research Notes

There is a surprisingly limited literature in English concerning the Soviet air force, and much of that is in journals devoted to aviation. Developments up to 1960 are covered in Asher Lee's *Soviet Air and Rocket Forces* (New York, 1959) and

The Soviet Air Force (New York, 1962) as well as in Robert A. Kilmarx' *History of Soviet Air Power* (New York, 1962). The Soviet involvement in the Berlin air-lift, the Korean conflict, the Cuban missile crisis, the Middle Eastern wars, and

Vietnam is treated in some detail in J. Scrivner, ed., *A Quarter of a Century of Air Power* (Maxwell AFB, Ala., 1973), and in K. Whiting, *The Development of the Soviet Armed Forces, 1917-1972* (Maxwell AFB, Ala., 1972). Soviet doctrine and strategy, including air power, is soundly treated in Thomas Wolfe's *Soviet Strategy at the Crossroads* (Cambridge, Mass., 1964) and *Soviet Power and Europe, 1945-1970* (Baltimore, 1970). The classic Soviet view is in V. D. Sokolovsky, ed., *Soviet Military Strategy* (New York, 1975), with translation and commentary by Harriet F. Scott. A rundown on Soviet military aid to the Soviet client states in the third world can be found in W. Joshua and S. Gilbert, *Arms for the Third World* (Baltimore, 1969). The organization of the VVS is dealt with in some of the above-mentioned works; more detailed discussions appear in John Erickson, "Soviet Military Power," *Strategic Review* 1, no. 1 (Spring 1973), and in A. Ghebhardt and W. Scheider, Jr., "The Soviet Air Force High Command," *Air University Review*, May-June 1973.

Soviet research and development in the aviation field and the role of the design bureau is dealt with by A. J. Alexander in *R & D in Soviet Aviation* (Santa Monica, Calif., 1970). Descriptions of Soviet aircraft are to be found in *Jane's All the World's Aircraft* (London, annual) and in various aviation journals, especially *Interavia, Flying Review International,* and *Aviation Week and Space Technology.* See also H. J. Nowarra and G. R. Duval, *Russian Civil and Military Aircraft, 1884-1969* (London, 1970), and Jean Alexander, *Russian Aircraft since 1940* (London, 1975). *Air Force* magazine (March 1975 and March 1976) has a new feature entitled "Soviet Aerospace Almanac," which provides an excellent overview of the Soviet air force. For those who read Russian, the Ministry of Defense's daily paper, *Krasnaya Zvezda* [*Red Star*], and *Aviatsiia i Kosmonavtika* [*Aviation and Cosmonautics*], a journal published monthly by the VVS, are informative, although less so than their counterparts in the West.

Illustration Credits

4. USN; 5. USN; 7. Sovfoto; 8. USAF; 11. USAF; 12. Sovfoto; 13. USN; 14. USAF; 15. USAF; 16. USAF; 17. USAF; 18. USAF; 19. USN; 20. USAF; 21. USAF; 22. USAF; 24. USAF; 25. USAF; 26. USAF; 28. USN; 29. USN; 30. USAF; 31. USAF; 32. USAF; 33. USAF; 34. USAF; 36. USAF; 37. USAF; 38. USAF; 39. USN; 40. USAF; 41. USN; 42. USN; 43. USN; 44. USN; 45. USN; 47. USN; 49. USN; 50. USN; 51. USN; 52. USN; 54. USN; 55. USN; 56. USN; 58. Aeroflot; 59. Aeroflot; 61. Aeroflot; 62. Aeroflot; 64. USAF; 65. USN; 66. Jerzy Toboloski; 67. USN; 68. USN; 69. USN; 71. USN; 72. U/K; 73. USN; 74. USAF; 75. USN; 76. DIA; 77. DIA; 79. DIA; 80. DIA; 81. DIA; 82. DIA; 83. DIA; 84. DIA; 86. DIA; 87. DIA; 88. DIA; 89. DIA; 91. DIA; 92. DIA; 93. Sovfoto; 94. Sovfoto; 95. Sovfoto; 96. Sovfoto; 97. USAF; 98. USAF; 99. USAF; 100. U/K; 101. USN; 102. USN; 104. Jerzy Toboloski; 105. Jerzy Toboloski; 107. USAF; 108. USAF; 109. USN; 111. USAF.

Index

This index was prepared by Maia Aleksandrovna Kipp and Naomi Ossar.